CRITICAL APPROACHES TO INTERNATIONAL RELATIONS

Studies in Critical Social Sciences Book Series

Haymarket Books is proud to be working with Brill Academic Publishers (www.brill.nl) to republish the *Studies in Critical Social Sciences* book series in paperback editions. This peer-reviewed book series offers insights into our current reality by exploring the content and consequences of power relationships under capitalism, and by considering the spaces of opposition and resistance to these changes that have been defining our new age. Our full catalog of *SCSS* volumes can be viewed at https://www.haymarketbooks.org/series_collections/4-studies-in-critical-social-sciences.

CRITICAL APPROACHES TO INTERNATIONAL RELATIONS

Philosophical Foundations and Current Debates

EDITED BY

M. KÜRŞAD ÖZEKIN AND ENGIN SUNE

Haymarket Books
Chicago, IL

First published in 2021 by Brill Academic Publishers, The Netherlands
© 2021 Koninklijke Brill NV, Leiden, The Netherlands

Published in paperback in 2022 by
Haymarket Books
P.O. Box 180165
Chicago, IL 60618
773-583-7884
www.haymarketbooks.org

ISBN: 978-1-64259-804-9

Distributed to the trade in the US through Consortium Book Sales and
Distribution (www.cbsd.com) and internationally through Ingram Publisher
Services International (www.ingramcontent.com).

This book was published with the generous support of Lannan Foundation and
Wallace Action Fund.

Special discounts are available for bulk purchases by organizations and
institutions. Please call 773-583-7884 or email info@haymarketbooks.org for more
information.

Cover design by Jamie Kerry and Ragina Johnson.

Printed in the United States.

10 9 8 7 6 5 4 3 2 1

Library of Congress Cataloging-in-Publication data is available.

Contents

Acknowledgements

Finalizing this book project has been a long and tiresome, but nevertheless pleasant and rewarding experience. The very initial idea for writing this book originated in the late 2018, almost one year after completing our PhD degrees at University of Sussex and Middle East Technical University respectively. As PhD candidates whose interests lie in both Critical International Relations and Marxist political economy, we got ourselves involved with diverse set of schools in critical thought and had been exposed to different perspectives and readings of the pioneers in critical IR scholarship. Particularly, the lively academic milieu and the critical thinking to which we had been exposed at our departments were quite rewarding and led us to further develop our interests in critical IR approaches along our professional lives. As we have become more and more familiar with what has been written on critical IR theories, we realized the need for a book that comprises the complex strands of critical theoretical approaches in IR with their respective philosophical foundations and future research directions. Indeed, much has been written so far in the existing literature of critical IR scholarship. Even though there are significant works that scrutinize theorists, concepts and configurations in critical IR thinking and that concentrate on the concepts of emancipation, power and other excluded subject matters, none of these studies provides a detailed account that easily extends our knowledge on different strands of critical IR scholarship by taking into account their separate but not mutually exclusive historical foundations, their respective critiques and contributions to IR scholarship and further research directions they offer. Furthermore, looking into the existing literature of critical IR scholarship, it is generally very uncommon to encounter with studies that treat imperialism as a critical theory of IR and analyze Marxism and its sub-theories such as dependency, imperialism and uneven and combined development as separate approaches.

Thus, meeting the need for such an essential resource eventually led us to embark on this book project by mid-2019. Indeed, many companions, colleagues and people have encouraged, advised, helped, criticized and supported our project throughout writing and publishing processes. To mention a few, encouragement and constructive comments of Prof. Ali Murat Özdemir, Prof. Nurcan Özgür, Assoc. Prof. Zeynep Arkan Tuncel and Assoc. Prof. İlhan Aras at the earlier stages of the project deserve special appreciation. Likewise, we are very appreciative to our friends and colleagues at our departments and the anonymous reviewers who generously devoted their time and shared their comments on the project. As editors, we owe a profound debt of gratitude to each of the contributors for their consideration and patience, particularly during tiresome and demanding process of revision. We are also very grateful to Derya Gürs, designer of the cover page illustration, for her patience in meeting our unremmiting requests gratuitously. Last but not least, this book project would not be finalized without the collaboration and support of Ms. Debbie de Wit, editor at the Social Sciences department of Brill publishers, as well as Prof. David Fasenfest, series editor of Studies in Critical Social Sciences. Indeed, Prof. Fasenfest's comments on the draft manuscript were quite precious, transforming the book into a much more solid contribution. For sure, the responsibility for any errors, interpretations, or omissions lies solely and entirely with the authors.

Figures

Notes on Contributors

Pınar Akgül
is Lecturer in the Department of International Relations at Giresun University. She holds a bachelor's degree in International Relations from Karadeniz Teknik University; MA degrees from Karadeniz Teknik University and King's College London and a PhD in International Relations from the University of Sussex at Brighton. She is the author of "The Criticism of EU's Efficiency in Region Politics: A Case Study of the Black Sea Region". Her research interests cover energy security, the concept of securitisation, the Black Sea Region studies and non-Western International Relations theories.

Zeynep Arıöz
is an Assistant Professor in International Relations at Bandırma Onyedi Eylül University, Turkey. She recieved her Ph.D. in International Relations from İstanbul University in 2016.

Neslihan Dikmen Alsancak
is currently a part-time lecturer at the Department of International Relations in Bilkent University. She received her Ph.D. in International Relations from Bilkent University in 2019. Her research focuses on International Relations theory, critical approaches to security, International Political Sociology and post-colonial/decolonial theory.

Altuğ Günar
is an Associate Professor in International Relations at Bandırma Onyedi Eylül University since 2018. He has numerous academic works, including articles, book chapters, book and book editorials in the field of the European Union. His main research areas are the European Union studies, International Relations and Economics, and Schumpeterian Economics. Dr. Günar is currently Vice Dean at the Faculty of Economics and Administrative Sciences in Bandirma Onyedi Eylul University, Director of the Mediterranean Policy Applications and Research Center, and Lecturer in the Department of International Relations. His most recent book is entitled "Creative Destruction, Crisis, and European Union: The 2008 Crisis within the Framework of the Schumpeterian Approach European Union and Globalization" and "Future of The European Union Integration: A Failure or A Success? Future Expectations".

Mine Nur Küçük

is Assistant Professor of Political Science and International Relations at Yeditepe University. She holds a Ph.D. from the Department of International Relations, Bilkent University. Her research interests include critical IR theories, critical approaches to security, and critical geopolitics.

Muhammed Kürşad Özekin

holds a bachelor's degree from Hacettepe University, an MA degree with distinction from King's College London and a PhD in international relations from University of Sussex. He previously worked at the Scientific and Technological Research Council of Turkey as a deputy of expert and at Uşak University as a lecturer in Politics and International Relations. Currently, he is an assistant professor at the Department of International Relations at Bandırma Onyedi Eylül University. His research interests include international political economy, political economy of development and Middle Eastern studies.

Çağdaş Özeniş

holds a bachelor's degree from Bilkent and SUNY Binghampton Universities, an MA degree with distinction from Middle East Technical University. Currently, he is a research assistant in the Department of Political Science and International Relations at Muğla Sıtkı Koçman University and a PhD candidate at Middle East Technical University. His research interests cover IR theory, theories of nationalism and development studies.

Engin Sune

is an Assistant Professor at the Department of International Relations at Hacettepe University. He holds his bachelor and graduate degrees from the department of International Relations at the Middle East Technical University. He was a visiting scholar at Harvard University, Center for Middle Eastern Studies from 2016 to 2017. His research interests are theories of globalization, international political economy, state theory, IR theories and the Middle East region.

Gözde Turan

has a PhD in International Relations from Bilkent University. Her research interests include international criminal law, critical theory, gender studies, international organizations, human rights and humanitarian law. She joined to Antalya Bilim University Department of Political Science and International Relations in 2017 as a full-time faculty member, and currently lectures Global

Governance and International Organizations, Politics of Human Rights, History of Political Thought, and Public International Law. She has published articles in Cooperation and Conflict, Journal of Gender Studies, and Feminist Legal Studies.

CHAPTER 1

Introduction

Foundations of International Relations Theory

M. Kürşad Özekin and Engin Sune

Although political philosophers, historians, jurists and policymakers have excessively written on international politics for many centuries, the field of International Relations emerged as a separate theoretical discipline at the beginning of the 20th century. Prior to the First World War, subject matters of International Relations had been studied by a number of old social science disciplines, including politics, philosophy, law, economics, and history, but it was the outbreak of the war which paved the way for the birth of International Relations as a distinctive scholarly discipline within the broad field of social sciences. Particularly, the extreme devastation and human cost of the Great War strengthened the conviction that little had been known about the nature of relationship between states and that systematic observation should be developed on an academic level. Indeed, the great catastrophe of the 1914–18 war led many to seek less-dangerous and more-effective means of conducting relations between societies, governments and states to serve human betterment in general. Thus, this increasing popularization of International Relations bears its very first fruit with the establishment of the Woodrow Wilson Chair of International Relations at the University of Wales, Aberystwyth in 1919. Throughout the 1920s, a series of other institutes, centres, schools and university departments were founded to promote teaching and research on issues related to war, peace and international cooperation. In addition to this, a number of private organizations were formed, and philanthropic grants were given to sponsor scholarly journals, conferences, seminars and academic trainings devoted to understanding and preventing international conflicts.

Primarily concerned with the puzzle of how and why the war began, International Relations scholarship in the early 20th century mainly focused on the causes and origins of war as well as its social, political, economic and psychological dimensions. As the Great War substantially undermined people's confidence in the prescriptions of power politics, many called for a 'clean break' with the old international order marked by the principles of secret diplomacy and classical balance of power. Mostly working in the U.S. and British universities, the first scholars in the field such as Sir Alfred Zimmern

(1936, 1938), Philip Noel-Baker (1934) and James T. Shotwells (1925) shared the conviction that a more peaceful and just world order could be created by democratizing inter-state relations and transferring the liberal principles of self-determination, rule of law and mutual respect to the realm of international politics. Thus, grew out of the liberal reaction to the War, the early phase of IR theorizing, during the 1920s and early 1930s, was largely predominated by the "idealist" or progressivist doctrines (Bull, 1972a, p.253). Central here was a shared commitment to the nineteenth-century belief that the mankind could achieve political progress by utilizing the power of human reason to develop common interest, good will and universal values in preventing international conflicts and making the world a more peaceful place for future generations. Concurrently, the increasing trust in human reasoning also reinforced the idea that IR scholarship was to assist this march of political progress by overcoming the ill-will, the prejudices, the ignorance and the sinister interests that stood in its way (Bull, 1972b, p.35).

The ascendency of political Idealism in International Relations was relatively short-lived and suffered a crisis of confidence with the breakdown of the League of Nations and the rise of aggressive dictatorships: Germany, Italy and Japan who sought to revise to the post-1918 global settlement made in the Paris Peace Conference. In fact, the real-life crisis of Wilsonian Idealism and the decline of the post-1918 settlement produced a strong reaction against liberal internationalism in world politics and against peace-inspired topics in the field of International Relations. The normative and visionary zeal inherent in the study of international relations was vehemently criticized as unrealistic and impractical. The moral idealism and liberal internationalism, dominated the discipline's early years, received a visceral attack for suggesting conception of international politics that bore little resemblance to the real conduct of international affairs. As the visionary world of moral idealism grew more distant from the hard facts of world politics, a new conception in the study of international relations, known as Realism, came to dominate the discipline. Perhaps one of the most trenchant criticisms in this direction was launched by Edward H. Carr, shortly before the outbreak of the Second World War. Following in the fashion of Thucydides, Machiavelli and Hobbes, Carr (1939), in his well-known book *The Twenty Years' Crisis,* revealed how utopian ideas of peace and cooperation among nations had been undermined by the realities of mistrust, insecurity and conflicting interests of states in the international realm. As one of the first modern Realist IR scholar, Carr blamed idealists or what he called 'utopians' for being exuberant and dangerously naïve in their analyses of international relations. Following the outbreak of the Second World War, Carr's critique of liberal internationalism was increasingly continued by various other scholars, mostly notably by Hans Morgenthau in the U.S., leading to what would later come to recognize as the first 'discipline-defining debate' in International Relations' history.

In fact, the Second World War not only brought about a drastic change in the agenda of world politics but also marked an important milestone for academic International Relations. The first great debate, which took place between Idealists and Realists during the late 1930s and 1940s, served as a starting point for the orthodoxy in the study of international relations which has been recurrently narrated in numerous "state of the disciple" articles. The war itself was seen as a severe crisis in the Idealist paradigm which rigorously brought the core concepts of national interest, survival and the struggle for power back to the centre of the discipline. Particularly, the post-war intellectual climate was characterized by a shift towards "power-politics" explanation of international relations which would eventually become a dominant part of the self-image of the field. Particularly, Hans J. Morgenthau's *Politics Among Nations* (1954) has significantly developed the main lines of the general theoretical framework of Realism in its classical sense. Central to Morgenthau's theory was the notion of power as the constituent nature and dominant goal of international politics. For Morgenthau, international politics is not governed by the universal values and moral laws, but guided by the logic of national interest, often defined in terms of power, security, survival and relative capabilities.

As one of the most long-lived text in the study of international relations, Morgenthau's (1954) work served as an essential exposition of Realist theory. In the decade or so after the World War Two, the Realist analysis became central within the field of IR theory offering easily adoptable insights particularly for the world of policymaking and statecraft. Numerous other contributors such as Raymond Aron (1967), Hedley Bull (1977), and Martin Wight (1977, 1978) in Europe and George Kennan (1979, 1982) and Reinhold Niebuhr (1953) in the U.S. have further systematized the notion of political Realism as the dominant explanation of international politics. Although Realists lack internal uniformity and do not constitute a homogeneous school of thought, they share a set of core premises about International Relations. Frequently drawing on the examples of the past, Realists suggest that humankind is actually held hostage to repetitive patterns of behaviour dictated by their nature. Unlike Idealists and liberal internationalists, Realists believe that humans are inherently self-interested and egoistic creatures driven by their desire or appetite to gain power over others. As humans are organized into states, the basic human characteristics have in turn an impact on state behaviour. In self-help system in which no sovereign power is in charge of the world order, states act selfishly and strive for survival, security and power, mostly to detriment of others. That is why mistrust, fear and disorder rules international relations and conflict is unavoidable and more common than peace and cooperation.

Although the basic premises of Realism found greater respect in academic and policy circles, its classical versions articulated by Morgenthau and others have subjected to a barrage of criticism, mainly on methodological, theoretical and empirical grounds. Particularly in the United States in the late 1950s and 1960s, a large influx of scholar from different disciplines got involved in the study of IR seeking to replace the "wisdom literature" of Classical Realists with scientific inquiry (Brown, 1992, p.35). Proponents of the scientific approach found theoretical frameworks of both Realism and Liberalism too impressionistic and expressed their dissatisfaction with the historical and interpretivist methodologies on which earlier accounts are based. Rather, they believed that mainly grounded in a theory of human nature, the earlier accounts of international relations lack of sufficient precision and rigor in their analyses. Overall, historical and philosophical elucidations had been used in a more impressionistic way to support rather than demonstrate presumptions about general patterns of international relations. Therefore, it is claimed that the study of IR lagged significantly behind other social science disciplines, most particularly economics which use the method of scientific inquiry to test specific hypotheses, develop general laws and predict human behaviours.

Thus, the scientific turn in IR during the mid-1950s to mid-1960s -the so-called "behavioural decade"- led to the second major disciplinary debate taking place between traditionalists or non-positivists and behaviouralists or positivists. Coming late to IR, at least compared to other areas of political science, behaviouralists sought to develop a more methodologically rigorous approach to theorize international affairs. They argued that the discipline was inordinately dominated by what they labelled as traditionalists, who had heavily drew on insights from interpretive historicist methods at the expanse of precision and accuracy. In the search for greater precision, behaviouralists rather relied on a positivist hypothetical-deductive methodology and emulated as much as possible the methodologies of natural sciences. Rooted in positivist methodology, behaviouralist distinguished between what can and cannot be observed. To put it more explicitly, the datum of behaviouralists is amenable to quantification, measurement, testing, and replication which let formulating rigorous relationships among clearly defined variables. Therefore, behaviouralists mainly rejected factors that could not be measured in empirical terms such as values, perceptions and motivations (Sanders, 2002). Rather, they examined the behaviour, actions and acts of states through the observation of systems, patterns, causalities based on empirical testing, mainly via falsification. Overall, they eschewed the uniqueness of particular episodes and guested for discoverable uniformities, regularities, and patterns of state behaviour that can be expressed in theories and generalizations with explanatory and predictive value (Singer, 1969, p.64).

For the behaviouralists, the main culprit in "traditional IR theory" is the field's attachment and grounding in history and philosophy, which inhibited it from formulating rigorous explications about international and political affairs and grounded its discourse in vague presumptions wherein notions such as human nature and power precluded scientific explanation. Thus, with the rise of behaviouralism, action and behaviour took ontological precedence over such conceptions as human nature, reason, power and freedom (Hamati-Ataya, 2012). The quest for precision has led many to turn their attention from human nature to appropriate models, analogies, metaphors and system analysis to explain regularities and patterns of state behaviour similar to laws observed in natural sciences. Adopting a descriptive and explanatory form of inquiry, behaviouralists gradually established a strong presence in the field of International Relations. By the mid-1960s, students and scholars of international politics had been already trained in quantitative research, game theory, simulation and statistical and mathematical techniques of the social sciences. Along with the changing international milieu and the advances in computational technology, the use of exploratory quantitative analyses in the study of international relations increased conspicuously. Consequently, a great number of studies sought for correlations between phenomena such as alliances and the outbreak of war, between levels of domestic violence and participation in international politics, between levels of economic development and political stability, between levels of political integration and levels of trade, communication and mobility.

This swift rise in quantitative methodology in turn provoked some anxiety and counterattack by Classical Realists and many other scholars associated with the so-called English School of International Relations. Thus, the main battle lines were broadly drawn between recognizable figures such as Hedley Bull and Edward H. Carr on the traditionalist side and Morton Kaplan and Thomas Schelling on the behaviouralist.[1] Defending the traditionalist approach, scholars such as Hedley Bull (1966) questioned the necessity or even the possibility of universal scientific theory of International Relations given

---

1 For the earlier debate between those insisting upon "classical historical-interpretive" analysis of IR and those who disdain all but "scientific-behavioral" approach see Hedley Bull, "International Theory: The Case for a Classical Approach," *World Politics*, Vol. 18 (April, 1966), pp. 361–377, and Morton Kaplan, "The New Great Debate: Traditionalism vs. Science in International Relations," *World Politics*, Vol. 19 (October, 1966), pp. 1–20.

the complexity of world politics, the uniqueness of each historical juncture and the role of leadership and contingency in diplomacy. Overall, traditionalists argued that historical conditions are so varied, diverse and complex that no scientific theory could ever capture the ebbs and flows of international politics. Behaviouralists, on the other hand, insisted that IR theory could only advance itself by adopting scientific methodology and empirical research which allows for greater intuitions and progress in theory development (Kaplan 1966, p. 380).

In fact, the behavioural revolution had a long-term impact on the study of international relations by contributing to theoretical advancement within the field. The behaviouralist programme did not completely replaced the classical approaches -particularly Realism- as many keen to discuss but gave rise to an assortment of empirical studies. As Ole Waever (1996, p.170) set forth, the study of IR was rather "conducted in a multitude of ways, many of which were on arch-realist premises (e.g. with power political, egoistic states fitted into models of a game theoretical or system theoretical nature)". Along with the behaviouralist turn, the basic tenets and assumptions of classical approaches such as Realism and Liberalism were reformulated relying on models and concepts barrowed from economics, rational choice theory, expected utility and theories of firms and markets. As a result, throughout the 1970s, the field of International Relations was increasingly marked by a renewed debate, mainly called 'the inter-paradigm debate' or 'the third debate'.

On one side of the dispute was a revival of Realist school of thinking under the name of neorealism or structural realism which gained wider recognition by Waltz's *Theory of International Politics* (1979) and Gilpin's *War and Change in World Politics* (1981). Overall neorealism represented an effort to relaunch more 'scientific' versions of Realism by injecting greater precision and conceptual rigour. In his seminal book, Waltz (1979) redefined the principal tenets of Realist enquiry of international relations by putting it on a more theoretically sound footing both in ontological and methodological terms. While retaining recognizable Realist features such as power and conflict as explanatory notions, Waltz discounts human nature as a meaningful variable for the sake of theoretical parsimony. Capitalizing on analogies from microeconomics and oligopoly theory, Waltz explicitly limits the focus of analysis to the structure of international system, which for him constrains the foreign-policy options available to states as principle unitary-rational actors and constitutes the underlying conditions of anarchy and self-help. According to Waltz and other neo-realists, human nature, therefore, is not the reason for why states are power-hungry. Rather, the reason stems from the structure and construct of the international system that obligates the states to seek power for the sake of survival and national security in a self-help anarchical world (Mearsheimer,

2007, p.72). In doing so, neorealists moved the intention away from expounding idiosyncratic motivations of government and instead examined the structural imperatives of international system to which all states are subjected as rational units whose functions are more or less similar.

On the other side of the controversy have been the neoliberal institutionalists who seek to present a more coherent reformulation of a liberal conception of international relations. In parallel with the neorealists, the neoliberal institutionalists also seek for precise and formula-like assertions which could be easily reduced to simple analytical explanations amenable to test. Up until now, works of numerous important individuals have contributed to this school of thought, but among them, works of Robert Keohane and Joseph Nye (1971 1977) are certainly the pioneers of this genre. Relying on models borrowed from rational choice approaches and game theory, neoliberal institutionalists aim to explain behaviour and policy choices of states both in conflict and co-operative situations. Although neoliberal institutionalists share many of the premises of neorealism, ranging from the centrality of states as the principal actors to the conception of anarchy as the underlying condition of international system, its adherents come to different conclusions in some instances. Neoliberal institutionalism – often shortened to just 'neoliberalism'– broadly acknowledge the structural condition of anarchy in international system but for them anarchy does not necessarily lead to competition and conflict as neorealists keen to argue. Rather as Keohane (1989, p.11) put forth the principal question that preoccupies neoliberals is how regimes and international institutions affect incentives facing states. Neoliberals consider international regimes and institutions as the means and the mediator to achieve co-operation among states under the condition of anarchy. Although neoliberals acknowledge the Realist conception of states as the key actors in a structurally anarchic international system, they argue that states are not the only significant actors and their behaviour can be restrained by interaction with international organizations such as the United Nations (UN), the European Union (EU), the World Trade Organization (WTO), and NATO.

The inter-paradigm debate between neorealists and neoliberal institutionalists has long preoccupied scholars' attention and has led to a plethora of works which argue for one or the other approach or intend to reconcile these two paradigms. Nevertheless, in the meantime, a third paradigm has also arisen as a "heretic voice" of IR discipline: Marxism or Radicals. Making powerful statements on international politics, Marxism was not indeed a new theory since Marxist thought on international relations pre-dates the foundation of the discipline as an institutionalised field of study. Particularly, the works of Lenin (1999), Kautsky (2007) and Luxemburg (1972) chiefly concerned themselves with analysis of imperialism and dominance which generated inter-state competition, colony grabbing and conflict in the capitalist world system. Nevertheless, despite its concern about inter-state rivalry, very few regarded Marxist accounts within the approaches of International Relations. For many traditional theorists of International Relations (see inter alia Wright, 1966; Waltz, 1979), Marxism was far too preoccupied with economic aspects of human affairs and its "utopian" assumptions underestimated the critical importance of the state, nationalism, power struggle and security for the structure of world politics.

Throughout the 1970s, however, Marxist accounts of world politics have been increasingly seen as an alternative theory of International Relations. Marxist and neo-Marxist accounts of international relations oppose the neorealist/ neoliberal conception of state conflict and cooperation and rather focus on material and economic aspects of international affairs. Unlike the established approaches of Anglo-American International Relations, Marxism identifies the causes of war as class conflict mainly taking place between and within the capitalist classes. That's why, Marxism holds a political, conflictual approach to IR. As long-established approaches argue, there are conflict of interests in international politics, but they do not take place between states or individuals, but between oppressed and oppressors within and across states. In this sense, class relations or more precisely social relations of production constitute the major unit of analysis for the Marxist accounts of international relations. Overall, Marxists question the very foundations of mainstream IR theory. For them IR is not just about states' foreign policy or their respective behaviour as "rational actors", but more about politics of dominant classes, reproduction of inequalities, class conflicts and the notion of survival in its broader sense. Thus, this in turn problematizes the dichotomized thinking in mainstream IR theory such as political/economic, international/domestic, sovereignty/anarchy and public/private as those categories obfuscate the ways in which states and foreign policies are designated by social relations of production and structure of capitalist world economy.

As the Marxism increasingly came to be seen as an alternative theory of international relations, the discipline has engaged in a triangular debate between these three main approaches. However, contrary to the two previous debates, "the third debate" or "the inter-paradigm debate", as Ole Waever (1996, p.155) notes, was "seen as a debate not to be won, but a pluralism to live with". To put it another way, the discipline itself was the debate between these incommensurable paradigms. Each paradigm formulates its own fundamental questions and concepts/units and thereby its own language and criteria of judgement. The discipline of IR thus became richer in the sense of having all three voices reflecting a triangular image. However, despite its triangular appearance, inter-paradigm debate was *de facto* mostly a debate alongside of the triangle, particularly between neo-realism and neo-liberalism. In fact, the three sides of the debate were never equal as the Marxists/radicals were mainly ignored in mainstream literature given the ideological aversion to this mode of thought particularly in the United States.

Starting from the early 1980s, such a constellation in the inter-paradigm debate became more apparent with the change of fronts. Throughout the 1980s, both neo-realism and neo-liberalism underwent a self-limiting reconstruction towards an anti-metaphysical, theoretical position by which they increasingly became compatible with each other. Both sought for more precise, formula-like contentions amenable to convert to simple analytical statement for testing and empirical research. As the previous lines of the debate became vague, the research programme of the 1980s was increasingly marked neo-neo synthesis. Eventually, two main poles came to appear. On the one hand of the debate was the neo-realist and neo-liberal synthesis and on the other the so-called radicals or what Keohane (1988) would later unite under the label of 'reflectivists'. As the dominant approaches of Anglo-American International Relations, the two main poles of inter-paradigm debate, namely neo-realism and neo-liberalism, were no longer 'incommensurable' but rather shared a 'rationalist' research agenda, a commitment to a unified conception of science, an agreed premise of anarchy and state which catalysed synthesis between them on many fronts. As dissenting voices of the discipline, Marxist or radical accounts on the other hand seemed to be on the margins of the field for a long time but they opened the way for a series of new critical approaches to international theory in the following decades.

Starting from the late 1960s, Marxist scholars have in fact served a crucial function in contesting the rationalist epistemology and politicized nature of International Relations as a discipline. To give an example, the earlier works of radical scholars such as Yergin (1977) and Chomsky (1969) have revealed how the prevailing political interests of the time, as defined by the dominant classes, acquire disciplinary dominance and hegemony at the expense of the expressible dissent voices and the interests of subordinate classes. In fact, the Realist-inspired Strategic Studies was seen as an illustrative case in point given its close connections with the 'military–industrial complex', particularly in the United States (Burchill and Linklater, 2005, p.14). From an epistemological point of view, Marxism has exercised immense impact on the development of critical thinking in International Relations theory and posed a serious alternative to the disciplinary orthodoxy. Unlike the mainstream IR theories, Marxism has revealed how theory itself is instrumental to power relations and how knowledge is incessantly conditioned by pre-existing social forces, political interests, and general beliefs tied to a particular place and time. Thus, this not only raises important issues about the claim of subject's neutral engagement with an objective reality but also questions the immutability of existing social structures as they are shaped predominantly by the dominant classes and underlying power relations. Therefore, in stark contrast to orthodox approaches in the field, Marxism pursues a normative and emancipatory interest in identifying the prospects for new forms of social and political order hopping that humanity could be free from vulnerability, exploitation and any other kind of social domination.

Consequently, the phase of inter-paradigm debate, as Banks (1985) and Hoffman (1987) claim, revealed that the early accordment about the nature of IR as a discipline has been replaced by a far wider range of critical or "reflectivist" approaches that survives until today. Particularly, the fourth debate[2] or what is commonly labelled as the post-positivist turn has made such a rapid theoretical expansion more prominent by posing ontological and epistemological questions about what IR theory is and what its purposes are. Emerged in the mid-1980s, the post-positivist turn has led a major disciplinary debate in which intellectuals such Robert Cox (1981, 1987, 1989) and Richard K. Ashley (1984, 1987) questioned the very possibility of an objective science of international relations as what is 'out there' in international politics is inevitably a political and value-laden question that depends on the matter of whose interest is protected and whose is neglected by the dominant social structures and power relations. In this pioneering article, Cox (1981, p.129) saliently propounds that "theory is always for someone and for some purpose". What Cox meant by this oft-quoted statement is that there is actually no such a thing as neutral theory concerning international affairs or no theory of universal validity. Rather, theories – even those that aim for objectivity – are actually rooted in specific time and space, reflecting views of the world which favour some political interests over others.

Addressing the politicized nature of IR theory, Cox identifies two main strains of theorizing. First, mostly associated with the established theories of

---

2   Confusingly, the disciplinary history of International Relations has lacked consensus on a widely acceptable typology of the Great Debates. This is particularly the case in the Fourth Debate as some scholars like Lapid (1989) reject the appraisement of the inter-paradigm debate as a Great Debate. However, following Wæver's (1996) typology we conceive a third debate occurring in the 1970s between neo-realists, neo-liberals, and radicals and a fourth debate arising in the 1980s mostly between positivists and post-positivist theories of international relations.

IR, there are problem-solving theories which take the existing world order and the prevailing social and power relations for granted as the given framework for action. For Cox (1981, p.128–129), the main purpose of problem-solving theory is to "make these relationships and institutions work smoothly by dealing effectively with particular sources of trouble". Therefore, by their nature, problem-solving theory has no intention of questioning how the existing social order came into being but instead aims to "arrive at statements of laws or regularities which appear to have general validity" constituting an ideological bias in favour of the status quo (Cox, 1986, p.208). Conversely, as the second strain of theorizing, the critical theory places itself above the prevailing power relations and dominant social order and questions how that order came into existence. Being self-consciously normative and reflective, the critical theories do not take the prevailing social order as an unchangeable natural fact, but seek to problematize existing power relations and dominant social structures asking whether and how they might be transcended. Thus, for critical theory, the main objective of theorizing is not only explaining the world as it is, but also criticizing repressive practices and institutions in the existing social order and seeking politically motivated action for an alternative set of social relations based on equality and universal justice (Yalvaç, 2015).

In fact, the critical and self-reflective tone in Cox's examination is widely shared also by various strands of post-positivist scholarship which set out to challenge the mainstream IR theorizing. Particularly, massive borrowings from social and political philosophy during the 1980s and the 1990s have not only re-embed international relations firmly in the wider social sciences but also triggered proliferation of a far wider range of critical approaches within the discipline. A broadly similar reflectivist purpose also runs through the post-structural/post-modern International Relations scholarship which explores how dominant framings of world politics are produced and reproduced a regime of power and vice versa (see inter alia, Ashley, 1981, 1984; Gregory, 1989; Der Derian and Shapiro, 1989; Campbell, 1992). As a critical discourse on disciplinary knowledge production, poststructural/postmodern approaches question the possibility of separating the 'subject' from the 'object' or the world of fact "out there" and the cognitive realm of theory. In a similar vein to other strands of critical scholarship, Poststructuralism/postmodernism seeks to expose the connection between hegemonic forms of knowledge production and the reproduction of power relations. By focusing on the relations between language, politics, and social structure, poststructuralism/postmodernism reveals how the so-called objective or knowable reality of international politics is discursively produced; and how power mechanisms of inclusion/exclusion produce dominant framings of world politics and legitimize certain forms of actions while marginalising other ways of thinking and acting (Gregory, 1989; Newman, 2010).

A similar concern is also presented by another school of intellectual tradition that emerged mostly as part of a wider critical turn in IR theory particularly starting from the late 1980s. Like other critical approaches- from Marxist and Frankfurt-school inspired critical theory to post-structural and post-modernist approaches, feminists voice not a dissimilar concerns about the exclusion of their presence and perspectives from IR theory, arguing that the study of international relations since its inception at the beginning of the 20th century, has tended to be a male-dominated realm in which the role of women is piecemeal and anything whatsoever related to gender is neglected as a subject of concern. Although not all feminists could be regarded as critical scholars, there are apparent affinities between the feminist concern of exposing the gender-based nature of IR theory and the broader critical project of reflectivist turn, considering the feminists' endeavour to theorise the untheorised in an effort to promote emancipatory change. Thus, in their pioneering scholarly works, feminist scholars like Cynthia Enloe (1989, 2000) Ann Tickner (1988, 1999, 2001) and Carol Cohn (1987) have brought gender concerns in the academic study of international politics by exposing socially and discursively constructed gender norms and identities in IR that the mainstream tended to take as a given.

Thus, the rapid expansion of critical approaches to International Relations has not only widened the disciplinary boundaries of the field in epistemological and ontological terms but also allowed a greater space for the dissent voices of marginalized and oppressed to be heard. The overall critical approaches do not simply observe and explain world of fact "out there", they pursue a broader purpose which is to question how and for what reasons the existing world order came into being and what possibilities exist for human intervention and action to change it in ways that improve the life-conditions of the excluded and vulnerable. In short, enhancing our ethical and practical horizons, the critical approaches- in all its various guises, have had huge implications for the scope of inquiry within the discipline of IR. Today, International Relations theory looks very different than what it was twenty or thirty years ago. Thanks to the wider intellectual plurality which has prospered by the rise of the critical turn, there is now a far greater space for more elaborate descriptions of social reality and more normative thinking on international issues.

No doubt, acknowledging the strength and praiseworthy outcomes of critical IR scholarship does not mean that the established theories of international relations is dead, but there is today a growing dissatisfaction with the intellectual imperialism of the so-called scientific rationality of IR orthodoxy that shapes the dominant images of "social reality" in our contemporary world. Therefore, a frank interest in various stands of critical IR scholarship is vital not only to free from the intellectual straitjacket of IR orthodoxy but to make a better sense of structures, actors, institutions, processes and interactions with the ultimate goal of transforming the world towards a better future for human existence. Thus, taking a sympathetic stance on such a self-reflective and emancipatory objective in critical IR scholarship, the main concern of this book is to explore the achievements of a wide variety of critical approaches in International Relations theory, discuss the barrage of criticism and theoretical openings they levied against the IR orthodoxy and suggest future potential of critical IR scholarship to improve not only our explanatory possibilities, but also our ethical and practical horizons. In line with this broad objective, the book examines a number of influential approaches within critical IR scholarship, including core strands of critical IR theory such as Marxism, post-structuralism, Feminism, post-colonialism and green politics as well as some sub-school approaches such as Marxist theories of imperialism, dependency perspective, uneven and combine development and non-western IR theory.

In this way, the book seeks to provide a comprehensive overview of the critical turn that has emerged in contemporary International Relations since the early 1980s and explores the overall theoretical openings it has achieved until now. In this regard, four main intellectual concerns seem to occupy our research agenda for launching this book project. The first is to examine the current state of International Relations theory in relation to a wide range of critical approaches that challenge orthodox problematics of knowledge production on global affairs. To that end, we aim to assess the extent to which the critical approaches, in all its various guises, have transcended and moved away from the intellectual dominance of the mainstream IR scholarship on both theoretical and practical grounds. The second is to provide a series of further reflections on dissent voices of marginalised in the contemporary theory of the international, assuming an emancipatory moral purpose for the betterment of human affairs based on more just and equal terms. Thus, with this purpose in mind, we seek to uncover how power relations privilege and legitimise certain points of view while others are silenced or excluded based on their race, class, gender, sexuality and or geographical location. The third is to discuss the major theoretical openings and achievements of various critical approaches and to assess their respective strengths and weaknesses vis a vis the parochial theories of the International Relations scholarship. Last but not least, the fourth concern of the book is to speculate about the future research directions within critical IR scholarship and to discuss prospective contributions that various critical approaches offer to move beyond the current confines of IR theory.

Although the book identifies major critical perspectives as a whole, we do not intent to give the impression that these schools of thought constitute a uniform or monolithic theoretical tradition. While the various critical approaches to international theory share some basic assumptions, they, at the same time, exhibit a wide variety of differing epistemological and ontological stands and even sometimes conflicting worldviews. To those who are new to the field, this diversity within the critical IR scholarship might be frustrating at first glance, but there is nothing abnormal about the plurality of different traditions of critical thinking as this is rather a strength and an obstacle to ossification in theoretical sense. To be sure, albeit their overall heterogeneity, differing critical approaches are not mutually exclusive and there are productive channels of conversation through which they engage in dialogue with one another. To give an example, the Frankfurt School inspired critical theory in IR presents a specific interpretation of Marxist philosophy with respect to some its key economic and political notions such as redistribution struggles, social emancipation, commodification, reification, and critique of mass culture. Similarly, it is not surprising to find further overlaps between Marxism, neo-Gramscian IR theory and postcolonialism. Again, whilst it seems a distinctive worldview, feminism, as a multidimensional school of thought engages in constant dialogue with Marxist, poststructuralist and postmodernist strands of critical IR theory.

Thus, recognising this dialogue of diversity within the broader critical IR scholarship, the book explores the merits of these overlapping but alternative forms of critical reflections and discusses their respective contributions to our understanding of contemporary world politics. In this sense, each chapter of the book is designed to be read separately and stands on its own but relates to all the other chapters as a part of broader critical theoretical inheritance that locates critical thinking and emancipatory possibilities at the centre of scientific inquiry.

Besides, there is uniformity among each chapter in terms of their formal organization and structural setting of the debates, as they all share a common objective and are motivated to explore responses to similar questions. First of all, acknowledging that knowledge is situated in time and space, each chapter begins with a depiction of the historiography of the theory. Beyond any doubt, any theoretical stand is built upon a vast and rooted philosophical inheritance and unveiling this historical background is believed to reveal the underlying ideational, as well as practical, mechanisms that set the basis for the formation of that specific critical approach. Thereof, each chapter commences with a historical analysis narrating the development of the theory, with a particular emphasis on the foundational texts and the studies by the pioneering scholars that led a new critical theoretical opening within IR scholarship.

The second concern of each chapter is to figure out the main critiques developed by that critical approach to the conventional theories of IR. Critical theories have always strived to make room for their scientific inquiry within IR scholarship as it has been overwhelmingly dominated by the conventional approaches; hence, they developed their theoretical arguments inevitably in a constant debate with the mainstream IR theories in order to transcend them. For instance, Robert Cox, as one of the leading figures of the critical scholarship in IR, clarified his theoretical position by comparison and in discussion with what he termed as the problem-solving theories. Similarly, before 1990s, in her seminal article, Ann Tickner (1988) analysed Hans Morgenthau's principles of political realism and tried to reformulate it through a feminist research agenda. In this regard, all chapters aim to put forth and compile the critiques of that specific approach to the conventional theories of IR.

Following the historical introduction of the theory and its critiques to the conventional IR scholarship, the purpose of each chapter is to explain the main premises of the approach and depict the modalities developed to capture the essence of international relations. As previously stated, there is a vast diversity among critical IR scholarship, and the theories analysed under the scope of this book are not an exception. Even though some critical approaches are inspired from the same epistemological and ontological traditions, they do not constitute a uniform theoretical understanding of international politics. Yet, regarding the emancipatory mission of overall critical scholarship, within this theoretical heterogeneity and richness, all the theories in this book aim to develop alternative ways of understanding international relations. In this respect, all these approaches strain to uncover the possibilities for constructing an alternative world, but they either concentrate on different spheres of social reality or they developed divergent sets of ideational mechanisms and theoretical tools to explain the nature of the subject matter. Therefore, within this rich theoretical corpus, the third objective of every single chapter is to introduce the main concepts and premises developed by each approach in order to explain the underlying mechanisms behind the apparent functioning of international relations.

Last but not least, the studies developed by the critical approaches are not limited to a certain historical period when the theory is originated or to a narrow field, as apart from their contributions to IR scholarship they pave the way for new theoretical openings and research. To give an example, while scientific realism is in and of itself an essential debate within the philosophy of science, it inspired conventional constructivists and various forms of Marxists

conceptualizations of the international sphere. In a similar vein, the literatures of uneven and combined development, as well as imperialism, which
are derived from various Marxist traditions, have encouraged new current
studies in the field of International Relations, especially those using the theoretical capacity and strength of the approach for conducting case studies.
Therefore, the last objective of each chapter is to introduce and explore these
new research directions and current studies that make use of the theoretical
findings and the conceptual framework of the approach that is under inquiry.

Herewith, the book covers the most influential approaches within critical IR
scholarship with a particular focus on the historical heritage they built upon
and their philosophical roots. However, this comprehensive study does not
provide an exhaustive survey of the critical IR literature and it does not claim
to represent all strands of critical perspectives. But the book still provides a
fresh insight into the underlying structures of the critical scholarship in IR
since it covers foundational theoretical debates that prepared the stage for the
development of critical approaches. All strands of critical theory engage in a
constant dialogue with the Marxist formulations and some of those can be
directly labelled as the sub-schools of Marxism. Furthermore, a good majority
of the critical theories under the scope of this book emerged in the IR after
the mid-1980s as a product of the post-positivist or reflectivist turn. Therefore,
the chapters of the book are grouped under two broader sections. While the
first section introduces the critical theories entirely affiliated with Marxism,
such as theories of imperialism, dependency and uneven and combined
development, the second section investigates critical approaches that have
become present in IR after the Great Debate between positivists and post-
positivists. This broad second section covers chapters scrutinizing far wider
range of critical approaches within the discipline, such as Post-structuralism,
Post-Colonialism, International Political Sociology, Feminism, Non-Western IR
theories and lastly Green Theory. In this setting, the book is composed of ten
separate chapters scrutinizing different branches of critical thinking.

In chapter two, Engin Sune and Kürşad Özekin introduce Marxism as a
scientific approach to International Relations. The radical criticism of Marx
and foundational texts of Marxism have paved the way for further critiques
in the various fields of social sciences, which produced a wide corpus of critical scholarship. Thereof, the chapter explores the original contributions of
Marxism to the study of IR by analysing the histography of Marxism and by
introducing the main concepts developed by Marxists for explaining the social
world. This introduction and discussion on Marxism and its contributions to
IR scholarship is further detailed in the following chapters.

In this context, in chapter three Engin Sune introduces theory of imperialism and discusses the possibilities of conceptualizing imperialism as a critical theory of the "international". While Sune admits that there are various studies and different perspectives on imperialism, he suggests that imperialism studies still form a single theoretical framework. Therefore, he explores how "theory of imperialism" depicts the nature of international politics with a peculiar focus on the historical transformation of the imperialism literature itself. The chapter also reveals the critiques of imperialism literature to the mainstream conceptualizations of the international relations and explores current research directions inspired by imperialism studies.

The fourth chapter analyses another crucial Marxist literature, namely the dependency approach, which emerged out of the intellectual heritage found in the critique of the liberal and diffusionist views of modernisation theory as the orthodox economic pensée of the 1960s. In this chapter, M. Kürşad Özekin meticulously documents how and in what ways the dependency tradition offers critical insights to IR scholarship. After reflecting on critical spirit of dependency perspective, the author discusses the enduring relevance and prospective research directions of dependency theory by putting a special emphasis on the current dynamics of global world.

In chapter five, Çağdaş Özeniş analyses the important yet understudied theory of Uneven and Combined Development (UCD) which argues that the historical development of capitalism should be studied as a non-linear, intersocietal and dialectical process. The chapter explores the contributions of UCD as an alternative theoretical framework that might replace the reified, ahistorical and supra-sociological understanding of the 'international' that mainstream theories put forward. Özeniş also provides a detailed account of the ontological, epistemological and methodological premises of the theory and discusses how UCD draws the boundaries of the 'international'.

The sixth chapter, which is also the first chapter of the second wider section, by Gözde Turan elaborates on Poststructuralism as a theory with its critical stance against not only mainstream theories, but also any approach with a claim of truth in IR. The author discusses how IR scholars attempted to display representations and symbols to configurate problems in International Relations by drawing on post-structural thinkers such as Michel Foucault and Jacques Derrida. The chapter presents how Poststructuralism ascribes power to discourses and thereby argues that the real source of power lies in the discourse which, inter alia, constructs particular subjects with particular identities. In this context, the chapter provides a detailed account of the language of poststructuralism itself in addition to the discourse analysis of poststructuralism.

Chapter seven introduces one of the fastest growing areas of research in IR, Postcolonial approaches, which emerged as a part of the critical strand of thought in the 1990s. In this chapter, Mine Nur Küçük investigates the key concepts of postcolonialism and presents the ideas of the classic postcolonial thinkers, such as Edward Said and Frantz Fanon. The chapter also reveals the problematization of mainstream theories by postcolonial IR critics; particularly with reference to the former's Eurocentrism. The author analytically discusses distinct contributions of postcolonial approaches to the discipline of IR and underlines the importance of colonial power relations in understanding world politics. This part of the book also elucidates the role of actors located in the Global South and clarifies recent research directions in the postcolonial IR studies.

Neslihan Dikmen Alsancak in chapter eight introduces International Political Sociology (IPS) as an understanding of international relations. The author in this chapter provides a detailed account of the historical background of IPS and sheds lights on its philosophical roots based on new materialism, relational sociology, practice turn, reflexivity, and micro-politics of the everyday. The chapter also figures out the problem of the international, the main critique developed by International Political Sociology to the conventional theories of IR and explains the main premises and concepts of the political sociology. Lastly, this part of the book explores new research directions of the approach and mainly focuses on its engagement with the sociology of science studies.

In chapter nine, Zeynep Arıöz analyses the trajectory and development of feminism in IR as a critical approach since the Post-Cold War era. The author reveals the engagement of feminism with IR and how gender has become a part of the analysis of international politics with the rise of feminist studies. The chapter provides an insight on the critiques of feminist approaches levied against philosophical and epistemological underpinnings of conventional IR theory. Arıöz, in this part of the book, also puts forth the key premises of the feminist perspective and its contributions to the apprehension of international politics.

In chapter ten, Pınar Akgül introduces non-Western IR theories which strive to overcome Western centrism in IR and generate a non-Western approach to International Relations. The chapter briefly provides a historical account of the development of critiques to Western-centrism and efforts to raise the voice of non-Western contributions to IR. The chapter presents how non-Western IR theories through their critique to ethnocentrism, false universalism and agency denial of the mainstream IR theories, provide a room for the theoretical contributions from different cultures and civilisations. Lastly, the chapter

discusses the possibilities of new future research directions triggered by theoretical contributions of non-Western conceptualizations in IR.

The last chapter of the book displaces one of the understudied approaches
to international politics, the Green Theory, which raises the concerns for the
global environmental issues. In this chapter, Altuğ Günar addresses the position of Green Theory in the field of International Relations and reveals its
fundamental theoretical assumptions. The chapter examines the historical
development of Green Theory with a particular focus on its foundational texts
and scholars. Moreover, the author presents the critiques of the theory to mainstream IR scholarship and discusses the new theoretical openings inspired by
the contributions of Green Theory to the field.

References

Aron R., 1967. *Peace and War: A Theory of International Relations*, translated from
the French by Richard Howard and Annette Baker Fox. New York: Frederick A.
Praeger.

Ashley, R. K., 1981. Political Realism and Human Interests. *International Studies
Quarterly*. 25 (2), pp. 204–236.

Ashley, R. K.,1984. The Poverty of Neorealism. International Organization. 38(2):225–286.

Ashley, R. K., 1987. The Geopolitics of Geopolitical Space: Toward a Critical Social
Theory of International Polities. *Alternatives*, 12 (4), pp. 403–434.

Banks, M., 1985. The Inter-Paradigm Debate. In: M. Light and A. J. R. Groom eds.
International Relations: A Handbook of Current Theory. London: Pinter, pp. 7–26.

Brown, C., 1992. *International Relations Theory: New Normative Approaches*. Hempstead:
Harvester Wheatsheaf.

Bull, H., 1966. International Theory: The Case for a Classical Approach. *World Politics*,
18 (3), pp. 361–377.

Bull H., 1972. International Relations as an Academic Pursuit. *Australian Outlook*, 26(3),
pp. 251–265.

Bull, H., 1972b. The Theory of International Politics, 1919–1969. In: B. Porter ed. *The
Aberystwyth Papers: International Politics 1919–1969*. London: Oxford University
Press, pp. 30–55.

Bull, H., 1977. *The Anarchical Society: A Study of Order in World Politics*. London:
Macmillan.

Burchill, S. and Linklater, A., 2005. Introduction. In: S. Burchill et al. eds. *Theories of
International Relations*. New York: Palgrave Macmillan, pp. 1–28.

Campbell, D., 1992. *Writing security: United States foreign policy and the politics of identity*. Minneapolis: University of Minnesota Press.

Carr, E. H., 1939. *The Twenty Year's Crisis 1919–1939: An Introduction to the Study of International Relations*. London: Macmillan.

Chomsky, N. 1969. *American Power and the New Mandarins: Historical and Political Essays*. New York: Pantheon Books.

Cohn, C., 1987. Sex and Death in the Rational World of Defense Intellectuals. *Signs: JournuL of Women in Culture and Society*, 12(4), pp. 687–718.

Cox, R., 1981. Social Forces, States and World Orders: Beyond International Relations Theory. *Millennium: Journal of International Studies*, 10(2), pp. 126–155.

Cox, R. W., 1986. Social Forces, States and World Orders: Beyond International Relations Theory, In: R. O. Keohane ed. *Neorealism and its Critics*, New York: Columbia University Press, pp. 204–254.

Cox, R. W., 1987. *Production, Power and Order: Social Forces in the Making of History*. New York: Columbia University Press.

Cox, R. W., 1989. Production, the State and Change in World Order. In: E. O. Czempiel and J. Rosenau eds. *Global Change and Theoretical Challenges: Approaches to World Politics*. Lexington: Lexington Books, pp. 37–50.

Der Derian, J. and Shapiro, M. J., 1989. *International/intertextual relations: postmodern readings of world politics*. Lexington, TN: Lexington Books.

Enloe, C., 1989. *Bananas, Beaches, and Bases: Making Feminist Sense of International Relations*. London: Pandora Press.

Enloe, C., 2000. *Maneuvers: The International Politics of Militarizing Women's Lives*. Berkeley: University of California Press.

Gilpin, R., 1981. *War and Change in World Politics*. Cambridge: Cambridge University Press.

Gregory, D., 1989. Forward. In: J. Der Derian & M. J. Shapiro Eds. *International/intertextual Relations: Postmodern Readings of World Politics*. New York: Lexington Books.

Hamati-Ataya, I., 2012. Behavioralism, In: R., Marlin-Bennetted. *Oxford Research Encyclopedia of International Studies*. Oxford University Press. Available at https://oxfordre.com/view/10.1093/acrefore/9780190846626.001.0001/acrefore-9780190846626-e-376.

Hoffman, M., 1987. Critical Theory and the Inter-Paradigm Debate. *Millennium: Journal of International Studies*, 16 (2), pp. 231–249.

Kaplan M., 1966. The New Great Debate: Traditionalism vs. Science in International Relations. *World Politics*, 19 (1), pp. 1–20.

Kautsky, K., 2007. *Ultra-imperialism*. Marlborough: Adam Matthew Digital.

Kennan, G. F., 1979. *The Decline of Bismarck's European Order: Franco-Russian Relations, 1875–1890*. Princeton: Princeton University Press.

Kennan, G. F., 1982. *The Nuclear Delusion: Soviet-American Relations in the Atomic Age*. New York: Pantheon Books.

Keohane, R. O., 1988. International Institutions: Two Approaches. *International Studies Quarterly,* 32(4), pp. 379–396.

Keohane, R. O., 1989. *International Institutions and State Power: Essays in International Relations Theory.* Boulder, CO: Westview Press.

Keohane, R. O. and Nye, J., 1977. *Power and Independence.* Boston: Little Brown.

Lapid, Y., 1989. The Third Debate: On the Prospects of International Theory in a Post-Positivist Era. *International Studies Quarterly,* 33 (3), pp. 235–54.

Lenin, V. I., 1999. *Imperialism: The Highest Stage of Capitalism.* Sydney: Resistance Books.

Luxemburg, R., 1972. *The Accumulation of Capital: an Anti-Critique.* London: Routledge.

Mearsheimer, J. J., 2017. Structural Realism. In: T., Dunne, M. Kurki, and S., Smith eds. *International Relations Theories: Discipline and Diversity.* New York theories: Oxford University Press, pp. 71–88.

Morgenthau, H., 1954. *Politics Among Nations: The Struggle for Power and Peace.* New York: Knopf.

Newman, S. 2010. *Power and Politics in Poststructuralist Thought.* London: Routledge.

Niebuhr, R., 1953. *Christian Realism and Political Problems.* New York: Charles Scribner's Sons.

Noel-Baker, P., 1934. *Disarmament.* London: League of Nations Union.

Nye, J. and Keohane, R. O., 1971. Transnational Relations and World Politics: An Introduction. *International Organizations,* 25(3), pp. 329–349.

Sanders, D., 2002. Behaviouralism. In: D. Marsh and G. Stoker eds. *Theory and Methods in Political Science.* Basingstoke: Palgrave Macmillan. pp. 45–64.

Shotwell, J. T., 1925. Plans and Protocols to End War: Historical Outline and Guide. *International Conciliation,* 10(208), pp. 78–109.

Singer, J. D., 1969. The Incompleat Theorist: Insight without Evidence. In: K. Knorr and J. Rosenau, eds. *Contending Approaches to International Politics.* Princeton, NJ: Princeton University Press pp. 66–67.

Tickner, J. A., 1988. Hans Morgenthau's Principles of Political Realism: A Feminist Reformulation. *Millennium: Journal of International Studies,* 17(3), pp. 429–440.

Tickner, J. A., 1999. Searching for the Princess? Feminist Perspectives in International Relations. *Harvard International Review,* Issue Fall, pp. 44–48.

Tickner, J. A., 2001. *Gendering World Politics Issues and Approaches in the Post-Cold War Era.* New York: Columbia University Press.

Waever O, 1996. The Rise and Fall of the Inter-paradigm Debate. In: S. Smith, K. Booth and M. Zalewski eds. *International Theory: Positivism and Beyond.* New York: Cambridge University Press, pp. 149–185.

Waltz, K., 1979. *Theory of International Politics.* Reading: Addison-Wesley Publishing Company.

Wight, M., 1966. Why Is There No International Theory? In: H. Butterfield and M. Wight eds. *Diplomatic Investigations: Essays in the Theory of International Politics.* London: Allen and Unwin, p.17–34.

Wight, M., 1977. *Systems of States.* Leicester: Leicester University Press.

Wight, M., 1978. *Power Politics.* New York: Continuum.

Yalvaç, F. (2015). Critical Theory: International Relations' Engagement with the Frankfurt School and Marxism. *Oxford Research Encyclopedia of International Studies.*

Yergin D., 1977. *Shattered Peace: The Origins of the Cold War and the National Security State.* Boston: Houghton Mifflin Company.

Zimmern, A., 1936. *The League of Nations and the Rule of Law 1918–1935.* London: Macmillan. Available at: https://archive.org/details/leagueofnationsa009378mbp/page/n5/mode/2up [Accessed 29 July 2020].

Zimmern, A., 1938. The Ethical Presuppositions of a World Order. In: L. Marquis et al. eds. *The Universal Church and the World of Nations.* Chicago: Willett, Clark & Company. Available at: https://archive.org/details/universalchurcha006907mbp/page/n7/mode/2up [Accessed 29 July 2020].

CHAPTER 2

Relevance and Contributions of Marxism as a Critical IR Theory

Engin Sune and M. Kürşad Özekin

1 Introduction

This chapter aims to present a comprehensive introduction to Marxism and its critical engagement with the field of International Relations (IR). Although Marxism is widely not considered as a full-fledged International Relations theory, it has much to say about world politics and international economic relations as a part of global social relations – or what Marx called social relations of production (Yalvaç, 2017, p. 9). No doubt, neither Marx nor his followers could be qualified as IR theorists in its contemporary sense, but the legacy of Marxism has indeed formed conceptual and analytical underpinnings for a wide array of critical approaches as its major offshoots in the twentieth century. In fact, number of the critical International Relations theories have either been inspired by Marxism or developed in a critical dialogue with it. Therefore, introducing and exploring the foundations of Marxism seems a tactical prerequisite for placing these critical approaches in social theory in general, and in IR in particular.

Bearing this fact in mind, the chapter commences with a short introduction to historical origins and development of Marxist thought as a critical social theory. Since the founder of this scientific approach is Karl Marx, along with his political companion and financial benefactor Friedrich Engels, this introductory section primarily focuses on their intellectual and political vision during the 19th century Europe. Besides, this first section provides an account of the historical and intellectual development of Marxism, and an outline of Marxist theoreticians who contributed to the development of Marxist theory over time. The second section of the chapter then scrutinizes the fundamental connection of Marxism to the critical explanations of the "international" – as a part of social relations of production. This section at the same time pursues a complementary objective of exposing the potential of Marxism as a critique of the mainstream IR scholarship. The third section, on the other hand, seeks to provide an overall -albeit being not sufficient- understanding of the main notions and premises of Marxism which are directly or indirectly related to the analysis of international relations. The detailed exploration of these notions and their respective positions within the theory in general would reveal the relevance and contributions of Marx's thought to the theory and practice of international relations. Lastly, in the final section, the chapter concentrates on relatively more recent studies of Marxist international relations theory. This final section presents current critical approaches which are commonly associated with Marxism by discussing the actual position and current validity of Marxism in I R discipline.

2   Origins and Historical Development of Marxist Thought as a Critical Social Theory

Marxism is a body of doctrine that uses historical materialism as a method of socioeconomic analysis to explain capitalist social relations in particular and the history of societies in general. As a critical social theory, Marxism is named after and developed by its founder, Karl Marx and, to a lesser extent, by his lifetime companion Friedrich Engels in the mid-19th century. However, the scientific feature of Marxism has made it a joint effort that has developed over time by getting beyond the works of its founding fathers and the period in which it was founded. Therefore, although the name of the theoretical approach derives from Karl Marx, the scholarly studies and scientific-practical struggles that constitute it transcend Marx's own life and his works.

Nevertheless, a close examination of the historical circumstances in which Marxism arose is essential to explain why and how such a scientific endeavour came into prominence. To that end, it seems necessary to give a special credit to the historic role of Marx and his work-companion Engels in the struggle of the working class and theorisation that have been made by their endeavour focusing on the historical facts of that era. First of all, European societies, during Marx's life, were undergoing dramatic and sometimes traumatic political, economic and social changes both at the domestic and international levels. While diffusion of industrialised production and so capitalist mode of production brought significant changes in the ownership and control of property, the expansion of European colonialism and the consolidation of "Westphalian states-system" occurred simultaneously at the international level. Undergirding these tremendous changes in the nineteenth-century Europe was an unprecedented economic transformation that brought the demise of feudalism and the gradual rise of modern industrial capitalism.

It should be noted that the process of transition from feudalism to capitalism implies the rise of the capitalist/bourgeois class[1] within European societies, as well as the emergence of the working class (proletariat) in large numbers on the stage of world history. Concurrently, it should be also noted that a series of liberal ideological *discoveries* (individualism, civil rights, free markets, freedom of thought, rule of law, etc.) upon which capitalism was built, constituted central tenets of the social relations during this era. On the other hand, socialism, which hinged and dwelled on the large masses of workers who had been "emancipated" from serfdom that was bound to the land and the petty bourgeois[2] strata of the society (with its new relations re-defined by capitalism), is also the product of this era.

Although the term socialism is often used interchangeably with Marxism, it had been formed under the dominance of petty bourgeois worldview and their movements in the above-mentioned era (Engels, 2003). It would not be wrong to state that these movements and ideological stances are still valid and influential today. Nevertheless, Marx and Engels rather opted for Communism, which is a revolutionary movement-ideology directly based on the proletariat and set out to distinguish "scientific socialism" from other forms of socialist movements and ideas.

> [Marx and Engels] both took a most active part in the then seething life of the revolutionary groups in Paris (of particular importance at the time was Proudhon's doctrine, which Marx pulled to pieces in his *Poverty of Philosophy*, 1999a [1847]); waging a vigorous struggle against the various doctrines of petty-bourgeois socialism, they worked out the theory and tactics of revolutionary *proletarian socialism*, or communism-Marxism.
>
> LENIN, 1968, pp. 10–11

Thus, the course of process brought Marx and Engels together with the international revolutionary workers' movement and imposed historic tasks upon them. *The Communist Manifesto* (1969), written in 1848, was of great importance in terms of both setting forth the creeds of the movement and forming a basis for the principles of a new scientific approach co-founded under the

---

1   For a detailed discussion on the process of transition from feudalism to capitalism, see Wood (2012a; 2012b).

2   In its traditional sense, the term petty bourgeois implies the social strata that makes a living from artisanship or self-employed jobs (lawyer, doctor, etc.). However, in contemporary debates, the term refers to the more complex and broader social relations (see, Poulantzas,1976; 2008).

baton of Marx. Indeed, Marx and Engels' work was not primarily about the formation of states or even their interactions, but what linked their interest to IR was the world-embracing development of capitalism that transcended national boundaries with it exploitative and unequal effects on labouring classes. Marx, with Engels, set forth a collection of revolutionary principles that transcend national differences and provide practical overtures on how to develop a transnational movement of people. This vision of linking the bulk of humanity as a global proletariat constituted the very first engagement of Marxist thought with IR scholarship from a distinct vantage point to the mainstream theories.

> With the clarity and brilliance of genius, this work outlines a new world-conception, consistent with materialism, which also embrace the realm of social life; dialectics, as the most comprehensive and profound doctrine of development; the theory of the class struggle and of the world-historic revolutionary role of the proletariat – the creator of a new, communist society.
>
> LENIN, 1968, p. 11

The works of Marx has emerged as a comprehensive study agenda and a scientific approach to explain social relations. Marx, who had dwelled on German Idealism in his early works, started to engage with subject matters of political economy, with the aim of explaining British capitalism in particular and capitalist mode of production in general, as a result of his personal experiences and scholarly endeavour in the following years. As Lenin (1968, p. 12) set forth, "Marx revolutionized science in his *Contribution to the Critique of Political Economy* (1999b [1859]) and *Capital* (Vol. I, 1999c [1867])". In addition to these works, Marx's discussions on political developments in France (French Trilogy – Marx (1871; 1969; 1999d) further constituted the last step of his theory and became sources of reference for the methodological ground that is still valid today in Marxist studies.

The work carried out by Engels in this process is also very important. In particular, Anti Dühring (1996) is a comprehensive response to the criticisms of scientific socialism originating from petty bourgeois socialism, which had a large group of followers in its era. Apart from this, his works such as *Condition of the Working Class in England* (1998 [1844]), *Origin of the Family, Private Property and the State* (2000 [1884]) are indispensable in studies of various branches of social sciences.

Regarding these developments, it should be noted that Marx and Engels' contributions to the analysis of the "International" sphere were very limited.

In their classical texts, when the state relations are concerned, the main emphasis was put on proletariat internationalism while the traditional subject matters of IR such as war and peace are neglected (Yalvaç, 2017, p.109). However, their leading work has paved the way for further critical accounts on the "International" as they meticulously documented the incentive of capitalism to extend to wider geographies. In the *Communist Manifesto*, the founding fathers of Marxism have stated that the need for constant profits trigger the capitalists to "nestle everywhere, settle everywhere, establish connexions everywhere" (Marx and Engels, 1969, p. 16). In this sense, they provided a basis for the upcoming generations of Marxist scholars to explain how capitalist social relations spread to the rest of the world and generate the capitalist world structure. Furthermore, Marx has produced immature and underdeveloped studies on British colonization in India, which may be counted as contributions to the study of IR (Marx, 2005 [1853]). However, these studies were criticised and discredited by the later Marxist scholars, as Marx seems to perceive colonization of India as a progressive historical occurring.

In this sense, the first comprehensive Marxist studies peculiarly concentrating on the international sphere are produced not by Marx himself, but by the first wave of Imperialism studies.[3] The first generation of imperialism scholars revealed the impact of capitalist mode of production on the relations between the states by delineating the mechanisms behind the rivalry between the European powers in the late 19th century (Lenin, 2005; Bukharin, 2001). At this point, Marxism commenced to deal specifically with the formation of monopolies at the capitalist centres which tend to expand to the rest of the world for new markets and resources. Theories of imperialism also shed light on the competition between the capitalist states, the so-called inter-imperial rivalry, by associating it with the development of monopolistic capitalism. In this sense, imperialism studies have carried classical Marxist analysis of the formation of capitalism to one step further by exploring the impact of this process on state relations.

Even though theories of imperialism are the first truly Marxist initiatives to conceptualize the international sphere, they have been criticized by the upcoming Marxist scholars for merely concentrating on the relationship between the core capitalist countries. Starting from 1960s, Dependency School theorists, with their critique to the dominant modernization discourses of their time, demonstrated how dominant social formations extract surplus

---

3   For a detailed account on imperialism literature, see Engin Sune's chapter on Imperialism in this book.

from the peripheries by exposing the latter to a constant process of underdevelopment.[4] In this sense, rather than focusing solely on the relations between the great powers, Dependency School analysed the global economic and political structures by exploring the dependent relationship between the core and periphery.

Another influential Marxist school, which emerged out of the studies on dependency and developed its main findings, is the World System Theory. While the theory is mostly associated with the works of Immanuel Wallerstein, Chase-Dunn and Hall (1997), Arrighi (2001), Emmanuel (1972), Amin (1976) are also pioneering figures of the approach. In addition to these, Gills and Frank (2003) are considered among the scholars of the school even though they moved away from the Marxist formulations of the World System School.

The World System School, similar to the dependency school, approaches to international relations as a single world system composed of underdeveloped and developed countries. For Amin (1976), the countries that make up the world economy are divided into two categories as developed and underdeveloped, and all these economies are attached to a system of a global financial and commercial capitalist network. In this sense, World System theory has developed a dichotomic approach between center-periphery, north-south, metropolitan-satellite and developed-underdeveloped countries in order to situate them within a singular system.

For World System theories, the main tenet of this single world system is its exploitative nature occurring between various states with different functions for the global capitalist structures. This organization stems from the tension between the mechanisms of global capitalist market that tends to integrate all the corners of globe and division of global whole among different nation states (Özdemir, 2010, p. 208). Thereof, while the World System perspective reproduces the dual categories of core and periphery, developed by the dependency theorists, it goes beyond this by situating those social forms into a single totality.

In addition to the core-periphery relations, the World System School also examines the relations in between the core countries. In this analysis, one of the important contributions of the World System analysis to the study of international relations is the concept of "semi-periphery". Accordingly, semi-peripheral countries are holding a middle ground position in the hierarchical world system. Based on this third category, World System theory perceives that

---

4   For a detailed account on Dependency School, see Kürşad Özekin's chapter on Dependency School in this book.

the positions of nation states within this hierarchical world order may change. As Wallerstein (2011, p. 179) claims, "many may try, but only a few succeed in significantly transforming the rank of their state in the world division of labor. This is because the very success of one eliminates opportunities and alternatives for others." Thus, despite of this possibility of change in the hierarchical positions of the countries, there are structural limits to this transitivity.

In this setting, semi-peripheral capitalist formations have a more developed industrial structure compared to the peripheries and they are less dependent on the core countries than the peripheral formations. Nevertheless, these countries, with their constant dependence on the core, should be considered within the scope of dependent development model introduced by the Dependency School. From the perspective of the World System, one of the functions of the semi-periphery is their contribution to the stability of the capitalist world order. Semi-peripheral capitalist formations have an ideological function since they legitimize the capitalist world system by demonstrating the possibility of development in a capitalist global economy. Moreover, they maintain a political function by preventing world-wide polarizations in between core and peripheries (Özdemir, 2010, p. 212).

In this context, even though the unit of analysis for the World System School is the global capitalism as a mega system, the analysis of states in this system still composes of a big portion of its theoretical formulation. The hierarchical positions of the states are determined by their place in the world economy and therefore they do not appear as independent actors of the international system. For example, since core countries have the capacity to produce more efficiently and with higher quality than peripheral countries, they appropriate more "surplus" produced on a global scale. The peripheral countries, on the other hand, lack this capacity and therefore, their activities within the system are limited. Therefore, while explaining the state relations, World System theory specifically gives prominence to the global system and its reflections on division of labour between states.

Another important contribution of the World System Theory to Marxist analysis is based on the discussions on "transition to socialism". According to Wallerstein (1979, pp. 348–350), the socialist project requires creation of a new participatory, egalitarian world system and world government, rather than the ubiquitous capitalist world system. Thereof, the school strived to reveal the conditions for transforming the international system. Contrary to the Dependency School, for which the emphasis on the continuity of underdevelopment is predominant, the World System theorists shed light on the ongoing transformations of countries with the changes occurring in the existing world order.

With this broad corpus of studies by imperialism theories, Dependency School and World System Theory, Marxism was able to bring International Political Economy to the agenda of mainstream IR theories, which transformed this branch of study into a sub-field of IR. However, as a result of this process Marxism is widely perceived as a reductionist theoretical approach, which establishes a mechanical relationship between economy and politics. Furthermore, it was accused of neglecting ideational factors or reducing them to mere reflections of capitalist economy. However, firstly emerged in 1923 and re-established in 1950s, Frankfurt School specifically concentrated on the role of ideology and culture which paved the way for the constitution of new critical theories emphasising the emancipatory mission of critical thinking. Philosophers such as Max Horkheimer, Theodor Adorno, Herbert Marcuse, Erich Fromm, and Jürgen Habermas were among the main figures of the Frankfurt School who were particularly concerned with the proletariat's declining and inhibited revolutionary consciousness and their support for right-wing movements (Yalvaç, 2015). In this sense, the role of ideology has started to appear as a central theme in the Marxist literature. With their critique to modernity, these scholars also revealed how the human 'rationality', which enlightenment discourse praises, has become an instrument of domination rather than emancipation. In this sense, Frankfurt School posed a challenge to the positivist epistemology prevalent in social sciences. Horkheimer (1972) believes the positivist understanding of scientific approaches perceive knowledge as an instrument of control by detaching facts from theory making. In doing so, theorising or science is portrayed as an activity independent from the dynamics of the outside world it studies. Frankfurt School criticises this notion by exploring how theories are themselves socially conditioned. Thereof, with an immanent critique to the social conditions, Frankfurt School sheds light on social contradictions in order to reveal the possibilities of emancipation. Frankfurt School's contribution to critical theory not only influenced Marxist scholarship but also post-positivist theories with its constant critique to the objectivity of knowledge production and theory making.

Lastly, with the advent of neo-Gramscian approaches, Marxism is more widely accepted as one of the critical approaches to International Relations. As the name speaks of itself, inspired from the Italian communist Antonio Gramsci, the neo-Gramscian approach, similar to the Frankfurt school, denounces Marxist techno-deterministic explanations, teleological conceptions of history and functionalist economism (Dofour, 2008). The most well-known IR scholar that contributed to neo-Gramscian studies is Robert W. Cox, who adopted the Gramscian concepts of hegemony, historic bloc, passive revolution, organic intellectuals and civil society into the study of IR. Cox

(1981) with his prominent comment "theories are for someone and for some purpose", challenged the objectivity (more precisely, impartiality) of not only mainstream theories but all theoretical initiatives. Furthermore, Cox's neo-Gramscian approach challenges the traditional unit of analysis of IR, namely the state, and propounds to concentrate on social forces in order to understand the nature of international relations (Cox, 1981, p.39). In this sense, neo-Gramscian studies inaugurated new Marxist theoretical openings and discussions both in critical scholarship and mainstream IR.

This corpus of Marxist studies has fed various schools of thought today, some of which holds on to its basic arguments and findings, while the others revised its premises and transformed it into a different theoretical stand. Today, there are Marxist studies carried out in many different fields, and a huge scientific effort is spent for the development of the theory and the analysis of the concrete social relations. The discipline of IR is among these fields, even though Marxism is mostly regarded as an "outsider" in this realm. Next section focuses on the possible critiques of Marxism to mainstream approaches in IR.

3   The Critique of the Mainstream IR Scholarship and the Notion of "International" in Marxist Thought

As indicated previously, taking Marxism exclusively as an IR theory poses certain challenges. It is controversial and equally problematic which schools or theoretical studies within the framework of Marxist thought should be included under the title of "International Relations Theory". For this reason, Marxist IR approaches tend to be limited to the work of theorists who share a strong commonality with the mainstream approaches of International Relations that excessively focus on *interstate* relations. However, this attitude towards "Marxist International Relations" falls short of understanding the relationship between the Marxist theory and its broad analysis of the social relations as a totality.

Indeed, even in the early periods when Marxist theory emerged, Marx and his followers perceived capitalism as an integrated global system in the pursuit of accumulation of capital.[5] For this reason, Marxism refuses to make a radical distinction between national boundaries and international sphere and seeks to analyse the dynamics of capitalism through the mutual interaction between

---

5   In his initial preparatory work on Capital, Grundrisse, Marx propounds that capitalism is the first globalized mode of production. (Marx, 1973).

these two with a transnational outlook and a political economy approach. In this context, it could be said that Marxism stands against the tendencies of excessive specialization and disciplinary exclusion between the fields of economics, sociology, political science, philosophy and International Relations. Indeed, while it is inescapable to dwell on any of these areas of social reality, the idea that a holistic analysis is essential for the scientific explanation of social reality is central to Marxist critical enquiry.

This is absolutely the case when it comes to Marxist critique of mainstream theories of International Relations, particularly for the case of political realism which believes that politics is autonomously governed by its "objective laws" (Morgenthau, 1985, p. 4). First of all, from a Marxist point of view, it seems problematic to define international relations as an exclusively distinct field of enquiry that is independent of underlying class relations and social relations of production. Thus, for the Marxist perspective, the fundamental notions of IR such as nation, state, sovereignty, power, war, peace and international law should not be taken for granted but should be rethought in their relation with the social and historical relations of production, underlying class relations and the structure of global economy. To put it differently, Marxism questions the very foundations of IR scholarship and its fundamental concepts that constitute it as a discipline. Rather, Marxism counter-argues that such concepts are problematic as they establish false presuppositions about the world itself. To give an example, the notion of anarchy generates the mirage that states are autonomous and rational entities whose actions can be predicted. This ignores, however, the sustainability of regional inequalities and the historical and structural relationships between states, conflict and key classes in the global political economy. Thus, such concepts that are taken with presuppositions by the mainstream approaches in fact stem from certain methodological-ideological fallacies that need a further critical scrutiny.

Drawing on the Marxist vantage point, it could be argued that the methodological-ideological positions of mainstream IR approaches primarily suffer from what would be called the fallacy of methodological individualism. Even though these approaches are built upon divergent epistemological foundations (positivism, hermeneutic etc.), the methodological basis of mainstream IR theories is mostly individualistic, and their effort to understand/explain the social phenomena is based more on the explanatory and predictive models of individualistic decisions and/or behaviours, than on the analysis of class relations or social dynamics. This sort of reasoning, which has strongly entrenched in neo-classical economics and liberal worldview, has certain repercussions on the mainstream explanation of the state "behaviour" in international politics. For instance, the rationality of states' decision and their desire for power derive from the assumed characteristics of the individual. For mainstream IR theorists, particularly for political realists, our selfishness, our appetite for power and our inability to trust others can be translated into the realm of state behaviour as individuals constitute state as a form of polity and human nature has certain impacts on the behaviour of states. According to political realists, the individual is self-interested, selfish, and acts in the pursuit of power; so, the state would also have similar characteristics (Morgenthau, 1985). In a similar vein, for liberals, the individual is compromising; although s/he is selfish, s/he is respectful to the rights and freedom of other individuals, s/he is peaceful; thus, would be the state.[6]

A further point that needs to be stressed in relation to the "individualistic" approach of mainstream IR is the false premise of the state and (civil) society dichotomy. For mainstream IR theorists, the state and the states system are constituted independently of or in isolation from the sphere of civil society and have a separate existence from it. That's why, the separation between the political and economic, state and society, or public and private seems problematic since these categories hide the ways in which state and foreign policies are shaped by the underlying social dynamics. Thus, the mainstream IR illusively assumes that international system consists of states that enjoy certain autonomy from their respective societies and behave in a standard manner that even sometimes run against the interests of key social forces. Seen in this way, the state is conceptualised in a Weberian sense as an institutionalised form of "monopoly of violence surrounded by legitimacy" that act for the general interest of the community, not for a specific group of people (Weber, 1978 cited by Pierson, 2004, p. 6).

In stark contrast to the mainstream IR theories, Marxism is primarily concerned with the role of social forces and class relations in explaining social structures. As the main driving force behind social evolution, class struggle presents a useful analytical concept for scrutinizing historical transformations and formation of social structures. Thus, Marxism seeks to explain the social facts by focusing on social relations of production and class dynamics,

---

6 Marxism tends to see the individual as a product of social relations. For this reason, to say that individuals are good or bad and to make inferences about human nature means to detach something that is actually historical (the individual and the concept of the individuality) from time and space (social context). In other words, the adjectives such as being rational, good or bad, which are determined by the above-mentioned approaches as characteristics of human nature, cannot be attributed to the human "species" from the beginning of humanity; instead they refer to the form in which people emerged at a particular stage in history. In addition, the social context of state cannot be understood by these concepts.

rather than the predictability of individual-based explanations. For Marxists, the ongoing relations between classes, class fractions, social groups and other social strata make up the social structure, and so the actions and behaviour of individuals cannot be explained without addressing them.

To put it another way, the behaviour of the individual that the mainstream IR assumes as the "explanatory" needs to be explained at first. Unlike the mainstream conception of human nature, Marxism conceives human as a "being of praxis" that s/he purposefully transforms and develops himself/herself and the world s/he lives in. Overall, Marxism dismisses the conventional conception of human existence as "a rational animal" and do not believe that rationality or any form of action constitutes the essence of humankind. Rather, human is a social being due to the form imposed by her/his relationship with her/his environment and herself/himself. In this sense, Marxism deduces that there are two main drives in human nature: individual's constant drives, such as hunger and sexual urge, that do not alter and individual's relative drives which are dependent on the respective social structures.

Seen in this way, the nature of the state and state-system are not shaped independently of, or cannot be conceived in isolation from, the wider social structure of the production and their relationship to the capitalist world economy. Thus, Marxism clearly denies the main arguments of the realist and liberal theories about the state and state-system. Rather, Marxist theory contextualised the state and the state-system within the wider framework of "material and social interpretation of history" that interconnects the substructure (base) of society (e.g. property relations, relations of production, division of labour, its corresponding social forces) with the superstructure of society, including its rituals, culture, political power structures, legal structure, institutions and the state.[7]

In this regard, Marxism views the state and the state-system as an expression of the changing ways in which societies organise their economic practices, in particular the way how they conceptualise property and relations of production. Therefore, in *Communist Manifesto*, Marx and Engels portrayed the development of the state, starting from the early epochs of history in which society was entirely organised in different ranks. In the early stages of evolution of society when production relations were mostly prosaic and

---

7   While the influence of the base seems predominant, the interaction between the two is not
    a strictly one-way relationship since the superstructure often has impacts on the base.

the mode of production was utterly rudimentary, there was no clear need for the state. With the need for labour force, due to the rise of agricultural production, the formation of state, so as to sustain slave labour system, has become necessary. Overtime this led to the metamorphosis from the tribal society to the feudal society and the pre-capitalist state-system as a super-structure determined by subject-kinship relations. With the expansion of commerce and industry, the bourgeoisie class grew large enough to edge out all the classes that remained from the middle ages. This marked the rise of capitalist societies and so the modern states as an apparatus sustaining the rule of the bourgeoisie who owns the means of production over the much larger proletariat.

Indeed, neither Marx nor Engels sought to analyse the state methodologi-cally, but their conception is essential for the nature of state and states-system and their respective relation with the society. Marx's conceptualisation tells us that the nation state and modern states-system came into existence at a par-ticular stage in the historical development of human society as concrete forms of capitalist class relations and the mode of production. As all other human institutions, states and states-system are not unchanging abstract entities but historical products that manifest underlying social relations of modern capi-talism and its class structure. To put it more clearly, modern system of private property and capitalist mode of production internally organised by the form of sovereign state and asserted itself in its external relations as nationality. Thus, placing class relations and struggles at the centre of its analysis, Marxism reveals that the international system is war-prone because of neither human nature nor its anarchical structure but due to the clashing class interests man-ifested as material needs of states.

To be sure, Marx did not make any systematic contribution to international theory, but his theory of historical materialism offers a radically insightful understanding of the evolution of states-system. Building on his under-standing, the pioneering studies of Nikolai Bukharin (2001), Rosa Luxemburg (2003), Karl Kautsky (1914) and Vladimir Lenin (2005) provided the first true initiatives to develop a class-based analysis of the states-system. Especially, Lenin's critique of imperialism and his theory of the unevenness of capital-ist development pointed out economic mechanisms, such as concentration of capital and formation of monopolies, as the underlying factors behind the geo-political competitions. Overall, Marxist theorists of the state and international relations, including relatively more recent theorists of world-systems, see the state and states-system as political forms that are inseparable from the devel-opment of world capitalism.

4   Main Notions and Premises of Marxist Thought

Marxism is one of the intellectual initiatives that have been constantly producing theoretical studies in various fields of social sciences. In any scientific
field that Marxism engages with, it comes up with its own set of concepts
and develops its theoretical stand in line with this conceptual framework.
Therefore, this section particularly introduces the fundamental concepts of
Marxist thought and sheds light on their contribution to the study of international relations.

In this regard, the first concepts to be familiarised for capturing the essence
of Marxist analysis are the notions of "historical materialism" and "dialectical materialism", which form the basis of Marxist philosophy. Marxist philosophical stand acknowledges the existence of reality independent of human
consciousness, which is itself a product of the material world. With this materialist formulation of the relationship between thoughts/ideas and appear-
ance/reality, Marxism reveals the constant change in the social world (Eroğul,
1992, p.312). Accordingly, historical materialism suggests approaching societies
within the context of social and historical relations or modes of production.
This understanding approaches human agency within the scope of social and
historical realities that permit or limit its activities. As stated by Marx (1999d),
"men make their own history, but they do not make it as they please; they do
not make it under self-selected circumstances, but under circumstances existing already, given and transmitted from the past." Through dialectical methodology, on the other hand, Marxism strives to theorise the dynamics of change
and interaction. In doing so, dialectical materialism approaches the social reality in its totality with a specific emphasis on the historical context and reveals
the contradictions immanent to social structures.

The historical materialist philosophy and dialectical materialism have
brought a new impulse to the study of international relations. First of all, the
conceptualisation of social reality in its totality encouraged structural analysis of the global structures, as it was visible in the structuralist World System
Theory of the 1970s (Wallerstein, 1979). Furthermore, due to its historical materialist approach, Marxism was able to go beyond the reified and ahistorical
conceptualisations of the international structure by the mainstream IR scholarship as it vociferously demonstrates the constant change in the social systems. Secondly, approaching the social reality in its totality steers Marxism
to transcend positivistic and mechanistic methodologies in IR, which divide
the social reality (international sphere) into pieces (among atomistic states)
and concentrate on the behaviour of the units (the state) in a deductive way
(with an individualistic ontology) to explain the characteristics of the totality

(international system). In this sense, dialectical methodology enables Marxism to disclose the formation of social structures in its historical context.

Aforementioned historical understanding of Marxism situates class struggle at the centre of the historical change and conceptualises it as the driving force of history. As stated by Marx and Engels in *Communist Manifesto* (1969, p. 14) "The history of all hitherto existing society is the history of class struggles." This emphasis on the class struggle has prompted Marxism to develop further concepts to capture the essence of class dynamics in social life. Thus, while analysing the historical transformation and dynamics of change, Marxism has developed concepts of productive forces, relations of production, modes of production and social formation. Productive forces refer to a combination of means of production (tools and equipment used in production, machines, soil, etc.) and labour, which takes different forms throughout the history. The relations of production, on the other hand, refers to the socialisation process during the production and reproduction of means of life. In this sense, productive forces and relations of production congregate and form the mode of production which invokes a specific composition of economic, political and ideological structures. Based on these concepts, in explaining historical structures Robert Cox (1981, p. 138) concentrates on the organisation of production, more particularly with regard to the social forces engendered by the production process. For the author, social forces, forms of state (derived from the study of state society complexes) and world orders (i.e. particular configuration of forces) should be the main units of analysis in understanding global relations.

In this sense, instead of approaching the state as a reified unit of international relations, Marxism perceives societies as complex social formations in which the dominant capitalist mode of production creates a capitalist class/bourgeoisie controlling the means of production and a worker class/proletariat selling its labour to access the means of production. For Marx, the essence of this social organisation is formed around the extraction of surplus value and exploitation. Thus, Marx developed the concept of base-superstructure metaphor, which renders a process that economic base generates a matching juridico-political superstructure, forms of life, and social consciousness (Jessop and Sum, 2018). In this account, the material (re)production of social life (economics) is perceived to determine other forms of social relations (politics, law and ideology). However, this mechanistic original formulation of Marx was criticized both by Marxist and non-Marxist circles for its economic reductionism. Later Marxist studies without ignoring the decisive role of economy, built a more complex relationship between the economic base and the other social structures. In this sense, for Marxism the capitalist system and social relations that constitute capitalism compose a totality in which all the components of the system are in a complex interaction (Yalvaç, 2017). To give an example, Gramsci criticises Marxist approaches that reproduce the liberal distinction between economic and political fields and strives to reveal the interaction between these two fields in line with his conceptualisation of hegemony (Yetiş, 2012). In fact, the Marxist conceptualisation of "relations of production" itself refers to many complex social relations, including extra-economic ones, that occur during the material (re)production of social life. For Marxism, sense and meaning making are co-constitutive of all social practices and interaction; therefore, it rejects treating the economic base one-sidedly and reifying culture as a mere reflection of the economy (Jessop and Sum, 2018).

This formulation enabled Marxist studies to capture the essence of the complex relationship between economic, political and ideological structures within the totality of global capitalist system. As capitalism is perceived as a global phenomenon, Marxist scholars relentlessly concentrated on the study of International Political Economy (IPE) in order to reveal the complex relationship between economic and political fields in their theorisation of IR. Especially with the contributions of imperialism studies, as well as dependency and world system scholars, political economy was brought up on the agenda of IR scholarship in the 1970s. This intrusion has been further intensified with the global economic turmoil of 1970s triggered by the end of Bretton Woods System and oil crisis, which drew the attention of mainstream IR theories on the role of economy in state relations and promoted IPE as one of the sub-fields of IR.

Marxism has also contributed to the study of state in IR with its distinctive ontological stand towards state. Mainstream IR narratives perceive states as a rational actor capable of recognising its interest and act accordingly. Conceptualising the state as an actor or an organism, as in Classical Realist thought, is to attribute them properties associated with human beings – rationality, identities, interests, beliefs, and so on (Wendt, 2004, p.289). For neorealism, on the other hand, "states are made function ally similar by the constraints of structure, with the principal differences among them defined according to capabilities" (Waltz, 1990, p.36). Unlike these formulations, Marxism perceives states neither as rational actors nor alike units. In line with its dialectical method, Marxism reveals how the state is itself a divided social structure in terms of class struggles. In this sense, rather than approaching state as a non-contradictory whole, or an ahistorical unit, Marxist IR presents the constant transformation and reproduction of state in accordance with the changes in social relations and class compositions.

Last but not least, for the Marxist philosophy, theorising IR should go hand in hand with the efforts of emancipating the field from any material and

ideological domination. As Marx and Engels (1998, p.571) stated "the philosophers have only interpreted the world, in various ways; the point is to change
it." In this regard, Marxism is not only a theoretical initiative aiming to conceptualise the outside reality but also a philosophy of praxis. Thereof, Marxism
emerged as the foundational critical IR theory, which opens up "the possibility
of choosing a different valid perspective from which the problematic becomes
one of creating an alternative world" (Cox, 1981, p. 128). This materialist interpretation of the emancipatory mission of theorising reformulated in an idealist way by the post-structuralist theories which aim to reveal the diffusion of
the political power to language and discourse. As discourses are intersubjectively produced, according to post-structuralist IR, change is possible due to
the contextuality of interaction. As Jenny Edkins (1999, p.24) affirms "change
takes place when there is a shift in the relationship between signified and signifier." In this context, the philosophical underpinnings of Marxism and the
emancipatory role it attributes to theorising paved the way for the development of a corpus of critical scholarship striving to change the very foundations
of social structures.

5   Contemporary Relevance of Marxist Approaches in International Relations

As alluded in the introduction, most of the critical approaches included in the
scope of this book are either influenced by Marxism or built their own positions based on its criticism. In this context, the upcoming chapters on the sub-
schools of Marxism, such as theories of imperialism, Dependency School and
the theory of uneven and combined development separately evaluate the new
theoretical openings and current research directions in Marxist IR theories.
However, there is still a considerable merit in presenting an overall assessment
of the current Marxist debates with a peculiar emphasis on their significant
contributions.

   One of the most striking and astonishing recent study by the Marxist scholars were produced on the relationship between capitalism and geopolitics.
These studies on the geopolitics of capitalist modernity meticulously problematise the role of state system in a capitalist world structure. The first initiative that explores the dialectical relationship between geopolitics and modes
of production was conducted by Justin Rosenberg in 1994 in his masterpiece
The Empire of Civil Society.

   The studies on geopolitics have been further developed in the following decades. In one of such studies, Alex Callinicos (2010) asked whether

capitalism needs a state system and depicted an anomaly between the capitalist economic system and international state system. In this sense, the author claims that geopolitical competition predates capitalism, which imposes different properties to geopolitical competition than capitalism (Callinicos, 2010, p. 19). This approach was ambitiously criticized by various Marxists due to its resemblances to Realism. As the approach attributes a different logic to the state system independent of capitalist social relations, at some point it turns into an amalgamation of Marxist and Realist arguments. Thus, Callinicos (2010, p. 21) states that "there is a necessarily realist moment in any Marxist analysis of international relations."

In fact, a similar approach is also visible in the studies on New Imperialism. There was a radical resurgence in the discussions on imperialism especially after the intervention of USA to Iraq and restructuring of Middle East in the Post-Cold War era. Specifically, the Marxist side of the debate concentrated on the transformations within capitalist international structures and analysed the role of neoliberalism on the exploitative global mechanisms. In one of such leading works on imperialism, David Harvey (2003) reproduces the division between geopolitical rivalry and capitalist competition. Based on Arrighi's (1990) categorical separation in between capitalist and territorial logics of power, Harvey strives to explore the role of both logics in the current imperialist policies. In this sense, he explains the motivations for the U.S. imperialism in the Middle East both in terms of search for profit and expansion of state power.

Even though it is not directly built upon the discussions on geopolitical competition, geopolitics also forms a significant portion of the new studies on Uneven and Combined Development (UCD). Problematising the geopolitical pressures on the domestic social structures of states, contributions of UCD gave a new impulse to the Marxist studies in IR, especially with the leading works of Justin Rosenberg (2013). The recent theoretical analysis of UCD has also contributed to the Marxist critique to mainstream IR scholarship, as it criticises the reified conceptualisation of the international structure by the neo-Realist scholars (Rosenberg, 2016). In order to go beyond such formulations, UCD explains how unevenness of the international system affects the interaction between states and their developmental levels.

It is worth mentioning that Cox's neo-Gramscian approach has also triggered new current studies. These new studies especially produced by the so-called Amsterdam School concentrated on the global structures and analysed its form with the theoretical capacity of Gramscianism. In one of these leading works, Stephen Gill examined the U.S. hegemony and revealed how American hegemony is transnationalised with the capacity of its capital power (Gill,

1993). Without any doubt, the most complex work on transnationalisation within Amsterdam School is produced by Kees van der Pijl (2005). Van der Pijl produced a significant Marxist account in explaining global rivalries from the Cold War to Iraqi intervention in 2003. He underlined the role of the rivalry between the Lockean heartland and the Hobbesian contender states for capturing the dynamo of the international system (Van der Pijl, 2006).

The debates on transnationalisation in the Marxist scholarship in recent years have also been reassured by the studies of William I. Robinson, who claims that capitalism has entered into a new transnational stage as the rise of transnational capital integrated every country into the global production and financial system (Robinson, 2007). His findings have brought the significant role of transnational capitalist classes into the agenda of Marxist IR scholarship. Furthermore, Robinson underlined the transformation in the relationship between space and power which cannot be captured with a nation-state centric perspective. In this sense, even though he accepts that states maintain their role in the current international structure, his account indicates that the interstate system is no longer the organizing principle of the capitalist development, or the primary institutional framework that shapes social and political dynamics (Robinson, 2001, p. 159).

Additionally, the contributions of the so-called Political Marxism to the Marxist IR scholarship in recent years deserve attention, especially those produced by Robert Brenner (1976) and Ellen Meikins Wood (2003). Political Marxism, while analysing the transition to capitalism, rejected the widely shared notion that capitalism, the sovereign state and the system of territorially organized societies are simultaneously emerged. In this context, Political Marxism indicated that class structures in distinct localities of medieval and early modern Europe followed fundamentally different trajectories which allows Marxists to recognize the emergence of capitalism as a much more localized and specific phenomenon (Teschke and Lacher, 2010, p. 31). To this scholarship Benno Teschke (2009) also made important contributions as he problematized the myth of 1648, which is accepted as the milestone of the modern international system in mainstream IR. Instead of approaching to Westphalia Peace as a treaty that formed the modern state system, Teschke presents its relationship with the tendencies of centralization of political mechanisms in the feudal societies.

Lastly, there are new theoretical openings and research directions in one of the sub-fields of IR, namely international law, by the Marxist scholars. In recent years a group of Marxist scholars exposed their criticisms to international law by critically approaching to the concept of state and sovereignty (See. Marks, 2008). Even though the central focus of these studies is not on the international law itself as a unit of analysis, they still problematise the field by challenging the concepts that it takes for granted.

6   Conclusion

This chapter has sought to present a comprehensive introduction to Marxist thought and its critical engagement with and contribution to the field of International Relations. As stressed throughout the chapter, Marxism could not be considered as a full-fledged International Relations theory. No doubt, neither Marx nor Engels sought to analyse the states-system methodologically, but Marxism has indeed much to say about world politics and international economic relations as a part of global social relations – or what Marx called social relations of production. In fact, number of the critical International Relations theories have either been inspired by Marxism or developed in a critical dialogue with it.

Thus, bearing this fact in mind, the chapter commenced with a short introduction to historical origins and development of Marxist thought by giving a special emphasis to works of Marx and Engels, and foundational texts of theoreticians who contribute to the development of Marxism as a critical social theory. In their classical texts, Marx and Engels' contributions to the analysis of the "International" sphere were very limited. When the state relations are concerned, the main emphasis was put on proletariat internationalism while the traditional subject matters of IR such as war and peace are neglected. However, what linked their interest to IR was the world-embracing development of capitalism that transcended national boundaries with its exploitative and unequal effects on labouring classes. Marx, along with Engels, have paved the way for further critical accounts on the "International" as they meticulously documented the incentive of capitalism to extend to wider geographies, and set forth a collection of revolutionary principles that provide practical overtures on how to develop a transnational movement of working class. This vision of expansion of capitalism as the dominating social relation and linking the bulk of humanity as a global proletariat constituted the very first engagement of Marxist thought with IR scholarship.

Dwelling on the classical works of Marx, the first generation of imperialism scholars have later revealed the impact of capitalist mode of production on the relations between the states by delineating the mechanisms behind the rivalry between the European powers in late 19th century. At this point, Marxism commenced to deal specifically with the formation of monopolies at the capitalist centres which tend to expand to the rest of the world for new markets and resources. In this sense, imperialism studies have carried classical Marxist analysis of the formation of capitalism to one step further by exploring the impact of this process on state relations. Perhaps as a truly IR theory, Marxism found its expression in the works of World System research which conceives the state and states-system as the political forms of the functionally integrated modern capitalist system that is governed by a single logic and set of rules associated with the relentless accumulation of capital.

As a critical social theory, Marxism questions the very foundations of IR scholarship and its fundamental concepts that constitute it as a discipline. Unlike the mainstream IR, Marxism does not believe that politics is autonomously governed by its "objective laws", and so it refuses to define international relations as an exclusively distinct field of enquiry that is independent of underlying class relations and social relations of production. Rather, Marxist IR theory adopts a holistic and political economic perspective of international relations which seeks to analyse the dynamics of states and states-system in their mutual interaction with the social and historical relations of production, underlying class relations and the structure of global economy. In this sense, as for the Marxist perspective, the fundamental notions of IR such as nation, state, sovereignty, power, war, peace and international law should not be taken for granted but should be rethought in their dialectical intercourse with social relations of production.

Overall, this formulation in Marxist enquiry has indeed offered valuable insights to IR scholarship and contributed critical thinking in International Relations by opening alternative ways of reasoning in many respects. Particularly, the historical materialist philosophy and dialectical materialism in Marxist thought have enabled the scholarship to capture the essence of the complex relationship between economic, political and ideological structures within the totality of capitalist system. As capitalism is perceived as a global phenomenon, Marxist scholars relentlessly concentrated on the study of International Political Economy (IPE) in order to reveal the complex interaction between economic and political realms in their theorisation of IR. Besides, in line with its dialectical method, Marxism, at the same time, reveals how the state itself is a divided social structure in terms of class struggles. In this sense, rather than approaching state and states-system as a non-contradictory whole, or an ahistorical unit, Marxist IR presents the constant transformation and reproduction of state and states-system in accordance with the changes in social relations and class compositions.

Last but not least, unlike the mainstream IR theorizing, Marxist enquiry does not only explain the world as it is but places itself above the prevailing power relations and dominant international order and questions the asymmetrical nature of international relations both in economic and political terms. Being self-consciously critical, Marxism, thus, is not only a theoretical initiative aiming to conceptualise the outside reality but also a philosophy of praxis that strives for the emancipation of IR scholarship from any form of material and ideological domination. Thereof, Marxism opened up new ways of reasoning about the question on global inequalities, the North-South divide and the hierarchical and asymmetric nature of international politics and constituted the foundational ground for a wide array of critical approaches as its major offshoots in the twentieth century.

References

Amin, S., 1976. *Unequal Development: An Essay on the Social Formations of Peripheral Capitalism,* Hassocks: Harvester Press.

Arrighi, G. 1990. The Three Hegemonies of Historical Capitalism, *Review (Fernand Braudel Center)*, Summer, Vol. 13, No. 3, pp. 365–408.

Arrighi, G. 2001, *Uzun Yirminci Yüzyıl: Para, Güç ve Çağımızın Kökenleri.* Translated by R. Boztemur. Ankara: İmge.

Bukharin, N., 2001. *Imperalism and World Economy.* [online] Available at: <https://www .marxists.org/archive/bukharin/works/1917/imperial/> [Accessed 21 December 2020].

Brenner, R., 1976. Agrarian Class Structure and Economic Development in Pre-industrial Europe, *Past and Present*, 70, pp. 30–75.

Callinicos, A., 2010. Does Capitalism Needs State System?, In: A. Anievas, ed. *Marxism and World Politics: Contesting Global Capitalism*, London: Routledge, pp. 11–26.

Chase-Dunn, C. and Hall, T. D., 1997. *Rise and Demise: Comparing World Systems.* USA: Westview Press.

Cox, R. W., 1981. Social Forces, States and World Orders: Beyond International Relations Theory. *Milennium: Journal of International Studies*, 10(2), pp. 126–155.

Dufour, F. G., 2008. Historical Materialism and International Relations. In: *Critical Companion to Contemporary Marxism*. Leiden, The Netherlands: Brill.

Edkins, J., 1999. *Poststructuralism & International Relations: Bringing the Political Back in*, Colorado: Lynne Rienner Publishers.

Emmanuel, A., 1972. *Unequal Exchange: A Study of the Imperialism of Trade.* New York: Monthly Revies Press.

Engels, F., 1996. *Anti-Dühring.* Translated by E. Burns. [online] Available at: <https:// www.marxists.org/archive/marx/works/1877/anti-duhring/> [Accessed 21 December 2020].

Engels, F., 1998. *The Condition of the Working Class in England.* [online] Available at: <https://www.marxists.org/archive/marx/works/1845/condition-working-class/> [Accessed 21 December 2020].

Engels, F., 2000. *Origins of the Family, Private Property and the State.* [online] Available at: <https://www.marxists.org/archive/marx/works/1884/origin-family/> [Accessed 21 December 2020].

Engels, F., 2003. *Socialism: Utopian and Scientific.* Translated by E. Aveling. [online] Available at: <https://www.marxists.org/archive/marx/works/1880/soc-utop/index.htm> [Accessed 21 December 2020].

Eroğul, C., 1992. Marksizmin Günümüzde Geçerliliği, *A. Ü. Siyasal Bilgiler Fakültesi Dergisi,* 47(1–2), pp. 311–316.

Frank, A. G. and Gills, B. K., eds., 2003. *Dünya Sistemi: Beş Yüzyıllık mı, Beş Binyıllık mı?.* Translated by E. Soğancılar. Ankara: İmge.

Gill, S., 1993. *Gramsci, Historical Materialism and International Relations.* Cambridge: Cambridge University Press.

Harvey, D., 2003. *The New Imperialism,* Oxford and New York: Oxford University Press.

Horkheimer, M., 1972. Traditional and Critical Theory. In: M. Horkheimer, ed., *Critical Theory: Selected Essays.* New York: Contiuum. pp. 188–243.

Jessop, B. and Sum, N., 2018. Language and Critique: Some Anticipations of Critical Discourse Studies in Marx, *Critical Discourse Studies,* 15:4, pp. 325–337.

Kautsky, K., 1914. *Ultra-Imperialism.* [online] Available at: <https://www.marxists.org/archive/kautsky/1914/09/ultra-imp.htm> [Accessed 21 December 2020].

Lenin, V. I., 1968. *Marx, Engels, Marxism.* Moscow: Progress Publishers.

Lenin, V. I., 2005. *Imperialism, the Highest Stage of Capitalism.* [online] Available at: <https://www.marxists.org/archive/lenin/works/1916/imp-hsc/> [Accessed 21 December 2020].

Luxemburg, R., 2003. *The Accumulation of Capital.* Translated by A. Schwarzschild. [online] Available at: <https://www.marxists.org/archive/luxemburg/1913/accumulation-capital/> [Accessed 21 December 2020].

Marks S., ed., 2008. *International Law on the Left: Re-examining Marxist Legacies.* Cambridge: Cambridge University Press.

Marx, K., 1871. *The Civil War in France.* [online] Available at: <https://www.marxists.org/archive/marx/works/1871/civil-war-france/index.htm> [Accessed 21 December 2020].

Marx, K., 1969. *The Class Struggles in France, 1848 to 1850.* [online] Available at: <https://www.marxists.org/archive/marx/works/1850/class-struggles-france/index.htm> [Accessed 21 December 2020].

Marx, K., 1999a. *The Poverty of Philosophy.* Translated by the Institute of Marxism Leninism. [online] Available at: <https://www.marxists.org/archive/marx/works/1847/poverty-philosophy/> [Accessed 21 December 2020].

Marx, K., 1999b. *A Contribution to the Critique of Political Economy*. Translated by S. W. Ryazanskaya. [online] Available at: <https://www.marxists.org/archive/marx/works/1859/critique-pol-economy/ > [Accessed 21 December 2020].

Marx, K., 1999c. *Capital: Volume I*. Translated by S. Moore and E. Aveling. [online] Available at: <https://www.marxists.org/archive/marx/works/1867-c1/> [Accessed 21 December 2020].

Marx, K., 1999d. *The Eighteenth Brumaire of Louis Bonaparte*. [online] Available at: <https://www.marxists.org/archive/marx/works/1852/18th-brumaire/index.htm> [Accessed 21 December 2020].

Marx, K., 2005. *The British Rule in India*. [online] Available at: <https://www.marxists.org/archive/marx/works/1853/06/25.htm> [Accessed 21 December 2020].

Marx, K., 2015. *Grundrisse*. Translated by M. Nicolaus. [online] Available at: <https://www.marxists.org/archive/marx/works/download/pdf/grundrisse.pdf > [Accessed 21 December 2020].

Marx, K. and Engels, F., 1969. *The Communist Manifesto*. Translated by S. Moore. [online] Available at: <https://www.marxists.org/archive/marx/works/1848/communist-manifesto/> [Accessed 21 December 2020].

Marx, K., and Engels, F., 1998. *The German Ideology*. New York: Prometheus Books.

Morgenthau, H., 1985. *Politics Among Nations: The Struggle for Power and Peace*, New York: Knopf.

Özdemir, A. M., 2010. *Ulusların Sefaleti: Uluslararası Ekonomi Politiğe Marksist Yaklaşımlar*. Ankara: İmge.

Pierson, C., 2004. *The Modern State*. London: Routledge.

Poulantzas, N., 1976. *Classes in Contemporary Capitalism*. Translated by D. Fernbach. London: NLB.

Poulantzas, N., 2008. *The Poulantzas Reader*. Edited by James Martin. London: Verso.

Robinson, W., 2001. Social Theory and Globalization: The Rise of a Transnational State. *Theory and Society*, 30, pp. 157–200.

Robinson, W., 2007. Beyond the Theory of Imperialism: Global Capitalism and the Transnational State, *Societies Without Borders*, 2, pp. 5–26.

Rosenberg, J., 1994. *The Empire of Civil Society: A Critique of the Realist Theory of International Relations,* London: Verso.

Rosenberg, J., 2013. The "Philosophical Premises" of Uneven and Combined Development. *Review of International Studies*, 39(3), pp. 569–597.

Rosenberg, J., 2016. Uneven and Combined Development: 'The International' in Theory and History, In: A. Anievas and K. Matin, eds. *Historical Sociology and World History*. London: Rowman&Littlefield, pp. 17–31.

Teschke, B., 2009. *The Myth of 1648: Class, Geopolitics, and the Making of Modern International Relations*. London: Verso.

Teschke, B. and Lacher, H., 2010. The Changing Logics of Capitalist Competition, In: A. Anievas ed., *Marxism and World Politics: Contesting Global Capitalism.* London: Routledge, pp. 27–41.

Van der Pijl, K. 2005. *Transnational Classes and International Relations.* London: Routledge.

Van der Pijl, K. 2006. *Global Rivalries From the Cold War to Iraq.* London: Pluto Press.

Wallerstein, I., 1979. *The Capitalist World-Economy.* Cambridge: Cambridge University Press.

Wallerstein, I., 2011.*The Modern World-System II: Mercantilism and the Consolidation of the European World-Economy, 1600–1750.* California: University of California Press.

Waltz, K. N., 1990. Realist Thought and Neorealist Theory, *Journal of International Affairs,* Vol. 44, No: 1, pp. 21–37.

Weber, M., 1978. *Economy and Society, Volume I.* New York: Bedminster.

Wendt, A., 2004. The State as Person in International Theory, *Review of International Studies,* 30, pp. 289–316.

Wood, E. M., 2003. *Empire of Capital.* London: Verso.

Wood, E. M., 2012a. *Liberty and Property,* London: Verso.

Wood, E. M., 2012b. *Kapitalizmin Arkaik Kültürü.* Translated from English by O. Köymen. İstanbul: Yordam.

Yalvaç, F., 2015. Critical Theory: International Relations' Engagement With the Frankfurt School and Marxism. *Oxford Research Encyclopedia of International Studies.* [online] Available at: <https://oxfordre.com/view/10.1093/acrefore/978019 0846626.001.0001/acrefore-9780190846626-e-109> [Accessed 21 December 2020].

Yalvaç, F., 2017. Uluslararası İlişkiler ve Marksizm: Marksizmi Uluslararasılaştırmak ve Marksist Bir Uluslararası İlişkiler Kuramı'na Doğru. In: F. Yalvac ed., *Marksizm ve Uluslararası İlişkiler Kuramları,* Ankara: İmge Kitapevi Yayınları, pp. 9–66.

CHAPTER 3

Imperialism as a Critical Theory of IR

Engin Sune

1   Introduction

At first glance, it is very challenging and controversial to approach imperialism within the scope of critical theories. This difficulty stems from two separate realities embedded in the imperialism literature. Firstly, imperialism is one of terms that have been widely accepted and discussed not only by the critical theories but also by the mainstream scholars of International Relations (IR). The first comprehensive study on imperialism was written by a liberal scholar, John Hobson (2005). Within liberal IR, Joseph A. Schumpeter (1951) discussed how the combination of liberalism with capitalism may prevent imperialism and war. On the Realist side, Hans Morgenthau (2005) spared a huge chapter to the discussion on imperialism in his leading work *Politics Among Nations*. Similarly, imperialism was one of the most significant concepts in Kenneth Waltz's (2001) keystone book *Man, The State and War*. It goes without saying that imperialism is also one of the most central issues in the Marxist studies. Furthermore, other sub-branches of critical theories such as post-colonialism has also taken imperialism as one of the central units of analysis. Therefore, it is very legit to question how imperialism, which has been widely accepted and used by such different theoretical schools, can be accepted as a critical theory on its own.

Secondly, imperialism is a vague term. For some, it is only a concept to define a political practice of international relations. To give an example, Morgenthau (1985) asserts that imperialism is a term that is indiscriminately used to define any foreign policy. However, for him also, imperialism is not a defining mechanism of the international sphere. Instead, it is a mere consequence of search for more power or a product of power politics. In this account, imperialism cannot be taken as a theory and is reduced to a loose concept. Therefore, within this perspective we cannot talk about a single theory of imperialism but various theories of imperialism which conceptualize it in different ways.

For some, imperialism is not a concept but a law of international relations. Laws aim to reveal dependency between two or more variables. If these dependent relations are repeatedly found, then the relationship turns into a law (Waltz, 1979). Within this framework, imperialism is generally regarded as a dependent variable that is constantly being reproduced by an independent variable. In most of the Marxist accounts, imperialism is perceived as a product of capitalism (Brewer, 1990). For these, imperialism can be perceived as a theory since theories cannot be reduced to the collections of laws. As underlined also by Waltz (1990, p.22), a "theory is an intellectual construction by which we select facts and interpret them." In this sense, a theory is a depiction of a certain domain; and it describes the organization of that domain and the connections among its parts (Waltz, 1979, p.8).

Regarding this definition, imperialism can be perceived as a theory of international within the scope of this chapter. First of all, even though it refuses the Realist distinction between the realms of domestic and international, imperialism as a theory concentrates on the form of social relations taking place at the international level. In this sense, theory of imperialism is a picture of a bounded realm. Moreover, it aims to depict the organization of that domain. Unlike the mainstream accounts of an anarchically organized world order, imperialism reveals the inherent hierarchies embedded in the global structure. This account also explains the determining principle of the relations among the parts of the domain. It brings forth accumulation of capital and exploitation as the foundational motives which determine the relations between the states. In this sense, it satisfies Waltz's (1979, p.8) criteria of being a theory, as it "indicates that some factors are more important than others and specifies relations among them".

In short, it is possible to perceive imperialism as a policy practice since the Roman Empire, or as a law of conduct of relations among states, or as a theory of international politics. While this study acknowledges this conceptual versatility, it approaches to imperialism as one of the critical theories of IR. While it admits that there are various studies and different perspectives on imperialism, it suggests that imperialism studies still form a single theoretical framework regarding the definition of what constitutes a theory as mentioned above. Therefore, instead of labelling this literature as "theories of imperialism", this study prefers to refer to one single "theory of imperialism".

Yet the question remains: If imperialism is a theory of the international, then why is Idealism widely accepted as the first theoretical school of IR? A close look at the schools of Idealism, Realism and Imperialism reveals that all of these theories were concerned with two Great Wars but developed different reasonings. Within these schools, both Idealism and Realism strive to find solutions to the problems of the existing system. Moreover, the theoretical borders of IR were drawn by the winning powers of two Great Wars, who excluded critical premises out of the field due to their emphasis on change. Unlike these problem-solving conventional theories, theory of imperialism viewed wars as products of the world capitalist system; therefore, suggested a total modification of the global relations. In this sense, imperialism, as a critical theory of IR, is totally excluded from the field and reduced to a policy practice.

In order to situate the theory of imperialism into its well-deserved place within the critical theories of IR, this chapter is divided into four sections. The first section concentrates on the history of imperialism, as a theory. Without any doubt, if imperialism is taken as a policy, its history would be very argumentative and much longer. The term *"imperium"* dates back to the political practices of the Holy Roman Empire. The first section neglects this comprehensive literature on the formation of imperialism as a policy practice, since it concentrates on the advent of imperialism as a theory. Therefore, it specifically examines the formation of imperialism as a theory of the international since early 1900s.

The second section focuses on the critical evaluation of the mainstream narratives of international relations by the theory of imperialism. When the first scholars of imperialism have started to write on the subject matter, there was no institutionalized field of International Relations. Therefore, there was no conventional theory that they were supposed to criticize. However, in the later generations of imperialism studies, the volume of this critique is much more visible. In this sense, the second section reviews those critiques of the theories of imperialism to the mainstream narratives.

The third section examines how the theory of imperialism depicts the "international". Within a century old corpus of studies on imperialism, it is impossible to talk about a single narrative. As time passed by, the theoretical formulations of imperialism have been developed and modified. Within this broad spectrum and historical divergences, this section puts forth how these different schools of imperialism have conceptualized international relations in a way to reveal the power struggles inherent in the existing global system.

Last but not least, there was a relatively stagnant period for the imperialism studies since early 1980s. However, there was a resurgence in early 2000s that produced a new body of work that is widely known as the new imperialism. Apart from the case studies that apply the analytical tools developed by these imperialism studies to the concrete historical developments, there are considerable numbers of theoretical initiatives that situate imperialism to the center of scientific inquiry. The aim of the last section is to introduce these new studies and new theoretical openings led by imperialism as a theory of the international.

2   Theory of Imperialism: A Brief History[1]

As mentioned earlier, it is very controversial to refer to a specific historical period as the milestone of imperialist political practices. Imperialism is etymologically derived from the Latin word *Imperium* that refers to commanding and capacity to make laws in a territory. In this sense, it depicts a rule in extensive territories which is a process of maintenance and expansion of empire. Regarding this, some scholars stress the resemblance of political practices of Roman Empire to Western Imperialism of the 20th century (Galtung, Heiestad and Rudeng, 1980). For the others, imperialism is a product of the global expansion of capitalism starting from the late 15th century (Amin, 2001). Based on this picture, imperialism can easily be associated with the colonial policies. However, colonialism, derived from the Latin word *colonus* (farming), refers to the permanent transfer of a segment of population from one region to another. Moreover, the second half of the 20th century has proven that imperialism is not dependent on colonialism, as imperialist policies prevailed in the age of decolonization. Especially imperialism analysis of the World System Theories associates imperialism mostly with free trade and unequal exchanges. In these accounts too, the roots of the exploitative world system dates back to the formation of world capitalist economy (Gills and Frank, 2014). In these narratives, imperialism emerged with the end of protectionism and the rise of world economic structures and trading networks.

It is obvious that imperialism as a policy practice has a long and argumentative history. However, when imperialism is taken as a theory of the international, things get clearer. Especially in the first decade of the 1900s, there were studies concentrated particularly on imperialism. This first group may be termed as the classical imperialism theories. The first comprehensive study on imperialism conducted by British economist and social scientist John A. Hobson (2005) was published in 1902. Even though he was not a Marxist, Hobson's pioneer work inspired the first generation of Marxist imperialism studies. The first Marxist studies on imperialism concentrated on the rise of monopolies and it was Hobson who first linked the rise of inter-imperial rivalry to the development of monopolies (Brewer, 1990, p.20). Hobson's aim was neither to develop a theory nor to explain the nature of international relations. He strived to discover the general principles which underlie the main drivers behind imperialist policies. Even before the First World War, or even before the

---

1   For a detailed account on the historical processes that led to the development of imperialism theories see (Sune, 2017).

emergence of Idealism and Realism as theories of the international, Hobson has tried to explain why states are competing at the international level.

A broad Marxist literature on imperialism has followed studies of Hobson, in the first decade of the 20th century. One of such leading studies was Austro-Marxist Rudolf Hilferding's (1981) the *Finance Capital,* first appeared in 1910. Hilferding (1981, p.21) addressed economic characteristics of the latest phase of capitalist development. Therefore, rather than an overall theory of the international, this study also appears as a detailed account of capitalism. His main focus was the formation of finance capital, as a distinct form from the industrial and commercial capital. He perceived this process as an end to free competition and put forth how the formation monopolies created new tendencies for crises.

In the following years, these pioneer studies were developed by Nikolai Bukharin (1971), Rosa Luxemburg (1972), Karl Kautsky (2007) and Vladimir Lenin (1999). These scholars concentrated on the structural causes of inequalities and destruction created by the rivalry between imperialist powers. These are the first true initiatives to develop a class-based analysis of the international. Especially, Lenin and Bukharin developed their theories in order to make sense of the First World War and to formulate counter strategies against the imperialist powers. This first generation of the theory of imperialism attributed the war to the rivalry among the states and associated the rivalry with the development of monopoly capital in the core capitalist states. Therefore, unlike the Classical Realist accounts of the international, which reduced the causes of the rivalries to search for power, theory of imperialism pointed out economic mechanisms, such as concentration of capital and formation of monopolies, as the underlying factors behind the geopolitical competitions.

The premises of this first generation of the theory of imperialism have been credited by the mainstream theories as well. For example, Robert Gilpin (1987, p.51) claimed that Lenin was right to attribute the causes of the First World War to imperialism. However, he adds that theories of imperialism and Realism share common arguments since both asserts that states compete for power and wealth. Also, in both accounts, unequal distribution of power is perceived as the source of international conflict and political changes (Gilpin, 1987, p.42). Similar arguments were put forward by Keohane (1984, pp. 41–46) who claimed that Lenin's version of Marxism is not much different than Realism. In fact, they were partially right since earlier accounts on imperialism perceived the state as an instrument of the dominant classes; and therefore, they also concentrated on the state policies. However, this overlap was mostly a product of the historical development. Even though imperialism studies developed a very different conceptualization of the international, the process of monopolization led them to concentrate on state as a unit of analysis. In this sense, unlike Realism, state-centered analysis of early imperialism studies was triggered by their class analysis. Despite apparent similarities, the ontological formulation of the international was much more different.

As the theory of imperialism has been developed at the second half of the 20th century, this resemblance has begun to disappear. Along with the decolonization process, new states have gained their independence, which signified the end of formal domination by the central capitalist states (Magdoff, 1975, p.73). However, this does not mean the end of imperialism. Even though direct political control has become invisible, undeveloped regions continued to experience economic domination. Therefore, new studies have emerged and concentrated especially on the relations between the first and the third world, which is claimed to be neglected by the first generation of imperialism scholars.

These new studies, which sprang up in the 1960s and 1970s, are composed of the variations of Dependency and World System Theories. Since these schools are analyzed in separate chapters within the scope of this book, they are not discussed in detail in this chapter. However, it should be noted that these schools have situated the issue of exploitation at the center of their inquiry in order to understand the nature of international relations. Thus, imperialism was one of the strongest themes in these studies. For example, a group of scholars organized around the journal of *Monthly Review* developed the monopoly capital-based analysis of the first generation of imperialism studies. In 1966, Paul Sweezy, together with Paul Baran, wrote *Monopoly Capital* (Baran and Sweezy, 1966) to discuss how capitalism has transformed from a competitive structure to the monopoly form. Similarly, within this literature, Harry Magdoff (2005) analyzed how imperialism functions without colonies.

Contrary to the hegemonic discourses of modernization, which attached the underdevelopment of the third world countries to their internal political, economic and social structures, imperialism studies in the 1960s aimed to demonstrate how the dependent relationship between the first and third world reproduces the existing developmental disparities. Andre Gunder Frank (1967, p.153), as one of the pioneering figures of the dependency school, claimed that capitalism is a worldwide monopolistic exchange and exploitation system. He asserted that contradictions immanent to the capitalist system create development in the central states, while the periphery is sentenced to underdevelopment. Unlike the first generation of imperialism studies, which concentrated on the field of production, dependency school specifically examined the exchange relations between hierarchically organized geographies.

Similar to the Dependency School, World System Theory has also based its core arguments on the nature of exploitation embedded in the global structures. However, Dependency School has reduced the dynamics of underdevelopment to the relationship between center and periphery. World System Theory, on the other hand, suggested locating the issue of exploitation and underdevelopment into the overall world structure. Pioneered by Immanuel Wallerstein (1974), Arghiri Emmanuel (1974) and Samir Amin (1976), World System Theory asserted that the centers and peripheries of the world should be examined as the components of a single system. To give an example, Amin (1976) put forth that while the world economy is divided between different development levels, all the economies are attached to globally organized trade and financial capitalist networks. In order to show its imperialistic character, the World System scholars revealed that the global system is hierarchically organized, in which there is a certain division of labor between and within centers, peripheries and semi-peripheries of the world.

Even though imperialism studies continued to exist within the academic circles, they started to lose their political popularity since imperialism has become invisible through democratic and humanitarian discourses. However, 2003 Iraqi intervention led to an upsurge in the studies on imperialism. These New Imperialism studies have touched upon wide range political and academic subjects, such as American imperialism, hegemony, humanitarian intervention, regime change, failed states, rogue states, neoliberalism, international organizations, empire, sovereignty, globalization and so on. As it can be deduced from these broad-spectrum issues, these new studies strive to put forth that imperialism has a political dimension together with the economic one (Öztürk, 2006, p.297). New imperialism studies can be categorized under three categories: a) Studies concentrating on the new imperial rivalries, b) studies on super imperialism, and c) post-modern narratives on imperialism.

Studies by David Harvey (2004) and Giovanni Arrighi (2001) are examples of research on imperialism that fits into the first category. Especially transformation to a neoliberal world economic order after 1970s is one of the central themes in these studies. These scholars analyze the current world structure by making a categorical separation between capitalist and territorial logics of power (Arrighi, 2001, p.62). Simply, while capitalist logic of power stems from the politics of production, exchange and accumulation, the territorial logic of power is related with state policies, which necessitates commanding a certain territory. In order to explain the rivalries between the states, these scholars concentrated on the dialectical relationship between the capitalist and territorial logics of power. Financial capital is also a central theme for these studies. To give an example, Harvey (2004) analyzed different periods of American hegemony and asserted that USA has lost its industrial superiority to Japan and Germany in the 1970s. As a result, USA used the capacity of its financial power to dispossess the others (Harvey, 2004, p.24). At this point, Harvey developed the concept of *accumulation by dispossession* and explained the characteristics of the *new imperialism* through the theoretical capacity of this notion.

Perspectives of Leo Panitch and Sam Gindin (2006) can be given as an example of the second category. Especially formation of the American Hegemony, regime change and the literature on rogue states are the central themes in these studies. These scholars claim that classical imperialism studies lost their validity. First of all, in the past the main imperial form of relations was between exploited and exploiting countries. According to these scholars, in order to understand the current form of imperialism, one must examine the connections between the imperialist states (Panitch and Gindin, 2006, p.25). They also criticize the reduction of state to an instrument of the monopoly capitalists by the classical imperialism studies. They emphasize that for establishing a connection between imperialism and capitalism, a state theory is fundamental. Therefore, according to the premises of super imperialism theories, American Empire restructured other nation states and attached them to an imperial center. With the transformation of nation states, or the internationalization of the state (Panitch and Gindin, 2006, p.21), the imperial power got the capacity to be represented within each nation state. As imperial power is diffused to distant state systems, the idea of super imperialism comes in sight. This new mode of imperialism functions through penetration of American Hegemony in distant geographies and cooperation between capitalist states (Panitch and Gindin, 2006, p.21). The states, which do not comply with the rules of neoliberal capitalist order, are labelled as rogues and forced for regime change (Panitch and Gindin, 2006, p.32).

While discussions on super imperialism are based on the unification of state structures under the aegis of the American Empire, the postmodern narratives on imperialism suggest total disappearance of localities. For example, Michael Hardt and Antonio Negri (2001, p.286) claim that nation states took a backseat with the rise of transnational companies. This process is perceived as the disappearance of national boundaries since localities are attached to a universal system with the rise of a new type of empire (Hardt and Negri, 2001, p.368). According to these studies, the new empire has no center and boundaries. It is a non-territorial form of rule that integrates every part of the world into its power. They also refute the premises of the classical imperialism studies, as they claim that imperialist policies are not governed by the nation states. Instead, imperialism takes place above the nation states (Hardt and Negri, 2001, p.197). Therefore, sovereignty is one of the central issues within these studies. They claim that with the establishment of a network by transnational classes, the functions of nation states have disappeared; and therefore, there is no "outside" anymore that may form the idea of national sovereignty. The political power of the new empire takes place at the transnational level and therefore forms a global sovereignty.

3   Critiques of Theory of Imperialism to Mainstream IR

It is impossible to talk about one single critique developed by the theory of imperialism to the mainstream narratives of IR. Since the beginning of the 20th century, there have been different perspectives on imperialism narrating international relations in different ways. However, the main aim of imperialism scholars was not to get involve into a debate with the mainstream IR theories. As mentioned above, the first generation of imperialism studies were conducted before Liberalism and Realism have emerged as separate schools of IR. Therefore, discussing the critiques of imperialism studies to conventional IR theories is also a difficult task. Still, within this multiplicity it is possible to sum up these critiques under certain themes.

The first critique of imperialism theories to the mainstream IR can be derived from their analysis of the causes of Great Wars. Wilsonian Idealism, which was the most dominant perspective in the post-War years, has attributed the First World War to the secret agreements and misunderstandings between the states. Therefore, what Idealism suggested as a prescription was to develop open diplomacy and a platform for states to discuss their problems. Classical Realism, on the other hand, criticized this perspective and searched the causes of military conflicts by concentrating on the human nature. According to them, war is an inevitable and unescapable feature of international politics that is triggered by the impulse of search for more power. Imperialism, on the other hand, have challenged these idealistic and ahistorical accounts of modern military conflicts. As indicated by Bukharin (1972), colonial annexation and war was a reflection of the inter-imperial rivalry. Therefore, it is a product of the historical development of capitalism at the world scale. Also, for Lenin, inter-imperial competition was central in explaining the outbreak of the World Wars (Kiely, 2010, p.59). In these accounts, imperialism has stimulated economic, military and political competition among states at the international level.

The second line of critique can be deduced from the mainstream perspectives on "national interest". Especially for the Realist narratives of IR, national interest is a key term with its explanatory power. Machiavellian forms of analysis assert that state policies represent the interest of the whole nation, which is mostly associated with the protection of state and its inhabitants. For these accounts, power of the states is crucial for the protection of national interest (Morgenthau, 1985). Even though Gilpin asserts that for both imperialism theories and realism states struggle for power and wealth (Gilpin, 1987, p.46), theory of imperialism in fact conceptualizes national interest in a very different way. According to the theory of imperialism, what is presented as the national interest is the limited interest of the dominant classes, who are able to present it as the interest of the whole nation by using the ideological apparatuses of states. Whilst Realist theory attaches territorial expansion to the necessity of increasing the power of the state, theory of imperialism demonstrates that expansionist policies do not serve to the whole nation. As Hobson (2005, p.46) states, "imperialism has been bad business for the nation, it has been good business for certain classes and certain trades within the nation".

The third critique can be derived from the discussions on the structure of the world system. Conventional approaches to IR portray a world structure organized according to the principle of formal sovereign equality between nation states. Even though they accept an imbalance in terms of distribution of power between nation states, they believe the international sphere is anarchically organized. Imperialism theory, on the other hand, uncovers the embedded inequalities and hierarchies hidden behind the principle of formal sovereign equality of states. Unlike the atomistic accounts of the international, theory of imperialism perceives world as a single system organized by the capitalist social relations under the dominance of the Western capitalist states. This whole system is hierarchically organized, in which unequal relations among the geographies are prevalent. As Lenin (1999) puts it, the whole world is divided into territories having different functions for the global capitalist system. In this system, the monopoly capitalists in the central capitalist states use the capacity of their nation states to share the world among themselves.

This brings us to the fourth critique, which is also based on this hierarchically organized world conceptualization. As noted above, according to the theory of imperialism, the world system has a stratified characteristic, in which different regions have different capacities and functions. Within this multilayered international division of labor, the conventional IR theories are criticized for reducing international relations only to the Great Power politics. This concentration on the Great Powers by the mainstream narratives hides other forms of unevenness which affect the rest of the world. Therefore, conventional IR theories have been criticized for ignoring "small" states. This Western-centric characteristic of the mainstream IR has also been criticized by Post-Colonial and Non-Western IR theories, as it has been discussed in separate chapters in this book.

The last line of critique of imperialism to the mainstream IR can be derived from their critical evaluation of human rights and democracy. Especially normative liberal formulations of international politics assert that IR should be governed by the norms of human rights and democracy. They perceive a close relationality among the principles of human rights, democracy and peace (Doyle and Recchia, 2011) and portray such Western initiatives as civilizational missions. Theory of Imperialism, on the other hand, problematizes this relationship. Especially new imperialism studies demonstrate how discourses of human rights, democracy and peace are intertwined with the imperialistic policies. New imperialism studies, which concentrate specifically on the neoliberal policies, show that interventions by the Western capitalist states to the rest of the world through humanitarian discourses are in fact policies of restructuring the dominated states. This restructuring facilitates the penetration by the international capitalist classes. This discussion created a whole literature on "humanitarian imperialism" (Chomsky, 2008). Furthermore, imperialism studies are also critical of the conceptualizations of "globalization" especially by the liberal theories, which perceive it as a homogenization process integrating distinct geographies into a single system. Scholars writing on imperialism, assert that each phase of globalization is triggered by the capitalist social relations, in which exploitation has a central role (Amin, 2001). For these, the term globalization hinders understanding the exploitative nature of the process and contradictions stemming from the current world structure.

4   Imperialism and the Theory of International Relations

Following the critiques developed by the theory of imperialism to the mainstream narratives of IR, this section analyzes how imperialism conceptualizes the "international". Similar to the critiques, it is not possible to talk about a single form of understanding developed by the theory of imperialism for conceptualizing the international. As previously indicated, in different historical periods there were different theories and perspectives on imperialism. Therefore, there are differences in their conceptualization of the international since historical developments stimulated development of different theoretical studies. Furthermore, there are essential ontological and epistemological cleavages among these studies. However, it is still possible to gather these conceptualizations under certain categories. This also supports the argument that imperialism forms a single theoretical framework capable of revealing the functioning mechanisms of the global structure.

Imperialism theory, while conceptualizing IR, does not separate domestic and international spheres. Instead, it concentrates on the internal dynamics of capitalism and its reflection at the international arena. One of the main themes in the theory of imperialism is the expansion of capitalism to the rest of the world and its transformation into a world system. For example, Bukharin (1972) analyzes how a single world economic system is formed with the geographical expansion of capitalism. In this sense, the dialectical relationship between the domestic and international has been established by the theory of imperialism. In the accounts of classical imperialism studies by Hilferding, Bukharin and Lenin, it is explicit that there is a dialectical relation between the development of monopolies at the domestic level and competition among states at the international level. To give another example, for Dependency School, underdevelopment is a domestic characteristic that is triggered by the global system. In this sense, theory of imperialism concentrates on both domestic and international sphere in order to capture the nature of IR.

Theory of imperialism also prioritizes a structural analysis of the international, instead of reducing international relations to a mere activity of the atomistic states or individual state leaders. Classical imperialism studies revealed structural grounds of the global inequalities and catastrophes triggered by the competition of imperialist states (Özdemir, 2010, p.130). Similarly, World System Theory perceives the world as a single system, mostly directed by the dynamics of capitalism. There is also a structural theoretical tendency in the new imperialism studies. These studies do not examine the world through the dichotomy of the central capitalist states versus the underdeveloped world. Instead, they start their examination with the accumulation of capital at the global level and its reflection at different geographies (Öztürk, 2006, p.297). Since theory of imperialism perceives the world as a single totality, it tries to reveal the contradictions immanent to it. In this sense, dialectical analysis plays a central role in their structural formulation of the international relations. To give an example, for Bukharin the inter-imperial rivalry and war between the capitalist states is a consequence of the dialectical relation between the internationalization tendency of the world economic system and nationalization tendencies that separate the world into distinct blocs (Özdemir, 2010, p.132). In this account, war is a structural outcome of the contradictions immanent to a single world capitalist system.

As indicated in the previous section, imperialism theory views international system as a hierarchically organized social structure. Even though there is a sort of "formal" sovereign equality between the states, this does not create an anarchical system. Instead, there are embedded hierarchies within the international system. These hierarchies are not reduced to unequal distribution of wealth and capabilities. Without any doubt, for the theory of imperialism, unequal distribution is central to the analysis of the international system. However, the hierarchical structure of the international system is also related with the ability of the Western capitalist states to determine the rules of the global system. This ability gives the central capitalist states the capacity to shape the economic, political and cultural forms in the rest of the world. As argued by Magdoff (2005, p.167), the global structures are organized in a way to serve the interest of the central capitalist states. In this sense, for imperialism theory, the hierarchical world structure is defined in terms of a social relationship which occurs between and within the states and social classes. To give an example, Sweezy (1962, p.252) states that the international system is formed around the mutual relationship between capitalist, semi-capitalist and noncapitalist states. This relationship is organized by an unequal division of labor, which sets the basis of hierarchies.

Within this hierarchical structure, theory of imperialism explains the nature of foreign policy making. The first generation of the imperialism scholars put forth that expansionist policies and competition between the states are triggered by the national monopolies. For them, concentration and centralization of capital created monopolies, which are capable of using the capacity of their nation states for their own economic interests (Brewer, 2011, p.128). As a result of this process, each national economy has turned into a private investment. In this sense, for the first generation of imperialism theory there is a competition between capitalist monopolies which control national economies as a tool for their expansionist policies. For this account, the motivation behind states' expansionist polices is not to increase the state power but to access to external markets. As for the mainstream IR, this struggle of the social classes is reduced to an ahistorical competition between states that search for more power. Explaining state policies through concentrating on the dynamics of class relations is also prevalent in the following generations of imperialism studies. Dependency studies, with their concentration on comprador bourgeoisie, strived to put forth how state policies are determined by class relations. A similar position can be derived from the new imperialism studies. Arrighi (2011, p.62) emphasized the importance of concentrating on the capitalist and territorial logics for understanding state policies. In this account, territorial logic may resemble to the Realist discourse of "state interest"; however, it does not reduce state policies to search for more power. Instead, it underlines the significance of analyzing the dialectical relationship between territorial and capitalist logics for explaining states' foreign policies.

In this sense, theory of imperialism does not perceive an ahistorical constant competition between states. Since it tries to reveal the historical and class-related aspects of state policies, it accepts that cooperation between the states is possible and even necessary at some certain circumstances. As stated by Panitch and Gindin (2006, p.21), one of the principles of the global system, which is shaped by the U.S. hegemony, is cooperation among capitalist states. This capacity of imperialism to present the changing nature of state policies is due to its flexible theoretical framework stemmed from historical materialist tradition. Concentrating on the globalization process, these scholars demonstrated the development of new sort of relations between states and classes. According to them, with the globalization of capital, national capitalist classes started to become more dependent upon other nation states. Similarly, nation states have become more dependent on the capitalist classes of other nations. This new form of dependencies necessitated new forms of cooperative mechanisms. In this sense, both competition and cooperation of nation states are triggered by the functioning mechanisms of the global capitalism.

Last but not least, imperialism theory perceives international relations as a process. According to the formulations developed by the different strands of imperialism studies, relations between states and the international structure are constantly being determined by the process of formation of world capitalist system. It can be derived from various studies on imperialism that the creation of the modern international system coincides with the formation of world capitalist system. For example, Amin (2001) suggests that there has been an internationalization process since the 15th century, whose roots should be found within the dynamics of capitalist development. According to the scholar, this process set the basis of the new global system. Moreover, this is not a constant, ahistorical global system as it is presented by the mainstream IR theories. Instead, for imperialism studies, understanding the dynamics of change within the international system has always played a central role in theoretical analysis. Within this account, since its establishment, the global capitalist system is transforming; and therefore, the nature of the relationship between the states is changing as well. In this regard, the centrality of the notion of change in the theory of imperialism gives it a flexibility that sustains its validity in different historical periods.

5 Contributions of Imperialism to the Current Debates in IR

Without any doubt, imperialism is still one of the most discussed and highly debated topics, particularly in IR and generally in social sciences. Even with a superficial glance, it is possible to find out the widespread studies produced on the topic in the recent years. This is due to the flexibility of theory of imperialism, which adapts itself and its theoretical stance according to the changes in social relations. As the previous sections put forth, theory of imperialism has modified its analysis according to the new developments in global relations. This transformation over the twentieth century has been discussed by the current studies that concentrate on the relationship between imperialism and globalization (Sundaram, 2014). However, this does not mean that classical studies produced by the first generation of imperialism studies lost their relevancy. There are still plenty of studies focusing on these classical texts and their explanatory capacity in analyzing today's world structures (An, 2015).

Among these, the first group of studies inspired by the theory of imperialism is centered around the discussions on globalization. The role of imperialism in the process of globalization, relevancy of imperialism under globalization and transformation of imperialist relation in the age of globalization are the core themes in these studies (Narayan and Huggins, 2017). They strive to establish a close link between capitalism, development, imperialism and globalization (Veltmeyer, 2019). In majority of these studies, globalization is understood as a different face of imperialism, arising out of a project of world domination that is triggered by the U.S. efforts to establish its hegemony (Veltmeyer, 2005). In other words, globalization in its current form is conceptualized as the new form of American Imperialism (Barrow, 2005). For some, globalization is viewed as an integral part of Europe's recent imperial past (Thomas and Thompson, 2014). However, not all the studies examining the globalization process perceive it as equal to imperialism. For instance, Pozo-Martin (2006) critically reviews the relationship between globalization and imperialism and underlines the importance of a state theory in order to conceptualize the form of inter-state relations. William Robinson (2006), on the other hand, criticizes this state-centric analysis and examines how the state-centric International Relations have been transformed in the globalization process.

New imperialism studies also led to further studies within IR, especially those focusing on the relationship between neoliberalism and imperialism (Fouskas, 2018). Some of these scholarly works reproduce the main premises of the new imperialism studies (Petras, 2020); however, there are quite number of studies built on criticizing this literature (Callinicos, 2009). These studies do not accept that Lenin's version of capitalism is outdated and believe that classical imperialism studies are indispensable for understanding today's global crises (Michael-Matsas, 2008). For instance, Kiely (2006) asserts that international order is still imperialist but the nature of it cannot be captured totally through the new imperialism studies. Other studies criticize Harvey's territorial logic and claim that nonterritorial character of imperialism is crucial to understand the current form of imperialism (Sakellaropoulos and Sotiris,

2015). This discussion on the new imperialism is not limited to the Marxist debates. Post-modern narratives on imperialism have also led to further studies within IR. These studies aim to analyze the role of imperialism in the age of globalization with a post-structuralist perspective (Hoogvelt, 2006). They particularly analyze the role of empire in IR with a specific focus on the function of the United States in the current world structure (Mabee, 2004). Lastly, discussions on return of imperialism with the war on terror have triggered further post-modern studies analyzing global relations with the concept of biopolitics (Reid, 2005).

Imperialism is also one of the main themes in the current non-Western IR studies. Especially in the last decade, there are varieties of studies critically evaluating colonialism and imperialism in order to create a non-Western IR theory (see. Shilliam, 2011). To give an example, there are some studies taking the issue of imperialism at the center of inquiry in order to create a Korean style of IR theory (Cho, 2015). There are also studies concentrating on the role imperialism in the foreign policy making in non-Western world (Wang, 2012). Furthermore, there are studies which perceive IR as a colonized field and therefore concentrate on imperialism in order to decolonize it (Capan, 2017).

Theory of imperialism has also created new concepts and studies on cultural imperialism, humanitarian imperialism and peace building. Even though the role of culture in imperialist policies has been widely discussed, the capitalist development and globalization has led to further discussions on the subject matter (Meyer, 1987). The interventions by the central capitalist states to the underdeveloped world in the name of human rights and peace have generated a literature on humanitarian imperialism and peace building. Discussions on peace building perceive such policies as the new form of imperialism (Schellhaas and Seegers, 2009). Similarly, there are current studies critically evaluating the issue of global human rights and analyzing how the humanitarian discourse is used as a tool for imperialist policies (Bush, Martiniello and Mercer, 2011).

In recent years, theory of imperialism has also led to the discussions on sub-imperialisms which refer to the states that are components of larger imperial power (Valencia, 2017). Even though sub-imperialism is an old term, in recent years these studies have concentrated on the political and economic policies of the new rising powers. Especially, studies on the foreign policy of Russia through the theoretical framework of theory of imperialism are apparent (Van Herpen, 2015). It should be noted that some of these studies perceive Russia as a new imperialist power by its own. There are also current studies combining the premises of uneven and combined development and sub-imperialism in order to examine different cases (Moldovan, 2018).

Last but not least, imperialism theory has also generated a wide literature on different case studies. To give an example, Veltmeyer and Petras' article on imperialism and capitalism centered on the changing forms of imperialism through analyzing the capitalist development process in Latin America (Veltmeyer and Petras, 2015). As indicated above, there are plenty of case studies on Russian imperialism as well (Sangramoso, 2020). In recent years, there are also case studies examining the policies of Europe in Libya within the scope of imperialism (Pradella and Rad, 2017). Besides, it is possible to come across further case studies discussing imperialism in very different countries such as India (Osuri, 2017) and Canada (Garrod, 2018).

6   Conclusion

This study approached to imperialism as one of the critical theories of IR. According to the definition of Waltz (1990, p.22), a theory should fulfill three qualifications. First of all, it should depict a certain domain. As discussed in the previous sections, the main concentration of theory of imperialism is the international domain. However, it does not perceive the international field as a separate entity from the domestic sphere. Unlike conventional IR theories' negligence of the role of domestic sphere, theory of imperialism demonstrates the dialectical relationship between the domestic and international. On the one hand, it shows how domestic political and economic structures determine the foreign policies of countries. For instance, the first generation of imperialism studies has put forth how the concentration and centralization of capital in the Western capitalist states has created expansionist foreign policies. On the other hand, it reveals that the hierarchical international system determines domestic social structures. While earlier accounts of imperialism analyze the impact of global capitalism on the dominated states, new imperialism studies, as in the accounts of Panitch and Gindin (2006), concentrate on the domestic transformations in the central capitalist studies.

The second trait of a theory is explaining the organization of aforementioned domain. Conventional IR theories portray an anarchically organized world order, in which each nation state is an atomistic unit under the principle of formal sovereign equality. Realist accounts of IR attribute this organization to the lack of a world state, which results in a constant conflict among states. Similarly, Liberal theory with its neoliberal variations accepts this anarchical organization of the global structures. However, by underlining the possibility of cooperation between states, Liberal theory diverges from the Realist accounts in terms of the impact of this organization on state behavior. Theory of imperialism, on the other hand, puts forth that the global structure is hierarchically organized. The rules of this hierarchical organization are set by central capitalist states, serving the limited interest of their monopoly capitalists. In this sense, for the theory of imperialism, the dynamics of global capitalism creates a stratified organization in which there is a certain division of labor. While this organization serves to the core states, peripheries are exposed to constant underdevelopment due to the extraction of surplus and its transfer to the central capitalist states.

The third qualification of a theory is its capacity to explain the connection and relation among the parts of the domain. In this sense, as the previous sections has proved, theory of imperialism explains the nature of relations among the states without reducing international relations to the mere activities of atomistic units. Theory of imperialism reveals that the pattern of relation among states is determined by the dynamics of global capitalism. For the theory of imperialism, capitalism is a dynamic system which is constantly changing; therefore, triggering transformations in the nature of relation among states. Unlike the conventional conceptualizations of IR, which conceive power politics as the constant motive in state relations, imperialism theory proves that the relations of the parts of the international domain is continuously being shaped by the changing dynamics of global capitalist relations. Therefore, unlike the ahistorical accounts of international politics, theory or imperialism historicizes the underlying dynamics of state relations.

This flexibility of theory of imperialism gives it the capacity to analyze each different period of international relations without changing the foundational theoretical premises of its perspective. This capacity is reflected in the current studies in IR which cling to the theoretical findings developed by the theory of imperialism. The historical materialist roots of imperialism theory enable it to explain the constant change. This characteristic proves that imperialism as a critical theory of IR will continue to exist within the academic circles of IR and will carry on stimulating new studies benefiting from its theoretical capacity.

References

Amin, S., 1976. *Unequal Development: An Essay on the Social Formations of Peripheral Capitalism*. Hassocks: Harvester Press.

Amin, S., 2001. Imperialism and Globalization, *Monthly Review*, 53 (2), pp. 6–24.

An, J., 2015. Lenin's "Theory of Imperialism": Historical Debate and Contemporary Appraisal. *Social Sciences in China*. 36 (3), pp. 20–36.

Arrighi, G., 2001. *Uzun Yirminci Yüzyıl: Para Güç ve Çağımızın Kökenleri*. Ankara: İmge.

Baran, P. A. and Sweezy, P. M., 1966. *Monopoly Capital: an Essay on the American Economic and Social Order.* New York: Monthly Review Press.

Barrow, C. W., 2005. The Return of the State: Globalization, State Theory, and the New Imperialism. *New Political Science*, 27 (2), pp. 123–145.

Brewer, A., 1990. *Marxist Theories of Imperialism,* London: Routledge.

Brewer, A., 2011. Marksist Emperyalizm Teorileri, Istanbul: Kalkedon.

Bukharin, N., 1971. *Imperialism and World Economy.* London: Merlin.

Bush, R., Martiniello, G. and Mercer, C., 2011. Humanitarian imperialism, *Review of African Political Economy*, 38 (129). pp. 357–365.

Callinicos, A., 2009. Imperialism and Global Political Economy. Cambridge: Polity.

Capan, Z. G., 2017. Decolonising International Relations?. *Third World Quarterly*, 38 (1). pp. 1–15.

Cho, Y. C., 2015. Colonialism and Imperialism in the Quest for a Universalist Korean-Style International Relations Theory. *Cambridge Review of International Affairs*, 28 (4). pp. 680–700.

Chomsky, N., 2008. Humanitarian Imperialism: The New Doctrine of Imperial Right. *Monthly Review*, 60 (4). Pp. 22–50.

Doyle, M. and Stefano, R., 2011. Liberalism in International Relations. in B. Badie, D. Berg-Schlosser and L. Morlino ed. *International Encyclopedia of Political Science*. Los Angeles: Sage. pp. 1434–1439.

Emmanuel, A., 1974. *Unequal Exchange: A Study of Imperialism of Trade*. London: New Left Books.

Fouskas, V. K., 2018. Neo-liberalism and Ordoliberalism: a Critique of Two Forms of Imperialism and Authoritarianism. *Critique*, 46 (3). pp. 397–421.

Frank, A. G., 1967. *Capitalism and Underdevelopment in Latin America: Historical Studies of Chile and Brazil.* New York: Monthly Review Press.

Galtung, J., Heiestad, T. and Rudeng, E., 1980. On the Decline and Fall of Empires: The Roman Empire and Western Imperialism Compared. *Review,* 4 (1), pp. 91–153.

Garrod, J. Z., 2018. Imperialism or Global Capitalism? Some Reflections from Canada. *Studies in Political Economy*, 99 (3). pp. 268–284.

Gills, B. and Frank, A. G., 2014. *The World System: Five Hundred Years or Five Thousand?*. London: Routledge.

Gilpin, R., 1987. *The Political Economy of International Relations.* Princeton: Princeton University Press.

Hardt, M. and Negri, A., 2001. *İmparatorluk,* İstanbul: Ayrıntı.

Harvey, D., 2004. *Yeni Emperyalizm*, İstanbul: Everest.

Hilferding, R., 1981. *The Finance Capital: a Study of the Latest Phase of Capitalist Development.* London: Routledge.

Hobson, J. A., 2005. *Imperialism: A Study*, New York: Cosimo.

Hoogvelt, A., 2006. Globalization and Post-modern Imperialism. *Globalizations*, 3(2), pp. 159–174.

Kautsky, K., 2007. *Ultra-imperialism*, Marlborough: Adam Matthew Digital.

Keohane, R., 1984. *After Hegemony: Cooperation and Discord in the World Political Economy*, Princeton: Princeton University Press.

Kiely, R., 2006. United States Hegemony and Globalisation: What Role for Theories of Imperialism? *Cambridge Review of International Affairs*. 19 (2), pp. 205–221.

Kiely, R., 2010. *Rethinking Imperialism*. London: Palgrave Macmillan.

Lenin, V. I., 1999. *Imperialism: The Highest Stage of Capitalism*. Sydney: Resistance Books.

Luxemburg, R., 1972. *The Accumulation of Capital: an Anti-Critique*. London: Routledge..

Mabee, B., 2004. Discourses of empire: the US 'empire', Globalisation and International Relations. *Third World Quarterly*, 25 (8). pp. 1359–1378.

Magdoff, H., 1975. Emperyalizm: Tarihsel bir Bakış. In A. Aksoy ed. *Azgelişmişlik ve Emperyalizm*. İstanbul: Gözlem Yayınları.

Magdoff, H., 2005. *Sömürgesiz Emperyalizm*. İstanbul: Devin.

Matsas, S. M., 2008. The New-Old Imperialism. *Critique,* 36 (1), pp. 45–61.

Meyer, W., 1987. Testing theories of cultural imperialism: International media and domestic impact. *International Interactions*, 13 (4), pp. 353–374.

Moldovan, A., 2018. Uneven and Combined Development and Sub-Imperialism: The Internationalization of Brazilian Capital, *Globalizations*, 15 (3). pp. 314–328.

Morgenthau, H. J., 1985. *Politics Among Nations: Struggle for Power and Peace*, 6th ed. New York: Alfred A. Knopf.

Narayan, J. and Huggins, L. S., 2017. Whatever happened to the idea of imperialism?. *Third World Quarterly*, 38 (11), pp. 2387–2395.

Osuri, G., 2017. Imperialism, Colonialism and Sovereignty in the (Post)Colony: India and Kashmir, *Third World Quarterly*, 38 (11). pp. 2428–2443.

Özdemir, A. M., 2010. *Ulusların Sefaleti*. Ankara: İmge Yayınları.

Öztürk, Ö., 2006. Emperyalizm Kuramları ve Sermayenin Uluslararasılaşması. *Praksis*, 15, pp. 271–309.

Panitch, L. and Gindin, S., 2006. Theorizing American Empire. In A. Bartholomew, ed., *Empire's Law: The American Imperial Project and the War to Remake the World*. London: Pluto Press, pp. 21–43.

Petras, J., 2020. *US Imperialism: The Changing Dynamics of Global Power,* 1st ed. Milton: Routledge.

Pozo-Martin, G., 2006. A Tougher Gordian Knot: Globalisation, Imperialism and the Problem of the State. *Cambridge Review of International Affairs*. 19 (2), pp. 223–242.

Pradella, L. and Rad, S. T., 2017. Libya and Europe: Imperialism, Crisis and Migration. *Third World Quarterly*, 38 (11). pp. 2411–2427.

Reid, J., 2005. The Biopolitics of the War on Terror: A critique of the 'Return of Imperialism' thesis in International Relations, *Third World Quarterly*, 26 (2). pp. 237–252.

Robinson, W. I., 2006. Reification and Theoreticism in the Study of Globalisation, Imperialism and Hegemony: Response to Kiely, Pozo-Martin and Valladão. *Cambridge Review of International Affairs*, 19 (3), pp. 529–533.

Sagramoso, D., 2020. *Russian Imperialism Revisited: From Disengagement to Hegemony.* London: Routledge.

Sakellaropoulos, S. and Sotiris. P., 2015. From Territorial to Nonterritorial Capitalist Imperialism: Lenin and the Possibility of a Marxist Theory of Imperialism. *Rethinking Marxism*, 27(1), pp. 85–106.

Schellhaas, C. and Seegers, A., 2009. Peacebuilding: Imperialism's New Disguise?. *African Security Review*, 18 (2). pp. 1–15.

Schumpeter, J. A., 1951. *The Sociology of Imperialism.* Cleveland and New York: Meridian Books.

Shilliam, R., 2011. *International Relations and Non-Western Thought: Imperialism, Colonialism and Investigations of Global Modernity*, London: Routledge.

Sundaram, J. K., 2014. Globalization, Imperialism and its Discontents. *Inter-Asia Cultural Studie*s, 15 (1), pp. 17–24.

Sune, E., 2017, "Emperyalizm Teorileri ve Uluslararası İlişkiler", Faruk Yalvaç (ed.) *Tarihsel Materyalizm ve Uluslararası İlişkiler,* Ankara: İmge.

Sweezy, P. M., 1962. *The Theory of Capitalist Development: Principles of Marxian Political Economy.* London: Dobson.

Thomas, M. and Thompson, A., 2014. Empire and Globalisation: from 'High Imperialism' to Decolonisation. *The International History Review*, 36 (1), pp. 142–170.

Valencia, A. S., 2017. *Sub-Imperialism Revisited: Dependency Theory in the Thought of Ruy Mauro Marini.* Leiden: Brill.

Van Herpen, M. H., 2015. *Putin's Wars: The Rise of Russia's New Imperialism,* Second ed. US: Rowman & Littlefield.

Veltmeyer, H. and Petras J., 2015. Imperialism and Capitalism: Rethinking an Intimate Relationship, *International Critical Thought*, 5 (2). pp. 164–182.

Veltmeyer, H., 2005. Development and Globalization as Imperialism. *Canadian Journal of Development Studies*, 26(1), pp. 89–106.

Veltmeyer, H., 2019. Capitalism, Development, Imperialism, Globalization: a Tale of Four Concepts, *Globalizations*.

Wallerstein, I., 1974. *The Modern World System.* London: Academic Press.

Waltz, K., 1979. *Theory of International Politics.* Reading: Addison-Wesley Publishing Company.

Waltz, K., 1990. Realist Thought and Neo-Realist Theory. *Journal of International Affairs*, 44 (1), pp. 21–37.

Waltz, K., 2001. *Man, The State and War: A Theoretical Analysis.* New York: Columbia University Press.

Wang, J., 2012. The Chinese Interpretation of the Concept of Imperialism in the anti-Imperialist Context of the 1920s. *Journal of Modern Chinese History,* 6 (2). pp. 164–181.

CHAPTER 4

The Achievements of Dependency Approach as a Critical IR Theory

M. Kürşad Özekin

1 Introduction

Dependency approach emerged out of the intellectual heritage found in the critique of the liberal and diffusionist views of modernisation theory as the orthodox economic *pensée* of the 1960s. While the origins of dependency analyses are usually traced back to ECLA's critique of the conventional theory of international trade and economic development during the late 1940s and early 1950s, much of dependency literature in fact draws inspiration from Marxist debate concerning the development of capitalism in backward nations and from the earlier theories of imperialism, mostly formulated by the writings of Lenin (1999). Bukharin (1971), Hilferding (1981) and Luxemburg (1972). Principally developed as an economic theory of underdevelopment, dependency approach criticises the progressive and liberal developmentalist proposition that capitalism and free trade internationalism will automatically bring growth, prosperity, convergence and peace among nations. Emphasizing the putative constraints mostly imposed by the global political and economic order, dependency approach rather points out the persistence of unequal development and hierarchical power relations between underdeveloped countries of South and advanced economies of North.

Spearheaded mostly by Latin American intellectuals (*pensadores*) who regard capitalist penetration as the root cause of underdevelopment, dependency approach attributes the difficulties of development in the Global South to the series of factors such as the precise nature of unequal exchange, the methods of surplus extraction between nations and the dominating role of transnational corporations in technological, managerial and marketing terms. By envisioning world as a hierarchical and imperialist system, dependency approach suggests that the global expansion of capitalism does not promote general and even development among countries, but rather produces and reproduces global asymmetries in which peripheral countries of the South remain economically and politically subordinated to the advantage of core countries of North. Thus, according to proponents of dependency perspective

(*Dependistas*), the original roots of underdevelopment in the global south do not only lie in the socio-economic and socio-political factors of poor countries such as policy inefficiencies, lack of entrepreneurial and technical skill, cultural traditions, class-structures and historical legacies, but also are a by-product of the functioning of the global capitalist system which is apt to favour a narrow group of core countries at the expense of others. In this view, becoming self-sufficient as much as possible, and breaking the cycle of dependency though autonomous development policies are thought to be the only possible solutions to overcome underdevelopment for peripheral economies.

Emerged as a post-colonial move and a nativist critical reaction from below, the ideas of dependency perspective had been initially taken with a pinch of salt, particularly by policy circles in the Northern hemisphere, but in time it made a tremendous impression in intellectual currents as an outstanding development paradigm of the time. Particularly, the original propositions of dependency perspective such as the centre-periphery paradigm, the peculiarity of development in peripheral economies and the unequal nature of exchange between nations profoundly influenced the development mindset in global south laying the foundations for the idea that industrialisation in peripheral countries should be boosted through state-led developmentalism (*desarrollismo*) and import-substitutions. As time passed by, the impact of dependency approach did not only confine to academic sanctuaries, but rather moved beyond to scholarly circles by gaining many adherents among statesmen, policymakers, civil servants and chief experts of development agencies.

Particularly after reaching campuses in the US and Europe, dependency perspective came to have far-reaching implications on critical thinking worldwide and enjoyed a high degree of popularity in the 1960s and 1970s. Given its mixed parentage and the diversity of its intellectual roots, dependency perspective in fact appealed to a broad church of writers and scholars from different disciplines ranging from economics to sociology, from development studies to International Relations. However, by the early 1980s the dependency approach began to lose its purchase both in analytical and practical terms. In fact, a new common sense began to crystallize by the mid-1980s on behalf of the benefits of open trade, foreign direct investment, less state intervention, rise of new wave of globalisation and emergence of NICs (Newly Industrialising Countries). Thus, it is hardly surprising that dependency approach has been subjected to a storm of criticism not only for falling behind the times but also for being intellectually and theoretically flawed in and of itself. And eventually, dependency approach lost its overall allure in analytical terms and has been almost relegated to footnote status in the fields of both development studies and International Relations.

Today, there is much talk both on the terrain of intellectual currents and within policy circles that we live in a world of convergence that spreads opportunities, wealth and capabilities globally across borders, and therefore stands at odds with notions of peripherality and dependency. The force of these arguments has particularly intensified in the 2000s with the rise of BRICs and BRIC-like countries such as Mexico, Turkey and Indonesia as new economic powerhouses and notable drivers of international economic and political order. However, despite the recent popularity of these contentions, this chapter counter-argues that critiques of the dependency school have gone too far, ignoring its overall critical contributions and contemporary relevance, and claims that albeit the need of refinement to account for the recent changes in today's global world, it still offers a certain degree of validity and heuristic value for scholars in critical IR scholarship. Bearing this objective in mind, the chapter commences with a retrospective overview of dependency approach which charts a brief survey of the rise and fall of the dependency school as a critical intellectual movement. Here the purpose is not to comprehensively review dependency literature, but to inform the readers in advance of the complex intellectual roots and variety of theoretical formulations that the dependency tradition embodies. Beginning with such an introductory section in fact seems to be a tactical prerequisite since any revisiting of this "archaic line of thought" might be quite easily subjected to an outright and sweeping dismissal beforehand. Thus, in doing so, the section does not aim to blindly defend obsolete formulations within the dependency tradition, but to reveal how critiques of the dependency school have gone too far to ignore its sophisticated variants, overall contributions and contemporary relevance.

Drawing on such a critical survey, the next section subsequently explores how and in what ways the dependency tradition offers critical insights to IR scholarship. Beyond any doubt, the dependency school of thought has not emerged as an exclusively IR theory, but it profoundly contributes critical thinking in international relations and opened new ways of reasoning about the question of global inequalities, the North-South divide and the structure and functioning of international system. By and large, the mainstream IR theories are mostly interested in explaining the world as it is and have little intention to problematize how the existing international order came into being. Being self-consciously critical, the dependency approach, on the other hand, places itself above the prevailing power relations and dominant social order and questions the very foundations of international relations both in economic and political terms. Directly emanating from the global south as an emancipatory approach, the primary motivation of theorizing for dependency tradition is not only to explain the world out there, but also reveal repressive

practices and institutions in the existing international order and transform circumstances of domination and exploitation, particularly for the sake of people
in the global south.

Last but not least, after reflecting on critical spirit of dependency perspective, the chapter concludes with a discussion on the enduring relevance
and prospective research directions of dependency theory by putting special
emphasis on the current dynamics of today's global world. More in particular,
this last section is purported to discuss how and in what ways dependency
approach offers important analytical and critical insights to explain the current structure and dynamics of today's global world. In this respect, this section dwells on the recent writings and the contemporary issues in the dependency debate in order to give a fresh look for new theoretical openings and
research. Thus, the overall section does not only provide a window into some
possible ways of thinking about dependency theory's relevance today, but also
hopes to inspire scholars as well as practitioners to revisit and use the viable
tenets of dependency approach for future research directions.

2   Dependency in Retrospect: The Historical Roots and Intellectual
     Foundations of Dependency Approach

In retrospect, the historical roots of dependency perspective could be traced
back to the 19th-century when Latin American subaltern groups – including
indigenous peoples, Afro-Latin Americans, artisans, campesinos, women, and
workers – built collective consciousness of resistance against imperial order of
European colonialism over the continent. As Cibils (2015, p.105) put forward
the debates on issues such as colonialism, economic backwardness, industrialisation, social segmentation, reform and revolution were rich and diverse dat-
ing back at least to the late 1800s. Nevertheless, if one treats dependency as a
scholarly approach, the propositions which can be grouped under the banner
of dependency theory emerged in Latin America during the 1960s and 1970s,
largely as a response to liberal and diffusionist dogmas of modernization theory (Kay, 2011). In this respect, the early foundations of dependency approach
had been put forward by a group of social scientists working for the Economic
Commission for Latin America (ECLA, or CEPAL for its name in Spanish), a
regional commission of the United Nations established in 1947 and headquar-
tered in Santiago, Chile (Seers, 1981).

From colonial times to the mid of the 20th century, many economic policies for the development of the Latin American countries have been applied
based upon unilinear-evolutionist and liberal prescriptions of modernization

theory which regard Western experience as the prototype of development for the third world countries. However, the overall situation of the continent did not change, rather it had been worsened in relative terms. Although there was a general dynamic of change at play, the terms of trade for the majority of the continent remained highly problematic and the intra- and inter-state disparities still remained broadly in place. Under the direction of its executive secretary Raúl Prebisch, a group of economists and social scientists associated with the ECLA challenged the classic theory of free trade and comparative advantage and enunciated an alternative explanation to the persistence of underdevelopment (*subdesarrollo*) across the Latin American countries. Sketching out the center-periphery model of world, Prebisch (1950), along with Hans Singer, a well-known heterodox economist, developed a theory of the secular trends of exchange relations propounding that the terms of trade had retrospectively deteriorated to the disadvantage of periphery-like countries. As a spatial metaphor, the centre–periphery model perceives the international system as one of advanced or metropolitan 'centre' and a less developed 'periphery' in which former dominates the latter based on political interference, trade power, technological supremacy and economic surplus extraction.

Although ECLA's propositions on the centre-periphery are initially treated with great scepticism, particularly by policy circles in the Northern hemisphere, it profoundly influenced development thinking and practice not only in Latin America but also in the wider global south (Bernecker and Fischer, 1998). The originality of Prebisch and ECLA's centre-periphery paradigm in fact lies in the notion that development and underdevelopment are two opposite sides of a single process in which the disparities between the core and peripherial countries are reproduced through hierarchically structured power relations in international trade and production. In this sense, ECLA's propositions (*cepalismo*) on the peculiarity of peripheral capitalism, declining terms of trade and underdevelopment enjoyed a high degree of popularity not only in Latin America as a whole but in the Third World in general as the first genuine school of thought directly emanating from the global south. Thus, Latin American countries pursued strategies professedly conducive to state-led, autonomous, self-sustaining development (*desarrollismo*). Likewise, they aspired to industrialise and diversify their export compositions behind high tariff walls and state-directed protectionism, with the ultimate goal of reducing the continent's dependence on multinational manufactures and thus on the developed north.

However, the goals and expectations of the ECLA's model of development ran into problems starting in the early 1960s. The situation in Latin American economies took a turn for the worse: the balance of payment crisis exacerbated, real wages did not increase far enough to stimulate aggregate demand, unemployment grew even more acute, and the industrialisation process lost its dynamism (Palma, 1978; Larrain, 1989). These developments sparked a new wave of pessimism, leading to trenchant criticism of old established paradigms, namely modernisation theories as well as the ECLA's structuralist approach. To put it another way, the real-life crisis of import substitution and *desarrollismo* generated new and possibly more dangerous forms of dependence that gradually converted the ECLA structuralists into dependency theorists (Seer, 1981, p.140).

Partly evolved out of ECLA's thinking on development, dependency perspective drew inspiration from complex sets of intellectual traditions, including classical sociology, Marxian political economy, earlier theories of imperialism and some structuralist and Keynesian theories of economics that are avowedly non-Marxist (Palma, 1989; Kay, 2011). Among these diverse traditions, two main features particularly worth mentioning as intellectual bases of dependency analyses. First, despite its eminently critical stance towards *Cepalismo*, dependency school kept a line of continuity with ECLA's structuralist thinking on development incorporating ECLA's formulations of centre-periphery paradigm and its asymmetrical trade relations as a starting point (Larrain, 1989). In this respect, Raúl Prebisch can be rightly credited not only as the leader of the ECLA's structuralist school but also a forerunner of dependency analysis. Similar to the ECLA's structuralists, dependency theorists utilised the center-periphery paradigm and the uneven nature of capitalist development to articulate their view. Nevertheless, dependency theorists, in general, focused more on country-specific factors such as politics, class structures and social dynamics as an explanation of underdevelopment than the ECLA's structuralists. In this way, the original contribution of the dependency analysis was to present a new conception of underdevelopment combining the structural analysis of economics with society and politics in specific historical circumstances (Cibils, 2015, p.107).

Secondly, much of the dependency school also drew inspiration from classical sociology, Marxian political economy analysis of backwardness, as well as earlier accounts of imperialism, by which dependency analyses sought to integrate determination of economic structures with the agency, social and political aspects of the development process and strategies of class domination (Palma, 1978). In this respect, the complementarity between the classical theories of imperialism and dependency perspective is striking, particularly given the theoretical writings of Baran (1968), Frank (1967), Amin (1974; 1976) and Marini (1972) on the consequences of imperialism for the countries of the periphery. As Munck (1999) discusses the dependency perspective emerged as not only a reaction to the inadequacies of 'one size fits all' neoclassical and modernisation theories but also as a response to the perceived Eurocentrism of the Marxist theories of imperialism. Thus, in a critical dialogue with earlier theories of imperialism, dependency scholars turned focus of analysis from the metropolitan countries to the third world countries by looking deep into implications of imperialism within particular national contexts.

Thus, having inspired by such a complex base of intellectual traditions, dependency perspective, by its very nature, does not constitute a coherent and unified school of thought. Rather, given its mixed parentage and the diversity of its intellectual roots, it appealed to a broad church of writers and scholars from different disciplines and political perspectives. Therefore, lacking internal uniformity, its formulations tended to be employed flexibly, meaning quite different things to different people. As Palma (1978) points out what is commonly known as dependency theory is in fact a very broad house of literature that could be classified into three different, but not mutually exclusive currents. The first current, best represented by Sunkel (1969) and Furtado (1970), grew out of the critique of the ECLA's analyses as a reformulation which put greater emphasis on the obstacles to national development stemming from exogenous factors. Being reformist in nature, this current of dependency analysis did not only add new elements (both social and political) into the analysis, it also sought to move beyond the ECLA tradition which in turn popularised the dependency paradigm throughout Latin America.

The second current within the dependency school, on the other hand, sought to uncover the general 'laws' of dependency and construct a unified theory of underdevelopment. The principal tenets of this variant are that capitalist underdevelopment in peripheral countries is inevitable, directly caused by their dependence on core economies and that the only way out of underdevelopment is a socialist revolution. Here Palma (1978) notes the works of A.G. Frank (1967; 1969), followed by Dos Santos (1970), Hinkelammert (1972), Marini (1972) and others. Most notable among them, U.S. Marxist A.G. Frank quickly became the well-known and most important representative of the dependency school as the reception of dependency analyses in the English-speaking world gave inordinate space to him, thanks to their higher accessibility vis-à-vis the literature in Spanish and Portuguese (Cardoso, 1977). As a staunch Marxist, Frank proposed a formalistic and 'fully-worked' out theory of dependency which was easily consumed by academic circles in the northern hemisphere as series of variables, isolated and measured through the full panoply of quantitative methods.

Lastly, the third current of dependency analysis conceives dependency as a method to understand specific situations of underdevelopment. This variant of dependency analysis is mostly associated with a particular line of thinking called associated-dependent development, originally proposed by Cardoso and Faletto (1979) and later adopted and crystallized by many others such as Evans (1979), Gereffi (1983), Bennett and Sharpe (1985), Lim (1985), and Gold (1986). For the authors in this current, dependency and underdevelopment is simply neither an external phenomenon nor an internal one, but is conceived through the interaction between internal and external elements, all of which form a complex and interwoven whole to be explored (Cardoso and Faletto, 1979). While the earlier currents of dependency mostly worked with ahistorical, economistic and stagnationist models, in which world economic structure is seen as determinative, the proponents of associated-dependent development adopt a more sophisticated conception of dependency by examining concrete situations of peripheral capitalist development that emerge within countries of the Global South based on historical specificities of domestic social formations, such as configurations of class forces, peculiarities of state-society relations and social relations of production.

Although these three main currents of dependency school are often at odds with each other in many respects, they share a number common, but albeit still contestable propositions which form the core of dependency analysis as a distinctive critical approach. First of all, all these three currents of dependency analysis refute the liberal and diffusionist views of neoclassical and modernisation theories arguing that they cannot fully account for the causes of underdevelopment both in Latin America and in the rest of the wider global south. Overall, the dependency theorists challenge the notion that the main obstacle to development is rooted in the domestic socio-political and socio-cultural conditions of traditional or underdeveloped societies which lack the characteristics of the advanced capitalist countries. While liberal and diffusionist accounts put the blame on the domestic social, political and cultural factors as the prime cause of underdevelopment, the adherents of dependency school place emphasis both on internal and external factors as well as their interaction. In other words, for the adherents of dependency perspective, underdevelopment is not just the outcome of intra-state factors but is also by-product of world capitalist system in which colonialism and external dominance of Northern hemisphere played a key role in shaping the overall dynamics of international development.

In this connection, another commonality between the three currents of dependency school is the structural division of the world into

a developed or industrialised core and an underdeveloped periphery as
the central characteristic of interstate relations. As a stratified social system, the centre-periphery paradigm distinguishes various states according to the different economic functions they perform within the hierarchically structured global division of labour. The countries of the center are
industrially and technologically advanced and deemed to the main beneficiaries of the capitalist world system as they are capable of exploiting
and expropriating economic surplus from the peripheral countries thanks
to their monopolistic power in world economy. Peripheral countries on the
other hand occupy the bottom rungs of the global ladder of production and
trade and they mostly rely on core economies in number of respects such as
technology transfer, industrial upgrading, access to global markets and capital
investment. Thus, within such a framework, the core-periphery relations are
conceived as hierarchically ordered system of dominance in which the underdevelopment of peripheral countries, to a significant degree, results from their
participation into world economy on terms that are asymmetrical and exploitative in favour of the centre.

This brings us to another common aspect within the dependency thinking, namely the asymmetric and polarizing tendency of the capitalist world
economy. Almost all strands of dependency analyses share the view that the
world capitalist system has always been polarising and that it tends to present
restricted opportunities for peripheral countries to catch up with those in the
advanced core. As a general tendency, the terms of trade in the world markets
are disposed to deteriorate to the detriment of the countries in the periphery. In other words, this means that the global trade between the core and
the periphery is in fact an unequal exchange between high-wage, high-profit
activities of production and low-wage, low-profit activities of production. The
implication of integrating these two kinds of activities is the extraction of sur-
plus-values from the peripheral zones of production to the core ones. Thus,
this implies that the value transfers of profits flow not merely from the workers
to the owners but from the owners of the peripheral productive activities to
the owners of the core activities. Therefore, development and underdevelopment are opposite sides of the same coin, each being the results of the other.

In fact, all these commonalities outlined so far have appealed to a broad
church of scholars and policymakers not only in Latin America but also in
the rest of the world. As a truly Latin American perspective, the dependency
approach is originally very much a product of a particular place and historical period, but later it eventually came to have far-reaching scholarly influence and policy implications particularly in other parts of the global south.
Particularly through the several think-tanks and research institutes linked to

CEPAL and various academic institutions,[1] the analysis of dependency came to be crystallised as alternative explanatory framework on the realities of international political economy and the matter of underdevelopment. As dependency perspective grew influential during the 1960s and 1970s, number of countries in Latin America and the rest of the global periphery adopted strategies nominally conducive to autonomous, self-sustaining development and sought to redefine their respective position in the world economy by increasing the role of manufacturing-exports in their economies, diversifying the range of goods they produce and adopting more technology-intensive and higher value-added productions techniques.

However, while the ideas of dependency perspective became popular throughout Latin America and other parts of the periphery, they did not receive due attention in western academia, especially within economics and politics departments in the U.S. In part, language was one of the main obstacles to the diffusion of dependency perspective, as much of the published works was in Spanish or Portuguese and very few of them were translated into English (Kay, 2011). Therefore, the well-known and most important representative of the dependency school outside Latin America was ironically André Gunder Frank who even considered himself a world system theorist not a native dependency theorist (Cibils, 2015). More importantly, the main reason for the neglect of dependency theories in North American and European academic circles is much more related to a certain degree of parochialism on the part of the white Western-centric social sciences than the language barrier. In fact, many economics and politics departments in North America and Europe are dominated by an orthodox, mainstream community of scholars who mostly follow positivist hypothetical-deductive methodology of science and dissociate themselves from left-leaning, politicised scholarly endeavour. Predictably enough, having its roots in Marxism, the dependency perspective is largely seen as an unscientific, tautological and politicized scholarly endeavour.

Thus, it is not surprising that dependency analyses have been prejudicially marginalised and then ultimately casted aside. In this respect, the 1980s and the 1990s especially marked a distinctly new phase in terms of both the policymaking space and the knowledge production in social sciences. Despite its

---

1   To mention but a few, the major think-tanks and research institutes which contribute the development of dependency analysis were CESO (Centre for Social and Economic Studies), linked to the University of Chile; ILPES (Latin American Institute of Social and Economic Planning), linked to CEPAL; FLACSO (Latin American Social Science Faculty); and CEREN (Centre for the Study of the National Reality), linked to the Catholic University. For further information see Cibils (2015).

lasting popularity in the late 1970s, particularly in the Global South, dependency perspective gradually lost its allure in analytical and practical terms as a
new common sense began to crystallize by the mid-1980s on behalf of the benefits of free-market economy, pro-globalisation policies and less state intervention. Particularly the ascendance of neoliberalism and emerging orthodoxy
of globalisation discourse placed the market forces at the heart of resource
allocation and growth policy and narrowed down the policy space for many
countries which sought an autonomous development path (Kay, 2011). Thus,
the next two decades, overall, witnessed the retrenchment of developmental
state institutions, the dismantling of collective social welfare provisioning and
the repression of labour movements, most pointedly in the global south.

Alongside the closing of policy space was the intellectual hegemony and the
self-proclaimed triumph of capitalism in knowledge production and dissemination. Most particularly in economics but explicit in other fields of social
science, the plurality of public discourse has been considerably constrained,
revealing the self-proclaimed triumph of Western capitalism and the demise
of any alternative and emancipatory projects associated with right/reformist
and revolutionary/Marxist positions. Thus, dependency, as an allied theory
of Marxism, experienced much the same fate, and eventually lost its entire
credibility among students and practitioners of development studies. The end
result of this fading popularity was an outburst of misplaced and sweeping
critiques and outright dismissal of the dependency tradition which has gone
so far as to ignore its overall contributions, more sophisticated formulations, as
well as its contemporary relevance.

In fact, given its diverse nature, it is hardly surprising that the dependency
approach has been subjected to a barrage of criticism from within and outside
of the dependency school on methodological, theoretical, empirical and sty-
listic grounds. Perhaps, one of the most trenchant and devastating critique of
the dependency school came from those scholars who adhere to the positivist
hypothetical-deductive methodology. For critics such as O'Brien (1975), Lall
(1975) Packenham (1992) and Sanchez (2003), having its roots in Marxist analysis of economic, social and political factors (including economic structures,
class dynamics, political configurations and colonial legacies), dependency
approach has been increasingly seen as a utopian, unfalsifiable and politicized theory in empirical and testifiable grounds. Moreover, the adherents of
dependency approach have been also charged with being economistic, static,
reductionist and mechanistic in their analyses of capitalist development and
underdevelopment in the periphery. Particularly, the global spread of production and the rise of new manufacturing powerhouses, first in the newly industrialised countries of East Asia and then in the rest of the developing world

such as China, Brazil, India, Mexico, Turkey, Malaysia and Indonesia cast doubt on ideas of peripherality and dependency. Thus, not a few critics (see inter alia Warren, 1980; Amsden, 1979; Haggard, 1990) propound that economic and social transformation that countries such as South Korea, Taiwan, Malaysia, Singapore and China experienced in the last couple of decades has undermined the propositions of the *dependentistas* by revealing that development is possible even within the existing global capitalist order.

While some of these critiques are instructive and thought-provoking to a certain extent, much of them have been sweeping and insensitive to the diversity and richness of modes of explanation in the dependency school. As suggested by many scholars (Larrin, 1989; Kay, 2011; Gosh 2001), the critique of the dependency perspective has in fact gone so far that even employable aspects of the dependency perspective have been defamed as an outcast way of thinking. To be more precise, much of these criticisms cannot be applied to the whole dependency school, since some eminent dependency authors such as Cardoso and Faletto (1979), Dos Santos (1970), Evans (1979, 1982) and Palma (1978) must be excluded due to their recognition of the possibility of development or the historical progressiveness of capitalism in the global south. In fact, given its complex intellectual roots and variety of analyses, the dependency approach has in fact a highly abstruse diversity within itself, which leads critics to treat this broad church of thought as if it was a single theory whose fundamental premises were shared by its adherents. Thus, the analytical value and contemporary relevance of the dependency tradition have remained largely clouded by the outright dismissal and misplaced critiques, particularly in today's academic literature.

3   Achievements and Contributions of Dependency Approach as a Critical IR Theory

Over the last 30 years or so since the heydays of dependency theory in the 1960s and 1970s, a substantial geopolitical and geoeconomic change has been taken place in the world political map, especially with the rise of new powerhouses in the global south. In today's International Relations literature, there is a growing perception that the global spread of economic capabilities and the emergence of new powerhouses in the global south has already altered the political landscape of the world reviving the contentions that we live in a world of convergence that spreads opportunities, wealth and capabilities globally across borders, and therefore stands at odds with ideas of peripherality and dependency. Therefore, both on the terrain of intellectual currents and within policy circles, the notions of dependency and peripherality have lost their momentum. And today most International Relations students have either never come across dependency perspective in their curriculum or have just learned of it as a theory used in the past. However, despite its waning importance today, having a critical and emancipatory intent, dependency approach has offered valuable insights to International Relations scholarship. As widely discussed in the preceding section, the dependency school has not indeed emerged as exclusively IR theory, but it has profoundly contributed critical thinking in International Relations and opened alternative ways of reasoning in many respects.

First and foremost, dependency approach has been influential in the development of critical and emancipatory research agenda in IR as it compelled students of International Relations to question the material inequalities and asymmetrical power relations that are in part created by the organisation of capitalist world system, and it consequently sought for alternative ways to build a more equal and just relations between and within nations. Unlike the mainstream IR theory, dependency approach was not only interested in explaining the international politics as it is but problematized the very foundations of asymmetries and hierarchical power relations in existing international order both in economic and political terms. In this respect, the study of global asymmetries through the core-periphery paradigm was a notable theoretical achievement. Drawing inspiration from the Marxian pretension that capitalism is an ever-expanding global system in which national economies take part as subsystems, the dependency approach unrevealed the processes by which peripheral economies in the south were incorporated into world capitalist system by Northern capitalist powers on unequal and exploitative terms. In this sense, the critical intervention of dependency approach is crucial for unveiling that impotency and economic backwardness of Latin American, African and Asian countries were not natural but a by-product of historical encounters with metropolitan capitalist states of Europe and North America as early as 16th century. Thus, the historical encounters between metropolitan capitalist states of Europe and North America and those other regions ended up with a pattern of dependency and subordination in which the preponderance of core states in the realm of technology, capital, production and trade ensures structural asymmetries in power over peripheral social formations, delimits the political sovereignty of dependent states and shapes their domestic social structures according to imperatives of global capitalist system.

Besides its self-consciously critical look to international political order, dependency approach has also provided a functionally integrative and holistic social science framework to examine the nexus between dependency and underdevelopment in global economic system. For the adherents of dependency theory, subordination and dependency is not simply seen as an external condition, but also as a political phenomenon that covers the whole institutional framework embodied in the periphery's political, economic, social and cultural structures. Thus, the appropriate level of analysis is neither the nation-state nor the international system as the mainstream IR theory would have it, but rather the interplay between nation-states, social classes and world capitalist system. More precisely, dependency perspective has two distinctive units of analysis, namely the nation-state and social classes both of which are viewed with regards to their manifold relationships with the world capitalist system. In underscoring an explanatory intercourse between domestic social formations and global capitalism, dependency analysis questioned state-centred conception of international relations. Particularly, the penetration of global class forces in peripheral societies and the subsequent fragmentation of peripheral social formations along with global class dynamics in turn challenged the pretension that the state can be regarded as either a unitary actor or the core analytical unit within international relations. Thus, dependency approach objected the conception of state as a unitary sovereign and insulated entity separable from societal dynamics and class conflict on one hand, and from the conditioning impacts and imperatives of the external world on the other.

Moreover, dependency approach, as a Marxian-inspired critical theory, has also exercised significant influence upon the discipline of International Relations by offering an emancipatory alternative to the existing structures in international order. As alluded earlier in the preceding section, dependency school of thought has originally emerged as a post-colonial move and a nativist reaction to the perceived immutability of existing structures in the social world which in fact serve to sustain inequalities of power and wealth between and within nations. Placing itself above the prevailing power relations and dominant social order, dependency theorists were inevitably troubled by the claims that social structures cannot be altered because they are deeply embedded in human nature or in an "objective" circumstance (such as anarchy) which human agency is deemed impotent to transform. Pursuing an explicitly emancipatory purpose in theorising, dependency approach has rather sought prospects for new forms of social ordering and political community in which individuals and states break with unjustified exclusion and exploitation, and enjoy higher degree of prosperity, wealth and freedom.

In fact, emancipatory orientation of dependency approach towards existing structural constraints is largely affected by the Marxian premise that human beings can change the imposed constraints upon them and make more of their own history under conditions of their own choosing. After all, from a dependency point of view, individuals and societies of global south are united in their oppression by capitalist world economy and preponderance of metropolitan capitalist states that sets out exploitative social practices and institutions, so the global south as a whole should be freed (or emancipated) from such a status. Therefore, dependency perspective has had a transformative and emancipatory dimension in the sense that it sought to replace the modern world system by promoting more just global economic, political and social arrangements and advancing more equitable forms of relations between and within states. Consequently, although dependency approach has been erroneously accused of being deterministic, it opposes to system determinism and acknowledges the capacity of human agents to act collectively to emancipate themselves from repressive social practices and institutions in the existing world order.

Last but not least, dependency approach has also enlarged the parameters of the discipline by giving special emphasis to the significance of history and, in particular, the historical legacy of colonialism in constructing the roles and positions of different countries within the global economic and political system. Thinking about history and sociology within the discipline of International Relations had always been a long and well-recognised endeavour but the ascendance of behavioural revolution (most notably prevalent in the U.S.) in the second half of the twentieth century largely swept aside historical and sociological analyses in favour of empiricist and so-called "scientific" approaches. The scientific turn in IR during the mid-1950s to mid-1960s -the so-called "behavioural decade"- led to the narrowing of the discipline's boundaries. Particularly, with the publication of Kenneth Waltz's (1979) *Theory of International Politics* the mainstream IR theory regressed sharply into a highly exclusive scholarly realm that ruled out the analytical value and utility of historical and sociological analysis. Mostly relying on positivist methodology, the mainstream approaches to IR guested for discoverable uniformities, regularities, and patterns of state behaviour and treats the nature of interstate system as if it was an eternal political verity rather than a socially and historically constructed entity which is brought about and sustained by a complex interaction between states, sub-state and trans-states factors.

In sharp contrast to the mainstream IR theorising, dependency perspective drew attention to the conditioning role of historical, colonial and sociological factors in the development of interstate system. Having its roots in Marxist political economy and classical historical sociology, dependency approach has indeed opened the door to an analysis of how historical, colonial, class-relational and socio-institutional specificities matter for explaining conditions and interstate dynamics in the present world. Thus, as one of its chief insights, dependency approach has been essentially concerned to reveal historical and sociological origins of the present interstate system and uncover the dynamic processes that underpin its development as well as its possible transformation in the future. At the same time, this in turn led to a form of theorising that was necessarily sensitive to specificities of different peripheral social formations, to their national histories and to their particular class configurations and socio-political structures. Particularly, the analysis of why a country occupies a certain position within the current interstate system and how its participation impacted possibilities for development has provided historically sensitive and rich accounts of interstate relations, especially for the global south.

As a result, despite not being an exclusively IR theory, dependency school of thought has had a significant impact on International Relations in general and international political economy in particular as a serious alternative to state-centric and ahistorical orthodox approaches in the field. Overall, given its critical and emancipatory aspect, dependency analyses have in part broadened the discipline's boundaries by opening up a discursive space within which questions about the asymmetries of power and wealth between the North and the South gave a further impetus to the development of IPE. Having its roots in the late 1960s and the early 1970s, IPE had been ad initium dominated largely by a realistic perception of IR in the sense that debates on international regimes and interdependence occupied the main research agenda and the state remained the principal unit of analysis. In fact, it is fair to argue that the intellectual dominance of realist and liberal approaches in the study of IPE has been partially undermined by the intervention of dependency perspective which shifted the research agenda of IPE towards a more radical and critical directions. Especially, despite not being the perfect representative of dependency tradition, easily consumed works of Andre Gunder Frank (1967, 1969, 1978), Samir Amin (1974, 1976), and Immanuel Wallerstein paved way for the development of a more critical enquiry especially in the field of international political economy.

While the ideas derived from dependency perspective offered a critical point of departure for the study of international relations, they paradoxically disappeared from the academic curricula and mainstream debates particularly with the rise of current wave of globalization since the late 1970s. As argued so far, the critique of the dependency school has in fact gone so far that even employable aspects of the dependency perspective have been defamed as an outcast way of thinking today. To put it more clearly, criticizing the dependency approach, as Haggard (1990, p.19) states, has become an academic industry of the worst sort. While its vulgar formulations have been vehemently denounced, its critical contribution and enduring analytical relevance today have been unfairly ignored. Thus, as many state, criticism of dependency theory has threatened to throw away the baby with the bath water (see Larrain, 1989; Ghosh, 2001; Abbott, 2003 Holloway, 2003). However, while theory of dependency as an explicit approach to development is currently regarded as a thing of the past, its legacy and critical analytical value is very much with us, making a comeback in both theoretical and applied works. Thus, the following section concludes with a particular discussion on the enduring relevance and prospective research directions of dependency theory. In this respect, the next section particularly dwells on the recent writings and the contemporary issues in the dependency debate not only to provide a window into some possible ways of thinking about dependency theory's relevance today, but also to inspire scholars as well as practitioners to revisit and use the viable tenets of dependency approach for future research directions.

4   Enduring Relevance and Contemporary Manifestation of
       Dependency Theory Today

As the forgoing discussion has shown, from the early 1980s onwards dependency approach has become less fashionable and eventually lost its overall allure for scholars and policy makers as an alternative development paradigm. Actually, the reasons behind this swift demise are miscellaneous but identifiable in broad strokes. As Stallings (1992, p.48) simply puts it, "the combination of intellectual critiques and reinforcing international trends had a devastating effect on dependency analysis". The ascendance of market liberalisation, coupled with the collapse of the Berlin Wall and so the overall Eastern Bloc, has created a totally different political, economic and ideological context which many were to characterise as the end of history and the decisive victory of neoliberal globalisation as the only feasible pathway to development. Indeed, it was this context of triumphalism of Western Capitalism in which left-wing progressive and emancipatory approaches such as dependency have been insensibly defamed and outcasted from mainstream debates on "globalization" and the academic curricula. However, being out of fashion does not necessarily mean that dependency approach is no longer irrelevant or does not offer inspirations for both current and prospective research.

Rather, after four decades of market-oriented neoliberal reconstruction in the global south, there has been a revival of interest in critical and emancipatory thinking of Latin American theories of economic structuralism and dependency. In other words, the failed promise of neoliberal globalisation and the polarising tendency of global capitalist system have resulted in a rebirth of the critical analyses that owe a direct debt to some of the basic insights of dependency perspective. Indeed, there is no doubt that the world economic map has witnessed tremendous change over the last 30 years so thanks to the meteoric growth of global production and trade and the dissemination of industrial and technological capabilities to the global south. Today, the complex nature of global production and trade has transformed peripheral social formations in the global south (whether scaled as nation-state, region or city), so that they have now appeared to become fully integrated into the global economic system as new growth centres in their own right.

Nevertheless, despite the global spread of production and the advances made by emerging economies of East Asia and the rest of developing world, the asymmetric and polarised nature of the capitalist world economy is still at work, continuing to generate economic, technological and social disparities between and within countries. Although the world has not been static and there has been an ongoing dynamic of change at play, old lines of inequality remain broadly in place as departure points for dependency analyses. To mention but a few, while developing world has converged with and even in some cases overtook the advanced countries of North in terms of industrialisation levels, the countries of the global south continue to overwhelmingly occupy the bottom rungs of the global accumulation ladder. Indeed, the global spread of production has been on the other hand accompanied by new asymmetrical power relations that mostly take place throughout hierarchically structured chains/ networks of global value relations. Having relatively restricted control over high profit-making nodes of global production, the overwhelming majority of countries in the global south relied on the advanced countries of the North in terms of accessibility to cutting-edge technologies, finance, patents, markets and global entrepreneur skills.

Seen in this way, many scholars (Kay and Gwynne, 2000; Gosh, 2001; Abbott, 2003; Fischer, 2015; Kiely, 2015) have returned to the notions of peripherality and dependency to argue that persisting asymmetrical power relations in the contemporary global capitalist system reflect forms of 'new' or 'neo' dependency. In this respect, the global economic and financial crisis in 2008–2009 particularly seems to have increased the interest in the critical analysis of worldwide capitalism and core-periphery relations that have always been the hallmark of dependency approach. To mention but a few, three main stands of contemporary research direction still reflect the critical spirit of dependency studies. First, with certain regularity, some scholars echo the changing nature of coreness and peripherality of the contemporary global capitalist system, by attaching special importance to recent bifurcation or differentiation within the global periphery. To name a few, St Andrews professor of International Relations Ian Taylor (2014) provides a window into some possible ways of thinking about dependency by unveiling the relationship between BRICS countries and Africa. Indeed, the recent growth in African economies has coincided with BRICS' cooperation and efforts throughout the continent. Nevertheless, as investors and trading partners, the BRICS have not really helped African states in structural and technological terms but rather "reify the continent's historical dependence on resource extraction, which has resulted in the jobless growth of the past decade and deindustrialization", and which has in turn diversified African dependency (Taylor, 2014, p. 139–141). In a similar vein, Patrick Bond (2015) contextualised BRICS' relations with Africa within dependency theory by reviving Ruy Marini's (1965, 1972) notion of sub-imperialism and dialectic of peripheral development. Bond points to BRICS being sub-imperialist, as they uphold global neoliberal policies and practices that favour both imperial powers and themselves. To put it another way, analogous to the "semi-periphery" of Wallerstein, the BRICS, as sup-imperialist powers, expand the capitalist mode of accumulation by brokering the extraction and exploitation of resources and people, by means of labour rights violations.

The second strand of research direction that reflects the central tenets of dependency and also world-system theory appears to be global commodity-chain or global value-chain (GCC/GVC) frameworks which examine how surplus value is added and captured from suppliers in the global south though hierarchically structured networks of global production and trade. Contemporary research in a 2014 special issue of the Journal of World-Systems Research has provided an evaluation of global commodity chains in particular of the way in which dependency scholars examined the exploitative potential of outsourcing between the 'core' economies and the 'periphery' in the global capitalist system. Citing evidence from global cotton industry, Amy Quark (2014) shows that the U.S. government and U.S. cotton producers, together with European and U.S. transnational merchants, maintained their dominance over the governance of the transnational commodity chain of cotton and managed to keep their main rivals – particularly China – from developing scientific, technological and institutional capacities to launch a counter-hegemonic alternative in the global cotton industry. Besides Clelland's research on the production of Apple tablets reveals how TNCs in the North retain the opportunity to extract the surplus value "offered" by the global south given their control over the commodity chains through design, marketing and sales as well as their 'monopsonistic externalisation of costs' (Clelland, 2014, p. 94). As another witness to this orientation, John Smith (2016) provides a contribution to our understanding of modern imperialism and dependency by showing how the surplus-value created by super-exploited workers in the so-called "developing" or "emerging" southern economies is captured TNCs and transferred through global value chains to the core counties of the North.

Last but not least, the third strand of research orientation that owes a direct debt to the principles of dependency perspective is institutional analysis of patterns of divergent development in the contemporary era of globalization. As discussed earlier, dependency perspective has offered an integrated, comprehensive social science framework that combines a focus on economic structures and imperatives of world economy with a focus on class configurations, state-society relations and modes of national integration into world economy. Thus, putting special emphasis on class configurations, political strategies and institutional arrangements, dependency perspective has not only harkened back to classical theory but also inspired a wide range of contemporary works which are commonly called the new institutionalism. Recent scholarship (Abbott, 2003; Bohle and Greskovits, 2012; Bruszt and McDermott, 2014; Bruszt and Langbein, 2017) inspired by the tradition of the historical structural dependency analyses has combined a focus on divergent patterns of national insertion in the global economy with a focus on domestic class configurations, the capacity of state institutions and state-society relations to explain the contrasting paths of development and global integration of countries in the "semi-core," "semi-periphery," and "periphery". Likewise, inspired by Latin American dependency thinking, and its offspring, World System Theory, recent works of Fernandez, Ebenau and Bazza (2017) has also provided a reconsideration of institutionalist "comparative capitalisms" literatures by analysing the structural, uneven, and hierarchical reproduction of capitalism and highlighting the significance of the division between centers and peripheries as a fundamental axis of differentiation in today's global capitalist system.

5   In Lieu of Conclusion

Taking dependency perspective as a critical IR theory, this chapter explores how and in what ways the dependency tradition offers useful insights and conceptual tools to IR scholarship. As discussed earlier throughout the chapter, the dependency school of thought has not emerged as an exclusively IR theory, and so has not engaged in a direct dialogue with conventional IR theories such as Realism and Liberalism. Rather, originally developed as an economic theory of underdevelopment, the dependency perspective, by its very nature, has emerged as a post-colonial move and a nativist critical reaction to the liberal and diffusionist propositions of modernisation theory that capitalism and free

trade internationalism would automatically bring growth, prosperity, convergence and peace among nations. Nevertheless, given its mixed parentage and
the diversity of its intellectual roots, dependency perspective in fact appealed
to a broad church of writers and scholars from different disciplines ranging
from economics to sociology, from development studies to International
Relations.

Having its roots in Marxist debate of the development of capitalism in
backward nations and the earlier theories of imperialism, the dependency
perspective has indeed offered valuable insights to IR scholarship and contributed critical thinking in international relations by opening alternative ways of
reasoning in many respects. In sharp contrast to the mainstream IR theorising,
dependency perspective does not only explain the world as it is, but places
itself above the prevailing power relations and dominant international order
and questions the very foundations of international relations both in economic
and political terms. Being self-consciously critical, dependency perspective
profoundly contributed critical thinking in International relations and particularly opened new ways of reasoning about the question on global inequalities, the North-South divide and the hierarchical and asymmetric structure of
international system. Besides its self-consciously critical look to international
political order, dependency approach has also provided a functionally integrative and holistic social science framework. The appropriate level of analysis
is neither the nation-state nor the international system as the mainstream IR
theory would have it, but rather the interplay between nation-states, social
classes and world capitalist system. More precisely, dependency perspective
has two distinctive units of analysis, namely the nation-state and social classes
both of which are viewed with regards to their manifold relationships with
the world capitalist system. Thus, underscoring an explanatory intercourse
between domestic social formations and global capitalism, dependency analysis questioned state-centred conception of international relations. Moreover,
despite erroneously accused of being deterministic, dependency perspective
questions the so-called immutability of existing structures in the social world
and acknowledged the capacity of human agents to act collectively to emancipate themselves from repressive social practices and institutions in the existing world order. Pursuing an explicitly emancipatory purpose in theorising,
dependency approach is inevitably troubled by the claims that social structures cannot be altered because they are deeply embedded in human nature
or in an "objective" circumstance (such as anarchy) which human agency is
deemed impotent to transform. Rather, dependency approach seeks prospects
for new forms of social ordering and political community in which individuals

and states break with unjustified exclusion and exploitation, and enjoy higher degree of prosperity, wealth and freedom.

Nevertheless, while the ideas derived from dependency perspective offered a critical point of departure for the study of international relations, they paradoxically disappeared from the academic curricula and contemporary debates of IR, particularly with the rise of current wave of globalization. As widely discussed throughout the chapter, despite its waning popularity, critiques of the dependency school have gone too far, ignoring its overall critical contributions and contemporary relevance today. Thus, mostly dwelling on the recent writings and the contemporary issues in the dependency debate, the chapter has revealed how and in what ways dependency approach offers important analytical and critical insights to explain the current structure and dynamics of today's global world. Overall, the chapter does not only provide a window into some possible ways of thinking about dependency theory's relevance today, but also hopes to inspire scholars as well as practitioners to revisit and use the viable and critical tenets of dependency approach for future research directions.

References

Abbott, J. P., 2003. *Developmentalism and Dependency in Southeast Asia: The Case ofthe Automotive Industry.* London: RoutledgeCurzon.

Amin, S., 1974. *Accumulation on a World Scale.* New York: Monthly Review Press.

Amin, S., 1976. *Unequal Development: An Essay on the Social Formations ofPeripheral Capitalism.* New York: Monthly Review Press.

Amsden, A. H., 1979. Taiwan's Economic History: A Case of Etatisme and a Challengeto Dependency Theory. *Modern China*, 5(3), pp. 341–379.

Baran, P., 1968. *The Political Economy of Growth.* New York: Monthly Review Press.

Bennet D. C. and Sharpe K., 1985. *Transnational Corporations versus the State: The Political Economy of Mexican Automobile Industry.* Princeton: Princeton University Press.

Bernecker, W. L. and Fischer T., 1998. Rise and Decline of Latin American Dependency Theories. *Itinerario*, 22(4), pp. 25–43.

Bohle, D. and Greskovits, B., 2012. *Capitalist Diversity on Europe's Periphery.* Ithaca: Cornell University Press.

Bond, P., 2015. BRICS and Sup-imperial Location. In P. Bond and A. Garcia eds. *BRICs: An Anti-Capitalist Critique.* London: Pluto Press.

Bruszt, L. and Mcdermott G., 2014. *Leveling the Playing Field: Transnational Regulatory Integration and Development.* New York: Oxford University Press.

Bruszt, L. and Langbein, J., 2017. Varieties of Dis-Embedded Liberalism. EU Integration Strategies in the Eastern Peripheries of Europe. *Journal of European Public Policy,* 27(2), pp. 297–315.

Bukharin, N., 1971. *Imperialism and World Economy.* London: Merlin.

Cardoso F. H., 1977. The Consumption of Dependency Theory in the United. *Latin American Research Review,* 12 (3), pp. 7–24.

Cardoso, F. H. and Faletto, E., 1979. *Dependency and Development in Latin America.* Berkeley: California University Press.

Cibils, A., 2015. The Resurgence of Dependency Analysis: Nostalgia or Renewed Relevance? In: C., Sunna and D., Gualerzi eds. *Development Economics in the Twenty-First Century.* New York: Routledge.

Clelland, D., 2014. The Core of the Apple: Degrees of Monopoly and Dark Value in GlobalCommodity Chains. *Journal of World-Systems Research,* 20(1), pp. 82–111.

Dos Santos, T., 1970. The Structure of Dependence. *American Economic Review,* 60(2), pp. 231–236.

Evans, P., 1979. *Dependent Development: The Alliance of Multinational Corporation, State and Local Capital in Brazil.* Princeton: Princeton University Press.

Evans, P., 1982. Reinventing the Bourgeoisie: State Entrepreneurship and Class Formation in Dependent Capitalist Development. *American Journal of Sociology,* 88, pp. 210–247.

Fernández, V. R., Ebenau, M., and Bazza, A., 2017. Rethinking Varieties of Capitalism from the Latin American Periphery. *Review of Radical Political Economics,* 50(2), pp. 392–408.

Fischer, A. M., 2015. The End of Peripheries? On the Enduring Relevance of Structuralism for Understanding Contemporary Global Development. *Development and Change,* 46(5), pp. 700–732.

Frank, A. G., 1967. Capitalism *and Underdevelopment in Latin America: Historical Studies of Chile and Brazil.* New York: Monthly Review Press.

Frank, A. G., 1969. *Latin America: Underdevelopment or Revolution.* New York: Monthly Review Press.

Frank, A. G., 1978. *World Accumulation, 1492–1789.* New York: Monthly Review Press.

Furtado, C., 1970. *Economic Development of Latin America.* Cambridge: Cambridge University Press.

Gereffi, G., 1983. *The Pharmaceutical Industry and Dependency in the Third World.* New Jersey: Princeton University Press.

Ghosh, B. N., 2001. *Dependency Theory Revisited.* London: Aldershot.

Gold, T. B., 1986. *State and Society in the Taiwan Miracle.* New York: M.E. Sharpe.

Haggard, S., 1990. *Pathwys from the Periphery: the Politics of Growth in the Newly Industrializing Countries.* New York: Cornell University Press.

Hilferding, R., 1981. *The Finance Capital: a Study of the Latest Phase of Capitalist Development*. London: Routledge.

Hinkelammert, F. J. 1972. *Dialéctica del Desarrollo Desigual*. Santiago de Chile: Ediciones Universitarias de Valparaíso : Centro de Estudios de la Realidad Nacional (CEREN).

Holloway, T., 2003. The Persistence of Dependency as a Useful Framework for Understanding Latin America paper presented to the Center for Latin American Studies, University of California, Berkeley. Available at: http://clasarchive.berke ley.edu/Events/spring2003/02-10-03-holloway/index.html [Accessed 15 June 2020].

Kay, C., 2011. *Latin American Theories of Development and Underdevelopment*. London and New York: Routledge.

Kay C. and Gwynne, R. N., 2000. Relevance of Structuralist and Dependency Theoriesin the Neoliberal Period: A Latin American Perspective. In: R. L. Harris and M. J. Seideds. *Critical Perspectives on Globalization and Neoliberalism in the DevelopingCountries*. Leiden: Koninklijke Brill.

Kiely, R., 2015. *The BRICs, US 'Decline' and Global Transformations*. London: Palgrave Macmillan.

Lall, S., 1975. Is Dependency a Useful Concept in Analysing Underdevelopment?.*World Development*, 3(11–12), pp. 799–810.

Larrain, J., 1989. *Theories of Development: Capitalism, Colonialism and Dependency*. Cambridge: Polity Press.

Lenin, V. I., 1999. *Imperialism: The Highest Stage of Capitalism*. Sydney: Resistance Books.

Lim, H. C., 1985. *Dependent Development in Korea 1963–1979*. Seul: Seul National University Press.

Luxemburg, R., 1972. *The Accumulation of Capital: an Anti-Critique*. London: Routledge.

Marrini, R.M., 1972. Dialéctica de la dependencia: La economía exportadora. *Sociedad y Desarrollo*, (1), pp.35–51.

Munck, R., 1999. Dependency and Imperialism in the New Times: A Latin American Perspective. *European Journal of Development Research*, 11(1), pp-56–74.

O'Brien, P., 1975. A Critique of Latin American Theories of Dependency. In: I., Oxaal, T., Barnett, and D., Booth eds. *Beyond the Sociology of Development: Economy andSociety in Latin America and Africa*. London: Routledge.

Palma, G., 1978. Dependency: A Formal Theory of Underdevelopment or aMethodology for the Analysis of Concrete Situations of Underdevelopment. *WorldDevelopment*, 6: 881–924.

Palma, G., 1989. *Development, Dependency and Marxism: a Critical Reappraisal andCase Study of Chile*. Unpublished PhD Thesis, University of Sussex.

Packenham, R., 1992. *The Dependency Movement: Scholarship and Politics inDevelopment Studies*. Cambridge: Harvard University Press.

Prebisch, R., 1950. *The Economic Development of Latin America and its Principal Problems*. Lake Success: United Nations.

Quark, A., 2014. Private Governance, Hegemonic Struggles, and Institutional Outcomes inthe Transnational Cotton Commodity Chain. *Journal of World-Systems Research*, 20(1), pp. 38–63.

Ruy, M., 1965. Brazilian 'Interdependence' and Imperialist Integration. *Monthly Review*, 17(7), pp. 10–29.

Ruy M., 1972. Brazilian sub-imperialism, *Monthly Review*, 23(9), pp. 14–24.

Sanchez, O., 2003. The Rise and Fall of the Dependency Movement: Does It Inform Underdevelopment Today? *EIAL*, 14(2), pp. 31–50.

Seers, D., 1981. *Dependency Theory: A Critical Reassessment*. London: Frances Pinter.

Smith, J., 2016. *Imperialism in the Twenty-First Century: Globalization, Super-Exploitation, and Capitalism's Final Crisis*. New York: Monthly Review Press.

Stallings, B., 1992. International Influence in Economic Policy. In: S. Haggard and R.R. Kaufmann eds. *The Politics of Economic Adjustment: International Constraints, Distribute Conflicts and the State*. Princeton: Princeton University Press.

Sunkel, O., 1969. National Development Policy and External Dependence in Latin America. *Journal of Development Studies*, 6 (1), pp. 23–48.

Taylor, I., 2014. *Africa Rising?: BRICS – Diversifying Dependency*. Rochester, NY: James Currey.

Waltz, K., 1979. *Theory of International Politics*. Reading: Addison- Wesley Publishing Company.

Warren, B., 1980. *Imperialism, Pioneer of Capitalism*. London: Verso.

CHAPTER 5

Uneven and Combined Development

A Dialectical and International Theory of Social Change

Çağdaş Özeniş

1 Introduction

Uneven and Combined Development (UCD) is a historical materialist theory which argues that the historical development of capitalism should be studied as an inter-societal, multi-linear and dialectical process. Laying the foundation for his "permanent revolution" strategy, the theory was initially formulated by Leon Trotsky at the beginning of 20th century, in the course of his attempts to make sense of Tsarist Russia's rather unorthodox transition to capitalism with its own idiosyncratic class dynamics. The idea that historical progression occurs in ruptures and leaps was already evident in Trotsky's earlier works, yet the most manifested formulation of the theory came in the first chapter of his 1930 book, *History of the Russian Revolution*, where he introduced 'the law of combined development' as an intrinsic and complementary outcome of uneven development: "the most general law of historic process" (2008, p.5).

Nevertheless, Trotsky's theory received limited academic interest up until the first time it was introduced to the discipline of International Relations (IR) by Justin Rosenberg in 1995. Following this revival there has been an upsurge of academic interest in UCD, turning it today into a school of thought which redefines the field of the discipline entirely. For Rosenberg, the theory of UCD has far greater implications for dialectical materialism then Trotsky had ever anticipated. Furthermore, he believes, apart from a well-established theory of capitalist development, UCD also provides an alternative theoretical framework which might replace the reified, ahistorical and supra-sociological understanding of the 'international' that mainstream theories put forth. Through this new sociological reconceptualization of the international, he argues, UCD does not only overcome the problems of domestic analogy and methodological nationalism, but also ruptures the ontological singularity of pre-existing conceptions of development.

This chapter aims to examine the main theoretical premises of UCD and what these imply for IR theory. First, it starts by tracing the evolution of the theory from early 1900s as it was initially sketched in Trotsky's writings, to early

2000s right before it became a full-blown research programme centred at the University of Sussex. Then, in the second part the contributions of UCD to IR theory are analysed through the works of the scholar who introduced it to this field; Justin Rosenberg. This section examines the critiques that UCD raised against mainstream IR theory together with the features that distinguish it from other critical approaches. The third part addresses the ontological, epistemological and methodological premises of the theory and discusses how UCD draws the boundaries of the 'international' and how it utilizes dialectical materialism to explain its functioning. The final section reviews the main lines of discussions regarding UCD and after covering the earlier debate regarding the trans-historicity of the theory and the later discussion initiated by political Marxists about the notions analytical value, it concludes by mentioning the new empirical trends and theoretical openings taking place in this fairly new research programme.

2   Trotsky, Permanent Revolution and the Emergence of the "Law of UCD"

It would be impossible to fully comprehend the theoretical and methodological implications of UCD for international and social theory, if we examine it detached from the political and historical context upon which it appeared. Anyone studying UCD should keep in mind, first and foremost, that UCD had not emerged out of solely academic concerns, but also provided the intellectual basis of Trotsky's political strategy of permanent revolution, an approach he first devised at the beginning of the 20th century. Trotsky was a revolutionary above anything else, and as a revolutionary he was not only expected to make abstract analysis of the changing material conditions or structural forces directing the course of history, but also obliged to put forth solid strategies through which he thinks, people might effectively insert their agency into this structural operation. "Marxism has proved to be right, and this is now past the need for discussion or proof", Trotsky wrote, as early as 1906. "The Marxists", he added, "are now confronted by a task of quite another kind: to discover the "possibilities" of the developing revolution by means of an analysis of its internal mechanism" (2010, p.41).

In this regard, although the theory took its final form in the late 1920s, the roots of the idea can be traced back to early 1900s, particularly to the aftermath of the 1905 Revolution. After the events of 1905–06, which later came to be known as the First Russian Revolution, Trotsky was convinced that the Russian revolution bears a unique character, which was wholly peculiar to herself, "a character which was the outcome of the special features of the entire [Russian] social and historical development" (2016, p.3).

In his *Results and Prospects* (1906), he was especially critical against the views of the Russian liberals, who try to identify the 1905 revolution with French and German bourgeois revolutions, by drawing analogies between them (2010, p.41). "History does not repeat itself", Trotsky asserted.

> However much one may compare the Russian revolution with the Great French Revolution, the former can never be transformed into a repetition of the latter. The 19th century has not passed in vain (Ibid, p. 59).

In the following years, explaining this distinctive character of 1905 revolution with its own peculiar class dynamics became the focal point of Trotsky's studies, since he believed it opened entirely new perspectives before us, regarding the historical development of capitalism in general.

In the process leading up to UCD's ultimate formulation in 1930, almost every book Trotsky wrote started with a chapter devoted on this peculiarity of Russian historical development. In these chapters, by taking Russia's historical backwardness as a given reality, Trotsky defined the comparative primitiveness and slowness of Russian historical development as its "principal distinguishing characteristics" (2016, p.3, 2010, p.42). This slow tempo of Russia's development according to Trotsky, most clearly manifested itself in its "economic backwardness, primitiveness of social forms, and low level of culture resulting from it" (2008, p.3). "It is difficult to say what shape Russian social development would have taken", Trotsky cynically states following these assessments, "if it had remained isolated and under the influence of internal tendencies alone" (2010, p.43). "Suffice it to say", he adds, "this was not the case" (2016, p.3).

On the contrary, Trotsky suggests, Russian social existence "has all the time been under the influence, even under the pressure, of its external social-historical milieu", which was dominated by the more developed social and state relations of Western Europe (2016, p.3, 2010, p.43). Given the relatively weak development of international trade, this pressure, which Trotsky later termed "the whip of external necessities", found expression, "first and foremost, [...] in the form of military technology" and "as time went on [it] became more and more powerful" (2016, p. 3–4).

In other words, the influence of these more developed countries took shape "in fierce struggle for the existence of the state before expressing itself in direct economic competition" (2010, p.47). When the Russian state, which "grew up on a primitive economic basis", entered into relations and came into conflict with these economically more developed state organizations, it only faced two possibilities. Either it was going to crumble in its struggle with these more developed state organizations or it had to outpace them in the development of its own economic relations (2016, p.4).

Fortunately for the Russian state, it had at its disposal, all the methods of government and administration that was previously developed by Western states in the course of centuries. Moreover, while economically enslaving Tsarist Russia,

> [...] European capital projected its main branches of production and methods of communication across a whole series of intermediate technical and economic stages through which it had had to pass in its countries of origin. But the fewer obstacles it met with in the path of its economic domination, the more insignificant proved to be its political role (2010, p.57).

This allowed Russian absolutism to copy these methods and equip itself with European technology and capital, "much earlier than economic conditions here permitted the rise of a capitalist bourgeoisie" (Ibid, p. 57). Because as Trotsky emphasizes, "[i]t was not the village craftsman, nor even the rich merchant, but the state itself which finally came face to face with the necessity of creating a large-scale industry" (2016, p.11).

As Trotsky put forth; "[i]n order to be able to survive in the midst of better-armed hostile countries, Russia was compelled to set up factories, organize navigation schools and publish textbooks on fortification" (2010, p.47). However, the Western economics could only influence Russian economics through the intermediary of the state. By the time the developing bourgeois society in Russia, "began to feel a need for the political institutions of the West", Trotsky pointed out, the autocracy which was armed with all the material might of the European technology and European capital, had already transformed itself into the largest capitalist entrepreneur, the largest banker and the monopoly owner of railways (2016, p.8, 2010, p.48). It was in command of a tremendous standing army and supported by a centralized bureaucratic and fiscal machine, and although these proved to be quite inefficient and in no way suited for regulating the new relations, they were "perfectly capable of applying systematic repression with considerable energy" (2016, p.8, 2010, p.49).

Besides, the Russian absolutism had conquered the vast dimensions of its geography through its telegraph and railway networks, which enabled it to transfer military forces and communicate through enormous distances at short notice. Neither of these technologies were available in the pre-revolutionary governments of Western Europe (2016, p.8, 2010, p.49). This financial and military strength of the Russian absolutism overwhelmed and blinded both the European bourgeoisie and the Russian liberals, since for them, "[t]he military and financial might of absolutism seemed to exclude any chance whatever for the Russian revolution" (2010, p.50). However, Trotsky states, what actually took place was the exact opposite. As Russian absolutism get more centralized and more independent from the ruling classes, "the more rapidly it is transformed into a self-contained organization placed above society" (2016, p.5).

Thus, despite what liberals believe, this administrative, military and financial might of Russian absolutism, "did not exclude the possibility of revolution [...] but, on the contrary, made revolution the only possible way of development" (2016, p.9). This Trotsky wrote in 1906, made "it possible for the workers to come to power in an economically backward country sooner than in an advanced country" (2010, p.71). Thinking that proletariats' rise to power is in some way mechanically dependent on the technical advancement of the material capabilities of a country, he asserted, "is a prejudice of economic materialism simplified to absurdity", and "[t]his point of view has nothing in common with Marxism" (ibid, p.71).

History proved Trotsky right, not only regarding the forecasts he made about how the proletariat will come to power in Russia, but also regarding his predictions on how the Russian revolution will trigger revolutions in other states. The political climate, however, has changed following Lenin's death, especially after Stalin became the General Secretary of CPSU. During late 1920s, when Trotsky was formulating the final version of the UCD, the political environment in Soviet Russia, left no room for uncertainty in his analysis. 'Socialism in one country',[1] a theory that Stalin and Bukharin formulated in collaboration, had recently become Soviet's official state policy, and this program was clearly signalling that this 'indefensible theory', in Trotsky's words, was about to shift

---

1 Socialism in one country, is a theory that Joseph Stalin and Nikolai Bukharin put forth in 1924. Following the defeat of proletarian revolutions in other European countries (especially in Germany) between 1917 and 1923, the theory argued that Soviet Union, "which found itself surrounded externally by a hostile capitalist world, and internally with a vast peasantry composing the overwhelming majority of population", (for more information check, https://www .marxists.org/archive/weisbord/conquest44.htm) was left without an option, but to build up the industrial base and might of the Soviet Union before exporting the revolution abroad. Accordingly, the theory claimed, if militarily defended, it is possible to build socialism in Soviet Union with the forces of that country alone (Joseph Stalin, Pravda, Nov. 12, 1926). To this end, Stalin rescinded the New Economic Policy (NEP) that was established by Lenin, began collectivization of Soviet agriculture, and embarked on a national program of rapid, forced industrialization (see, https://www.britannica.com/topic/socialism-in-one-country).

the immediate strategy of the Communist International as well, from world revolution to the military defence of the Soviet state (Ibid, p.22).

Under such dire circumstances, Trotsky felt compelled to voice his critique with absolute determination and scientific precision. The general premises of UCD were already fully apparent in his *Third International After Lenin* (1928/ 1996). Trotsky's real concern here is to prove that Stalin's and Bukharin's theory is established on a crude and narrow understanding of uneven development, "based on the one-sided and false non-Marxian and non-Leninist interpretation of the law", as it overlooks the combined character of capitalist development altogether (1996, p.18).

Capitalism, Trotsky stated, "finds various sections of mankind at different stages of development, each with its profound internal contradictions." For him, this extreme diversity in the levels of development attained by different societies during various epochs, serves as the starting point of capitalism. However, he pointed out, "capitalism gains mastery only gradually over the inherited unevenness, breaking and altering it, employing therein its own means and methods." This is because contrary to previous economic systems, Trotsky put forth, capitalism intrinsically and continually aims at economic expansion; "at the penetration of new territories, the surmounting of economic differences, the conversion of self-sufficient provincial and national economies into a system of financial interrelationships" (Ibid, p.19).

In doing so, Trotsky asserts, it brings the rapprochement of these societies through levelling out economically and culturally "the most progressive and the most backward countries." However, he points out, while doing that, capitalism "operates by the methods of its own." That is to say, in Trotsky's words,

> [...] by anarchistic methods which constantly undermine its own work, set one country against another, and one branch of industry against another, developing some parts of world economy while hampering and throwing back the development of others (Ibid, p.19–20).

According to Trotsky, these two fundamental tendencies are intrinsic to capitalist development, and only their correlation can explain to us "the living texture of the historical process." Without understanding this he argued, neither "the relative levelling out, first, of Europe with Great Britain, and then, of America with Europe", nor "the industrialization of the colonies" which led to "the diminishing gap between India and Great Britain" can be comprehended holistically (1996, p.20).

Furthermore, when one realizes the complementary nature of these two contradictory tendencies, Trotsky hoped, it will not be difficult to understand that both unevenness, or the "sporadic historical development" and the "organic interdependence" of countries "developing toward an international division of labour, excludes the possibility of building socialism in one country ... [and] all the more so now, in the modern epoch", since imperialism "has developed, deepened, and sharpened both of these antagonistic tendencies" (Ibid, p.22). Thus, he argued without a world revolution on an international scale, even the socialism in Russia is doomed to perish, given its economic backwardness (Ibid, p. 39).

In the opening chapter of his famous History of the Russian Revolution, which was published two years later, Trotsky took this certainty a step further and this time introduced both of these tendencies as historical laws (2008, p.5). Nonetheless, Trotsky's theory received little attention, especially in Western academia, until it was introduced to the field of International Relations by Justin Rosenberg at the turn of the next century. The most remarkable exception in this sense, is of course Isaac Deutscher's well known "Prophet" trilogy, which traces the intellectual development of Trotsky in an extensive three-volume biographical account.[2] Other notable exceptions may include; David Romagnolo's 1975 critique in *Latin American Perspectives* entitled "The So-called 'Law' of Uneven and Combined Development"; George Novack's (1976) response to this critique in the same journal a year later; and Michael Löwy's (1981) phenomenal work on the theory of permanent revolution; "The Politics of Combined and Uneven Development."[3] However, other than a handful of scholars, no one really made a comprehensive theoretical reading of Trotsky's work or bother to examine the analytical significance of UCD's postulates for social theory. As a result, for many like Jon Elster, UCD has remained a concept which belongs "to a class of Marxist notions whose suggestiveness is equalled only by their elusiveness" (Elster, 1986, p.55). Yet, as will be discussed in the next section, this situation has started to change towards the end of 1990s.

---

2 Deutscher, I (1954) *The Prophet Armed, Trotsky: 1879–1921*; (1959) *The Prophet Unarmed, Trotsky: 1921–1929*; (1963) *The Prophet Outcast, Trotsky: 1929–1940*, Oxford: OUP.

3 Other studies may include; Knei-Paz, B. (1978) *Social and Political Thought of Leon Trotsky*, Oxford: Clarendon Press, Thatcher, I. (1991) 'Uneven and Combined Development', *Revolutionary Russia*, 4: 2, pp. 235–258, and Savran, S. (1986) "Azgelişmişlik: Eşitsiz ve Bileşik Gelişme". *11. Tez, 3. Kitap*. İstanbul: Belge Yayınları.

3   The Main Critiques Levied against Conventional IR Theory

In 1995, Justin Rosenberg introduced UCD to the discipline of International Relations (IR) for the first time, in an epochal speech he delivered at the Isaac Deutscher Memorial lecture. Following the views of Martin Wight, one of the foremost scholars of the English school, Rosenberg started his speech by emphasizing the moral and intellectual poverty of international theory. "In the entire period of its existence", Rosenberg stated, the discipline of IR has "produced no great books" or "inspired no classics of the political or historical imagination" (1996, p.4). Nevertheless, Rosenberg pointed out, for many mainstream theorists, such as Wight, this intellectual barrenness is not a consequence of the insufficiencies of individual theorists, but rather, an outcome of the tragic nature of the international dimension itself (ibid, p.4).

In this prevalent line of thinking, it is presumed that the domestic field formed by the existence of a central political authority allows more room for agency, thus permitting societies to a certain extent, to determine their own paths of development within their national boundaries. In the international sphere, on the other hand, where the reign of anarchy deemed undisputed, actors' behaviour is mainly believed to be determined by the structural imperatives of this extremely hostile environment. In which of course, the struggle for survival, "ultimately overrides the moral requirements of any political theory" and necessarily reveals and consolidates a balance of power mechanism among the actors (ibid, p.4).

And just like that, Rosenberg asserted, by utilizing this inevitable pursuit of the balance of power, the orthodox international relations theory, not only persuasively argued for the evacuation of moral choice from international theory, but it could also claim to explain the behaviour of states in a scientific manner, due to its "drastically descriptive simplification" (Ibid, p.4). The moral and intellectual poverty of international theory, compared to legal and political theories in this regard, is deemed "necessary" and "irremediable" for most mainstream theorists, including Wight (Ibid, p.5). Since they believe this poverty also gives IR theory its scientific parsimony.

According to Rosenberg however, it was not IR's subject matter, but instead, its central paradigm that has stunted the development of international theory, by promoting a reified understanding of the international. "The intellectual centrality of balance of power", Rosenberg explained, which is considered to be the "masterpiece of international politics" by conventional approaches, has in fact been the major cause underlying the underdevelopment of international theory (Ibid, p.5). In this regard, he argued, Trotsky's theory carries some ground-breaking ontological implications for international theory, which can finally emancipate the discipline from the "necessary poverty" that it was condemned by mainstream theoretical approaches. The explanatory power of UCD was so self-evident for Rosenberg, that 25 years ago, while giving the above-mentioned speech, he was actually wondering, why UCD had not emerged in an earlier date, considering the "retrospective simplicity" it provides as a theory of social and historical development (1996, p.6).

The point of departure in Rosenberg's analysis is the analytical separation between domestic and international spheres, since he believes this internal/ external dichotomy, is not only constitutive for the field of IR, but also foundational for all disciplines of social sciences. Underlying this distinction, Rosenberg suggests, is the 'predominance of internalism' across social sciences, or more precisely, "the explanation of social phenomena by reference to the inner characteristics alone of a given society or type of society" (2013a, p.1). Inherited from the tradition of classical social theory, this internalist thinking (which Rosenberg also refers as methodological nationalism or ontological singularity) essentially conceptualizes society as a "singular, unitary and self-contained" entity, in which the international becomes "not just a spatial but also a theoretical externality" (2013b, p.188). According to Rosenberg, this internalist conceptualisation of society in both classical and subsequent social theory, "has prevented the theorisation of the space of inter-societal relations"; and therefore, "deprived the social sciences of a proper understanding of the international dimension of their subject matter" (2013a, p.2).

The most elaborate version of Rosenberg's critique first appeared in his 2006 article; "Why is There No International Historical Sociology?" As the title implies, while problematizing the lack of the international in classical social theories, Rosenberg was once again tracing the footsteps of Martin Wight. As "[r]emarkable as it seems in retrospect", Rosenberg concluded following Wight's views,

> [N]one of the major classical social theorists systematically incorporated the fact of inter-societal coexistence and interaction into their theoretical conception of social causality – with regard either to explaining the constitution of social orders, or to theorizing the dynamic process of their ongoing historical development (2006, p. 311).

In short, he argued, "the classical tradition never formulated theoretically the multilinear and interactive dimension of social development as a historical phenomenon" (2006, p. 308).

But what did this general neglect in social theory indicated for international theory? For Rosenberg, its theoretical implications were twofold. Firstly, it allowed Realism to construct "its own edifice of geopolitical reification" on the ontological ground that was "left unoccupied by sociology" (Ibid, p.308). As Rosenberg points out, the discipline of IR which ought to fill this theoretical gap in inter-societal relations, paradoxically, has itself been partly misshaped by it, since,

> Over the years, this neglect of the international in other disciplines, has promoted a realist self-definition of IR, in explicit contrast to Sociology, with the implication that its subject matter, lying beyond the reach of social theoretical categories, is somehow 'supra-sociological' in nature (2013a, p.2).

Secondly, classical social theory also "bequeathed a correspondingly prob-lematic conception of society" for potential challengers of Realism, making them easy prey to charges of reductionism whenever they tried to expand the explanatory reach of this social substratum into IR theory (2006, p.309). For Rosenberg, this inevitable reductionism, which Hedley Bull (1977/2002, p.44) also refers as *'fallacy of the domestic analogy',* is another direct consequence of the singular ontology of the classical social imagination, which could never be extended to encompass those properties of social existence that "arises specifi-cally from the coexistence of more than one society" (Rosenberg, 2006, p.308).

"This dual circumstance", Rosenberg suggested, is what obstructed "a sociological definition of the international" (Ibid, p.309). Moreover, it led both sociological and international theory to deliberately define their object domains independent from each other, providing the traditional (positivist) justification for separated theories of these 'autonomous' academic fields, and encouraging them to theorize systematically "the very phenomena which the other externalizes as untheorizable contingent variables" (2006, p.313; 2013b, p.185). This in turn, further reinforced the analytical separation of domestic and international politics, while consolidating a reified (or "ahistorical") con-ception of international relations that is unable to conceptualize historical change. In this anomalous conception, the international dimension which was defined through the essentialization of anarchy, "subsists without sociological foundations" mirroring in a way "Sociology's tendency to reductionism with its own, equal and opposite, tendency towards the reification of 'the interna-tional'" (2013a, p.2).

This analytical distinction has been challenged by almost every theoreti-cal approach available in IR theory, including dependency theorists, histor-ical sociologists, Marxists, post-colonialists, post-structuralists, feminists, constructivists, liberals and even some realists. In this regard, the domestic/

international divide is not only ontologically but also epistemologically constitutive for the field, considering IR theory mainly revolves around this debate.

According to Rosenberg however, "this founding and continuing great debate" is "not only lop-sided (with realism being allowed to monopolise the definition of the international), but also non-progressive" (2013a, p.4). In fact, Waltz's theory allowed more interaction between domestic and international object domains than many of its critics have acknowledged. What Waltz actually claimed was that "inside-out forms of explanation were unable, by their nature, to grasp any causal factors that were specifically international in their constitution," a claim he primarily directed against classical realists as much as anyone else (2013b, p.186). As Rosenberg explains (quoting Waltz), the argument was simply built "on the oft-repeated grounds that 'if you can't think of [international politics] in itself, then you can't have a theory of it' " (Ibid, p.187).

According to Rosenberg, this is the point where the lop-sidedness begins. Since the above-mentioned critical approaches, while "reacting against the essentialising of 'anarchy', grant little or no theoretical significance to the multiplicity of societies itself which composes the international" (2013a, p.3). Instead of providing an alternative non-realist account, they have argued that "the consequences of anarchy are either increasingly mitigated or even directly configured by social and cultural developments which originate outside the international domain" (Ibid, p.3). In short, Rosenberg argues, a "false reification of geopolitics holds the field because its challengers offer no alternative conceptualization of that feature of the social world which has been reified" (Ibid, p.4).

Moreover, Rosenberg explains, the critiques of realism almost always tend to operate, by importing forms of thought that is developed in other disciplines of social sciences. However, he points out, as a result of the continuing hold of internalist thinking over social sciences, these imported resources could never bring alternative conceptual tools for capturing the implications of social phenomena that are specifically international in their constitution (2013a, p.2). Inevitably, these critical approaches largely focused on "explaining the changing historical forms and dynamics of geopolitical behaviour", instead of "explicitly theorizing the existence and causal significance of the international dimension itself" (2013b, p.184).

Therefore, Rosenberg argues, these imported elements paradoxically served to strengthen the dichotomization of the internal and domestic spheres quite contrary to their original intention. Since, in the words of Hall, "although international and domestic forces interact or combine to produce a certain outcome" within these theories, they still remain "analytically distinct." This is why, Rosenberg asserts, "[t]hree decades later, the force of

Waltz's original critique stands out more strongly than ever" (Rosenberg, 2013b, p.184). Because it still remains the case, as Ole Weaver has argued, that "today, articles use lots of theory, and apply or test it – only it is not IR theory" (Rosenberg, 2013a, p3).

How is it possible then, to overcome these shortcomings of other critical theories? How can we develop an approach which "neither reifies nor downplays the international but instead grasp it as a sociologically intelligible dimension of the human world?" (Ibid, p.4). Rosenberg argues that "such a theory of international relations can nevertheless be constructed, using Trotsky's idea of 'uneven and combined development,'" a theory which "reconceptualizes the international [...], defining it sociologically," as a "dimension of social reality which arises specifically from the co-existence within it of more than one society" (2006, p. 308; 2013b, 185). By doing so, Rosenberg emphasizes, Trotsky's theory provides an alternative ontological framework, which ruptures the singular ontology of existing development theories, and overcomes the problems of methodological nationalism and domestic analogy simultaneously (2013a, p.5).

4   The Philosophical Premises of UCD

After exploring the historical background of UCD and reviewing the main critiques its more contemporary proponents levied against social and international theory, we may now finally proceed to examine the main philosophical premises of the theory. In order to do that, we shall return to the opening chapter of Trotsky's "History of the Russian Revolution", which for Rosenberg, constitutes the "locus classicus" of the idea, as it contains "Trotsky's most concentrated and pregnant formulation of the 'laws' of unevenness and combination", along with "an application of these to the long-term history of Russian development" (2013a, p.15).

So now, let's take up where we left off in the second section, and scrutinize the text of this introductory chapter, which Trotsky titled, in his customary manner, "Peculiarities of Russia's Development". Only this time, through the lens of Rosenberg, since examining how Rosenberg interpreted this ten-page long text, will clearly show us that he actually attributes UCD a much broader meaning than Trotsky has ever anticipated. Hence, it will be argued, Rosenberg's theoretical contribution to UCD actually points to a substantial revision, rather than a simple reformulation of Trotsky's original idea.

4.1 *Ontological Premises of* UCD*: Causal Mechanisms & Social Structures*

Today, we often speak of UCD as a uniform and monolithic theory (as the abbreviation itself clearly manifests). Hence, the first thing that should be underlined in the above-mentioned text is that, Trotsky defined 'uneven' and 'combined' development as two distinct but interrelated laws of capitalist development. "From the universal law of unevenness", Trotsky wrote, "thus derives another law which, for the lack of a better name, we may call the law of *combined development*", and then, he elaborated,

> [...] by which we mean a drawing together of the different stages of the journey, a combining of the separate steps, an amalgam of archaic with more contemporary forms. Without this law, to be taken of course in its whole material content, it is impossible to understand the history of Russia, and indeed of any country of the second, third, or tenth cultural class.
>
> TROTSKY, 2008, p. 5

This conceptual distinction between "uneven development" and "combined development" is critical in two regards. Firstly, as discussed in the second section, it played a political/strategic role against the limited understanding of uneven development that was promoted in Stalin and Bukharin's strategy of "Socialism in One Country." Yet, secondly and more importantly, this conceptual distinction also played a methodological role in Trotsky's overall abstraction of capitalist development as a dialectic-historical process. The rest of this section will dwell on this second point, since nothing demonstrates the dialectical materialist logic inherent in Trotsky's methodology better than the way how he theoretically associates these two contradictory but complementary historical laws.

In fact, according to Rosenberg, the true theoretical potential of UCD lies precisely in this dialectical association, in which the causal significance of the international is interpreted through the interactive coexistence of multiple societies with different levels of development. In his 2013 article, which was devoted to explaining UCD's main philosophical premises, Rosenberg argues that UCD actually involves an innovation for dialectical thought in this regard; a "fundamental revision", which he believes Trotsky introduced "unintentionally" (2013a, p.5). Moreover, for Rosenberg, this innovation is not only crucial for Marxist dialectics, but also for other branches of social theory, as it provides "a general solution to some of the most basic problems in social and international thought" (2013a, 1). This claim will be examined further in the ensuing section.

As Figure 5.1 illustrates, based on the dialectical correlation Trotsky established between these two antithetical laws, Rosenberg identifies three main axioms regarding UCD. The apparent fit between these three main axioms (unevenness-combination-development) and those of the triadic equation (thesis-antithesis-synthesis), can be extended even further, since development functions both as thesis (where unevenness became antithesis) and synthesis (where unevenness act as thesis) in Rosenberg's analysis. In "The Philosophical Premises" (2013a), for instance, where Rosenberg argued that UCD involves a fundamental reworking of the triadic equation, 'development' corresponds to the opening term or the 'thesis', as Rosenberg holds 'development' to be the starting point of Trotsky's idea (p.13). However, in most of Rosenberg's own analysis, *'unevenness'* constitutes the first postulate, thus serves as the thesis itself (2006, p. 313; 2013b, p. 208; Rosenberg & Boyle, 2019, p.7).

As stated earlier, Trotsky considers unevenness to be "the most general law of the historic process." In his words, this law "reveals itself most sharply and complexly in the destiny of the backward countries." Since 'the whip of external necessity', embodied in their geopolitical vulnerability against more

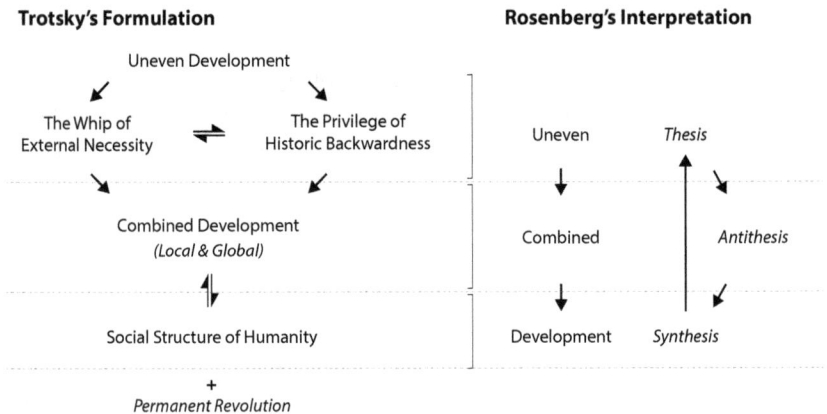

FIGURE 5.1   Main axioms of UCD
The above table is a combination of two figures which are used by Rosenberg in two different presentations; his professorial lecture on UCD which was delivered at the University of Sussex on 02.02.2014, and the speech he delivered on 06.09.2019 titled, "China, Brexit and Trump in the Mirror of Uneven and Combined Development, in the conference, *Uneven and Combined Development for the 21st Century,* University of Glasgow, September 5th–7th, 2019.

developed state organizations, compels their backward cultures to assimilate "the material and intellectual conquests of these more advanced societies" in order to survive (Trotsky, 2008, p. 4–5).

For Rosenberg though, the axiom of unevenness, "illustrates a much wider fact about human social existence." By defining uneven development as a 'universal law', Rosenberg points out, Trotsky indicates that "at any given point in time social development will have reached different levels and taken different forms in different countries" (Rosenberg, 2013a, p.17). Moreover, these different levels of development, in Rosenberg's point of view, "are not simply a latent, descriptive feature of the empirical world", but since "the countries making up a given pattern of unevenness co-exist and interact, their internal development is causally affected by their co-existence with each other." "Refracted through societal multiplicity", he puts forth, "the spatio-temporal unevenness of historical development becomes multi-centered and interactive" (Ibid, p.17).

In this context, Rosenberg suggests, the axiom of unevenness, also comprises an ontological premise of multiplicity, as it extends "the referent" of the term 'development' by widening its conceptual space to incorporate "multiple instances" or multiple societies, which "frames the logical core of any idea of the international" (2006, p. 318). In doing so however, Rosenberg explains, unevenness,

> [...] also reveals that the plane of number (multiple instances) is only one of several dimensions across which this essential multiplicity of the idea is expressed. For the unevenness of development also entails, distributed across (and ultimately also within) its instances, multiplicity of cultural form, geographical scale, developmental level and historical temporality (Ibid, p. 318).

Besides, Rosenberg points out, this ontological premise of unevenness, also postulates a causal mechanism for explaining an irreducibly international force; the 'whip of external necessity', which compels the backward country to follow after a course of development that is initiated elsewhere.

Of course, this does not mean that the latecomers have to follow the course of early industrializers slavishly, by "reproducing all the stages of their past." As Trotsky asserts, even though compelled to go after advanced countries (due to whip of external necessity), a backward country "does not take things in the same order." Since, 'the privilege of historic backwardness' (a second "specifically international" causal mechanism, as Rosenberg points out) permits backward countries to adopt "whatever is ready in advance of any specific date", allowing them to skip "a whole series of intermediate stages" (Trotsky, 2008, p. 4).

"Savages", writes Trotsky, "[...] throw away their bows and arrows for rifles all at once, without traveling the road which lay between those two weapons in the past" (ibid, p. 4). When you look at the following sentences, it becomes evident that the metaphor also defines this 'privilege' and the resulting 'combination' (combined development) as a corollary of uneven development. So, savages or the less developed did not only upgrade their weapons when they encountered civilized man, but also altered their way of life, their means of production. In addition, due to their privilege of historic backwardness, they even occasionally outpaced the more developed in their own game, for instance, in economic growth, intellectual and technical advancement and cultural hegemony. One way or another, the privilege of historic backwardness, which comes along with the whip of external necessity (two inherently international factors) thus leads us to the second law of Trotsky; the law of combined development. By the virtue of this law, Trotsky does not only acknowledge the possibility of skipping over intermediate stages, but also rules out the repetition of the previous forms of development in different societies (Ibid, p.4).

Rosenberg derives his second axiom, from this second fundamental law, and argues that with the postulate of "*combination*", Trotsky establishes the necessarily 'multilinear' character of the historic process. "The 'law' [of combined development] itself", Rosenberg writes, which can be also transcribed as "societies do not exist in isolation", "arises directly from the anterior premise of unevenness", or more precisely from the multiplicity of social existence. Yet, he adds, "its operation deepens and multiplies the latter's implications" (2006, p. 327). In a way, Rosenberg points out, "through its corollary of 'combined development'", Trotsky "redraws the sociology of 'development' in line with the consequences of" ontological multiplicity (2013b, p.193).

According to Rosenberg, through this second axiom, "the static multiplicity" of inter-societal coexistence fully resolves into a "dynamic multilinearity" of social development. We can now picture, in Rosenberg's words.

> [...] the different instances of development emerging and disappearing within the common frame- expanding, contracting, mutating and changing their positions relative to the others, in the shifting constellations making up the now moving whole (Ibid, p. 319).

Furthermore, Trotsky's conception of combined development, Rosenberg argues, also brings a "sociological definition of the international" within reach. Understood within the context of combined development, the "object domain of the international is no longer delimited to the field of geopolitics" (2013b, p. 193). As a dimension it arises from the inherent multilinear and interactive nature of human social development, as a transhistorical phenomenon. Therefore, "[i]t subsists neither at a level above, nor in a space between societies, but rather in [...] the 'domestic' constitution of those societies themselves" (2006, p. 327). This way, the separation of domestic and international spheres is pre-empted from both directions (2013b, p. 193).

At this point however, it must be emphasized that Rosenberg's interpretation of combined development also starts to become controversial. Because in Trotsky's writings, the term 'combined development' corresponds to a very particular meaning. As Rosenberg himself states, "[i]t refers to the sociological outcome of international capitalist pressures on the internal development of non-capitalist societies", or more specifically to "the sociological amalgam of capitalist and non-capitalist forms which resulted from these pressures" (Rosenberg, 2006, p. 319). Therefore, in his works, Trotsky seems to argue that combined development is an outcome of capitalist development alone. After all, pre-capitalistic cultures he explains "was in fact bound up with the provincial and episodic character of that whole process", allowing "a certain repetition of cultural stages in ever new settlements." Capitalism, however, signifies an "overcoming of those conditions" for Trotsky. It is not surprising, therefore, that most scholars have considered uneven and combined development to be a specifically modern phenomenon, or as Rosenberg describes, "a side-effect of distinctively capitalist social logics" (Rosenberg, 2013a, p.18).

According to Rosenberg however, that would be a misreading of Trotsky's theory. First of all, Trotsky's analysis "operates via a two-step process of abstraction." In the first step, the peculiarities of Russia's development "are argued to reflect a more general experience of backward countries within the unfolding of capitalist development." Then, in the second step, the multi-linear character of this process is represented to mirror the more general exigencies of social development and universalized as outcomes or upbringings of historical laws (ibid, p.18).

Besides, Rosenberg argues, Trotsky has insistently asserted that "combined development was an intrinsic, emergent property of uneven development." And if uneven development is a universal law, then Rosenberg concludes, the phenomenon of combined development "must also have a more general existence" (Rosenberg, 2006, p.319). Following this line of logic, Rosenberg goes beyond the limits of Trotsky's own formulation and reconstructs the meaning of combined development as a *general* abstraction, which reflects the transhistorical "significance of inter-societal coexistence per se" (ibid, p.319).

Here, Rosenberg extends the conceptual reach of combined development by tracing its existence back to the earliest historical stages of human development and claims that "the phenomenon is grounded in the condition of inter-societal coexistence itself, rather than in any given historical form or level of development" (Ibid, p.320). Through this new perennial conception of combined development, Rosenberg rejects "at the deepest theoretical level any notion of the constitution of society as analytically prior to its interaction with other societies" (Ibid, p.325).

Yet, whether transhistorical or not, combined development, conceptualized as a "geopolitically interconnected, temporally compressed and sociologically hybridized" process, has signified a major innovation, both for the classical Marxist notion of uneven development and for social theory in general (Rosenberg, 2013b, p. 198). Because this concept, not only interpolated inter-societal interaction into development theory, but also indicated that social progress is not a unilinear process, in which societies are obliged to pass through some definitive historical stages respectively. What combined development suggested in this regard, is not simply a leap over consecutive stages, but rather, the rejection of the stagist approach all together.

Therefore, what Trotsky meant by 'skipping over inter-mediate stages', should not be perceived as a rupture in the space-time continuum of human history, rather it should be viewed as a spatio-temporal compression occurring in between different historical continuums. Since, in Trotsky's view, "[t]he possibility of skipping over intermediate steps is by no means absolute". "It's degree", he argued, "is determined in the long run by the economic and cultural capacities of the country" (Trotsky, 2008, p.4). In this context, combined development rather implied the "drawing together of the different stages" as Trotsky himself has asserted; or "a combining of the separate steps", as its very name signifies (Ibid, p.5).

Moreover, the latecomers often encounter social resistance while adjusting to the new production relations and incorporating the institutions they imported from more developed societies. Thus, as Trotsky states, the backward nation usually "debases the achievements borrowed from outside in the process of adapting them to its own more primitive culture." This way, he argues, "the very process of assimilation acquires a self-contradictory character", leading to "an amalgam of archaic with more contemporary forms" (ibid, p. 4–5). For instance, in the case of Tsarist Russia, the introduction of Western industrial technology and European armaments did not give rise to bourgeois-liberal institutions or class relations as they did in their countries of origin. Instead, they led to the strengthening of serfdom and tsarist absolutism, even though these forms of organizations are based on feudal production relations.

According to Rosenberg however, we do not need to look that far, in order to find some other striking examples of combined development. For him, the most peculiar example in this regard, is of course China. As Rosenberg (2016, p. 20) states:

> Using the privilege of historic backwardness, Chinese industrialization is now occurring on an even more accelerated, compressed scale than the other late developers before it. And like others before it, Chinese combined development is also producing a peculiar hybrid social formation. Capitalist industrialization organized by a semifeudal Czarist monarchy was peculiar enough; capitalism presided over by a *communist* state is surely the most peculiar, most paradoxical combination so far.

Undoubtedly, there are numerous other peculiar hybrids that exist today. This, in a way, clearly demonstrates how combined development operates via its "anarchistic methods", as Trotsky had previously argued (Trotsky, 1996, p. 19). Rosenberg's two most favorite examples in this sense are Saudi Arabia; where he states, "a tribal system of politics has been grafted onto an industrializing society, so that the state, which owns the wealth of society, is itself the property of a 7000-strong extended family of princes", and Iran; an Islamic republic, that "has been locked in a confrontation with the great powers over its use of advanced nuclear technology" (Rosenberg, 2016, p. 20). "The forcing together of the old and the new", Rosenberg states, "the fusion of traditional and modern elements", cannot manifest itself more extreme than these examples (Ibid, p. 20).

In short, by carrying forward the theoretical implications of unevenness, combination also reveals the dialectical nature of capitalist development as a historical process, since it reproduces the existing unevenness, while altering it with its own contradictory methods. By this way, asserts Rosenberg, "anarchy, a quality earlier seen to be latent in unevenness, was now activated across a range of socio-cultural dimensions by the corollary of combined development" (Rosenberg, 2006, p.327). Furthermore, he explains, anarchy is now conceptualized as "an emergent property of social development, rather than being an extraneous condition operating over and against it" (Rosenberg, 2013b, p. 195).

After all, Rosenberg argues, it was "anarchy", which "had allowed for the historical proliferation of paths and temporalities of socio-cultural development", while ensuring "that the transmission of social and technological elements between societies produced innovative fusions, rather than sociological photocopies of the originating developmental process" (Ibid, p. 200). In fact, he argues, "the ability of U&CD to visualize both anarchical structures – the geopolitical and the social developmental –", entails "in a further paradoxical twist [...] an even larger significance for 'anarchy' than has been argued by Waltz himself" (Ibid, p186). Considering how unpredictably combined development could splice different developmental temporalities into each other (Rosenberg, 2014), or how it ends up producing unique historical forms in each society, "anarchy in general no longer appears as a circumstance arising beyond the conceptual reach of sociology", for now "it is visibly a basic and systematic ingredient of social development", resulting from its uneven and combined nature (Rosenberg, 2013b, p. 194 & p.201).

But what does all this tell us about historical development? How should we utilize this information to make sense of what Trotsky calls the "social structure of humanity"? This brings us to the third and final axiom of Rosenberg, namely to 'development'. If "the existence of 'the international' arises ultimately from the 'unevenness' of human sociohistorical existence", Rosenberg argues, and if "its distinctive characteristics can be derived from analysis of the resultant condition of 'combined development'", then he states, "its significance, thus sociologically redefined, entails a reconceptualization of 'development' itself" (2006, p. 307 & p. 313). In the simplest terms, this last element of the idea stresses that "interaction and combination between societies itself is a driver of historical development and change", and it would be impossible to have a comprehensive understanding of the social world without taking this fact into account (Rosenberg, 2014).

The most crucial aspect that unevenness and combination has revealed about socio-historical development in this regard, is that, although it is inter-societal, multi-linear and dialectical, it is still a holistic and unified process. As Rosenberg pointed out, "the more capitalism was expanding into a world system of production and exchange", and the more "this scrambled the social structures of the societies involved",

> the more it was incorporating into it strange contradictory hybrids like Tsarist Russia [...] and the more the integration of those hybrids was modifying the overall structure of world development.
> ROSENBERG, 2014

So, Marx and Engels were indeed right, when they wrote that capitalism "creates a world after its own image", through drawing all "even the most barbarian, nations into civilization", by compelling them "to adopt the bourgeois mode of production" (Marx and Engels, 1970 p.37). Only that, in effect, "the country that is more developed industrially" was not simply showing "to the less developed the image of its own future", as Marx has predicted in his oft-quoted passage from the Preface of *Capital* Volume I (Marx, 1982, p. 91). Because, instead of the world increasingly looking like a version of a Western European society, it resembled more and more of an interconnected hybrid, with conflicting and contradictory elements. But as the uneven and combined nature of capitalist development has proven us, is not that the true image of capitalism after all?

As Trotsky's analysis of capitalist development in Russia clearly demonstrated, uneven and combined development occurring in a given society often leads to the most drastic unintended consequences in the overall course of global capitalist development. "In the midst of better armed hostile countries", the semi-feudal Tsarist state was compelled to launch a program of industrialization in order to extend its own survival (Trotsky, 2010, p. 47). And even though, it managed to do that in the short run through strengthening serfdom and tsarist absolutism, in the long run, the very process of industrialization that it imported with its own hands, led to the vaporization of the social relations to which its hegemony rests upon, and resulted with its virtual disappearance from the stage of history (Ibid, p.167). Furthermore, it was succeeded by the very first socialist state, which then in return affected the general trajectory of capitalist development radically.

Similar formulations of causal relationships between unevenness, combination and development can also be found in most studies conducted by Rosenberg, where he demonstrates the profound effects of unevenness and combination on the unfolding of historical development as a whole (See for instance, Rosenberg 2013(b), Rosenberg and Boyle, 2019). Nevertheless, it would not be wrong to suggest that there exists a fundamental element which distinguishes the Trotsky's approach from Rosenberg's. When Trotsky was analyzing how uneven and combined development of Tsarist Russia ended up producing a socialist revolution, he was actually aware of the fact that such a revolution cannot live up to fulfil its promises. What he presumed instead, was that the Russian Revolution, because of all the economic, social and political interconnections that now existed, might have the effect of triggering other revolutions in the advanced capitalist countries, which could then initiate a wider process of world revolution (Trotsky, 2010, p. 313). In other words, he did not only associate unevenness and combination with the social structure of humanity, but he also based his political strategy of permanent revolution on this very association. However, as it will be further elaborated in the concluding section, it is quite hard to speak of such revolutionary strategy within Rosenberg's analyses.

But for now, let's stick with what Rosenberg's interpretation has to offer, instead of focusing on what it lacks. As already noted above, among other things, Rosenberg had derived an ontological premise of multiplicity out of uneven development, while simultaneously conceptualizing two specifically international causal mechanisms associated with it, namely; 'whip of external necessity' and the 'privilege of historic backwardness' – it should not be forgotten that Trotsky refers each phrase only once in his work. Also, he reconstructed Trotsky's concrete abstraction of combined development as a general abstraction, thereby universalized it as a transhistorical law. Moreover, he took the reified neo-realist understanding of anarchy, and through UCD he reconceptualized it as an emergent phenomenon of social development, even though Trotsky had never used such language of anarchy in his own analyses. However, as it will be discussed in the following section, incorporating the premise of multiplicity into dialectical methodology, maybe constitutes the most far-reaching (most farfetched for some critiques) innovation that Rosenberg have introduced in this regard.

4.2   *Epistemological & Methodological Premises: UCD as an innovation in Dialectical Thought*

As mentioned earlier, in "The Philosophical Premises", Rosenberg (2013) argues that UCD actually involves an innovation for dialectical thought; a "fundamental revision", which he believes Trotsky introduced "unintentionally" (2013a, p.5). Moreover, according to Rosenberg, this innovation is not only crucial for Marxist dialectics, but also for other branches of social theory, as it provides "a general solution to some of the most basic problems in social and international thought" (2013a, 1).

The main lines of Rosenberg's argument can be mapped out in three parts. The first part commences with an examination of Trotsky's own conception of dialectics. After briefly summarizing the dialectical worldview through Robert Heilbroner's four philosophical premises, Rosenberg claims that, "Trotsky's own writings on dialectics rehearse all four of these", namely, *praxis, motion, contradiction* and *method*.[4]

However, since Trotsky himself had nowhere explicitly drawn out on the dialectical premises of UCD, Rosenberg rather focuses on Trotsky's later works

---

4   Praxis: refers to a view of thought not as passive contemplation of the world, but rather as an active (and interactive) engagement with reality – an unending back and forth between concepts and their objects, a fundamentally creative process of interrogation. Motion: refers to the principle that all of reality – physical, social, and ideational – is in endless movement. Contradiction: refers the ontological claim that in reality, opposing (but internally related) tendencies co-exist, pulling things in different ways, their tension playing into the movement of change. Method: refers to a distinctive method of analysis that could capture the reality described in the previous three points, usually represented with the Fichtean formula of thesis-antithesis-synthesis (Rosenberg, 2013a, p.6).

and bases his analysis primarily on two texts, in which he believes Trotsky, "albeit fragmentarily" attempted to expound his views on the philosophy of dialectics; his notebook between 1933–1935 (Trotsky, 1986) and a piece that he wrote on December 1939 titled, "A Petty-Bourgeois Opposition in the Socialist Workers Party" (1942, pp. 43–63). While reviewing these works, Rosenberg especially dwells upon Trotsky's threefold premise of "non-identity", a conceptual framework that he developed through his critical engagement with Aristotelian logic.

Embodied in its most general axiom "A=A", Aristotelian formal logic, Trotsky argues, relies on the assumption that the attributes of things can be abstracted in the mind as fixed quantities and qualities for purposes of comparison and classification (Trotsky, 1986, p.87). This axiom ("A=A"), which also forms the basic building block of *syllogistic logic*,[5] constitutes "the point of departure for all our knowledge", according to Trotsky. Yet, the very same axiom he asserts, simultaneously appears to be "the point of departure for all the errors in our knowledge" (Trotsky, 1942, p.49).

This is why, he puts forth, the logic of dialectics should take off from the exact opposite axiom and attempt to explain, why in reality, "A" is never equal to "A" (A≠A). Since saying "a thing is equal to itself" necessarily implies that it does not change over time, for Trotsky, this means it does not exist in material reality, but only in mathematical abstraction. After all, he asserts, "everything exists in time; and existence itself is an uninterrupted process of transformation" (ibid, p. 49). On these grounds, Trotsky defines dialectics as "the logic of development". Formal logic, in this context, is interpreted as a particular case of dialectics, "the dialectic of motionlessness" (as in A=A), where "motion and change enter into the formula as '0'" (Trotsky, 1986, p.111).

According to Rosenberg, this inequation (A≠A), which he also refers as the "principle of non-identity", is the point where all the aforementioned four premises of dialectics become prominent in Trotsky's approach. Based on Trotsky's views, Rosenberg (2013a, p.7) identifies the three underlying elements (or dimensions) of this principle as follows (Figure 5.2);

---

5   Syllogism, in logic, refers to the formal analysis of logical terms and operators and the structures that make it possible to infer true conclusions from given premises. Developed in its original form by Aristotle in his Prior Analytics (Analytica priora) about 350 BCE, syllogistic represents the earliest branch of formal logic. In syllogistic reasoning, a valid deductive argument has two or more premises that are assumed to be true, and a conclusion which is arrived through simple declarative statements of these premises. Most famous example in this regard, "All men are mortal; no gods are mortal; therefore, no men are gods". For more information check; https://www.britannica.com/topic/syllogistic & https://www.britannica.com/topic/syllogism.

1st Principle	Applies to the equation of objects with each other	No two physical or social objects are ever exactly identical with each other. A stronger microscope, more sensitive scales, or a closer analysis will always reveal a difference, however small.
2nd Principle	Applies to their equation with themselves	All material and social reality is subject to continuous change over time; the same object differs, however infinitesimally, at one point in time from what it was, or will be, at another.
3rd Principle	Applies to their equation with the concepts by which they are apprehended	What applies to the relations between things in the world applies also to the relations between these things and the concepts by which they are apprehended in the human mind. No concept corresponds fully with the empirical reality which it seeks to grasp – and of which it is itself a simplified abstraction.

FIGURE 5.2   Principles of non-identity

As Rosenberg suggests, this account of dialectics might appear to disclose the philosophical premises of UCD at first sight, especially considering how much the first two elements of non-identity; "change over time and variations across instances", resemble "the ontological precursors to the categories of 'development' and 'unevenness' respectively". Furthermore, he points out, there is also an apparent fit between UCD's core components (development-unevenness-combination) and "those of the triadic equation itself (thesis-antithesis-synthesis)" (Ibid, p. 10).

This brings us to the second part of Rosenberg's argument, where he introduces the fundamental innovation that UCD has introduced to dialectics. In formulating the theory of UCD, Rosenberg points out, Trotsky in fact "tacitly inserted an extra philosophical premise" into his "inherited dialectical conception of motion and change" (ibid, p.5). This premise, Rosenberg asserts, corresponds "in effect, to a fourth principle of non-identity, one that cannot be derived from the previous three". Moreover, he argues, when we examine UCD as a concept, "we find that it involves a quite fundamental reworking of the triadic equation itself – a reworking produced above all by the (unannounced) interpolation of this fourth principle" (Ibid, p. 10). According to Rosenberg, this "hidden premise", which Trotsky "unwittingly presupposed" is the premise of multiplicity (Ibid, p. 13).

So, for Rosenberg, the relationship of inequality that Trotsky established between concepts and objects ($A \neq A$) were not limited to time, space or their relation to each other. Since, he explained, this fourth premise (of multiplicity) indicated that the objects of comparison, cannot be abstracted as fixed quantities, simply due to the fact that, as a result of their co-existence they would be inevitably interacting with each other. In other words, what renders A=A impossible, is not only the cumulative change or conceptual differentiation that occurs over time, but also the fact that these objects cannot be conceptualized in isolation from each other.

The third and final part of Rosenberg's argument is devoted to a detailed analysis of Trotsky's opening chapter of the History of the Russian Revolution. Here, Rosenberg demonstrates how UCD, through this fourth premise of multiplicity, succeeds in overcoming the internalism of traditional conceptions of development (either dialectical or non-dialectical) and integrates "the conceptual space of interaction" into its theoretical framework "as a dimension of change" (Ibid, p.12–13). By doing so, Rosenberg argues, it does not only extend Trotsky own argument about dialectics, but it also "directly overcomes the problems of domestic analogy, methodological nationalism, and the realist reification of the international" (Ibid, p.5).

Well, did Trotsky really insert this fourth premise unwittingly, or is it Rosenberg who forged it out of Trotsky lines? The answer is up to the reader. However, one way or another, it is an undeniable fact that Rosenberg's interpretation has taken UCD to a whole new level. As discussed in this section, Rosenberg's analyses have made remarkable contributions to the theory of UCD, both in terms of its revival and its reformulation as an IR theory. In fact, it would not be wrong to suggest that, although Trotsky is the one who discovered the law of UCD, it was Rosenberg who formally turned it into an inter-disciplinary theory of social sciences, by defining its theoretical premises and causal mechanism more structurally. In that regard, Rosenberg deserves credit for reconstructing UCD formally as a grand theory of IR and for making it more applicable to different instances by identifying its general postulates and principles. And, what is more admirable is that he did this in an era when the very phrase "grand theory" was considered to be a taboo, not only within the discipline of IR, but also across other fields of social sciences. Needless to say, Rosenberg's reconstruction of UCD aroused much controversy, especially among the scholars working within the field of historical sociology. The next chapter addresses the main lines of these discussions.

5   Contemporary Discussions, New Theoretical Openings and Research Directions

The ongoing debates about UCD are centred around three particular issues: the temporal scope of the theory, its interrelation with neorealism, and its analytical value. Actually, all three issues are deeply interrelated with each other.

So much so that, rather than independent areas of discussion they actually resemble "intersecting fault lines", as Brophy describes it, underlying almost every theoretical discussion with regards to UCD (Brophy, 2018). Therefore, instead of focusing on each controversial point individually, it might be a better idea to adopt a chronological approach and examine how these discussions unfolded sequentially.

The very first theoretical debates on UCD were actually triggered by a series of correspondences that took place between Justin Rosenberg and Alex Callinicos in 2006. This exchange of letters got published in the Cambridge Review of International Affairs in 2008 and led to a special section on UCD in the same journal a year later. In this regard, it would not be wrong to suggest that this interchange of ideas between Rosenberg and Callinicos constitutes one of the key texts of contemporary UCD literature, especially considering that it ignited, what amounts to be the "first great debate" of UCD. However, since this correspondence is initiated by an earlier article from Callinicos, it might be more appropriate to begin with briefly explaining how Callinicos (2007) integrates UCD to his own theoretical framework within this article, titled "Does Capitalism Need the State System?".

Here, Callinicos utilizes UCD only partially, in order to argue that capitalist development inherently has a tendency "to keep the states plural", as a result of its uneven and combined character (Callinicos, 2007, p. 544). His main concern was rather to demonstrate, "a way of non-reductively incorporating the state system within the capitalist mode of production" through using the method, which he claims, Marx used within the Capital (Ibid, p. 532).

According to Callinicos, the sociological abstractions of Marx in Capital indicate that his work should be "conceived as a multi-levelled theoretical structure, in which successive levels represent increasing degrees of complexity". For Callinicos, there is no reason why the same method of 'non-deductive concretization' should not be applied to any Marxist conception of the state system. After all, in his view, the international is "one among a number of dimensions of the social world which, though not deducible from Marx's concept of 'capital', must (and can) be critically incorporated in the course of his concretization" (Callinicos and Rosenberg, 2008, p. 77). Consequently, Callinicos argues, the state system should "be understood as a distinct determination [...] within the larger enterprise of developing a satisfactory theory of the capitalist mode of production" (2007, p. 542). This indicates, above all, that the logic of geopolitical competition cannot be reduced to that of class exploitation alone (Ibid, p. 538). Since, as Callinicos points out; "geopolitical competition predates capitalism" (p. 540). Thus, he explains, although the logic of geopolitical competition intersects or interacts with the logic of economic competition, it nevertheless posits a distinctive logic which cannot be explained solely with the previously introduced determinations of capitalist production relations.

After reading this article, Rosenberg writes a letter to Callinicos, which starts by praising his above-mentioned approach. According to Rosenberg, Callinicos' article clearly illustrates that, "what Marxism (and other non-realist approaches) has yet to provide is a sociological answer to the question of why 'international' dimension of social reality exists in the first place" (Ibid, p. 80). However, for Rosenberg, two points in Callinicos' article still demands further explanation. First of all, he points out, the question " 'Why are there many states?' is not fully reducible to the question 'Is there anything in capitalism that tends to keep states plural?' " (Ibid, p. 81). This is why he argues, if we conceptualize geopolitical competition as a transhistorical phenomenon with a distinctive logic, this means that UCD, which Callinicos himself associates with the social logic of capital, "simultaneously captures, at a more general level, a sociological characteristic of all historical development" (Ibid, p.80). At least, Rosenberg states, this is the only means that he had yet found, in order to "crack the shell" of geopolitical reification, given that its "historical referent extends back beyond capitalism" and that it cannot "be done exhaustively by working from a theory of capitalist development" (p. 81).

Secondly, Rosenberg claims, although Callinicos' intellectual method of progressive but not-deductive concretization demonstrates an ingenious example of broaching "the issue of 'the international' at the more fundamental level of historical materialism" (Ibid, p. 81), it still begs the question, why it needs, in the first place, the determinations that are admitted to, what Callinicos refers as, "the necessary 'realist moment' of a Marxist analysis" (Callinicos, 2007, p. 542). Moreover, Rosenberg emphasizes, it is still unclear how this necessary moment should be captured within the larger theoretical framework. "To put it another way: where comes the positive non-Realist theorization of the geopolitical determinations, which Realism rightly emphasizes but wrongly conceptualizes?" (Ibid, p. 81).

These two points that Rosenberg raised in his letter, also lays the foundations of the two main discussion areas of the 2009 CRIA forum. The first point; whether UCD could be treated as a transhistorical general abstraction or not, appears to be the claim which provoked most controversy, considering that the forum practically revolved around this topic. Here, as opposed to Rosenberg's position, scholars such as Sam Ashman and Neil Davidson argued that the theoretical usefulness of UCD "depends on understanding the limits of its spatial and chronological reach" (Davidson, 2009, p. 9). According to these scholars, by conceptualising it as a general abstraction, Rosenberg ascribed UCD a transhistorical characteristic which it does not possess (Ibid, p. 9). As a concept, they emphasised, UCD is "best understood within the relations, processes and tendencies of capitalist mode of production" (Ashman, 2009, p. 29). More importantly they argued, overextending UCD's temporal and spatial reach can only diminish or dilute the explanatory power of the theory (Davidson, 2009, p.16), as it will undermine those qualities of "capitalist social relations and political forms", which are "historically unique in their capacity to generate both combination and unevenness" (Ashman, 2009, p. 31).

The article of Jamie Allinson and Alexander Anievas from the same forum constitutes, in a way, the middle ground between the two poles of the debate. Although they admit that the distinct causal determinations of UCD "are only fully activated under the specific socio-historical conditions of generalised commodity production", they argued, it might nevertheless represent "a truly transhistorical phenomenon", as it does actually seem to reflect the general characteristic of historical development (Allinson & Anievas, 2009, p. 49). For these scholars, the theoretical implications of the UCD phenomenon, if carefully expended and enriched, might "provide a useful basis, from which to apply the concept for future research" as they would be particularly apposite in illuminating many theoretical problems that Marxist's theory cannot explain solely relying on a theory of capitalist development – such as; state formation and changing forms of geopolitical rivalry (Ibid, p. 64).

Callinicos on the other hand, stands on Rosenberg's side in this discussion. In his response letter, Callinicos strongly supports Rosenberg's attempt to utilize the concept as a transhistorical perspective on inter-societal relations. Nevertheless, he warns Rosenberg about the risks of general abstractions, as they often tend to give rise to essentialism. Callinicos' suggestion to Rosenberg in this regard, is to contextualize the referent of the general abstraction through a mode of production analysis, since he thinks, Rosenberg's approach will push the idea in this direction eventually (Callinicos and Rosenberg, 2008, p. 82).

Callinicos maintained this stance also throughout the 2009 forum. His article, (2009) once again demonstrated that the disagreements between him and Rosenberg is rather "tactical [...] than strategic". "Despite the strictures expressed" in their correspondence, Callinicos states, he still regards Rosenberg's transhistorical approach as an important step in Marxism's necessary reconciliation with the realist theories of the international. (Callinicos, 2009, p. 93) According to Callinicos the main difference between their approach is; while Rosenberg took the 'high road' by widening the stage and "liberating UC&D from [it's] primarily capitalist context", he, himself preferred to take the " 'low road' of more focused analysis centred on the prevailing mode(s) of production", by grounding his analysis of UCD in the structure and tendencies of capitalism (Ibid, p. 89 & p. 93).

A year later, Rosenberg replied to the first controversial issue arising from the 2009 Forum, by presenting a depth model in which he addresses "the relation between sociological unevenness and the existence of the international" in three different levels (Rosenberg, 2010, p. 166). The first and the most superficial of these levels, is the "external" level, where "[d]ifferential development *among* societies impacts upon development *inside* societies through its consequences for political and military relations *between* them" (Ibid, p.168). In this level, "dynamics of political multiplicity over-determine processes of uneven and combined development [only] from without" (Ibid, p.167). In the second and more fundamental level, "political multiplicity is no longer treated as an external influence on development but is rather posited as one of its *intrinsic* properties" (Ibid, p. 169). Here, political multiplicity is defined as a perennial aspect of human social development. Thus, it becomes "an internal (but untheorized) aspect of uneven and combined development" (Ibid, p. 167), while overcoming the "regnant premise of ontological singularity" (Ibid, p. 169). In the last and the deepest level, political multiplicity becomes an *emergent* property of the wider process of social development. In this level, political multiplicity is no longer regarded as a factor effecting development from within or from outside, but as a phenomenon arising from uneven and combined quality of social development itself. At this level, UCD becomes more than just a concept that explains how the international works, it becomes an emergent expression of development that explains why the international exists in the first place (Ibid, p. 170–175).

Rosenberg's reply for the second controversial issue however, which focuses on the relationship between UCD and realism, was reserved for a future instalment, which unfortunately never appeared. In fact, in this "first great debate" of UCD, this second issue surprisingly got relatively less attention than one would expect, considering that such reconciliation with realist thought is quite controversial for any critical theory of IR, yet alone for a Marxist theory. Among all these scholars dwelling upon the higher, more abstract metatheoretical debate on trans-historicity, Allinson and Anievas was the only ones in the forum, who addressed the problematic nature of the relationship that Rosenberg's approach established between UCD and structural realism. Here, Allinson and Anievas (2009) argued that, while trying to transform UCD into a transhistorical theory of the inter-societal, rather than offering an alternative to realism, Rosenberg unwittingly affirmed realisms' assumptions, by "equating U&CD with realism's multiplicity-anarchy-competition syllogism" (p. 64). "Elevated to this level of a transhistorical social logic of anarchy", they pointed out, "U&CD accounts for not only the historical existence of the discourse of realism but also its 'normative resources'" (Ibid, p. 62–63).

However, the strongest reaction in this regard, has come from Andrew Davenport, who joined the discussion in 2013. According to Davenport, what is ultimately at issue in the above-mentioned discussions within Marxist IR theory and remains unresolved (even unacknowledged) is "the nature of the relationship between Marxist thinking and Realism, the core theory of the discipline" (Davenport, 2013, p.27). After reviewing how the major strands of Marxism within IR (such as neo-Gramscian theory, political Marxism and UCD) have approached to the problem of realist essentializing of the international, and examining "[w]hat conceptions of the political are operative in their work" (Ibid, p. 34), Davenport comes to the conclusion that Marxism in IR theory might be condemned to a realist fate, considering that the "question of the political remains a theoretical blind spot" within all of its major approaches (Ibid, p. 27).

As you can see the first two front lines of controversy with regards to UCD, was already evident at the end of the 2009 Forum. The third one however, regarding the concepts of analytical value, only came to fore in the later debate between political Marxists and UCD scholars, even though Ashman addressed this issue in the forum while discussing the limited value of trans-historic abstractions for Marxist theory.

The antipathy of political Marxists such as Lacher and Teschke (2007) towards UCD's conception as an inherent feature of capitalist development, begins with their polemic with Callinicos (2007) within the broader "capitalism vs state-system" debate. In their 2007 article, Lacher and Teschke argued that, contrary to what Callinicos suggests, UCD is not an intrinsic feature of capitalism, which simply "tends to keep states plural." If anything, they claimed,

> capitalism developed unevenly not because it is in its nature – conceptually, of course (that is, abstracted from history and agency), it should even itself out internationally through world-price formation and the long-term equalization of profit rates – but because its spatio-temporally differentiated historical origin and expansion was from the first suffused with non-capitalist (and often anti-capitalist) elements that produced and kept reproducing unevenness, manifested in differential strategies of late development and catching-up.

In fact, for these scholars, the very idea of UCD, is only meaningful "due to something that lies outside the pure notion of capitalism", considering that it primarily aims at explaining the integration of non-capitalist regions, "within and through an antecedent geo-territorial configuration that is not of its making" (Lacher and Teschke 2007, 579).

Meanwhile, within the discussions among UCD scholars a particularly critical view of political Marxism has started to emerge. In 2010, Allinson and Anievas wrote a book chapter, in which they sought to elaborate the criticisms they raised in their original contribution to the 2009 Forum. Here, while remaining committed to their previous line of argument, and their overall critique regarding the ambiguities in Rosenberg's use of UCD as a general abstraction, they particularly confronted political Marxism, and especially the above-mentioned works of Teschke and Lacher. According to Allinson and Anievas (2010) the conceptualization of the absolutist state which "follows from Lacher and Teschke's collapsing of the basis-superstructure relation into the social property relations", was actually a product of "their commitment to an almost 'platonic' conception of capitalism as a theoretical abstraction, of which empirical reality must conform or remain something outside." Moreover, it was not entirely clear within this conceptualization, "why a single economic structure (in this case, feudalism) cannot have varying 'corresponding' state forms, as Lacher and Teschke allow for capitalism" (p.201).

Besides, what is particularly concerning about this "restrictive conception of capitalism", according to Allinson and Anievas, is "its relationship with the states system and geopolitical rivalry." Since, for Lacher and Teschke, "there is neither any structural connection between capitalism and multi-state system, nor anything inherent to the nature of capitalism which would necessary perpetuate it." Simply put, "the relationship is conceived as an entirely contingent one" (Ibid, p.201–202). Allinson and Anievas, argues that this was actually an inherited deficiency of the political Marxist understanding.

Following this criticism, Allinson and Anievas presented their alternative way of extending UCD as a transhistorical phenomenon, in a manner compatible with their position in the 2009 Forum, by arguing that although "unevenness – and hence the potential or simple form of U&CD extends in time and space beyond modes of production", only under capitalism it comprises "essentially within it the impulse to transform all others" (ibid, 208). After noting, how more advanced Eastern "principles of mathematics, navigational inventions, arts of war, key military technologies, and even haute cuisine" diffused across Europe predominately during the Christian Middle Ages, Allinson and Anievas stated that,

> "Such examples demonstrate the advantages of historic 'backwardness' (Hobson 2004 [*Eastern Origins*], 192), accrued to the late-developing Europeans as a result of the transhistoric fact of unevenness, and given sufficient interaction ('combined development') between the uneven poles" (Ibid, 209).

In that regard, they pointed out, no one can claim that these diffusionist processes are insignificant for European development. Nevertheless, according to these scholars, it still "seems theoretically problematic to deny the massive qualitative differences between pre-capitalist and capitalist U&CD". After all, "although conflict between Islamic states and Europe's feudal and later absolutist polities were a feature of Europe's entire history between the antique and capitalist epochs", Allinson and Anievas assert, "this did not result in imitative attempts at social re-organization by [European] polities" (Ibid, 2010).

At this point Hobson also decided to took part in the discussion. In a way, Hobson (2011) felt obliged to intervene in the ongoing debates within what he calls, "neo-Trotskyist circles". (p. 147). Since, he believed, these discussions concerning to what extend the concept of UCD should be historically generalized, actually amounts to be a 'third wave' of historical sociological approaches in IR (p. 150). And the above discussed understanding of Allinson and Anievas was clearly demonstrating that, this third wave was about to get contaminated, with the same set of thoughts, which shaped the historical narrative, and thus the shortcomings, of first two waves; the "Eurocentric logic of immanence" (p. 154).

This is why, he argued that "[f]ailure to historically generalize U&CD, at least to some extent, necessarily leads the analysis into a Eurocentric cul-de-sac" (Ibid, p.148). "In the end, it turns out", Hobson asserted, "that at best Allinson and Anievas provide only a very weak case for applying U&CD to the 'pre-capitalist' era, or at worst they simply deny its relevance altogether" (ibid, p.157). In order to advance his "third-wave non-Eurocentric historical sociological approach", and as a direct response to Allinson and Anievas' approach, in the final section of his paper, he provides his own conceptualization of UCD, through an alternative reading of "the rise of the West (p.158–165).

Almost around the same time, Bhambra (2011) also accused UCD with the same crime of Eurocentrism. According to Bhambra, "any model that posits a world historical center from which developments diffuse outwards is problematic, especially when such a model does not address the 'others' with which it comes subsequently to engage" (p. 667). In this regard, Bhambra argued, "the concept of 'uneven and combined development' is seemingly sensitive to the issues of difference, development and underdevelopment in a global context." Nevertheless, she emphasized, it continued to "retain an account of the logic of capitalism derived from European experience", as "its underlying framework is one of a linear stadial theory" (p. 675 & p.667). Even though "the social relations of colonialism, imperialism and slavery are coextensive with capitalism", UCD "renders them peripheral to the development of capitalist modernity", as the " 'unevenness' in 'uneven and combined' is argued to be a consequence of the modes of production *internal* to societies, not a consequence of relations between societies" (p. 676).

After these criticisms, Anievas seemed to reconsider his position. In the 2013 article he co-authored with Nisancioglu, he decided to take up with the challenges that Hobson and Bhambra raised, by "engaging with anti-Eurocentric critiques in developing a more 'international' approach to the origins of capitalism." In this article, by building upon UCD, Anievas and Nisancioglu (2013) sought to develop "a distinctly non-Eurocentric account of the genesis of capitalism", which, "as Bhambra puts it, 'brings the non-West more thoroughly into understandings of the construction of the modern world' " (p. 80). Anievas and Nisancioglu's attempt to generalize UCD "beyond its original capitalist temporality", thus moved the field of discussion to the debate on transition to capitalism, as if deliberately to offer a critique of political Marxist approach, which is mostly associated with the "Brenner thesis"; "arguably the most influential (if controversial) interpretation of capitalism's origins" (p. 82).

After this critique, Anievas and Nisancioglu provided their alternative reading of the so-called 'Rise of the West'. They started their analysis, by explaining how the emergence of Pax-Mongolica in 13th century provided the favorable geopolitical conditions for growing trade and commerce, "linking the West and East together as interactive components of a unified geopolitical system." Following this, they demonstrated how the plague pandemic known as the Black Death, "spread from East to West through the intersocietal interactions facilitated by the Pax Mongolica", while generating decisive shifts in the balance of class relations which will eventually serve as the basis of capitalist social relations that arise in Northwestern Europe (Ibid, p. 82). This longue durée analysis then continues with scrutinizing the Ottoman-Habsburg rivalry over the long 16th century and how this opened up geopolitical space to the north-western European states within which modern developments could take place. Anievas and Nisancioglu concludes this extended historiography by examining how the Ottomans "unwittingly facilitated the development of English agrarian capitalism and brought about a structural shift to Atlantic trade and north-west European dominance", by focusing on "the development of specific social forces in England, tied to colonial trade and plantation production", as these will eventually "play a decisive role in the making of the English 'bourgeois revolution' " (Ibid, p. 82).

Two years later, Anievas and Nisancioglu (2015) further elaborated this analysis in their celebrated book, *How the West Came to Rule*, along with the scope of their criticisms towards Marxist-inspired theorizations of the transition to capitalism. Here, in addition to Brenner's thesis of transition to capitalism – which they also refer as 'capitalism in one country' following Perry

Anderson – they also put World-System Theory and post-colonialism under critical scrutiny. This, of course, did not in any way soften the tone of their critique against the political Marxist conception of capitalism.

Meanwhile, things were getting flared up on the political Marxist side of the debate, as well. In 2014, Teschke presented his thorough and trenchant critique of UCD, in which he held UCD responsible for paving the way towards an "integrated super-discipline of International Historical Sociology (IHS)." According to Teschke, UCD remains problematic and, ultimately, misleading on at least below listed five points:

- Its positivistic conception social theory – modelled on the criteria of theory-production specified by Kenneth Waltz's
- Its conflation as a law (identifying recurring patterns) and as an explanation (theory), rendering the argument circular and neutralising its capacity to explain social change
- Its under-theorization of agency; resulting in a failure to theoretically incorporate the human sources of change and development
- Its inability to bridge the gap between theory and history, which manifests itself in an absolute dualism between abstract general theory and particularities that surface in empirical narratives, which have to be either subsumed under the general law, ignored, or declared extra-theoretical, rendering the approach empirically opportunistic, confirmationist and self-validating
- Its reification and ontologisation (rather than historicization) of "general abstractions", and a corresponding hollowing out of their explanatory power, as the inflation of substantive social categories into space-time indifferent and invariant general abstractions deflated their historically specific meanings.

Leave aside the post-positivist critique which characterizes Teschke's overall argument, these five points actually boils down to one general fundamental problem, which also forms the basis of the third main area of discussion with regards to UCD; the concepts analytical value. Indeed, as Brophy (2018) points out, Teschke's critique actually raises a problem, "which others have already flagged" in the previous discussions; "the hypostatization of the abstract law that loses sight of the concrete." According to Teschke, since UCD is simultaneously, but unwittingly, presented as a law (a collection of observable empirical regularities) and a theory (a statement that explains them), "it remains unclear what drives UCD", leading to an inevitable flat tautology that "UCD explains UCD" (Teschke, 2016, p. 32).

6   Conclusion

Debates on UCD continue today mainly, though not exclusively, in these three areas. Nevertheless, the theory has already managed to establish itself as a distinct school of thought in critical IR theory, inspiring the studies of numerous scholars and the subjects of doctoral dissertations, books and conference panels. This chapter sought to examine the theoretical premises of UCD and their implications for IR theory. It started by explaining how Trotsky coined the term and advanced it as the basis of his political strategy, considering that any understanding of UCD would be incomplete, if it overlooks this revolutionary rigor underlying its ontological and epistemological premises. Following this it went on to explore its contemporary contributions to IR theory through surveying the works of Justin Rosenberg, the scholar who introduced it to the field. After briefly reviewing the critiques that Rosenberg raised against mainstream and critical approaches, the chapter continued by addressing the ontological, epistemological and methodological premises of the theory and discussed how UCD draws the boundaries of the 'international' and how it utilizes dialectical materialism to explain its functioning. As this chapter clearly put forth, the theory of UCD owes no small debt to Rosenberg, both in terms of its revival and its reformulation as an inter-disciplinary theory of social sciences.

Of course, as the above-mentioned discussions have indicated, UCD continues to have its own pitfalls and shortcomings. Afterall it is still a theory in progress. However, this does not change the fact that it has unlocked a whole new field of research that was left unexplored by mainstream social and international theories, as it fell in between the cracks of their disciplinary boundaries: the inter-societal dimension of social development. Moreover, as the contours of its growing literature keep expanding, the theoretical framework which was initially sketched by Rosenberg continues to broaden and deepen as well. This trend has already manifested itself in numerous empirical studies where scholars applied UCD to provide alternative historical readings (See for instance; Allison, 2015; Allison and Anievas, 2010; Anievas & Saull, 2019; Brown, 2009; Cooper, 2013; Davidson 2006, Goksel, 2018, Matin 2010, 2012). Besides these, UCD has also led to new theoretical openings in other fields of research including but not limited to; geography, anthropology, legal theory, political economy, industrial relations, nationalism studies, dependency and post-colonial theory and philosophy of science (See; Antunes de Olivera, 2019; Bieler & Morton, 2014, Brophy, 2017; Dufour, 2007; Taylor, 2014; Yalvaç, 2016).

One thing remains to be problematic, however. As mentioned before, unlike Trotsky's theory, Rosenberg's approach to UCD lacks a political strategy, which incorporates UCD into our conception of political agency. Rosenberg himself is well aware of this problem. In his 2019 speech, he acknowledges that, "only when we have [UCD] as a many-sided political debate will we have recovered the full potential of Trotsky's theory, which is not just an abstract theoretical schema or a tool of historical and contemporary analysis but also an enabler of political agency". As Rosenberg states, "25 years into the revival of UCD", it seems like "that is now the last big piece of the jigsaw that we need in order to complete the picture" (Rosenberg, 2019).

References

Allinson, J., 2015, *The Struggle for the State in Jordan: The Social Origins of Alliances in the Middle East.* London: I.B. Tauris.

Allinson, J. and Anievas, A., 2009, "The Uses and Misuses of Uneven and Combined Development: An Anatomy of a Concept", *Cambridge Review of International Affairs*, 22:1.

Allinson, J. and Anievas, A., 2010, "The Uneven and Combined Development of the Meiji Restoration: A Passive Revolutionary Road to Capitalist Modernity", *Capital & Class*, Special Issue 'Approaching Passive Revolution', No. 102.

Allinson, J. and Anievas, A., 2010, "Approaching 'the International': Beyond Political Marxism" in Alexander Anievas (ed) *Marxism and World Politics: Contesting Global Capitalism*, London: Routledge.

Anievas, A. and Nişancıoğlu, K., 2013, "What's at Stake in the Transition Debate? Rethinking the Origins of Capitalism and the 'Rise of the West'", *Millennium – Journal of International Studies*, 42:1.

Anievas, A. and Nişancıoğlu, K., 2015, *How the West Came to Rule: The Geopolitical Origins of Capitalism.* London: Pluto.

Anievas, A. and Saull, R., 2019, "Reassessing the Cold War and the Far-Right: Fascist Legacies and the Making of the Liberal International Order after 1945", *International Studies Review*, DOI: 10.1093/isr/viz006, pp. 1–26.

Antunes de Oliveira, F., 2019, "Development for whom? Beyond the developed/under-developed dichotomy", *Journal of International Relations and Development*. https://link.springer.com/article/10.1057/s41268-019-00173-9.

Ashman, S., 2009, "Capitalism, Uneven and Combined Development and the Transhistoric", *Cambridge Review of International Affairs*, 22:1.

Bhambra, G. K., 2011, "Talking among Themselves? Weberian and Marxist Historical Sociologies as Dialogues without 'Others'". *Millennium – Journal of International Studies*, 39:3.

Bieler, A and Morton, A. D., 2014, "Uneven and Combined Development and Unequal Exchange: the second wind of neoliberal 'free trade'?", *Globalizations*, 11:1.

Brophy, S., 2017, "An Uneven and Combined Theory of Law: Initiation", *Law Critique,* 28:2.

Brophy, S., 2018, The Explanatory Value of the Theory of Uneven and Combined Development. *Historical Materialism,* [online] Available at: https://www.historical materialism.org/blog/explanatory-value-theory-uneven-and-combined-developm ent [Accessed, 22 December 2020].

Brown, W., 2009, "Reconsidering the Aid Relationship: International Relations and Social Development", *The Round Table,* 98:402.

Bull, H., 1977/2002, *The Anarchical Society: A Study of Order in World Politics,* New York: Palgrave.

Callinicos, A., 2007, "Does Capitalism Need the State System?", *Cambridge Review of International Affairs,* 20:4.

Callinicos, A. and Rosenberg, J., 2008, "Uneven and Combined Development: The Social-Relational Substratum of 'the International'?: An Exchange of Letters", *Cambridge Review of International Affairs,* 21:1.

Callinicos, A., 2009, "How to Solve the Many-State Problem: A Reply to the Debate", *Cambridge Review of International Affairs,* 22:1.

Cooper, L., 2013, "Explaining the Paradox of Market Reform in Communist China: The Uneven and Combined Development of the Chinese Revolution and the Search for 'National Salvation'. PhD Thesis, University of Sussex.

Davenport, A., 2013, "Marxism in IR: Condemned to a Realist Fate?", *European Journal of International Relations,* 19:1.

Davidson, N., 2006, "China: Unevenness, Combination, Revolution?" in Bill Dunn and Hugo Radice (eds) *100 Years of Permanent Revolution: Results and Prospects,* London: Pluto.

Davidson, N., 2009, "Putting the Nation back into 'the International'", *Cambridge Review of International Affairs,* 22:1.

Deutscher, I., 1954, *The Prophet Armed, Trotsky: 1879–1921;* Oxford: OUP.

Deutscher, I, 1959, *The Prophet Unarmed, Trotsky: 1921–1929;* Oxford: OUP.

Deutscher, I., 1963, *The Prophet Outcast, Trotsky: 1929–1940,* Oxford: OUP.

Dufour, F., 2007, "Social-property Regimes and the Uneven and Combined Development of Nationalist Practices", *European Journal of International Relations,* 13:4.

Elster, J., 1986, "The Theory of Combined and Uneven Development: A Critique", in Roemer, J., ed., *Analytical Marxism.* Cambridge: Cambridge University Press.

Goksel, O., 2018, "Uneven Development and Non-Western Modernities: A Historical Sociology Guide to the New Turkey", *New Middle Eastern Studies,* 8 (1).

Hobson, J. M., 2004, *The Eastern Origins of Western Civilization,* Cambridge: Cambridge University Press.

Hobson, J. M., 2011, "What's at Stake in the Neo-Trotskyist Debate? Towards a Non-Eurocentric Historical Sociology of Uneven and Combined Development", *Millennium,* 40:1.

Knei-Paz, B., 1978, *Social and Political Thought of Leon Trotsky*, Oxford: Clarendon Press.

Löwy, M., 1981, *The Politics of Combined and Uneven Development: The Theory of Permanent Revolution*, London: Verso.

Marx, K, 1982/1867, *Capital: A Critique of Political Economy Volume I*, New York: Penguin Books.

Marx, K. and Engels, F., 1970/1848, *Manifesto of the Communist Party*, Peking: Foreign Languages Press.

Matin, K., 2010, "Decoding Political Islam: Uneven and Combined Development and Ali Shariati's Political Thought", in Shilliam, R., ed., *International Relations and Non-Western Thought: Imperialism, Colonialism and Investigations of Global Modernity*. London: Routledge.

Matin, K., 2012, "Democracy without Capitalism: Retheorizing Iran's Constitutional Revolution", *Middle East Critique*, 21:1.

Novack, G., 1976, 'The Law of Uneven and Combined Development and Latin America', *Latin American Perspectives*, Spring 1976, Vol. III, No. II.

Romagnolo, D., 1975, 'The So-Called 'Law' of Uneven and Combined Development', *Latin American Perspectives*, Spring 1975, Vol. II, No. I.

Rosenberg, J., 1996, "Isaac Deutscher and the Lost History of International Relations", *New Left Review* 1:215.

Rosenberg, J., 2006, "Why is There No International Historical Sociology?", *European Journal of International Relations*, 12: 3.

Rosenberg, J., 2010, "Basic Problems in the Theory of Uneven and Combined Development. Part II: Unevenness and Political Multiplicity", *Cambridge Review of International Affairs*, 23:1.

Rosenberg, J., 2013a, "The 'Philosophical Premises' of Uneven and Combined Development", *Review of International Studies*, 39:3.

Rosenberg, J., 2013b, "Kenneth Waltz and Leon Trotsky: Anarchy in the Mirror of Uneven and Combined Development", *International Politics*, 50:2.

Rosenberg J. "Professorial Lecture on U&CD", University of Sussex, on February 2, 2014.

Rosenberg, J., 2016, "International Relations in the Prison of Political Science", *International Relations*, 30:2.

Rosenberg, J. "China, Brexit and Trump in the Mirror of Uneven and Combined Development, in the conference, *Uneven and Combined Development for the 21st Century*, University of Glasgow, September 5th-7th, 2019.

Rosenberg, J and Boyle, C., 2019, "Understanding 2016: China, Brexit and Trump in the History of Uneven and Combined Development", *Journal of Historical Sociology*, 1–27.

Savran, S., 1986, "Azgelişmişlik: Eşitsiz ve Bileşik Gelişme". *11. Tez, 3. Kitap*. İstanbul: Belge Yayınları.

Taylor, N., 2014, "Theorising Capitalist Diversity: The Uneven and Combined Development of Labour Forms", *Capital & Class*, 38:1.

Teschke, Benno., 2014, "IR Theory, Historical Materialism, and the False Promise of International Historical Sociology". *Spectrum: Journal of Global Studies*, 6:1.

Teschke, B and Lacher, H., 2007, "The Changing 'Logics' of Capitalist Competition", *Cambridge Review of International Affairs*, 20:4.

Thatcher, I., 1991, "Uneven and Combined Development", *Revolutionary Russia*, 4: 2.

Trotsky, L., 1942, *In Defense of Marxism: Against the Petty-Bourgeois Opposition*, New York: Pioneer Publishers.

Trotsky, L., 1986, *Trotsky's Notebooks, 1933–1935. Writings on Lenin, Dialectics and Evolutionism*, edited by Philip Pomper. New York: Columbia University Press.

Trotsky, L., 1996/1936, *The Third International After Lenin*, New York: Pioneer Publishers.

Trotsky, L., 2008/1932, *The History of the Russian Revolution*, Chicago: Haymarket Books.

Trotsky, L., 2010, *The Permanent Revolution* (1930) *and Results and Prospects* (1906), Seattle: Red Letter Press.

Trotsky, L., 2016, *1905* [sic], Chica: Haymarket Books.

Yalvaç, F., 2016, "Ibn Khaldûn's Historical Sociology and the Concept of Change in International Relations Theory," in Deina Abdelkader et. al. (eds.) *Islam and International Relations: Contributions to Theory and Practice*. London: Palgrave.

CHAPTER 6

Poststructuralism and the Poststructuralist Turn in IR

Gözde Turan

1   Introduction

Today, it seems to remain disquieting to observe that the scholars, intentionally or unintentionally, end up founding their gated communities with Critical scholars communicating primarily with other Criticals, Realists and Liberals continuing to debate with each other though uniting in their disapprobation of post-positivist theories, or Feminists paying tribute to fellow Feminists. Poststructuralist IR stands out as one of the most marginalized approach amongst these different strands not only due to its allegedly abstract and complicated assumptions, but also not so easily accessible written texts. Instead of being just a retrospective summary of Poststructuralist approaches in general and repeating the debates on Poststructuralism's contributions in IR, this chapter, therefore, will further aim to incite a self-questioning by Poststructuralist writers on the impotency of their communication with non-Poststructuralists. This incitement is premised on the argument that the difficulty of post-positivist interrogations in IR to outreach an extensive audience and to share their insights on different modes of oppression in current world affairs is connected more to how these interrogations are discussed than is acknowledged. To this end, the first part will investigate in a basic setting how Poststructuralism entered into IR, how it differs from other theoretical positions including but not limited to Structuralism, and what it implies to follow a Poststructuralist approach. The second part will focus on Poststructuralist approaches in IR, its critique on the mainstream, and what implies to develop a Poststructuralist critique which will be followed by a discussion on its effectiveness in the Conclusion.

2   The Poststructuralist Turn in IR

If the discipline of IR is referred to as production of knowledge about world politics, it is possible to briefly summarize Poststructuralist studies of IR as a critical investigation on "how the subject – in the dual senses of the subject-matter and subject-actor – of international relations is constituted in and through the discourses and texts of world politics" (der Derian and Shapiro, 1989, p. ix). Challenging the traditional divisions between private and public, international and national, theory and practice, Poststructuralist IR scholars focus on, for example, the war discourse, not wars; security discourse, not security itself; anarchy discourse, not anarchy; or diplomatic discourse rather than *corps diplomatique*. The investigation on how the discourses and texts of world politics are constituted is not simply and exclusively an intellectual curiosity lacking any further motivation since Poststructuralism is "about disclosing the assumptions and limits that have made things as they are, so that what appears natural and without alternative can be rethought and reworked" (Campbell, 2013, pp. 232–233).

The Poststructuralist turn within the discipline should be traced back to 1980s with postmodern scholars who took their inspiration from the challenge against positivist foundations of science in social sciences and literature. It would not be incorrect to reason a potential connection between the critique against positivist foundations of so-called scientific knowledge in social sciences and the already established critique in natural sciences in early 20th century. Thus, it is plausible to depict the Poststructuralist and Postmodern turn in IR less as a timely disposition than as a belated initiative which might be partly due to the young discipline's need of incorporating the modernist and positivist approaches prior to Postmodernism and post-positivism, and also due to the heavy pressure from the mainstream paradigms dominating the Cold War political environment. Whether it is a need of intellectual maturement in terms of internalizing first the premises of modernity and only then the contradictions of modernity, or a need of a dramatic change of political environment, critiques on positivist and modernist thought in IR apparently gained momentum particularly with the demise of Cold War and its accompanying mainstream theoretical approaches.

In parallel to a general dissatisfaction with mainstream theories in IR and drawing on founding figures of Poststructuralist thought such as Jacques Derrida, Michel Foucault, Gilles Deleuze, Jean Baudrillard, Giorgio Agamben and Jacques Lacan, Poststructuralism entered to IR through the works of Richard Ashley (1981, 1984), James Der Derian (1987), Michael Shapiro (1988), and R. B. J. Walker (1987, 1993). However, a comprehensive understanding on the impact and evolution of Poststructuralism in IR requires an initial look at the genesis of Poststructuralism in Humanities.

3   What Is Poststructuralism and What Defines the *Post* of
     Poststructuralism

Poststructuralism is registered as a challenging attitude or perspective rather
than a theory on its own with its critical stance not only against foundational
theoretical approaches, but against any approach with a universal truth claim in
International Relations (IR) including also the Critical Theory. Poststructuralism
problematizes any grand theory since theory building is seen as a social practice next to being an intellectual attempt to make sense of the things happening in the world. When the social world is taken as operating not independently
of how human beings think about it, all observations and all theoretical systems assuming the possibility of impartiality from the research subject will
be challenged from the start. Thus, the primary assumption Poststructuralists
are unconvinced of is the possibility of observing from outside. It is the imper-
sonal and objective relationship between the observer and the inquired entities as a point of departure which determines also the divergent yet ongoing
relationship between Structuralism and Poststructuralism (Howarth, 2013,
p. 7). Although the name Poststructuralism suggests a certain kind of relationship to Structuralism, the latter assumes that entities under the inquiry of the
scholar have a distinct and natural essence. Structural analysis, finding its very
first examples in Western thought with Durkheim's and Montesquieu's studies, focuses on the "number," the "nature," and the "interrelations" of parts or
"elements" in a system of "things" or "facts" each of which hold a distinct and
natural essence (Maryanski and Turner 1991, p.107). The interrelation between
the elements characterizing and differentiating Structuralism from other
approaches such as essentialism which also treats things as distinct and natural since "[s]tructures are never mere aggregates, accidental bunches of elements and their properties" (Merquior, 1986, p. 189). A structural system, as self-
regulative and transformative, is able to self-stabilize without the use of any
external element while the researcher strives for finding out the rules of such
self-stabilization (Merquior, 1986, p. 190). Against this, Poststructuralists, rather
than assuming the natural essence of entities as well as embracing academic
work as an intellectual attempt to grasp the relationality of the entities, begin
with questioning the very processes and practices that produce entities as natural and distinct. Still, some writers question to what extent it makes sense to
describe the approach as "Poststructuralist" instead of anti-Structuralist which
radically rejects all premises of Structuralism, or neo-Structuralist[1] which

---

1   Habermas was one of the figures calling Poststructuralism as neostructuralism, not to under-
     line the parallels between two, but to disparage it with the accusation of "undermining

modifies while maintaining certain structural features (Merquior, 1986, p. 192). However, anti-Structuralism or neo-Structuralism does not seem to capture the real essence of Poststructuralism. Although the prefix "post" suggests a relationship with Structuralism without a hint on the nature of that relationship, Poststructuralism differs both from *anti* and *neo* forms with its avoidance of any enduring explanation on the structure on account of its versatile and indecisive nature. Moreover, Poststructuralist authors see it as an advantage not to break from modernity in order to re-present the historical rupture, to critically reinscribe the forgotten and repressed pasts (der Derian and Shapiro, 1989, p. xx).

Language plays the major role for both Structuralism and Poststructuralism in constructing the entities and the relations of the entities, *vis a vis* each other. To begin with, speech itself is not natural; "language is a convention", including but not limited to speech next to other apparatuses of gestures and visual symbols used for communication. Speech is an instrument of language and a social product which is both arbitrary and rational at the same time (de Saussure, 2011, pp. 10, 73–75). It is arbitrary in the sense that it limits attempts of modification and there is no solid ground to discuss why we attribute a particular meaning to a given word though it also reflects a collective rationality assigned to social conventions (de Saussure 2011, pp. 73, 68). The connection of language to social conventions indicates that who shares a common social system of meanings are only able to use the same sounds and words. Sounds, in the Saussurean terminology "signifiers", are complex acoustical-vocal units of language that arise from ideas to reflect particular meanings (de Saussure, 2011, p. 8). Furthermore, it is not only the social and political phenomena standing as tangible and taking a particular set of meanings and implications through language, but the text is also a tangible entity reflecting forms of images and ideas of the language (de Saussure, 2011, p. 15). Another critical point to underline here is that the signified concepts do not simply correspond to objects in the world, but they depend on language to have a particular meaning. The quest to disclose the relationship between language and external world continues with Levi-Strauss's work on myths (Levi-Strauss 2008), and Barthes's analysis of sign systems (Barthes, 2010), which, together with de Saussure's theory of language, constitutes the linguistic turn in social and political theory. However, it has been Poststructuralism pioneered by Derrida, Barthes, Lacan, and Foucault to introduce a specific understanding of language, discourse and the role of contingency.

---

reason, destroing universality and renouncing the hope for emancipation" (Davis, 2004, p. 34).

Derrida, initially disputing the distinction between language and the world of objects, then challenging the closed nature of linguistic systems, deconstructs Structuralist analysis of language to show that language represents a process of production rather than a product in itself. The major share of producing reality falls on the text: "There is nothing outside of the text" (Derrida, 1997, p. 158). Yet, this is neither because of the fact that the lives of the authors of the text are of no importance, nor lies the only way to have access to their real existence in the text (Derrida, 1997, p. 158). Instead of being just mediums of communication, language operates as a way of making sense of the world. Taking language as a vantage point of departure does not imply that it is impossible for tangible social and political phenomena to exist independent of our sensory experiences. We convey values, perceptions and preferences which shape the nature and implications of such social and political phenomena. Beyond this, Poststructuralism considers the distinction between the material world and discursive complexes not only insignificant but also incorrect and meaningless. Nietzsche refuses the traditional philosophical distinction between reality and appearance arguing that what is apparent is the only world (Bleiker and Chou, 2010, pp. 10–12). Laclau and Mouffe (2001, pp. 107–108), taking this position a step further, argues that the distinction between discursive and non-discursive practices which they argue to have found in Foucault's writings is also inconsistent. Following Derrida's point on the non-existence of a world outside of the text, Laclau and Mouffe conclude that the object as a product of the discourse does not imply a separate world out of discourse. Such an approach would bring us close to the traditional controversy between idealism and realism and a debate on whether objects do or do not exist externally to thought. Objects indeed exist externally to our thoughts; however, what these objects imply is a discursive practice.

Because speech is more immediate and directly connected to our thoughts, Derrida privileges speech over writing (Howarth, 2013, p. 53), whereas there are other ways to arouse discursive power. For Baudrillard, the main implementation to construct the social world is through simulation, which is "the generation by models of a real without origin or reality" (Baudrillard, 1983, p. 2). While reality, or hyperreality as Baudrillard calls it, is continuously reproduced through simulation, power lies in the multiplication of signs in the play of simulation (Baudrillard, 1983, pp. 43–44). Rather than referring to material manufacture, production means to "render visible, to cause to appear and be made to appear" while "[s]eduction is that which is everywhere and always opposed to production; seduction withdraws something from the visible order" (Baudrillard, 2007, p. 37). Thus, irrespective of Baudrillard's use of a different terminology as "seduction" in contrast to production, Poststructuralism in general underlines the power dimension of producing signs of resemblance (Baudrillard, 1983, p. 45), which considers rendering invisible equally and as a matter of fact even more important as rendering visible. Rendering (in)visibility might give a deceptive impression that the human subject has the power to control, alter and put into force discourses. Indeed, Nietzsche concedes two main functions to language first of which is to have knowledge of the world. Yet, the world we develop knowledge of is not and cannot remain as the same world after we look at and make sense of by using our language. The second function of language is, therefore, complementary to the first, which is to grant the tools to men to deal with, in other words to master the world (Nietzsche, 2005). If humans cannot have any word to describe what is happening, then it would be impossible for them to formulate any knowledge of what is happening to them, which would then deprive them of any means to control these happenings (Strong, 1984, p. 86). However, the mastering human who, with modernity, is endowed with free, complete and conscious agency is also a discursive product in a similar way as the subordinated, dependent and incapable human in an incomplete structure transcending any foundational centre.

Along these lines, a summary definition of discourse can be formulated as "representations and practices through which meanings are produced, identities constituted, social relations established, and political and ethical outcomes made more or less possible" (Campbell, 2013, pp. 234–235) which cannot be restricted to linguistic forms, but should be expanded to include gestures, simulations, visual tools and the like. The observing subject cannot be detached from the observed entities throughout the discourse production process since the subject is simultaneously produced as part of the world it takes part in producing (Edkins, 2007, pp. 89–90). Besides the lack of impartiality of the subject and the contingency of the entities in social life, the relationship between them also posits a heterogeneous nature opposed to a fixed or closed ontological assumption (Howarth, 2013, p. 10). The unpredictable nature on the relationality between discourses and structure disconnects Poststructuralists not only from the Structuralist paradigm but also from other critical perspectives. Meanwhile, discourses are controlled, selected, organized and redistributed by certain people (Foucault, 1971, p. 8) whom Mc Morrow does not refrain from calling as elites. Elites can come from various backgrounds and occupy different positions in society such as government ministers, doctors or scientists (McMorrow, 2017, p. 56). The identity and position of elites, on the other hand, should not be considered to be stable and fixed as Poststructuralism attributes an "ontological uncertainty to authorship" (Weber, 1999, p. 439), which infers a further obliteration next to the selective process about things of the constructed reality and which separates Poststructuralism from Constructivism as well. There is no individual author of texts or scripts; discourses are intersubjectively produced that enables also change since interaction is contextual. If the interaction, therefore the discourse, is spacio-temporally specific, it will be possible to have a stabilized meaning only through forgetting, or in other words, silencing (Shapiro, 1989), which is the type of violence Poststructuralism is concerned of the most.

Despite a not too narrow employment of discourse analysis by scholars from different strands, it is Poststructuralism which undertakes to unfold discursive power with an emancipatory intention. Still, it is not easy to discern the power games put into force by discourses and find a straightforward answer to Derrida's question "what links writing to violence" (Derrida, 1997, p. 101), or Foucault's question "[w]here is the danger in [discourse]" (Foucault, 1971, p. 8). Violence, in fact, starts with speech, or lack of speech; we cannot speak about everything, "not everyone has the right to speak of anything whatever" (Foucault, 1971, p. 8). This is not merely related to prohibition but includes procedures of exclusion, rejection and division. The words of the madman, since Middle Ages, are not simply prohibited but classified as irrational and thus rejected, invalidated in legal terms, which enables the division between madness and reason (Foucault, 1971, pp. 9–10). When reason and madness is separated from each other via particular concepts and words, the one endowed with standards consistent with rationality will be honoured while the others will be excluded, subordinated and exposed to techniques of silencing. That means, power games reflect a contestation over words and concepts such as determining which words correspond to reason, what sort of practices fall into the sphere of reasonable actions, and who is fit as a rational agent. But beyond framing what and who is rational, "exercise of power over another involves the limiting or impairing of the recipient's capacity for choice or action" that is carried out with persuasion, internalization and naturalisation unlike manipulation, coercion or threat (Connolly, 1984, p. 140).

Exclusions, rejections and divisions move through discourses in every domain of life which are neither arbitrary, nor lack of violence while they are performed through different institutions including but not limited to medicine, incarceration, and law (Foucault, 1971, pp. 9–10). Power operates not just in order to discipline its subjects but to construct a productive subject/individual who then will be represented as normal and healthy, and whose life will be promoted as part of generating, shaping and controlling *healthy* human populations as part of *biopower* (Foucault, 1978). Foucault, in his quest for exploring the excluded, marginalized, and forgotten history, brings the idea of *archaeological* analysis, which is not intended to refer to simply studying archives, but to denote to a particular method of gathering "the things said and written on a particular subject in a particular context by a particular group of people (often political elites), in order to try to interpret what is being done politically through such statements" (Neal, 2009, p. 166). Without abandoning the archeological method, Foucault invents *genealogical* study to concentrate on how power operates through discourses over time (Foucault, 1991). Genealogy studies history not as a representation of a single, unitary line of events of continuity, but as a combination of discontinuities and accidental events with no essence or an underlying *telos* in history to be uncovered (Huysmans, 1997, pp. 364–65).

Inasmuch as "[p]olitics is performing substitutions within the sign or making foundational claims about the sign" (Weber, 1999, p. 439), it should be the main task of the analysis to rediscover and restore the text (Barthes 1981), to see the organic relationship between politics and signs, and decipher "the language of politics and the politics of language" (Connolly, 1984, p. 139). Only then, it will be possible to "draw attention to the depoliticising moment of the politics of 'reality' " (Zehfuss, 2004, p. 197) and to look for the relations of power between theory building and the social world which is shaped not only by the things, but how the things are seen and interpreted by human beings.

4   Poststructuralist IR against Mainstream IR

Poststructuralist IR scholars, rather than framing potential solutions to the problems in international relations, attempt to display, first, how representations and symbols configurate these problems and second, how such configurations produce and reproduce relations of power. Representations and symbols in international affairs might be a state leader or the state itself, sometimes an ethnic conflict or genocide, other times human societies who are taken to be primitives to be civilized. Reflecting on the contingency of an impartial inquiry on representations and questioning their political implications have enabled to put the most accustomed issues of IR and their highly arbitrary nature under careful scrutiny. The effort is geared towards displaying what is kept out of sight and how alternative representations are possible. Wars, diplomatic summits, state-rivalry, for example, have been regarded as the main representations which managed to escape from such scrutiny until the Poststructuralist turn. It has become possible to see how particular cultures of violence as well as their state-centric and masculine nature are reproduced only with the exploration of the subjectivity of the representations of most conventional actors and issues of IR (Bleiker, 2001, pp. 509–510).

Campbell's (2013, p. 229) legitimate warning that Poststructuralism, rather than advocating an altogether rejection of foundations attempts to demonstrate their historical production is a reminder that the aim is not to replace IR's major issues for alternatives. It is not a nihilist interpretation designed to discard reality but rather a discussion how different realities are constructed throughout historicopolitical processes. The reality of IR is a complex, ambiguous, incomplete and heterogeneous matrix of existence against mainstream IR theories' simplistic and universalized image (George, 1994, p. 11). As a matter of fact, Poststructuralist IR attends to the most common issues and actors of IR even more carefully and skeptically than mainstream IR theories. Rather than taking the state for granted, for example, and naturalizing the mantralike perspective "a state is a state is a state" like realism or liberalism have done before, Poststructuralism focuses on the state's historical foundations and raises the question how the universalized, essentialist and totalized understanding on state has come forward (Campbell, 2013, p. 226). In a similar vein, Poststructuralism does not deny the concept of "interest" playing a crucial role in IR. What it does is to engage with interests as discursive artefacts which are articulated in language by foreign policy actors (Hansen, 2013, p. 99). "War", likewise, is a signified concept, in other words, a discursive artefact in Poststructuralist analysis. Mainstream theories define war as a particular type of armed violence; yet this particular meaning attributed to the word of "war" depends on a social convention which continuously should remind us that there had been, there are, and there will be alternative ways to define it.

When common concepts and issues in IR such as war, security, anarchy, diplomacy and the like are taken as discursive artefacts rather than timeless and objective "facts", the Poststructuralist analysis will attempt to disclose the power-knowledge relationship between the signified, which will be the "disciplined conversation *among* these authors and writings" (Ashley, 1995, p. 95) and signifier, who are the beneficiaries of the relationship. The subject-actor as the signifier is not fully in control of the signified which distinguishes the Poststructuralist reading of power-knowledge relationality in a radical way from other approaches, such as neo-realism. Waltzian neo-Realist IR judges knowledge in terms of its utility and technical applicability which turns it into a commodity used as a power tool by states (Devetak, 1999, p. 63). Although Poststructuralism also agrees that "[p]ower in a specific field is practical, not arithmetic" (Abrahamsen and Williams, 2011, p. 316), subjects of IR, in other words its practitioners, are produced via designated competencies: "there is no doer before the deed" (Duvall and Chowdhury, 2011, p. 338). Power, here, understood in the Foucauldian fashion, is decentred and pluralized, exercised in a wide variety of forms disciplining and normalizing its subjects (Neal,

2009, p. 163). Performances stabilize identities beyond simply producing them, however, this is not a completed process but opens up a space for change that Poststructuralist IR attempts to provoke (Braun, Schindler, and Wille, 2019, p. 794). Besides, "every signified is but another signifier in a whole chain of signifiers" (Devetak, 1999, p. 68) whereby the contingent reality is constituted.

Noticing "the incessant sliding of the signified under the signifier" (Lacan, 2005, p. 117) nonetheless does not imply that Poststructuralism ignores or underestimates material violence, horrors of wars or terrorism as some of the most common issues of mainstream IR theories. What is at stake here is getting mesmerized by such horrors which likely brings about missing "the significance of the aftermath, when the calculus of the state, force-multiplied by the media and the fear of the body politic drops like a stone through the web of its own sovereignty myth " (Der Derian, 1995, p. 364). Whether it is a symbol or a linguistic medium, discourses frame what seems to be possible for actors rather than displaying their genuine intentions or objectives. In other words, discourses play a crucial role in enabling and disabling certain kinds of decisions and actions without denying or excluding the material conditions.

In politics, discourses, which position supposedly antithetical concepts against each other, impair critical thinking besides justifying power mechanisms conditioning society in a particular direction. The notorious security-liberty dilemma, for example, is a discursive construct which presumes that the higher level of civil and political liberties correspond to insecurity as the argument is that former will curb the state capacity to duly respond to threats such as illegal migration, crime, terrorism (McMorrow, 2017, p. 57). In such a discursive design, which imposes a choice between two mutually exclusive possibilities, what is at stake is not only the potential to transcend the conventional thinking with regard to what constructs security and liberty. In other words, we are not just deprived of an alternative world where security encompassing extensive liberties is possible. Confinement of the security-liberty debate to the political domain also maims our capacity to see how divisions between political and apolitical matters are artificial constructs with real consequences. And, as a matter of fact, the argument that discursive power is in operation not only in the political domain but in every aspect of everyday life would fail to capture what Poststructuralism tries to underline since the act of designating what is political and what is apolitical is itself a political decision therefore cannot be considered to be immune to power games. In other words, there is nothing which is not essentially political; only depoliticized things that need to be deconstructed to reveal the politics underneath.

5   How to Set Apart Poststructuralist IR from Other Critical Approaches

How to interpret the contribution of Poststructuralism to IR depends more on understanding what Poststructuralism, less than what IR, is all about. As already emphasized, Poststructuralism's main concern is on different forms of power and how these different forms relate to knowledge production. Poststructuralist IR, in the footsteps of Foucault's archeological and genealogical studies, disrupts the common IR concepts such as sovereignty, power, war, diplomacy, or state, and problematizes not just the common subjects of IR but the discipline of IR itself. Thus, it would be implausible to argue that Poststructuralist IR's purpose is to formulate alternative concepts or study areas to the discipline since the latter itself is at the centre of the Poststructuralist critique.

It is not quite easy to draw unsurmountable boundaries between Poststructuralism and Postmodernism, Postcolonialism, Critical Constructivism or other critical approaches as the overlapping zones might look more common than their differences initially (Buzan and Hansen 2009, p. 197). Critical IR scholars are not immune from confusions on how to cover and categorize post-positivist approaches to IR, let alone the mainstream theories.[2] It is not fully the case that post-positivist approaches critical to the Enlightenment Project's commitment to a unified view of science, which assumes that ontological, epistemological and methodological positions of natural sciences can well be adopted to social phenomena, represents a coherent grouping against positivist studies. Being critical to any notion of privileged access to truth, Critical Theory, Postmodernism and Poststructuralism share a common ground in challenging the positivist attempts to separate facts from values, to introduce value-neutral concepts, and to test truth claims using a certain protocol (Viotti and Kauppi, 2012, p. 330). The ultimate goal of emancipation, plus the concerns for the use of language that connects to power dimension of knowledge also bring together these different strands to a similar

---

2   Robert Keohane's (1988) featured Presidential address at the ISA in 1988 distinguishing studies in IR under two groups – the *rationalism* and *reflectivism* – is a relevant representation of mainstream IR theoreticians' perspective of generalizing all critical approaches under the same category. On the other hand, some post-empirical research has paired Poststructuralism with Postmodernism or Postcolonialism showing a similar tendency with that of Keohane (see, for example, George, 1994). Recognizing the differences of Poststructuralism Richard Wyn Jones suggests still to call all critical approaches as a constellations Critical IR Theory depending on the commonalities rather than their differences (Jones, 2001, pp. 9–12).

line of argument. Although all the post-positivist approaches share a strong commitment to the belief that for a genuine emancipation there needs to be a transformation which can only be achieved through a permanent state of criticism, what is understood from a critique differs for each and every critical approach. Taking into consideration how Habermas has recently become "the most vocal and persistent defender of the Enlightenment commitment to reason" (Jones, 2001, p. 3), Poststructuralism might be called as a radical challenge not only to the "mainstream" IR, but also to the "mainstream" of critique in IR.

Poststructuralist critique, through expanding its scrutiny to include rational assumptions and transcending how the social world is constructed, becomes a critique not only to the mainstream but also to any rational and foundational assumption including the Frankfurt School Critical Theory and Social Constructivism. Pointing out the crucial role that thought plays in our lives and how a change of perspective opens the door for a further change, Foucault (1988, pp. 154–155) draws attention to the overestimation of the social:

> A critique is not a matter of saying that things are not right as they are. It is a matter of pointing out on what kinds of assumptions, what kinds of familiar, unchallenged, unconsidered modes of thought the practices that we accept rest. We must free ourselves from the sacralization of the social as the only reality and stop regarding as superfluous something so essential in human life and in human relations as thought. Thought exists independently of systems and structures of discourse. It is something that is often hidden, but which always animates everyday behavior. There is always a little thought even in the most stupid institutions; there is always thought even in silent habits.

For Poststructuralist IR, the fields of battle are commonly described as international theory which operates to frame a particular type of truth to silence its alternatives. The critique, thus, should contribute in our understanding on how "one theory comes to stand above and silence other theories but also how theory as a knowledge practice has been historically and often arbitrarily separated from 'events', that is, the materially inspired practices comprising the international society" (der Derian and Shapiro, 1989, p. 6). The critical attitude of Poststructuralism overarching positivism and social constructivism differentiates it also from Postmodernism. Interpreting the indeterminate, pluralistic and tremendously globalized culture of modernity which is accompanied by a deep frustration after horrors of the two world wars, Postmodernism investigates the results of accelerated and rearticulated time-space relations, however, cannot catch up with the Poststructuralist engagement with the production and implications of these relations (Campbell, 2013, p. 231). Poststructuralism, holds Hansen (2010), is not confined to any particular historical period like Postmodernism.

As aforementioned, discourse plays a uniquely critical role in the production and implications of knowledge-power relation for Poststructuralism whose main concern is to unfold how particular subjects are empowered while others are subjugated and how particular issues are prioritized while others are marginalized. It is possible to outline discourses as both linguistic and non-linguistic systems which determine the confines, the rules, as well as the reflections and outcomes of knowledge rather than what knowledge actually is. Though language appears to be the primary medium to make sense of social world, means other than language in the form of representations and symbols also take part in construing subjects and events in the social environment. It is recognized that reality is mediated by modes of representations, however, representations have an even deeper critical role since "[they] are not descriptions of world of facticity, but are ways of making facticity" (Shapiro, 1989, pp. 13–14). The pre-formed properties of subjects that supposedly shape the observed practices and at the end what we see as reality engender a misconception with regard to the relationship between the representation(s) and reality. Turning upside down this relationship and interrogating how the representations contribute to the formulation of reality involving the subject properties is a major step in emancipation *a la* Poststructuralist (Dillon, 2013, p. 21). Challenging the pre-formed properties of subjects also signifies the main difference between Critical Constructivism and Poststructuralism. It should be noticed that Critical Constructivists who express a certain degree of suspicion towards liberal assumptions and who have significant affinities with linguistic studies also look into discourses as constituting identities, and concepts such as security or sovereignty. However, the conceptions of identity, security, or national interest are Constructivist rather than Poststructuralist in that actors are granted a certain degree of agency independent of the discourse. Thus, for Critical Constructivists, identities constructed by the states are in control of the latter, while for Poststructuralists states are also constructed as subjects through discourses (Buzan and Hansen, 2009, p. 199). Poststructuralism ascribes power to discourses, not to actors using discourses, and thereby argues that the real source of power lies in the discourse which, *inter alia*, constructs particular subjects with particular identities.

Therefore, perplexing it would be to see a Poststructuralist IR scholar who would not consider it as problematic to be labelled with a particular theoretical position even though it is sorted as a Critical, Post-modern or Poststructuralist theory. The alienation from theories of IR despite the concern with how these theories construct and confine the main issues of the field should be interpreted in relation to Poststructuralism's approach to disciplines. A discipline, Foucault (1971, p. 15) states, "is a domain of objects, a set of methods, a corpus of propositions considered to be true, a play of rules and definitions, of techniques and instruments" which provides possibilities for formulating new propositions though within narrow confines. Hence, it is not that scholars with a Poststructuralist perspective are inclined to be indifferent to labelling, but their self-restraint represents a more conscious, deeper and deliberate position not to be connected to a trait which both limits and controls the confines of a discipline while at the same time empowers its practitioners and theorists. It is this theory-knowledge-power triangle which plays a crucial role in setting the Poststructuralist critique apart from other critical approaches in IR, and which brings a meta-theoretical dimension to its contribution.

6   Poststructuralist Perspectives and Research

Poststructuralism strives to unfold the power relations in a vast spectrum of areas which is not necessarily limited to conventional understanding of politics amongst nations, and which will naturally *problematize* the problems formulated by the mainstream IR. The opulent and protean research agenda with highly fragmental outlook, which is in fact matching with its challenge against the *great* texts of *grand* theories, represents an unprecedented openness and diversity distinct from mainstream IR theories. Poststructuralist interpretations on security, war and militarization (Dillon, 1996, 2008, 2009; Shapiro, 1997); political economy and development (Escobar, 1995; Ferguson, 1996; De Goede, 2005, 2006); Postcolonial politics (Doty, 1996); diplomacy (Der Derian, 1993; Constantinou and Der Derian, 2010); environmental politics (Bennett and Chaloupka, 1993; Kuehls, 1996; Dalby, 2002); UN, humanitarian intervention and international law (Grovogui, 1996; Debrix, 1999; Orford, 2003, 2006); foreign policy and national identity (Campbell, 1992, 1998; Weldes, 1999), citizenship (Cruikshank, 1999) are only examples to such diversity. In order to draw critical attention to mainstream IR theory, Poststructuralists have not only extended the scope and application of critical inquiry with new methods and techniques, but furthered the critique by incorporating intersecting relations between different domains such as film-tabloid-cartography-geopolitics-security (Debrix, 2008; Shapiro, 1997, 2009; Bleiker et al., 2013; Bleiker, 2018); security-feminism (Stern, 2006); justice and security (Shapiro, 2015) or gender-IPE (Griffin, 2007).

Poststructuralist scholars' estrangement from mainstream IR is not confined to how IR has hitherto been studied, and to what extent the conventional issues and actors have been left behind in order to propose a much more inclusive and critical overview of international affairs. Poststructuralism, as it has already been underlined, is a radical approach with a meta-theoretical insight which strives against any truth claim and any universal foundation for knowledge since knowledge of truth is regarded as contingent, contextual with an organic linkage to power games. Every text depends on a dichotomy which implicitly or explicitly imposes a hierarchy; therefore, the Poststructuralist IR scholar deconstructs the text by showing the dichotomies as well as disguised hierarchies in order not to get rid of the theory, but to reinscribe it in a totally new way (Hansen, 1997, p. 340). To set an example, Ashley (1995) interrogates how the domestic-international analogy, which represents a dichotomization of international relations-domestic politics, has been constructed through mainstream IR theories and how this privileged interpretation of international affairs – such as Hedley Bull's anarchical society concept – limits alternative constructions with its subjective agents and structural institutions in operation at the international level. Walker (1993) unravels the role of the sovereign state discourse in this dichotomization whereby states repeatedly manage to consolidate their power through ascribing identity, universality, unity, presence to the inside as opposed to outside of the state domain.

On similar lines, Weber (1995) looking into intervention practices in three different phases – the Concert of Europe, the Wilson administration, and the Reagan-Bush administration – investigates how state power has been reconstituted historically through the ambivalent relationship between the sovereignty concept and intervention. Duffield (2001), Dillon and Reid (2009) trace how the Western knowledge on war constructs non-Western *Others* with a developmental differentiation of societies. *War/truth* is a more recent conceptual and analytical framework that aims to unravel the constitutive circuits between war making, politics and society (Barkawi and Brighton, 2011; Brighton, 2013, 2019). While constructing the *Others* both to be invaded and rescued, Brighton (2019, p. 136), for example, shows how the military consumes, organizes, privileges and resources the knowledge of a variety of actors to formulate its own truth about war. Self/Other dichotomies and the ontological as well as epistemological significance of the relationality of Self and Other cannot be limited to these examples, and it extends to further studies such as of Diez's (2004) analysis on Europe and its others; Campbell's (1992) and Der Derian (2009) insights on foreign policy, terrorism, and media; or Shapiro's (2004) investigation on how indigenous subjects are constructed. Feminist Poststructuralists interrogate how IR frames raced, gendered and sexualized knowledges; how, for example, the subject "woman" is constructed through gendered discursive practices, and how the definition of "woman" leaves many out of sight as defining who the "human" is simultaneously brings forward dehumanization (See, Butler, 1993, 2011).

The Poststructuralist nuance here is that, there is no single, autonomous, or consistent concept of sovereignty as is the case with other IR concepts like domestic/international affairs, diplomacy, or anarchy, which are exemplifications of dichotomous extremes constructed through IR theory. All these dichotomies are co-existent and in fact work for the maintenance of the system which turns IR theory as a form of power politics itself (O'Loughlin, 2014, p. 16). Moreover, it is not only that the concepts do not consist of any single, autonomous, or consistent content, but that the concepts and also emotions attached to these concepts do not correspond to a linear history. Poststructuralist IR, while studying how identities are (re)produced over time through non-stable dichotomies, display that collective losses, phantasms, or traumatic memories are narrativized and reflected onto the future rather than being part of the past (Eng, Kazanjian and Butler, 2003).

7   Conclusion: A Further Critique

In the opening pages of *International Intertextual Relations*, Der Derian and Shapiro declare "[i]t is up to the reader/writer to decide if there is some wisdom [in Poststructuralism] for world politics" (der Derian and Shapiro, 1989, p. xi), which is a noteworthy reminder on the possibility of transcending the text despite the Poststructuralist premise on the interconnected nature of textual and political relations. However, it seems to be a contradiction or weakness of Poststructuralism, which in its every attempt tries to unveil the sensitivity of politics to textuality, to do very little to look upon its own textuality when trying to alert readers on the power of texts or discourses in general. This is not to claim that there is hardly any consideration on the limits of writing and how these limits might be overcomed to outreach a wider audience. Noticing the significance of developing alternative ways of writing and communicating in a disciplinary establishment that is to be challenged, Darby (2016, p. 5), for example, states that "scholarly conventions stand in the way of breaking from disciplinary moorings and taking a chance with the unorthodox."

Poststructuralism has been mainly criticized for engaging with theory for its own sake, being distanced from the concrete international realities (Halliday, 1994), or transmuting "the disillusionment of the structuralist world-view into nihilism" (Merquior, 1986, p. 238). The attacks on Poststructuralism on the pretext of its continuous critical stance without a consensual theoretical ground, a solid research agenda and methodology, accompanied by a not so uncommon estrangement of writers with such labelling notwithstanding, Poststructuralism is now seen as an alternative establishment on its own (Hansen, 1997, p. 339). Beyond its divergent ontological and epistemological assumptions, it is precisely the competency to make a difference in terms of deconstructing the power mechanisms which renders Poststructuralism not a nihilist approach. One should do justice to Foucault when he calls to our attention the fact that after writing on problems of the relationship between mental illness and psychological normality, the problem of prison, the problem of medical power, or the problem of the relationship between the sexes, things are not the same (Foucault, 1988, p. 154). The Poststructuralist analysis, *a la* Foucault, tries to find out how a particular set of practices and discourses constitute a model out of which a discipline is carved such as medicine, psychiatry or penal system. Tracing the process necessitates a precise collection of cases, which implies a meticulous empirical study of sites, locations and techniques of power. This archeological study leads to series, which then leads to models in order to discern the discontinuity and irregularity next to continuity and regularity as to who speaks, who then is silenced, what is controlled and what is left out of sight. It is one thing to recognize the significance of endeavours "that explore how representative practices (...) have come to constitute and shape political practices" (Bleiker, 2001, p. 510). It is quite another to question the success of these endeavours to reach to a wide audience and inspire as many as possible to reset their way of thinking on world politics.

Despite its not insignificant contributions to the field of IR by challenging fixated truth claims and problematizing how IR maps a particular world of actors and issues, there still seems to be a substantial space for unnoticed or disregarded subjects. Through de-centering the human and focusing on the human/non-human interactions, Calkivik (2017, p. 20) argues Poststructural research agenda will be able to address emerging political issues "such as the global ecological crisis, uncertainties, and anxieties affected by the Anthropocene, globally circulating viruses, and health epidemics" in a field which has followed the anthropocentric tradition like other disciplines, thus will continue to push the disciplinary boundaries to move beyond the human perspective. However, it is not only the problem of stretching the inclusiveness of Poststructuralism in terms of subjects or problematizations in the field, but also to open a discussion on the way such subjects and problematizations can be communicated to a wider audience through a more accessible language. Here, controversy arises in Poststructuralism's failure in its outreach to the ones who are subordinated considering its main purpose of emancipation. One cannot avoid calling

Rorty's overall warning about the philosopher's endeavour to find something larger out of space and time whether it is named as "truth" or "God", or even a "method" like deconstruction (Brassett, 2009, p. 279). If it is indeed the case that the Poststructuralist privileges the questions *what we do*, or *how we do*, over the question *why we do*, then it might be not just a timely endeavour but also an indispensable need to discuss the discourse of Poststructuralism itself beyond Poststructuralism's address to various discourses. In order to "confront and engage the hidden effects and tendencies of dogmatism and militant orthodoxy in world politics" (Roach, 2020, p. 2), an equally militant yet neither dogmatic nor orthodox strategy needs to be advanced comprising a better communication without falling into the Habermasian communicative action trap. Militancy requires convincing the masses though to convince should not imply that the message has to be formulated with the same jargon or discursive patterns which are oftentimes the very target to attack for the Poststructuralist. The type of militancy and convincing effort mentioned here entail a much more meticulous work on the so far highly philosophical and theoretical writing to be transformed into a readable and straightforward message. Only then, the Poststructuralist author talks to the reader, and only then, the Poststructuralist reader stops to be merely a reader and begins to write his/her own text.

References

Abrahamsen, R. and Williams, M. C., 2011. Privatization in practice: power and capital in the field of global security. In: E. Adler and V. Pouliot, eds. *International practices*. Cambridge: Cambridge University Press. pp. 310–331.

Ashley, R., 1981. Political realism and human interests. *International Studies Quarterly*, 25(2), pp. 204–236.

Ashley, R., 1984. The poverty of neorealism. *International Organization*, 38(2), pp. 225–286.

Ashley, R., 1995. The powers of anarchy: theory, sovereignty, and the domestication of global life. In: J. Der Derian, ed. *International theory: critical investigations*. New York: New York University Press. pp. 94–106.

Barkawi, T. and Brighton, S., 2011. Powers of war: fighting, knowledge, and critique. *International Political Sociology*, 5(2), pp. 126–143.

Barthes, R., 1981. Theory of the text. In: R. Young, ed. *Untying the text: a post-structuralist reader*. Boston: Routledge. pp. 31–47.

Barthes, R., 2010. *Roland Barthes by Roland Barthes*. New York: Macmillan.

Baudrillard, J., 1983. *Simulations*. New York: Semiotext(e).

Baudrillard, J., 2007. *Forget Foucault*. Cambridge: MIT Press.

Bennett, J. and Chaloupka, W. eds., 1993. *In the nature of things: language, politics, and the environment*. Minneapolis: University of Minnesota Press.

Bleiker, R., 2001. The aesthetic turn in international political theory. *Millennium*, 30(3), pp. 509–533.

Bleiker, R. and Chou, M., 2010. Nietzsche's style: on language, knowledge and power in international relations. In: C. Moore and C. Farrands, eds. *International relations theory and philosophy: interpretive dialogues*. London: Routledge. pp. 8–19.

Bleiker, R., Campbell, D., Hutchison, E. and Nicholson, X., 2013. The visual dehumanisation of refugees. *Australian Journal of Political Science*, 48(4), pp. 398–416.

Bleiker, R. ed., 2018. *Visual global politics*. New York: Routledge.

Brighton, S., 2013. War/truth: Foucault, Heraclitus and the hoplite Homer. *Cambridge Review of International Affairs*, 26(4), pp. 651–668.

Brighton, S., 2019. Critical war studies. In: J. Edkins, ed. *Routledge handbook of critical international relations*. New York: Routledge. pp. 129–142.

Brassett, J., 2009. Richard Rorty. In: J. Edkins and N. Vaughan-Williams, eds. *Critical theorists and international relations*. London: Routledge. pp. 278–291.

Braun, B., Schindler, S. and Wille, T., 2019. Rethinking agency in international relations: performativity, performances and actor-networks. *Journal of International Relations and Development*, 22(4), pp. 787–807.

Butler, J., 1993. *Bodies that matter: on the discursive limits of sex*. London: Routledge.

Butler, J., 2011. *Gender trouble: feminism and the subversion of identity*. London: Routledge.

Buzan, B. and Hansen, L., 2009. *The evolution of international security studies*. Cambridge: Cambridge University Press.

Calkivik, A., 2017. Poststructuralism and postmodernism in international relations. In: *Oxford research encyclopedia of international studies*. Oxford: Oxford University Press.

Campbell, D., 1992. *Writing security: United States foreign policy and the politics of identity*. Minneapolis: University of Minnesota Press.

Campbell, D., 1998. *National deconstruction: violence, identity, and justice in Bosnia*. Minneapolis: University of Minnesota Press.

Campbell, D., 2013. Poststructuralism. In: T. Dunne, M. Kurki and S. Smith, eds. *International relations theories*. Oxford: Oxford University Press. pp. 223–246.

Connolly, W., 1984. The politics of discourse. In: M. J. Shapiro, ed. *Language and politics*. New York: New York University Press.. pp. 139–167.

Constantinou, C. and Der Derian, J. eds., 2010. *Sustainable diplomacies*. New York: Palgrave Macmillan.

Cruikshank, B., 1999. *The will to empower: democratic citizens and other subjects*. New York: Cornell University Press.

Dalby, S., 2002. *Environmental security.* Vol. 20. Minneapolis: University of Minnesota Press.

Darby, P. ed., 2016. *From international relations to relations international.* London: Routledge.

Davis, C., 2004. *After poststructuralism: reading, stories and theory.* London: Routledge.

De Goede, M., 2005. *Virtue, fortune, and faith: a geneaology of finance.* Vol. 24. Minneapolis: University of Minnesota Press.

De Goede, M., 2006. *International political economy and poststructural politics.* London: Palgrave Macmillan.

De Saussure, F., 2011. *Course in general linguistics.* New York: Columbia University Press.

Debrix, F., 1999. *Re-envisioning peacekeeping: the United Nations and the mobilization of ideology.* Vol. 13. Minneapolis: University of Minnesota Press.

Debrix, F., 2008. *Tabloid terror: war, culture, and geopolitics.* New York: Routledge.

Der Derian, J., 1987. *On diplomacy: a genealogy of western estrangement.* Oxford: Blackwell.

Der Derian, J., 1993. Anti-diplomacy, intelligence theory and surveillance practice. *Intelligence and National Security,* 8(3), pp. 29–51.

Der Derian, J., 1995. A reinterpretation of realism: genealogy, semiology, dromology. In: J. Der Derian, ed. *International theory: critical investigations.* Basingstoke and London: Macmillan. pp. 363–396.

Der Derian, J., 2009. *Critical practices in international theory: selected essays.* New York: Routledge.

Der Derian, J. and Shapiro, M. J., 1989. *International/intertextual relations: postmodern readings of world politics.* Lexington, TN: Lexington Books.

Derrida, J., 1997. *Of grammatology.* Baltimore: The John Hopkins University Press.

Devetak, R., 1999. Theories, practices and postmodernism in international relations. *Cambridge Review of International Affairs,* 12(2), pp. 61–76.

Diez, T., 2004. Europe's others and the return of geopolitics. *Cambridge Review of International Affairs,* 17(2), pp. 319–335.

Dillon, M., 1996. *Politics of security: towards a political phiosophy of continental thought.* London: Routledge.

Dillon, M. and Neal, A. eds., 2008. *Foucault on politics, security and war.* New York: Palgrave Macmillan.

Dillon, M. and Reid J., 2009. *The liberal way of war: killing to make life live.* New York: Routledge.

Dillon, M., 2013. *Deconstructing international politics.* London: Routledge.

Doty, R. L., 1996. *Imperial encounters: the politics of representation in north-south relations.* Vol. 5. Minneapolis: University of Minnesota Press.

Duffield, M. R., 2001. *Global governance and the new wars: the merging of development and security.* London: Zed Books.

Duvall, R. D., and Chowdhury, A. 2011. Practices of theory. In: E. Adler and V. Pouliot eds. *International Practices*. Cambridge: Cambridge University Press. pp. 335–354.

Edkins, J., 2007. Poststructuralism. In: M. Griffiths, ed. *International relations theory for the twenty-first century: an introduction*. New York: Routledge. pp. 88–98.

Eng, D. L., Kazanjian, D. and Butler, J. eds., 2003. *Loss: the politics of mourning*. Berkeley: University of California Press.

Escobar, A., 1995. *Encountering development: the making and unmaking of the third world*. Vol. 1. Princeton: Princeton University Press.

Ferguson, J., 1996. *The anti-politics machine: 'development', depoliticization and bureaucratic power in Lesotho*. Minneapolis: University of Minnesota Press.

Foucault, M., 1971. Orders of discourse. *Social Science Information*, 10(2), pp. 7–30.

Foucault, M., 1978. *The history of sexuality, the will to knowledge*. Translated by Robert Hurley, Vol. 1. New York: Random House.

Foucault, M., 1988. *Politics, philosophy, culture: interviews and other writings, 1977–1984*. L. D. Kritzman, ed. Translated by Alan Sheridan et al. New York: Routledge.

Foucault, M., 1991. Nietzsche, genealogy, history. In: P. Rabinow, ed. *The Foucault reader*. London: Penguin, pp. 76–100.

George, J., 1994. *Discourses of global politics: a critical (re) introduction to international relations*. Boulder, CO: Lynne Rienner Publishers.

Griffin, P., 2007. Sexing the economy in a neo-liberal world order: neo-liberal discourse and the (re) production of heteronormative heterosexuality. *The British Journal of Politics and International Relations*, 9(2), pp. 220–238.

Grovogui, S. N., 1996. *Sovereigns, quasi sovereigns, and Africans: race and self-determination in international law*. Vol. 3. Minneapolis: University of Minnesota Press.

Halliday, F., 1994. *Rethinking international relations*. London: Macmillan.

Hansen, L., 1997. R. B. J. Walker and international relations: deconstructing a discipline. In: I. B. Neumann and O. Wæver, eds. *The future of international relations: masters in the making?*. London: Routledge. pp. 339–360.

Hansen, L., 2010. Poststructuralism and security. In: *Oxford Research Encyclopedia of International Studies*. Blackwell Publishing. Available at: https://oxfordre.com/inter nationalstudies/view/10.1093/acrefore/9780190846626.001.0001/acrefore-978019 0846626-e-278 [Accessed 28 November 2020].

Hansen, L., 2013. Discourse analysis, post structuralism, and foreign policy. In: S. Smith, A. Hadfield and T. Dunne, eds. *Foreign policy: theories, actors, cases*. Oxford: Oxford University Press. pp. 94–109.

Howarth, D., 2013. *Poststructuralism and after: structure, subjectivity and power*. London: Palgrave Macmillan.

Huysmans, J., 1997. James Der Derian: the unbearable lightness of theory. In: I. B. Neumann and O. Wæver, eds. *The future of international relations: masters in the making?*. London: Routledge. pp. 361–383.

Jones, R. W. ed., 2001. *Critical theory and world politics*. Boulder: Lynne Rienner Publishers.

Keohane, R. O., 1988. International institutions: two approaches. *International Studies Quarterly*, 32(4), pp. 379–96.

Kuehls, T., 1996. *Beyond sovereign territory: the space of ecopolitics*. Vol. 4. Minneapolis: University of Minnesota Press.

Lacan, J., 2005. *Ecrits: a selection*. London: Routledge.

Laclau, E. and Mouffe, C., 2001. *Hegemony and socialist strategy: towards a radical democratic politics*. London: Verso.

Lévi-Strauss, C., 2008. *Structural anthropology*. New York: Basic Books.

Maryanski, A. and Turner, J. H., 1991. The offspring of functionalism: French and British structuralism. *Sociological Theory*, 9(1), pp. 106–115.

McMorrow, A., 2017. Poststructuralism. In: S. McGlinchey, R. Walters and C. Scheinphlug, eds. *International relations theory*. Bristol: E-International Relations. pp. 56–61.

Merquior, J. G., 1986. *From Prague to Paris: a critique of structuralist and post-structuralist thought*. London: Verso.

Neal, A. W., 2009. Michel Foucault. In: J. Edkins and N. Vaughan-Williams, eds. *Critical theorists and international relations*. London: Routledge. pp. 161–170.

Nietzsche, F., 2005. Twilight of the idols, or how to philosophize with a hammer. In: A. Ridley and J. Norman, eds. *The anti-christ, ecce homo, twilight of the idols, and other writings*. Translated by J. Norman. Cambridge: Cambridge University Press. pp. 153–230.

O'Loughlin, A., 2014. *Overcoming poststructuralism: Rawls, Kratochwil and the structure of normative reasoning in international relations*. London: Palgrave Macmillan.

Orford, A., 2003. *Reading humanitarian intervention: human rights and the use of force in international law*. Vol. 30. Cambridge: Cambridge University Press.

Orford, A. ed., 2006. *International law and its others*. Cambridge: Cambridge University Press.

Roach, Steven C., 2020. Introduction to the handbook of critical international relations. In: S. C. Roach, ed. *Handbook of critical international relations*. Cheltenham Edward Elgar Publishing. pp. 1–10.

Shapiro, M. J., 1988. *The politics of representation: writing practices in biography, photography and policy analysis*. Madison: University of Wisconsin Press.

Shapiro, M. J., 1989. Textualizing global politics. In: J. Der Derian and M. J. Shapiro, eds. *International/intertextual relations: postmodern readings of world politics*. Lexington, TN: Lexington Books. pp. 11- 22.

Shapiro, M. J., 1997. *Violent cartographies: mapping cultures of war*. Minneapolis: University of Minnesota Press.

Shapiro, M. J., 2004. *Methods and nations: cultural governance and the indigenous subject*. New York: Routledge.

Shapiro, M. J., 2009. *Cinematic geopolitics*. New York: Routledge.

Shapiro, M. J., 2015. *War crimes, atrocity and justice*. Cambridge: Polity.

Stern, M., 2006. Racism, sexism, classism and much more: reading security-identity in marginalized sites. In: B. A. Ackerly, M. Stern and J. True, eds. *Feminist methodologies for international relations*. Cambridge: Cambridge University Press. pp. 174–198.

Strong, T. B., 1984. Language and nihilism: Nietzsche's critique of epistemology. In: M. J. Shapiro, ed. *Language and politics*. New York: New York University Press. pp. 81–107.

Tuathail, G. Ó., 1996. *Critical geopolitics: the politics of writing global space*. London: Routledge.

Viotti, P. R. and Kauppi, M. V., 2012. *International relations theory*. Harlow: Pearson.

Walker, R. B. J., 1987. Realism, change and international political theory. *International Studies Quarterly*, 31(1), pp. 65–86.

Walker, R. B. J., 1993. *Inside/outside: international relations as political theory*. Cambridge: Cambridge University Press.

Weber, C., 1995. *Simulating sovereignty: intervention, the state and symbolic exchange*. Cambridge: Cambridge University Press.

Weber, C., 1999. IR: the resurrection: or new frontiers of incorporation. *European Journal of International Relations*, 5(4), pp. 435–450.

Weldes, J., 1999. *Constructing national interests: The United States and the Cuban missile crisis*. Minneapolis: University of Minnesota Press.

Zehfuss, M., 2004. *Constructivism in international relations: the politics of reality*. Cambridge: Cambridge University Press.

CHAPTER 7

Postcolonial Approaches in International Relations

Mine Nur Küçük

1   Introduction

This chapter aims to introduce the postcolonial approaches in the discipline of International Relations (IR). Emerged in the 1990s as a part of the critical strand of thought, postcolonial IR approaches are considered as "the fastest growing areas of research in IR" (Sabaratnam, 2020, p. 161; Rutazibwa and Shilliam, 2018, p. 9). The chapter uses "postcolonial approaches" rather than "postcolonial theory" as postcolonialism in the discipline of IR does not refer to one singular theory but to "plurality of perspectives emerged from the different interpretations about postcolonial conditions" (Wilkens, 2017, p.2).

The name "postcolonialism" indicates that the colonialism does not end by the period of decolonization in which the formerly colonized countries became independent from the colonizing powers starting from the mid- 20th century.[1] Instead, the term postcolonialism is based on the argument that colonialism has continuously and persistently shaped the world (Chowdhry and Nair, 2002, p.11; Seth, 2013). Put differently, postcolonialism refers "to the multiple, contending and overlapping legacies of colonial rule and imperial administration that inform contemporary global politics" even though we live "in an era where, formally speaking, colonialism has mostly ended" (Rutazibwa and Shilliam, 2018, p. 1).

Following this definition, one needs to explain how colonialism is understood and defined in postcolonial IR studies. Colonialism "is a historically specific set of processes and practices associated with the expansion and conquest by European powers" which began with the conquest of Americas in 1492 and

---

1   Throughout the chapter, the terms "formerly colonized", "non-core", "Third World", "Global South", "non-West" on the one hand, and "colonizer", "core", "First World", "Global North" and/ or "West" have been used interchangeably, even though I remain cognizant of the problematic nature of these concepts and their different usage in the literature. In the chapter, while the former set of terms will refer to those parts of the world which are "less influential", "non-dominant" and/or "non-privileged" in world politics (Waever and Tickner, 2009, p. 1), the latter will refer to "Western Europe and North America" (Bilgin, 2016a, p.1).

continued with other parts of the world from Australia to Africa (Persaud and Sajed, 2018, p. 3). It is possible to identify three main characteristics of colonialism, namely capitalism, racism and knowledge production, which are interrelated with one another. Firstly, colonialism is about the capitalist economic system in that it is based on the desire for profit through using raw materials and human labor in the colonized countries. According to Persaud and Sajed (2018, p. 3) "European colonialism introduced the capitalist system as the dominant mode of production, which altered – with indelible and long-term consequences – the economic, social, cultural, and political dynamics of many societies around the world." The second characteristic of colonialism is racism. In fact, the beginnings of racism in world politics can be traced back to the start of colonialism with the conquest of Americas in the 15th century. As such, argues Shilliam (2020, p. 287), racism is a "fundamental ordering principle of world politics in that it divides humanity into a hierarchy of distinct groups" which leads to "discriminatory and exclusionary" practices. Lastly, colonialism is about a particular way of producing knowledge which enables justifications for colonial actions. Accordingly, European colonial powers have justified their domination of and violence in the colonized societies through certain representations. In these representations, Europeans attribute themselves with "all the virtues and achievements of enlightenment, such as reason, science, progress, universality, beauty, truth", while associate their others ("the Orient", "the rest", "the non-West") with "dark irrationality, superstition, backwardness, particularity, ugliness, and myth" (Ling, 2002, p.70).

According to postcolonial IR approaches, this kind of ideas and practices of "colonialism, imperialism, racism, patriarchal domination, and civilizational claims of superiority" (Persaud and Sajed, 2018, p.15) are not events of the distant past. As opposed to that, they can all be traced in our current world politics. In other words, from the postcolonial perspective "the current world system is built on multiple layers of institutions, experiences, practices, and most importantly, memories of those experiences and practices from the past" (Persaud and Sajed, 2018, p.14). For this reason, postcolonial IR approaches analyze world politics starting from both material as well as ideational legacies of colonialism, and they question the ways through which the inequalities, hierarchies, and oppressions colonialism has been generating can be overcome. These engagements also manifest themselves in postcolonial scholars' problematizations of the discipline of IR.

Postcolonial IR scholars argue that imperial and colonial structures have shaped academic knowledge and practices, including the study of world politics (Grovogui, 2010, p. 241). For them, IR "does not so much explain international politics" but it "seeks, rather to parochially celebrate and defend or promote the West as the proactive subject of, and as the highest or ideal normative referent in, world politics" (Hobson, 2012, p. 1). This has led to a situation within IR that "no disciplinary thought is possible without the filters of the Western gaze" (Grovogui, 2006, p. 5). According to Grovogui (2006, p. 6), one reason for that is related with not including memories, understandings, and interpretations of "non-Western" experience on international events. For the author, non-Western contexts are included in the disciplinary narratives and theories as long as they affect great power relations, and when they are included, they are represented as unified "traditions and cultures as deviations from Western standards" (Grovogui, 2006, p. 36).

Following these discussions, this chapter aims to present the dominant themes in postcolonial IR approaches. Before going into the details, two caveats have to be made explicit. Firstly, underscoring the dominant themes in postcolonial IR approaches will necessarily result in leaving a range of postcolonial thoughts aside. As such, the chapter confines itself to introduce the reader with the central arguments of postcolonialism as it is studied in IR. Secondly, it is necessary to underscore that postcolonial IR does not mean "non-Western IR". For postcolonial scholars "postcolonial theory is not an attempt to foster 'non-Western IR' " as "a non-Western IR would still be IR; it would mobilize the concepts and categories of IR ... but now from the viewpoint of the poor and weak nations of the world, or of the emergent but not yet hegemonic powers" (Seth, 2013, p. 2).

The remainder of the article is set up in four sections. Following this introduction, the second section presents some of the classic postcolonial thinkers and their foundational works. The third section of the chapter discusses the ways in which postcolonial IR scholars problematize both conventional as well as other critical theories which exist in the discipline. The fourth section reflects on the main arguments of the postcolonial approaches so as to reveal their distinct contributions to the discipline of IR. The last section will elaborate on the research directions of postcolonial IR scholars by looking at examples conducted through postcolonial frameworks.

2   The Classical Works of Postcolonialism

Postcolonialism did not start as a branch of IR discipline. Instead, postcolonial approaches in IR "have been shaped through borrowings from many academic disciplines, from literary studies to social history to French philosophy to psychoanalysis" (Sylvester, 2014, p.194). In addition to that, postcolonial thinking has also been influenced by "the extra-academic intellectual work" of people who were part of "the anti-racist, anti-colonial, independence and liberation struggles of the late nineteenth and twentieth centuries", such as Jawaharlal Nehru in India, Che Guevara in Cuba, Steve Biko in South Africa, Kwame Nkrumah in Ghana, and Ho Chi Minh in Vietnam (Rutazibwa and Shilliam, 2018, p. 9). Given these extensive intellectual roots of postcolonialism, it would be impossible to summarize each thinker at length. For this reason, this section aims to briefly introduce some of the most significant postcolonial thinkers whose studies in different disciplines have influenced the analyses of scholars in IR.

W. E. B. Du Bois' article namely "Worlds of Color" which was published in 1925 in the journal of *Foreign Affairs* is one of the earliest examples of the postcolonial thinking (Du Bois, 1925). In this article, Du Bois underscored the centrality of race relations in world politics, particularly in explaining the reasons of the First World War (Shilliam, 2020, p. 288). That said, it is possible to argue that postcolonial studies have mostly emerged starting from the mid-1950s. Some notable examples of early postcolonial works include Aimé Césaire's book called *Discourse on Colonialism* (Césaire, 1955) in which he "discussed the devastating impact of capitalist expansion on the colonies where raw materials and human labor were extracted under regimes of slavery, systematic violence, and ruthless exploitation from colonial societies" (Persaud and Sajed, 2018, p. 3); and Frantz Fanon's *Black Skin, White Mask* (Fanon, 1952) and *Wretched of the Earth* (Fanon, 1961) in which Fanon analyzed the mechanisms through which the colonized people were dehumanized by the colonizers, the psychological processes through which the colonized people internalized this "sense of inadequacy and backwardness" (Persaud and Sajed, 2018, p. 4); and how they can resist against this "totalizing form of violence" (Sabaratnam, 2020, p. 167).

Another foundational text in postcolonial studies is Edward Said's Orientalism which was published in 1978 (Said, 1978; Krishna, 2009, p. 80; O'Hagan, 2002, p. 185). In this book, Said revealed the ways in which "the Orient" was constructed and represented in Western knowledge by analyzing a diverse set of sources, from novels to academic writings. These representations, argued Said, were based on assigning essentialized negative characteristics, such as being backward or irrational, to the non-Western societies. It is through such representations that the West also presented itself as "superior". According to Said, such essentialized representations were not innocent in the sense that they enabled the emergence and development of imperialism and colonialism in different parts of the world. Put differently, "the discourse of Orientalism was not so much about the verifiable truth of Eastern or Oriental societies, their religions, economy, politics, languages, grammars, and texts, but rather a rhetoric of Western self-fashioning and enabling of its dominance and control over the rest of the world" (Krishna, 2009, p. 74).

Emerged in the 1980s, Subaltern Studies is considered another significant group in the genealogy of postcolonial studies. Including scholars such as Ranajit Guha and Dipesh Chakrabarty, Subaltern Studies Group has challenged the dominant and elitist historical narratives in India which are written from the perspectives of former colonial powers or local elites. Instead, Subaltern Studies offer to engage with the experiences of those people who are located at the lowest strata of Indian society (i.e. the subalterns). In other words, Subaltern Studies Group is interested in the question of "what does history and contemporary life look like when it starts from subaltern points of view, from the bottom up instead of from the top down?" (Sylvester, 2014 p. 188).

In the 1980s, postcolonial studies witnessed the interventions of women who voiced the gender aspect of colonialism. Chandra Talpade Mohanty's article "Under Western Eyes: Feminist Solidarity and Colonial Discourse" was published in 1984, where the author problematized the ways in which the "Western Feminist" misrepresented the Third World women by taking them as "traditional", "ignorant" and "backward" (Mohanty, 1984, p. 352) and treating them as a homogenous group in a way that overlooks different experiences in different Third World contexts. Gayatri Chakravorty Spivak's article "Can the Subaltern Speak?" was firstly published in 1985 (Spivak, 1988). Her answer to this question is negative as the positions of the subalterns "in a system of power relations is so marginal that their voice is simply inaudible" (Persaud and Sajed, 2018, p. 8). For Spivak, due to the dominance of Western-centric frameworks in social sciences, even the most sympathetic analysts "can reinforce neo-colonial patterns of domination, exploitation, and social erasure for the very groups they seek to free of those conditions" as "the researcher might think she or he is being attentive to the subaltern but, in fact, it might be impossible to escape making the West and its ways of understanding others the real (though hidden) subject of a subaltern study" (Sylvester, 2014, p. 191).

3   The Main Criticisms to Conventional and Critical IR Theories

As discussed above, although the postcolonial approaches in different disciplines have emerged mostly starting from the mid-20th century, postcolonialism arrived in IR in the 1990s. On the one hand, this rather late arrival can be explained with reference to the dominance of "the ahistorical conception and particular focus on the Westphalian state-system of IR theories" which resulted in "an ontological and epistemological obstacle" for engaging with postcolonial insights (Wilksens, 2017, p. 7). On the other hand, IR has been unable to account for "the role of colonialism, neocolonialism, and various postcolonial responses to colonialism and its legacies" (Inayatullah and Blaney, 2004, p. 2). This is because, suggest Inayatullah and Blaney (2004, p. 2), IR is "partly a legacy of colonialism" which shapes what kind of knowledge is produced in the field. The studies informed by postcolonial insights have started their analysis by presenting various criticisms to such obstacles and limitations generated by the conventional IR approaches. This section aims to present the contours of such critiques of postcolonial scholars. While the section mainly focuses on the problematizations of conventional theories of the discipline, it also introduces some of the criticisms levelled against other critical theories by postcolonial IR scholarship.

One of the central criticisms that postcolonial IR scholars voice against conventional theories is related with their "relative neglect of questions concerning inequality and justice" (Chowdry and Nair 2002, p. 1). This neglect is related with the centrality of "anarchy" in the analyses of conventional approaches according to which the absence of an overarching authority shapes the main dynamics in international relations. For them, world politics consist of nation-states which are "locked in competition amidst an overall milieu of anarchy" (Krishna, 2018, p. 19). What follows from this assumption is that the "national security" and "national interest" are taken to be both "the non- negotiable *sine qua non* of every state" (Krishna, 2018, p. 19) and central concepts for the discipline of IR.

Given this focus, the conventional accounts in the discipline fall short in "investigating relations of dominance and subordination in the world" (Sylvester, 2014, p. 185) and overlook the hierarchies in world politics which are shaped by colonialism and imperialism. According to postcolonial approaches, these hierarchies are shaped by (and shape) different power relations stemming from by race, class, and gender. However, since conventional accounts view power only with reference to material capabilities, they pay "no attention to the role of history, ideology, culture in shaping state power and practices in international relations" (Chowdry and Nair, 2002, p. 4). Put differently, postcolonial scholars problematize the ways in which the notion of power is understood in the conventional accounts, and relatedly, the lack of attention to ideational factors such as history and culture that shape power relations in world politics.

Another significant challenge levelled against conventional theories concerns the ontological questions of the discipline, that is the actors we consider significant when studying world politics and their characteristics. In here, two central arguments can be identified: Firstly, conventional approaches treat sovereign states (which are considered as "alike") as the main actors of world politics. This view leaves no space for considering the ways in which non-state actors shape world politics. Secondly, not all states matter in the accounts of these approaches: Great powers are the only significant actors of world politics. As Sylvester (2014, p. 194) aptly puts it:

> great powers held colonies, but those colonies were not studied as centres of power and agency unless they caused difficulties for individual great powers. The histories, peoples, and cultures of what are known as Third World countries (or countries of the South or underdeveloped countries) were all but invisible to International Relations until the 1980s.

This centrality of great powers and their security and interests in the analyses of conventional theories led to the reproduction of status quo in world politics through naturalizing the already existing relations of domination (Chowdry and Nair, 2002, p. 1) and "draw[ing] our attention away from the deeply hierarchical, racist and colonial character of the interactions between different peoples and parts of an interconnected planet" (Krishna, 2018, p. 24).

The last criticism that this section focuses on is related with the questions of epistemology, or how do we generate knowledge about the world. In here, postcolonial approaches problematize the "Eurocentric" assumptions found in the conventional theories. Postcolonial IR scholars identify and challenge different types of Eurocentrism in the discipline. Rutazibwa and Shillliam (2018, p. 2) groups them into two, namely "imaginary and methodological Eurocentrism." What they mean by "imaginary Eurocentrism" is "an inability to conceive of reality outside of a gaze that assigns superiority and exceptionality to Europe – and by extension the Global North – and a belief that it developed in isolation." Methodological Eurocentrism, on the other hand, "refers to a systematic reproduction of this bias in the chosen tools and approaches to study the 'global', favouring scholars, questions, theories and concepts derived from a (putatively) European – and 'Northern' – experience to make sense of the 'Rest' ". As a result of methodological Eurocentrism, the ideas and experiences of other people (Bilgin, 2016a) and different ways of knowing the world (Shilliam, 2011a) are neglected in the discipline.

Even though postcolonial IR scholarship shares a great deal in common with other critical theories with regards to certain epistemological, ontological and methodological understandings, it also identifies several limitations in the critical approaches of IR. For instance, in one of the earliest examples of a postcolonial IR work, Krishna problematizes poststructuralism for several reasons such as starting their analyses "from a remarkably self-contained and self-referential view of the West" and being "oblivious to the intimate dialogue between 'Western' and 'non-Western' economies, societies, and philosophies", for its preoccupation with representations at the expense of overlooking "physicalistic sense of the violence that accompanies war", and for their "postmodernist suspicion of subjectivity and agency" which might disempower "peoples that are not so advantageously placed in the global hierarchy of late capitalism" (Krishna, 1993, p. 388).

Frankfurt School IR theory has been subject to criticism for its limited engagement with material inequalities resulted from imperial structures and practices, even though the theory builds on the promotion of universal equality and justice (Gruffydd Jones, 2011, p. 50). Postcolonial IR also challenges this theory for being Eurocentric, in that its main assumptions mostly draw on the European experiences at the expense of non-European ones (Munro and Shilliam, 2011). Neo-Gramscian IR is also criticized for its neglect on the issue of race (Chowdhry and Nair, 2002), for its unidirectional approach to hegemony through which "the West" is placed at the center of world politics (Ling, 2002, p. 56), and for its disinterest on how identities other than workers "become included or affirmed as potential agents of class struggle" (Agathangelou, 2002, p. 146). Certain feminist IR approaches, especially "western feminism", are questioned for their neglect on the issues of culture and race on the one hand, and on its disinterest the issue of class, on the other (Ling, 2002; Chowdhry and Nair, 2002).

4   The Main Arguments of the Postcolonial IR Approaches

Following the criticisms of the postcolonial IR approaches to the other IR theories, this section aims to reflect on the main arguments of this scholarship so as to reveal their distinct contributions to the discipline. Here, two central contributions are highlighted: Firstly, the importance of colonial relations of power (which include material and non-material aspects) in shaping world politics, and secondly, the role and agency of actors located in the Global South for understanding international relations. Each contribution will be treated in turn.

As discussed in the previous section, the neglect of colonialism and imperialism by conventional theories in the discipline constitutes one of the most significant points of criticism to the discipline by postcolonial scholarship. By challenging this neglect, postcolonial IR scholars underscore the centrality of colonialism which has not only affected material relations between "the colonizer" and "the colonized" but also led to "psychological, social, cultural destruction" of the latter (Sabaratnam, 2020, p. 167). Put differently, colonialism created, and has continued to create, various hierarchical relations between different groups in different parts of the world. By understanding hierarchy as "deep structures of organised inequality", this scholarship suggests that "Hierarchies create the actors of world politics and/or their repertoires for action. They also produce the boundaries that define who and what belongs where in world politics" (Zarakol, 2017, p. 7).

With regards to the material type of hierarchies, think about how capitalism has shaped the colonial world: "The integration of colonial societies into capitalist circuits has permanently changed and restructured local economies with tremendous consequences both for the short term and, more importantly, for the long term" (Sajed, 2020). To understand such long-term consequences, the concept of "neo-colonialism" can be useful. First coined by Kwame Nkrumah, the anti-colonial leader of Ghana, in the 1960s; neo-colonialism refers to the continuity of economic and political suppression of the formerly colonized societies. This domination is realized via multiple different ways from the existence of military troops (such as humanitarian interventions) in formerly colonized countries to structuring of their economies (e.g. IMF's structural adjustment policies) despite they gained independence legally during the period of decolonization (Sabaratnam, 2020, p. 167). As another example, consider the issue of development and how "discourse about development-and its most recent agenda of 'good governance'- has naturalized the structures of global inequality and exploitation that were the product of European expansion and formal colonialism" (Gruffydd Jones, 2006, p. 9–10). As Gruffydd Jones (2006, p. 9) puts it, these relations show the "persistence of imperialism in its neocolonial forms" in current world politics.

From a postcolonial perspective, such hierarchies established in material (i.e. economic and military) realm do not constitute the only area where we can trace the colonial relations of power. In fact, for this scholarship there is an interconnection between such material inequalities and non-material ones, such as culture, ideas, and representations. Put differently, postcolonial IR scholars suggest that the material inequalities are enabled by certain ideational structures in world politics. For instance, as we saw in the case of Said's analyses on "orientalism", postcolonial scholars are interested in how "colonial representations of the (formerly) colonized are institutionalized as instruments and/or features of cultural dominance" (Grovogui, 2010, p. 245). According to Grovogui (2010, p. 246), one example to the persistence of such non-material structures in current world politics can be found in discourses on terrorism which emerged after 9/11 attacks. The author argues that these discourses reproduce "separate, unequal, hierarchical spheres of civilizations" by drawing boundaries between the "virtues" of "Western civilization" and "corrupted" Orient. These instances indicate the subordination of "the others" at the level of representation which, in turn, inform the policies that are conducted (such as the invasion of Iraq by the USA and others in 2003).

These hierarchical ideational structures can also be found in the discipline of IR. As we noted before, according to postcolonial scholars, IR is a Eurocentric discipline in that it positions Europe at the center of human existence (Grovogui, 2006, p. 4) and it overlooks ideas and experiences of non-Western actors in thinking conceptually about world politics (Grovogui, 2006, p. 6). For instance, by utilizing a house analogy, Agathangelou and Ling (2004, p. 35) show how the theories of IR constitute a house in which "colonial erasures, violences, and desires underwrite IR as a discipline, a source of knowledge production, and a field of politics". Following this argument, the authors underscore that postcolonial IR does not seek an acceptance into this house; rather it seeks to challenge it by interrogating how the relations of race, class, gender, and culture constitute it (Agathangelou and Ling, 2004, p. 32).

That being said, from a postcolonial perspective "the others" located in the Third World or the Global South are not passive agents who remain subordinated as a result of the material and ideational dominance of the core actors. In this sense, postcolonial IR scholars are also interested in "recovery, resistance, agency" (Chowdry and Nair, 2002, p. 15) of the non-core actors such as their struggles against the colonial domination. As such, "postcolonialism opens up possibilities for resisting dominant discourses of representation and power by framing its own 'counter-narratives'" (Chowdry and Nair 2002, p. 26).

This point about agency brings us to another significant argument of the postcolonial scholars in the discipline of IR, namely the co-constitution of world politics by core and non-core actors. Co-constitution refers to the ways in which non-core actors, together with the core ones, shape world politics despite the fact that the role of the former has been extensively overlooked in the conventional accounts. As opposed to this neglect, postcolonial IR scholars suggest that "west and non- west were produced coevally and through a dialectical relationship to each other" and therefore "everything about our material and social lives, have to be understood contrapuntally, that is, as results of global and interrelated processes that suffuse the entire world" (Krishna, 2018, p. 22).

Postcolonial IR scholars have been analyzing both the co-constitution of world politics (Barkawi, 2004; Hobson, 2004) and the knowledge about world politics (Grovogui, 2006; Shilliam, 2011a). Those scholars who study the co-constitution of our knowledge about world politics analyze how the ideas of the non-core actors shape the knowledge about world politics either by contributing or contesting it (Bilgin, 2016b, p. 174). For instance, Shilliam (2011b, p. 4) points to the "*global*, rather than European or Western, context within which knowledge of modernity has been develop" and underscores how "capitalist world market and the systems of states" as "routes into modernity" emerged as a result of the "co-constitutive processes" of imperialism and colonialism. Similarly, Seth criticizes the conventional accounts in IR (in particular the English School) according to which "the international society" emerged in Europe and then "expanded" to the different parts of the world. To challenge such arguments, Seth suggests:

> Just as the period that saw the development of capitalism coincided with colonial conquest and trade, so too did the events and processes privileged in the conventional account of IR – the peace of Augsburg and the settlement of Westphalia – roughly coincide with the subjugation and settlement of the Americas, the rise of the slave trade, the founding of the British East India Company and the Dutch East India Company, Macartney's mission to the Middle Kingdom, and so on.
>
> SETH, 2011, p. 173

In other words, it is the very processes of colonialism and imperialism, through which "the international society" and its institutions, such as the state-system, came into being and structure world politics. Seth, by underscoring the role of the non-core parts of the world contributing to these processes, challenges those studies which confine their analysis solely to Europe or "the West" by overlooking the interconnections between different parts of the world. Barkawi (2004, p. 156) makes a similar point by focusing on the practice of war as a "form of international interconnectedness". What he traces is how war transforms and shapes diverse realms from economy to culture both in core and non-core contexts.

5   The Research Directions of the Postcolonial IR Approaches

Since its inception in the 1990s, postcolonial IR scholars have been examining the central issues in world politics by mobilizing postcolonial insights. These issues include, but not limited to, globalization (Muppidi, 2004; Krishna, 2009); foreign policy (Doty, 1996); war (Barkawi, 2005); security (Barkawi and Laffey, 2006; Bilgin, 2016a); weapons of mass destruction (Biswas, 2014); international law (Grovogui, 1996), international political economy (Inayatullah and Blaney, 2004), race and racism (Anievas, Manchanda and Shilliam, 2015), intervention

(Sabaratnam, 2017), and subjecthood (Jabri, 2013). While doing so, they both provide accounts on how colonialism and imperialism have continued to shape these issue areas, what kind of challenges and resistance emerge as a response to this continuity, and how these issues are understood and experienced in different parts of the world.

Postcolonial IR scholars have been interested in the ideas, perspectives, experiences and practices of those non-core actors who have been neglected by the conventional accounts of the discipline as their analyses are "largely rooted in the experiences of the West and the North" (Smith and Tickner, 2020, p. 5). In that sense, they both point to the agency of the non-core actors in shaping world politics and discuss the different ways of thinking about the central issues in international relations from their perspectives. While doing so, different scholars engage with different kinds of sources, such as traditional worldviews as found in the Global South, the ideas of non-Western thinkers, and/or policy practices of the non-core actors.

L. H. M. Ling's book *The Dao of World Politics: Towards a post-Westphalian, Worldist International Relations* (2014) is an example of how traditional worldviews are engaged with in the postcolonial IR studies. Ling draws on "Daoist yin/yang dialectics" which

> shows two polarities-yin and yang- meeting each other in an S-shaped curve. Black represents yin, white yang. Together, they constitute the whole that is the circle. Each half of the diagram also retains within it an element of the other: a white dot in yin, a black one in yang. Each dot signifies, in postcolonial terms, the Other in the Self.
>
> LING, 2014, p. 45

Through engaging with "Daoist yin/yang dialectics" Ling highlights the existence of "Multiple Worlds" in world politics, as oppose to conventional theories which only see "Westphalian world" where liberal world order, state-centrism, and great powers prevail. Recognition of the "Multiple Worlds" is significant as it shows us how different actors in world politics constitute world politics together. In this sense, the framework offered by the "Multiple Worlds" is presenting "alternative ways of relating to and resonating with Others" (Ling, 2014, p. 22), hence making a space for thinking about world politics in a different way.

The edited volume by Robbie Shilliam, namely *International Relations and Non-Western Thought: Imperialism, Colonialism, and Investigations of Global Modernity* (2011a) is an example to the studies which look at how "non-Western" thinkers understand the central concepts and categories (such as state, power, nation) in IR. For instance, in their contribution to the volume,

Munro and Shilliam (2011) look at the Francophone Caribbean thinkers' ideas, and discuss how non-core actors understand the notion of "cosmopolitanism". By challenging the prevailing understandings of cosmopolitanism which examine the concept with reference to experiences in Europe, and problematizing the disinterest in how people in different parts of the world contribute to this concept, the authors underscore the existence of a more inclusive view on cosmopolitanism. While doing so, the authors note, their analysis does not aim

> to substitute the Caribbean for Europe as the universal representative of cosmopolitical potential. Rather, the point has been to show that not all post-national ruminations and cosmopolitical projects start within or are derived from the contested cultivation of the European self. There are other intellectual traditions that have had to make far more foundational and urgent sense of the modern self through a cosmopolitical orientation. And there might, then, be other – perhaps deeper – sources of normative power running through the making of the modern world.
>
> MUNRO and SHILLIAM, 2011, p. 176

Shampa Biswas's article " 'Nuclear Apartheid' as Political Position: Race as a Postcolonial Resource" (2001) and her book *Nuclear Desire: Power and Postcolonial Nuclear Order* (2014) are exemplifying postcolonial IR studies which analyze the practices of decision-makers in the Global South. For instance, in her article, Biswas examines India's decision to nuclearize the country in the year of 1998. By challenging the conventional explanations in IR which associate this decision with reference to "external threats", Biswas highlights the importance of "the global structural and racial hierarchies" (Biswas, 2001, p. 487–488) which shaped the decision of Indian policymakers and enabled them to justify such a decision. Accordingly, Indian decision-makers argued that there is a "nuclear apartheid" regime in world politics which refers

> to the material inequities in the distribution of global nuclear resources – inequities that are written into, institutionalized, and legitimized through some of the major arms-control treaties, creating an elite club of nuclear 'haves' with exclusive rights to maintain nuclear arsenals that are to be denied to the vast majority of nuclear 'have-nots'.
>
> BISWAS, 2001, p. 486

This regime is based on the idea according to which the actors in the Global South are not "rational" enough to have the nuclear capacities. By arguing that the country is challenging such "racialized inequitable global order", suggests Biswas, Indian government justified its nuclear policy. The author also shows the connection between this nuclear policy and Indian nationalism. Accordingly, in justifying their nuclear policy, Indian decision-makers claimed to protect the "Indian nation" which is defined with reference to Hindu nationalism. This definition represents certain groups in India, such as Muslims, as "non-Hindu others" which in turn enables exclusionary policies within the country. As such, Biswas (2001, p. 509) exposes the "mutually constitutive co-construction of racialized domestic and international hierarchical orders".

To recapitulate, reworking on the central concepts and issues in world politics starting from the ideas, experiences, and practices of people from different parts of the world has been one of the most important research directions in postcolonial IR studies. While doing so, postcolonial IR scholars continue to highlight the centrality of current forms of imperialism and colonialism in understanding world politics, the role and agency of different actors (both from the Global North and Global South) and the interconnections between them in shaping international relations, and the necessity for widening our theoretical horizons in studying how the world works.

6   Conclusion

This chapter introduced the postcolonial approaches in the discipline of IR. The chapter started with examining how the notions of colonialism and post-colonialism are understood by postcolonial IR scholarship. It then introduced some significant thinkers whose studies have influenced the postcolonial approaches in world politics. The chapter then continued with a discussion about the ways in which postcolonial IR scholars have challenged both the conventional, as well as critical, theories of IR and what kind of novel contributions they have made to the discipline. The last section of the chapter looked at the studies conducted by scholars who engage with postcolonial insights in studying world politics.

Emerged in the 1990s, postcolonial IR scholarship has become one of the most significant theoretical approaches in the field. This is not surprising given the current situation in the world where various inequalities, injustices, hierarchies, dominations and violence based on colonial outlook and practices have been maintaining to shape the lives of many people in different places. Being a theoretical approach which "made its entry into academe as the voice of the dispossessed" through providing a "discourse of those who had been stripped of their authority, culture, and history" (Darby and Paolini, 1994, p. 393), postcolonialism in IR does not only provide us with tools to understand the underlying mechanisms of hierarchies stemming from capitalism, racism, and essentialized and exclusionary knowledge claims, but also gives us cues as to how we can overcome relations of domination which emerge from these ideas and practices.

References

Agathangelou, A., 2002. Sexing globalization in international relations: migrant sex and domestic workers in Cyprus, Greece, and Turkey. In: G. Chowdhry and S. Nair, eds. 2002. *Power, Postcolonialism and International Relations: Reading Race, Gender, and Class*, London: Routledge. pp. 142–169.

Agathangelou, A. M. and Ling, L. H. M. 2004. The house of IR: From family power politics to the poisies of worldism. *International Studies Review*, 6, pp. 21–49.

Anievas, A., Manchanda, N. and Shilliam, R. eds., 2015. *Race and racism in international relations*. Oxon: Routledge.

Barkawi, T., 2004. Connection and constitution: locating war and culture in globalization studies. *Globalizations*, 1, pp. 155–170.

Barkawi, T., 2005. *Globalization and war*. Lenham, MD: Rowman &Littlefield.

Barkawi, T. and Laffey, M., 2006. The postcolonial moment in security studies. *Review of International Studies*, 32 (2), pp. 329–352.

Bilgin, P., 2016a. *The international in security, security in the international*. London: Routledge.

Bilgin, P., 2016b. Unpacking "the global." In: J. Hönke and M. Müller, eds. 2016. *The Global Making of Policing: Postcolonial Perspectives*. London: Routledge, pp. 167–177.

Biswas, S., 2001. "Nuclear apartheid" as political position: race as a postcolonial resource? *Alternatives*, 26, pp. 485–522.

Biswas, S., 2014. *Nuclear desire: power and the postcolonial nuclear order*. Minneapolis: University of Minnesota Press.

Césaire, A., 1955. *Discourse on colonialism*. Translated by J. Pinkham., 2001. New York: Monthly Review Press.

Chowdhry, G. and Nair, S., 2002. Introduction: power in a postcolonial world: race, gender, and class in international relations. In: G. Chowdhry, S. Nair, eds. 2002. *Power, postcolonialism and international relations: reading race, gender, and class*. London: Routledge. pp. 1–32.

Darby, P. and Paolini, A. J., 1994. Bridging International Relations and Postcolonialism. *Alternatives: Global, Local, Political*, 19(3), pp. 371–397.

Doty, R. L., 1996. *Imperial encounters: the politics of representation in north-south relations*. Minneapolis: University of Minnesota Press.

Du Bois, W. E. B., 1925. Worlds of color. *Foreign Affairs*, 3 (3), pp. 423–44.

Fanon, F., 1952. *Black skins, white masks*. Translated by C.L. Markmann., 1967. New York: Grove Press.

Fanon, F., 1961. *The wretched of the earth*. Translated by C. Farrington., 1963. New York: Grove Press.

Grovogui, S. N., 1996. *Sovereigns, quasi sovereigns, and Africans: race and self-determination in international law*. Minneapolis: University of Minnesota Press.

Grovogui, S. N., 2006. *Beyond eurocentrism and anarchy: memories of international order and institutions*. London: Palgrave MacMillan.

Grovogui, S. N., 2010. Postcolonialism. In: T. Dunne, M. Kurki, S. Smith, eds. 2010. *International relations theories: discipline and diversity*. 2nd ed. Oxford: Oxford University Press. pp. 238–256.

Gruffydd Jones, B., 2006. Introduction: international relations, eurocentrism and imperialism. In: B. Gruffydd Jones, ed. 2006. *Decolonizing international relations*. New York: Rowman& Littlefield Publishers. pp. 1–22.

Gruffydd Jones, B., 2011. Anti-racism and emancipation in the thought and practice of Cabral, Neto, Mondlane, and Machel. In: R. Shilliam, ed. 2011. *International relations and non-western thought: imperialism, colonialism, and investigations of global modernity*. Oxon: Routledge. pp. 47–63.

Hobson, J. M., 2004. *The eastern origins of western civilization*. Cambridge: Cambridge University Press.

Hobson, J. M., 2012. *The Eurocentric conception of world politics: western international theory, 1760–2010*. Cambridge: Cambridge University Press.

Inayatullah, N. and Blaney, D. L., 2004. *International relations and the problem of difference*. London: Routledge.

Jabri, V., 2013. *The postcolonial subject: claiming politics/governing others in late modernity*. London: Routledge.

Krishna, S., 1993. The importance of being ironic: a postcolonial view on critical international relations theory. *Alternatives: Global, Local, Political*, 18(3), pp. 385–417.

Krishna, S., 2009. *Globalization and postcolonialism: hegemony and resistance in the twenty-first century*. Lanham: Rowman &Littlefield Publishers.

Krishna, S., 2018. Postcolonialism and its relevance for international relations in a globalized world. In: R. B. Persaud and A. Sajed, ed. 2018. *Race, gender, and culture in international relations: postcolonial perspectives*. Oxon: Routledge. pp. 19–34.

Ling, L. H. M., 2002. *Postcolonial international relations: conquest and desire between Asia and the West*. London: Palgrave Macmillan.

Ling, L. H. M., 2014. *The Dao of world politics: towards a post-Westphalian, worldist international relations*. London: Routledge.

Mohanty, C. T., 1984. Under western eyes: feminist scholarship and colonial discourses. *Boundry 2*, 12 (3), pp. 333–358.

Munro, M. and Shilliam, R., 2011. Alternative sources of cosmopolitanism: nationalism, universalism, and créolité in francophone Caribbean thought. In: R. Shilliam, ed.

2011. *International relations and non-western thought: imperialism, colonialism, and investigations of global modernity*. London: Routledge. pp. 159–177.

Muppidi, H., 2004. *The politics of the global*. Minneapolis: University of Minnesota Press.

O'Hagan, J., 2002. *Conceptualizing the west in international relations: from Spengler to Said*. Houndmills, Basingstoke: Palgrave.

Persaud, R. B. and Sajed, A., 2018. Introduction: race, gender, and culture in international relations. In R. B. Persaud and A. Sajed, ed. 2018. *Race, gender, and culture in international relations: postcolonial perspectives*. Oxon: Routledge. pp. 1–18.

Rutazibwa, O. U and Shilliam, R., 2018. Postcolonial politics: an introduction. In: O. Rutazibwa and R. Shilliam, eds. 2018. *Routledge handbook of postcolonial politics*. Oxon: Routledge. pp. 1–15.

Sabaratnam, M., 2017. *Decolonising intervention: international statebuilding in Mozambique*. Lanham, MD: Rowman and Littlefield.

Sabaratnam, M., 2020. Postcolonial and decolonial approaches. In: J. Baylis, S. Smith, and P. Owens, eds. 2020. *The globalization of world politics: an introduction to international relations*. 8th ed. Oxford: Oxford University Press. pp. 160–175.

Said, E., 1978. *Orientalism*. New York: Vintage Books.

Sajed, A., 2020. From the third world to the global south. *E-International Relations*, [online] Available at: < https://www.e-ir.info/2020/07/27/from-the-third-world-to-the-global-south/ > [Accessed 20 August 2020].

Seth, S., 2011. Postcolonial theory and the critique of international relations. *Millennium-Journal of International Studies*, 40 (1), pp. 167–183.

Seth, S., 2013. Introduction. In: S. Seth, ed. 2013. *Postcolonial theory and international relations: a critical introduction*. London: Routledge. pp. 1–12.

Shilliam, R. ed., 2011a. *International relations and non-western thought: imperialism, colonialism and investigations of global modernity*. London: Routledge.

Shilliam, R., 2011b. Non-Western thought and international Relations. In: R. Shilliam, ed. 2011. *International relations and non-western thought: imperialism, colonialism, and investigations of global modernity*. Oxon: Routledge. pp. 1–11.

Shilliam, R., 2020. Race in world politics. In: J. Baylis, S. Smith, and P. Owens, eds. 2020. The *globalization of world politics: an introduction to international relations*. 8th ed. Oxford: Oxford University Press. pp. 287–302.

Spivak, G. C., 1988. Can the subaltern speak? In: C. Nelson and L. Grossberg, eds. 1988. *Marxism and the interpretations of culture*. Basingstoke: Macmillan Education. pp. 271–313.

Smith, K. and Ticker, A. B., 2020. Introduction: international relations from the global south. In: A. B. Ticker and K. Smith, eds. 2020. *International relations from the global south: worlds of difference*. Oxon: Routledge. pp. 1–14.

Sylvester, C., 2014. Post-colonialism. In: J. Baylis, S. Smith, and P. Owens, eds. 2014. *The globalization of world politics: an introduction to international relations*, 6th ed. Oxford: Oxford University Press. pp. 184–197.

Waever, O. and Tickner, A. B., 2009. Introduction: geocultural epistemologies. In: A. B Tickner and O. Waever, eds. 2009. *International relations scholarship around the world*. London: Routledge. pp. 1–31.

Wilkens, J., 2017. Postcolonialism in international relations. *Oxford Research Encyclopedia of International Studies*, [online] Available at: https://oxfordre.com/ internationalstudies/view/10.1093/acrefore/9780190846626.001.0001/acrefore -9780190846626-e-101 [Accessed 05 August 2020].

Zarakol, A., 2017. Theorising hierarchies: an introduction. In: A. Zarakol, ed. 2017. *Hierarchies in world politics*. Cambridge: Cambridge University Press. pp. 1–14.

CHAPTER 8

International Political Sociology and International Relations

Neslihan Dikmen Alsancak

1 Introduction

Didier Bigo and R.B.J. Walker (2007a; 2007b) initially developed International Political Sociology (IPS) as an approach to the political sociology of the international (often capitalized and denominated by its acronym). With its increasing influence in the discipline (with its ISA section), international political sociology, as a field of study, has further evolved into an interdisciplinary intellectual project "opening up lines of inquiry and lines of thought" between other disciplines and research areas (Guillaume and Bilgin, 2017, p. 2–3).

International political sociology is not a new synthesis or a school of thought of international relations (Huysmans and Nogueira, 2012). Instead, it is an intellectual project, which problematizes disciplinary boundaries between IR and other disciplines such as sociology, political science, and criminology. It questions how these boundaries limit our understandings of power, authority, and sovereignty. In other words, "by putting at the same time, the international, the political and the social in conjunctive and disjunctive tensions, international political sociology is a mode of inquiry of the interstices" (Guillaume and Bilgin, 2017, p. 3). Thus, international political sociology as an intellectual project looks at transversal lines between disciplines, between categories, between levels of analysis, between the national and the international, agency and structure, discourse, and practice (Basaran et al., 2016).

The chapter aims to explore the contributions and main premises of international political sociology as a field of study. It begins with the historical background of international political sociology, which was initially developed as an approach to the political sociology of the international and then expanded into a field of study. As a field of study, international political sociology is influenced by different philosophical traditions and social theories, namely, relational sociology, practice theory, new materialism, and (methodological) reflexivity. Its philosophical inherence is mainly grounded on the works of Pierre Bourdieu, Michel Foucault, and Bruno Latour. The chapter, thus, focuses on the foundational assumptions in international political sociology that led

to a new opening within critical IR scholarship. Second, the study strives to figure out the main critiques developed by international political sociology. This
section focuses on "the question of the limits," which underscores those critiques of conventional understandings of international relations in IR. Third,
the chapter explains the central premises of international political sociology,
such as bordering, policing, power, authority, and sovereignty. Last, the chapter explores new research directions of this intellectual project and focuses
on its engagement with the sociology of science that can open a new research
agenda in IR and security studies in times of "post-truth."

2   The Historiography and Philosophical Underpinnings of
         International Political Sociology

The discipline of IR's self-critique of its disciplinary boundaries has been
backed before Bigo and Walker's seminal study (2007a). In the early 1990s,
R.B.J. Walker (1993) and other representatives of poststructuralist IR scholars
pointed to how the discipline's presumptions about inside/outside, domestic/
international, and the political/the international have shaped the boundaries of the discipline itself. These early studies reveal how these binaries have
shaped our understandings of limitations and possibilities of political life (for
these earlier studies, also see Ashley and Walker, 1990; George, 1994).
    Initially formulated by Didier Bigo and R.B.J. Walker (2007b) as two found-
ers of IPS (and the journal), "the problem of the international" has become
another central concern of the discipline's self-critique. This problem is the
imperative of IR discipline (itself). It makes possible IR a particular discipline
(as a policy science) since it identifies the concept of the international as an
object of study. According to Bigo and Walker (2007b), the concept of the
international is reduced to the definition of the object to be studied, and this
move is significantly related to the discipline of IR that draws boundaries and
limits of political life. Framing the international as a specific object defines the
precise boundaries of the object studied and deploys specific methodologies
to study the object. In this respect, as Bigo and Walker (2007b) note, the definition of international defines the social in terms of levels of analysis and distinct spheres of social life that make the analysis of politics possible. However,
the discipline's fragmentation of the social (fragmentation into parts rather
than relations) reduces the analysis of social structures on politics to analyse
the professionals of politics solely.
    The reduction of political sociology to the analysis of the professionals of
politics, Bigo and Walker (2007b) argue, has ramifications for IR (its drawing of

boundaries and limits of political life). Accordingly, this reduction reinforces "the capacity of the discipline to claim to be able to know about states, nations and society in its own specific way" (Bigo and Walker, 2007b, p. 729) since it is believed that the professionals are acting on behalf such states. The use of narratives of "a permanent struggle between institutions representing populations and having a specific authority over a particular territory" (Bigo and Walker, 2007b, p. 729), in turn, affirms the object and the problem of the international. The discipline actually celebrates the boundaries, limits, and borders set by the IR discipline. For instance, Waltz (1979), in his definition of theory, argues that theory should define the boundaries of the field it is studying. Bigo and Walker, thus, point to the necessity of questioning how we think about the international in relation to boundaries and limits it draws.

This questioning of the international and implications of its definition for our understandings of possibilities and limits of political life turned into a field of study by scholars' collective works. By the 2000s, a specific section has been established under International Studies Association (ISA), one of the leading associations of International Relations scholars worldwide, and essential collective works on other sub-fields such as security studies (under CASE Collective, 2006) have been done. Scholars of international political sociology are especially interested in "how to move from theorizing to the actual reconstruction of practice", how one relates theorizing as a form of practice into other forms, "and moves from academia to the world one wants to make sense of (and back)" (Bueger, 2017, p. 332).

As mentioned, earlier studies on the political sociology of the international have critically investigated how the discipline's boundaries have led to analyses of professionals of politics and their practices, which redrawn our understanding of limits and possibilities of political life, security, and politics. As a field of study, international political sociology extends this investigation of the boundaries between the political, the social, and the international by looking at everyday politics, other agents than the professionals, even non-humans. While doing that, it is interested in moving away "from -abstractions- such as the state or the international, to focus on the relational ways by which they are given a specific shape" (Guillaume and Bilgin, 2017, p. 3; see also Huysmans and Nogueira, 2012).

Due to its nature as an intellectual and collaborative project, international political sociology has been influenced by diverse sources. Based on recent writings on the field of study, this chapter identifies four key approaches to social theory that shape international political sociology's intellectual project and its philosophical assumptions. These are, namely, relational sociology, practice theory, new materialism, and (methodological) reflexivity. All these approaches have somehow poststructuralist lineages. This continuing critique of structuralism informs ontological, epistemological, and methodological assumptions of international political sociology in its dealing with the political, social, and international interstices (Huysmans and Nogeuira, 2016, p. 304–305). The remaining part of this section touches upon these four approaches and their influence on the development of international political sociology as a field of study in turn.

First, relationalism or relational sociology is one of the central philosophical underpinnings of international political sociology. Relational sociology studies social processes and relations (Emirbayer, 1997). How they study these social relations and "what precisely mean by 'social relations,' varies considerably from one relational sociologist to another" such as Pierre Bourdieu, Michel Foucault, Seyla Benhabib, Bruno Latour (Powell and Depelteau, 2013, p.1). For relational perspectives, "it is the relations between agents that permit us to understand their practices and what constitutes and transform their identities" (Basaran et al., 2016, p. 4).

There are two essential aspects of relationalism. First, relationalism does not assume that social substances form the social world. Instead, "relationalism starts with interactions and relations and sees those interactions or relations as constitutive" (Go, 2016, p.118). This assumption is the key to relational thinking, considering Marxist thought; for instance, capital has only properties in relation to labor. Thus, relational thinking addresses the analytical bifurcation between capital and labor in Marxist thought. Second, "relationalism does not posit that the multiple relations add up to a singular system with a single logic or unchanging properties" (Go, 2016, p.120). Thus, for instance, we could not consider relational thinking of world-system analysis as an approach of relational social theory (Emirbayer, 1997) since, in the end, multiple relations between the core and the non-core ends up with a singular logic. This latter aspect of relationalism in international political sociology opens up spaces for seeing the "persistent fluidity and the ever-present possibility of change" (Go, 2016, p.120).

Second, this understanding of relational sociology has implications for analyses of the relationship between power and practices. Scholars in international political sociology argue that social power does not precede action. However, action and practice as "networks" or "fields" generate power. In other words, the distribution of power among actors does not determine their position in social relations (main or less influential actors). Instead, actors' positions in relation to each other and the relationship itself generate power of certain actors. For instance, in Bourdieu's formulation, a social field is characterized by its capacity to define what can be said about the field. His theory "studies positions of social actors in relation to each other" and "the exchanges that occur in fields, to assert authoritative knowledge, provide some structure to these relations" (Rajanam, 2017, p. 93).

There is no general theory of power in Bourdieu's analysis. Terminologies used for the analysis of the power are identified and used historically. Thus, Bourdieu's concepts of field and habitus are different from structure and agency. Instead, Bourdieu's relational approach, Bigo (2011, p. 237) notes, focuses on "the moment of the making of action and will consider the agents only when they act in relation to each other." Thus, scholars of international political sociology also question how social relations can take the form of entities like the state or the international (Rajaram, 2017, p. 92). Agents and structures are the effects of practices. Here, there is a rejection of "the attempt by the structuralist writers to discover the center or the organizing principle that enables practices" (Wight, 1999, p. 123).

Third, since there are entanglements of social, cultural, political, and economic phenomena (which are in flux and changing), these social relations are also mediated by material objects (as a socio-technical phenomenon). This understanding of materialism, called the "new materialism", has become another philosophical underpinning of international political sociology. The new materialism differs from earlier representatives such as historical materialism and feminist studies. While the latter conceives material objects, "offering some measure of firmness and durability shifting social and political worlds," the former questions "beliefs in the stability of materials" like "their human or discursive counterparts" (Schouten and Mayer, 2017, p. 309).

Influenced mainly by Bruno Latour, Actor-Network Theory (ANT) and Science and Technologies Studies (STS), some studies in international political sociology informed by the new materialism underscores "the role of non-human elements and artefacts in constituting power relations" and "the composition of the international as 'facts' "(Schouten and Mayer, 2017, p. 310). Put differently, rather than understanding social facts as things, new materialist theories "consider things as social facts" (Schouten and Mayer, 2017, p. 311). ANT questions "the social." Furthermore, it is an approach against the categorization of the social (within mainstream and critical sociology) and the assumptions of presumed social structure or social agent (with various attributes) (Law and Hassard, 1999). Thus, the entanglements of the material and social realms point to "a broader claim of the profound diversity of co-existing and competing ontologies in social worlds" (Schouten and Mayer, 2017, p. 311). Rather than the opposition between discourse and materiality, new materialism studies offer "how to move beyond the assumed material/discursive divide, to interrogate how politics is situated in (what may be called) human and non-human assemblages" (de Goede, 2017, p. 360).

A critical aspect of both practice theories and new materialism is their emphasis on the micro-politics of the everyday. These theories question, "what people actually do and say when they engage in practices such as diplomacy, war or organizing the international" (Bueger, 2017, p. 330). The emphasis on the micro-politics of the everyday is not limited to practice theories since the new materialism studies, especially those influenced by ANT, also point to the significance of the interplay between macro and micro politics. As de Goede notes, the individual and the local "are key sites where global power is practiced and where political reality is constituted" (de Goede, 2017, p. 356). For new materialism studies, thus, analysis of "the complex connections between the 'big' and the 'small' in international politics" is "indispensable to understanding the power of big issues" (de Goede, 2017, p. 356).

Fourth and last, all these social theories informing international political sociology, relational sociology, new materialism, and practice theory are faced with challenges of methodological reflexivity, as they are sceptical of disciplinary regimes of truth in knowledge production. Methodological reflexivity is the fourth philosophical underpinnings of international political sociology. According to Huysmans and Nogueira (2012, p. 1), especially emphasis on practice, "invites an epistemological stance based on reflexive scholarship." This stance critically interrogates the claims to knowledge by examining how the interaction between research objects and subjects contributes to the formation of authoritative knowledge (also see, Mutlu and Salter, 2014). In one of the examples of "reflexive empirical work on researchers" practices in international political sociology, Büger and Villumsen (2007, p. 418) "develop the notion of a dense web of practices in which scientists and politicians partake" with the help of works of Pierre Bourdieu and Bruno Latour. This study shows how US peace researchers, the Clinton government, and NATO formed a "web of democratic peace practice" during the 1990s and stabilized the democratic peace "thesis as a fact."

In international political sociology, methodological reflexivity is also related to methodological turn in the scholars' research. This turn understands methods in research as performative practices. Rather than distinguishing between methodology and methods and putting methods in second place to the debates on ontology, epistemology, and theory, this turn makes apparent knowledge and political stakes of the methods used by IR scholars (Aradau and Huysmans, 2013, p. 603). Thus, methods as "devices" and "acts" "are instruments not for creating common grounds, but for power struggles, competing enactments of worlds and/or creating disruptive positions in the worlds of international politics" (Aradau and Huysmans, 2013, p. 598). By presenting methods as devices of enactments and acts for disruption into the worlds of knowledge and politics, the authors have "shifted focus on philosophical assumptions to a focus on political effects" since methods carry with them "particular visions of politics and critique" (Aradau and Huysmans, 2013, p. 613).

With the influences of different philosophical sources, international political sociology has been developing as an interdisciplinary intellectual project. The following section interrogates the foremost critics of international political sociology against conventional IR theories and IR discipline.

3   The Main Critics Levied against the Discipline of IR

Extending its foremost critics against conventional IR approaches to a disciplinary critique, for this project, "the question of limits" is vital. The question of limits reveals the "international theories' claims about the limits of the political is a condition of possibility of its knowledge about international relations" (Huysmans and Neguiera, 2016, p. 303). International political sociology takes making limits and boundaries themselves the object of analysis. These analyses focus on boundaries (such as inside/outside distinctions) and practices that take place on boundaries and examine how these practices reconfigure the limits and possibilities of political life. Thus, international political sociology and its critiques differ from poststructuralist and constructivist IR perspectives. While pointing to these differences, this section highlights the three essential aspects of the question of limits and interstices analysis between the international, the social, and the political.

First, international political sociology "calls to go beyond the sovereignty problematique" (Huysmans and Noguiera, 2016, p. 302). Poststructuralist IR theories mainly focus on the sovereignty problematique in terms of understanding how the binaries between inside/outside constitute our views on possibilities and limits of political life (beyond the sovereign state). In addressing the boundaries of the discipline, they address "language and speech as the main site of meaning", whereas scholars of international political sociology focus on the role of "the materiality of the social" (Bueger, 2017: p. 329). International political sociology's questioning of these limits is not limited to boundaries, but also the practice of bordering itself. This move of going beyond the sovereignty problematique means "questioning practices that delimit a realm with clear boundaries as grounds for making claims about world politics" (Huysmans and Noguiera, 2016, p. 299). Accordingly, this move leads to new discussions on political authority. Due to its focus on bordering practice itself, international political sociology "offers as an alternative view of decentering of the state and the diffusion of social practices of authority" (Huysmans and Noguiera, 2016, p.302). According to Walker (2010, p. 2–3),

> (There is need for paying) greater attention to what goes on at the boundaries, borders and limits of a politics orchestrated within the international that simultaneously imagines the possibilities and impossibilities of a move across the boundaries, borders and limits distinguishing itself from some world beyond.

Walker argues that modern claims to sovereignty, its subjectification, and rearticulation occur at the boundaries of the international. Thus, "it is not only the modern sovereign state that has made it easy to affirm separations and so difficult to affirm a politics of relations but also the modern system of states" (Walker, 2010, p. 51). Put differently, the constitutive outside of the international is "the world" (Walker, 2010, p.10).

Second, unlike substantive accounts of the "international," which conceive it as an autonomous realm of state interaction in which the entities "remain fixed and unchanging throughout this interaction," international political sociology underscores that actors and entities are constituted by exchange relations (Rajaram, 2017, p. 92–93). However, international political sociology differs from IR constructivism, which also conceives entities are constituted by social relations. While the latter relies on an "individualistic understanding" of practice, which conceives practices as "purposeful activities of individuals" (Bueger, 2017, p.329), for the former, practice's indeterminacy is central (Doty, 1997). Hence, scholars of international political sociology do not only question how social relations within the international constitute entities and their identities, but also problematize how these social relations make possible the representations of an act or an actor being of the "international." Thereby, these social relations also produce the "international" itself.

As in Pierre Bourdieu's notion of the field, the international indicates a social topography. This social topography highlights that "the meaning and boundaries of social space are by no means fixed; both are determined by the way actors relate to each other... The exchanges that occur in fields, to assert authoritative knowledge, provide some structure to these relations" (Rajaram, 2017, p.93). For instance, Bigo and Walker (2007b) developed the metaphor of Mobius Ribbon from a specific topology of the Mobius strip, which frames the border as a horizon to point to the intermingled nature of "inside" and "outside." It is impossible to know on which face of the strip the one is located, inside or outside of it. However, this bordering practice itself provides the structure of the international and its politics constituted through these processes.

Third, it is also necessary to highlight where politics lies in these processes. Accordingly, Guzzini notes, "when this drawing of boundaries is related to the constitution of order and/or to the (dis)empowering of people, they constitute politics" (Guzzini, 2017, p. 373). It is not to claim that international political sociology as a field of study points to an enlarged field of politics. Instead, "by making the drawing of boundaries a potential issue of politics," international political sociology "sees in the constitution of things the potential for politics, and this across different fields" (Guzzini, 2017, p. 374). Since international political sociology is based on an open social ontology, analysis of international order points to "the power politics of constitutive processes" (Guzzini, 2017, p. 375).

4   The Main Premises of International Political Sociology

This section focuses on the central premises of international political sociology: power, authority, bordering, and policing with particular questions and cases which leading scholars of international political sociology engage with. This section starts with analyses of power and questions of authority and sovereignty. While doing that, it also examines relevant studies on bordering, policing, and surveillance in critical security studies due to the organic relationship between this field of study and security studies (Mutlu and Lüleci, 2017, p. 81).

Bourdieu's theory of domination and concept of field provide thinking tools for analyzing power in international political sociology. For this theory, there is always competition not only within the fields but also among fields (especially the political field of "the state") about the counters and borders of a field (Rajanam, 2017: p.94). According to Bigo and Madsen, "Bourdieusian encounter with the international" helps for "mapping the international in terms of unique fields" (Bigo and Madsen, 2011, p. 220–221). In his analysis of practices of power among transnational professionals in their respective fields, Bigo (2016) opens up an understanding of "international," which is analytically based on the rejection of the dichotomy between domestic and international arenas. Respectively, the author (Bigo, 2011, p. 247) questions "to what extent are the fields of power restricted to the boundaries of a national state?" and describes the international in terms of various fields of power and politics.

For Bigo, fields of transnational expertise are not limited to state boundaries and its territory. Rather, these fields of power operate in multiple contexts

in addition to the state boundaries. Depending on their historicity and relations to other fields such as the field of economic elites, or field of security
professionals, they are "reconfiguring the web of intertwined fields of power
and challenging the field of politics" (2011, p. 250). For instance, Bigo examines
the European Union and the emergence of its transnational bureaucracies.
Accordingly, for the author, these bureaucracies have gained more autonomy
from the national state governments and their effects and have functioned
along with the formers' corporatist interests. In the EU, there is de-govern-
mentalization of the national state with the differentiation between the
meetings of specialized councils of ministers and the councils of heads of
states.

Using thinking tool of "field," Bigo, with his colleagues, also developed a
sociological approach to security practices (CASE, 2006). For this approach,
the field of security offers to be attentive to the practices of security professionals. According to Bigo, there is increasing entanglement of internal and
external security since the 1970s. The boundaries between internal and external fields of security have been blurred between the enemy and the criminal,
between civil protection in the case of an emergency and civil defense in the
case of a threat. De-differentiation, thus, indicates "a redrawing of boundaries
of a field of practices which follows a different logic or a different topology,"
and for tracing this "new topology of security" (Bigo, 2001, p. 95), Bigo also
uses the metaphor of the Mobius Ribbon (Bigo, 2001, p. 97). Exploring social
exchange processes, this new topology of security includes analysis of both
non-discursive and discursive practices of (in)securitization imposed by the
configuration of the balance of social forces in the specific field of security
(Bigo, 2001, p. 99). This process of (in)securitization is central to understanding those discursive and non-discursive practices that draw the lines between
security and fear.

Using the notion of the security field; therefore, this sociological approach
to security practices makes a horizontal differentiation of the social and distinguishes the field of security from other fields that emerged in the social context.
In this sense, the security field is also a field of domination over other social
fields. Since it monopolizes the legitimate definition of insecurities in terms
of authorizing what insecurity is, the field excludes other actors who cannot
claim technocratic or expert knowledge of security (Bigo, 2000, p.197). As Bigo
underscores, "there is no process of securitization independent of a field of
security constituted by groups and institutions that authorize themselves and
that are authorized to state what security is" (Bigo, 2000, p.195). There is only
one source of authority, and this is the special knowledge and expertise of the

field. Besides, the security field is a field of power struggles among competing security agents, reflecting on security routines and practices.

The conditions of the possibility of the performativity of these security narratives and everyday practices of social agents are also "rooted in a certain form of governmentality," which is routinized practices of everyday politics in calling for freedom and democracy. In this literature, Foucault's notion of governmentality is essential because it provides an understanding that could bridge between discourse and practice. Governmentality, a neoliberal technology of power, means the ensemble of institutions, data, and analyses that makes the exercise of a specific form of power possible (Mutlu and Lüleci, 2017: p. 86). (In)securitization processes as techniques of government show that security practices are forms of governing, including liberal and illiberal practices. It shows how controls of populations are routinized and how unequal access to fundamental rights, such as creating the waiting zones in France, is a defining feature of the liberal state. Thus, security is a practice that does not protect life but rather determines which life can and should be protected (or that regulates what kind of life can be recognized as life) (Burgess, 2017, p. 235).

Another preeminent representative of international political sociology, Jef Huysmans, interrogates the securitization of free movement of persons regarding the construction of the European modality of government. This Foucauldian framework analyzes political decisions and processes related to the application of visas and databases, professional skills, and technocratic routines "that are themselves constitutive of modalities of government" (Huysmans, 2004, p. 295). By his analysis, Huysmans shows how two technologies of security governing the free movement in the EU connect "between security and freedom in everyday policy practice" (2004, p. 313–314). The first one is the externalization of security through technologies of border control. Its governing rationality is based on "judicial distinctions between legal and illegal forms of free movement" and identifies the Union as a territorial and judicial identity (Huysmans, 2004, p. 314). The second one is the internalization of security through biopolitical and statistical technology. This technology provides the development and management of a European population "through practices of monitoring and profiling 'problematic' categories of people" (Huysmans, 2004, p. 296). At the interstices of these two practices and security technologies, the EU is constructed both as a territory and a population.

Another critical study that uses Foucault's governmentality analysis in international political sociology is Mark Salter's study on airports. The author shows how this analysis of the airport problematizes the connections between the national and the international, and the domestic and the foreign. For Salter, the airport is one of the institutions where politics is enacted in particular intersections of the national, and the international wherein power and authority is diffused (Salter, 2007, p.50). It is a combination of both sovereign and governmental modes of power that the airport represents. Considering as a sovereign power, Salter notes, the airport qualifies "the rites of passage of entry into and exit from the territory of the state," and it identifies deviant subjects (Salter, 2007, p. 52). As a disciplinary and policing power of the sovereign state, the airports "contain the dangerous or risky elements of the unknown, and that render certain mobilities visible and other impossible or invisible" (Salter, 2007, p. 53). While doing that through various policies and agencies of civil aviation security, Salter underscores, the airport makes acceptance of self-policing and self-limitation of the liberties of the population possible.

Another strand of studies on power and authority in international political sociology investigates the politics of exception. In this respect, there are different ways of problematization Carl Schmitt's understanding of sovereignty and the political (Huysmans, 2008, p.167). One of these problematizations vital in understanding the issue of bordering in international political sociology is coming from Roxanne Lynn Doty's (2007) analysis on the US-Mexico border. In her study, "States of Exception on the Mexico-US Border: Security, 'Decisions,' and Civilian Border Patrols," Doty (2007) focuses on civilian border patrol groups on the US-Mexico border and their impacts on the immigration issue in the US, such as anti-immigrant movement. In her analyses, Doty notes that civilian groups' decision to patrol the border is implicated in numerous other decisions such as various local legislation or national immigration reform bills (Doty, 2007, p.125). All these decisions refer to the undocumented migrant as the enemy, which in turn gave "the intensity that is essential to the political" (Doty, 2007, p. 128) and "function to create exceptions that apply to a certain group of people within the society" (Doty, 2007, p.125).

However, different from Schmitt's notion of sovereignty and the political, for the author, first, these decisions indicate that there is no center of decision, which is sovereignty itself. Instead, there are numerous decisions made in a variety of locales. There is no crystallizing moment of decision (Doty, 2007, p.130). Thus, diffused forms of decisions indicate a different form of a sovereign in the late Western capitalist modernity due to its contradictions as well as opportunities. In this sense second, Doty also raised that one cannot say precisely who the enemy is in all these decisions. There is an ambiguity.

As an illustration, perhaps the enemy is the newly born infant whose parents are undocumented. Nevertheless, these babies are citizens of the United States and thus legally part of the "we." At the moment, representatives of the anti-immigrant movement name these babies as "enemies," they are also arguing against the members of "we" (Doty, 2007, p.132). Thus, Doty's study also indicates how "bordering" as a politics of demarcating "the relations between groups, the sovereign power, the legitimacy of institutions" (Burgess, 2017, p. 236) emerges and intertwines with the traditional geo-security meaning of borders. More importantly, as Burgess (2017, p. 236) also underscores, opening up these complex currents and relations of power underlying the politics of demarcating makes the problematization of sovereignty, race, nation, and otherness possible in analyses of international political sociology.

5   The New Theoretical Openings and Research Directions

International political sociology as a project is very fruitful in developing new theoretical openings and research directions (Huysmans and Nogueira, 2020). The inherited central concern of the project, which focuses on the transversal lines, is yet to be fully explored and continuously emerging with new forms of social relations in the political, social, and international interstices. This section focuses on the new theoretical openings and research directions in international political sociology, which are related mostly to the debates on "post-truth" regimes of knowledge and its implications for making sense of these transversal lines. Debates on "post-truth" regimes of knowledge add one more traversal line to existing ones. It is through the line between truth and non-truth, which complicates our understandings and analysis of power we face to new research questions in the field of international political sociology.

Post-truth has been defined as the word of the year 2016 by Oxford Dictionaries as "relating to or denoting circumstances in which objective facts are less influential in shaping public opinion than appeals to emotion and personal belief." With the developments of Brexit and Trump's presidency, scholars analyze "post-truth" politics for interrogating the "new" dynamics of politics shaped by fake news, conspiracy theories, and the new wave of far-right political populism. These studies mainly focus on the false dichotomy of emotions and rationality and suggest emphasizing the importance of understanding people's everyday experiences, postcolonial and feminist insights to racism and sexism, and emotions to access how truths are mobilized (Crilley, 2018). This section does not focus on "post-truth" politics and its implications for international politics. The attention, instead, will be given to the debates on scholars' role in stimulating "post-truth" regimes of knowledge, primary reflections of the discussions on "critique" (Latour, 2004) by critical IR scholars (poststructuralist and critical-emancipatory IR scholars) in general, and international political sociology as a field of study in particular. This focus also helps us to clarify the latter's approach to the critique.

In his well-known article, Bruno Latour (2004), "Why has critique run out of steam? From Matters of Fact to Matters of Concern", self-reflexively claimed that his works showing "the lack of scientific certainty inherent in the construction of facts" led to "distrust of good matters of fact" (Latour, 2004, p. 227). Dangerous extremists and conspiracy theorists, Latour argues, now use this lack of certainty. Accordingly, Latour asks what the real difference between conspiracists and critics is.

Latour's article does not only open debate within science studies but also in the discipline of International Relations recently, especially among critical IR theorists and critical security scholars discussing the implications of critique for politics and security practices. Among them, some argue for the defense of poststructuralism against Latour's self-blame claims. For instance, Crilley and Chatterjee-Doody (2019, p. 167) argue, "poststructuralism is not a dogma that demands that we all reject facts." For the authors, "the point is rather to recognise how particular ideas and practices gain the status of 'facts' or 'common sense' knowledge as a result of the way in which they are represented, abstracted or interpreted." Accordingly, for Crilley and Chatterjee-Doody, this inquiry into representations and the destabilizations of these representations reveals how structures of power and authority make "post-truth" politics possible and necessary for some groups and their political ends.

On the other side, some IR scholars specifically focus on the notion of critique in relation to its emancipatory potential. These critical IR scholars do not blame critique for the present "post-truth" politics. Instead, their emphasis is to highlight the significance of critique as a critique of ideology, especially during these post-truths. In his recent study, Schindler (2020) shows the similarities between post-truth regimes and 19th-century totalitarian regimes and their respective claims for truth (ideologies). For Schindler, in both cases, the problem is the relativization of facts, and this relativization has been shared as an ideology. The author notes that the ideology shared by "post-truth" politics combines the naturalization and the relativization of facts.

The problem with critical approaches and their limited reflection to "post-truth" times, for Schindler, is because critical scholars solely focus on critiquing the naturalization of facts and respectively de-naturalize the prevalent accounts of "facts". However, they do not engage with the relativization of facts or "the uncritical relativization of all truth claims on the other" (Schindler, 2020, p. 377). For the author, critique has to focus on these two aspects in the sense that while denaturalizing the facts, it should not lead to the uncritical relativization of all truth claims. Thus, the critical theory is aiming at pointing to the relativity of other perspectives and "moving beyond the relativity of its own standpoint to achieve a perspective on perspectives" (Schindler, 2020, p.380). By doing so, the author says, "a critique of ideology allows us to make our own knowledge of society more objective" (2020, p.390- 391).

While poststructuralist arguments focus on revealing the power structures that make particular ideas and practices as "facts" and not others, critical IR theorists with emancipatory insights point to the necessity of problematization of the relativization facts as well. Unlike these two insights to the debate on "post-truth" knowledge regimes, Aradau and Huysmans (2018), as two significant representatives of international political sociology, have questioned the role of the validity of (scientific) knowledge in line with Bourdieu's sociology of knowledge perspective.

As mentioned in the first section, methodological reflexivity and methodological turn in international political sociology also bring out new techniques and standards for gathering knowledge (reflexivity, criticality, concreteness) (also see Salter and Mutlu, 2013). However, for Aradau and Huysmans, this turn also leaves the concern for facts remained with questions of epistemology and methodology and as problems of relativization or naturalization of facts. Instead, the authors question how certain knowledge becomes credible (and not others). For inquiring into this process, they conceive "science" as a field not only limited to internal science wars (as Latour mainly focuses on) and extended to external (socio-political) struggles for claiming what credible knowledge is. Thus, rather than solely focusing on epistemological debates on what science is, for Aradau and Huysmans, interrogating the assembling of credibility is vital for the democratization of knowledge and inclusion of lay actors into knowledge production. To clarify, rather than starting with questioning the relativization and the naturalization of facts, they initially question how the field of science (its practices and relations with other fields) defines what "facts" are. Thus, what they focus on is not knowledge wars about epistemology and methodology, but the politics underlying boundaries between "science" and "non-science." Accordingly, Aradau and Huysmans (2018, p.15) underscore,

> Assembling credibility places knowledge claims within transepistemic conversations, negotiations, and disputes rather than knowledge wars. Post-truth is then not really about truth but about whether one is prepared to support a less hierarchical and more horizontal transversal practice of knowledge creation and circulation.

This brief debate on "post-truth" politics in IR indicates that the meaning of criticality, the notion, and the nature of critique in broader critical IR theories is still an apparent issue of debate. What scholars in international political sociology bring out in this debate on critique is going beyond the conversation on positivist-social constructivist epistemology (and epistemological relativity). They have done so by first inquiring into the multiplication of facts through the analysis of their assembly. Second, they investigate the validity of knowledge production by analysis of this assembling of credibility. This move, I think, opens up new questions about the role of critique, and of the intellectuals in critical IR theory in general, and about interrogating new transversal lines between human, non-human; material, ideational in the analysis of the international in particular.

6   Conclusion

This chapter has underscored the main premises and assumptions underlying international political sociology as a field of study. Not an approach to international relations, but as a critique of the discipline of IR itself (as well as disciplinary divisions in general), international political sociology has suggested transdisciplinarity. Compared to other critical IR approaches, international political sociology differs from other critical IR perspectives in three ways. First, it differs from some versions of poststructuralism in IR because international political sociology not only focuses on boundaries of the discipline but also the practice of bordering itself. Second, international political sociology differs from IR constructivism, and historical materialism, by virtue of its emphasis on transversal lines between discourse/practice, the material/the ideational, the national/the international, agency/structure as well as the political, the social, and the international. Third, while international political sociology has also emphasized the reflexivity of scholars, different from other critical approaches to IR (except feminist theories), it has focused on methods in research as performative practices. This focus interrogates and re-questions the relationship between theory and practice, lay actors, policy practitioners, and IR scholars.

Sharing the assumption on scholars' reflexivity and concerns over the debates on "post-truth" regimes of knowledge with other critical IR scholars, international political sociology also helps us reconsider the role of critique. International political sociology does not limit the debate on critique to a conversation of epistemological relativity; instead, it opens up new insights beyond the positivist and social constructivist epistemology debate. By interrogating "science" as a field, it provides new ways to rethink the relationship between knowledge, power, authority, and science.

References

Aradau, C. and Huysmans, J. 2013. Critical methods in International Relations: The politics of techniques, devices and acts. *European Journal of International Relations*, 20(3), pp. 1–24.

Aradau, C. and Huysmans, J. 2018. Assembling credibility: Knowledge, method and critique in times of 'post-truth'. *Security Dialogue*, pp. 1–19.

Ashley, R. and Walker, R. B. J. 1990, "Conclusion: Reading Dissidence/Writing the Discipline: Crisis and the Question of Sovereignty in International Studies", *International Studies Quarterly*, 34 (3): 367–416.

Basaran, T., Bigo, D., Guittet E. P. and Walker, R. B. J. 2016. Transversal Lines: An Introduction. In: T. Basaran, D. Bigo, E.P. Guittet and R.B.J. Walker eds. 2016. *International Political Sociology: Transversal Lines*. London and New York: Routledge. pp. 1–9.

Bigo, D. 2000. When Two Become One: Internal and External Securitisations in Europe. In: M. Kelstrup and M. C. Williams eds. 2000. *International Relations Theory and the Politics of European Integration, Power, Security and Community*. London: Routledge, pp. 171–204.

Bigo, D. 2001. Internal and External Security(ies): The Möbius Ribbon. In: M. Albert, Y. Lapid and D. Jacobson eds. 2001. *Identities, Borders, Orders*. Minnesota: University of Minnesota Press, pp. 91–116.

Bigo, D. 2011. Pierre Bourdieu and International Relations: Power of Practices, Practices of Power. *International Political Sociology*, 5(3), pp. 225–258.

Bigo, D. 2016. International Political Sociology: Rethinking the International Through Dynamics of Power. In: T. Basaran, D. Bigo, E.P. Guittet and R.B.J. Walker eds. 2016. *International Political Sociology: Transversal Lines*. London and New York: Routledge. pp. 24–48.

Bigo, D. and Madsen, M. R. 2011. Introduction to Symposium 'A Different Reading of the International': Pierre Bourdieu and International Studies, *International Political Sociology*, 5, pp. 219–224.

Bigo, D. and Walker, R. B. J. 2007a. "International, Political, Sociology", *International Political Sociology*, 1 (1): 1–5.

Bigo, D. and Walker, R. B. J. 2007b. Political Sociology and the Problem of the International. *Millienium-Journal of International Studies*, 35, pp. 725–739.

Bueger, C. 2017. Practice. In: X. Guillaume and P. Bilgin eds. 2017. *Routledge Handbook of International Political Sociology*. London and New York: Routledge, pp. 328–337.

Büger, C. and Villumsen, T. 2007. Beyond the gap: relevance, fields of practice and the securitizing consequences of (democratic peace) research. *Journal of International Relations and Development*, 10, pp. 417–448.

Burgess, P. J. 2017. Security studies. In: X. Guillaume and P. Bilgin eds. 2017. *Routledge Handbook of International Political Sociology*. London and New York: Routledge, pp. 233–244.

CASE Collective. 2006. Critical Approaches to Security in Europe, A Networked Manifesto. *Security Dialogue*, 37(4), pp. 443–487.

Crilley, R. 2018. Book Review Essay: International relations in the age of 'post-truth' politics. *International Affairs* 94(2): 417–425.

Crilley, R. and Chatterje-Doody, P. 2019. Security studies in the age of 'post-truth' politics: in defence of poststructuralism. *Critical Studies on security* 7(2), pp. 166–170.

De Goede, M. (2017). Afterword: transversal politics. In: X. Guillaume and P. Bilgin eds. 2017. *Routledge Handbook of International Political Sociology*. London and New York: Routledge, pp. 355–367.

Doty, R. L. 2007. States of Exception on the Mexico-U.S. Border: Security, "Decisions," and Civilian Border Patrols. *International Political Sociology*, 1(2), pp. 113–137.

Emirbayer, M. 1997. Manifesto for a Relational Sociology. *American Journal of Sociology*, 103(2), pp. 281–317.

George, J.1994. *Discourses of Global Politics: A Critical (Re)Introduction to International Relations* (Boulder, CO: Lynne Rienner Publishers).

Go, J. 2016. *Postcolonial Through and Social Theory*. Oxford: Oxford University Press.

Guillaume, X. and Bilgin, P. 2017. Introduction. In: X. Guillaume and P. Bilgin eds. 2017. *Routledge Handbook of International Political Sociology*. London and New York: Routledge, pp. 1–14.

Guzzini, S. 2017. Afterword: international political sociology, or the social ontology and power politics of process. In: X. Guillaume and P. Bilgin eds. 2017. *Routledge Handbook of International Political Sociology*. London and New York: Routledge, pp. 368–377.

Huysmans, J. 2004. A Foucauldian view on spill-over: freedom and security in the EU. *Journal of International Relations and Development*, 7, pp. 294–318.

Huysmans, J. 2008. The Jargon of Exception-On Schmitt, Agamben and the Absence of Political Society. *International Political Sociology*, 2, pp. 165–183.

Huysmans, J. and Nogueira, J. P. 2012. International Political Sociology: Opening Spaces, Stretching Lines. *International Political Sociology*, 6(1), pp. 1–3.

Huysmans, J. and Nogueira, J. P. 2016. Ten Years of IPS: Fracturing IR. *International Political Sociology*, 10(1), pp. 299–319.

Huysmans, J. and Nogueira, J. P. 2020. International Political Sociology as a Mode of Critique: Fracturing Totalities. *International Political Sociology*, doi: 10.1093/ips/olaa017, pp. 1–20.

Latour, Bruno. 2004. Why has critique run out of steam? From Matters of Fact to Matters of Concern. *Critical Inquiry* 30, pp. 225–248.

Law, John, and Hassard, John, (eds) 1999. *Actor Network Theory and After*, Oxford: Blackwell Publishers.

Mutlu, C. E. and Salter, M. B. 2014. Commensurability of research methods in critical security studies. *Critical Studies on security*, 2(3), pp. 353–355.

Mutlu, C. E. and Luleci Ç. 2017. International Political Sociology of Security Studies. In: X. Guillaume and P. Bilgin eds. 2017. *Routledge Handbook of International Political Sociology*. London and New York: Routledge, pp. 81–91.

Powell, C. and Depelteau, F. 2013. Introduction. In C. Powell and F. Depelteau eds. *Conceptualizing Relational Sociology: Ontological and Theoretical Issues*. New York: Palgrave Macmillan, pp. 1–12.

Rajaram, P. K. 2017. Sociology. In: X. Guillaume and P. Bilgin eds. 2017. *Routledge Handbook of International Political Sociology*. London and New York: Routledge, pp. 92–101.

Salter, M. B. 2007. Governmentalities of an Airport: Heterotopia and Confession. *International Political Sociology*, 1(1), pp. 49–66.

Salter, M. and Mutlu, C. E. 2013. (eds.) *Research Methods in critical security studies: An Introduction*. Abingdon: Routledge.

Schindler, S. 2020. The task of critique in times of post-truth politics. *Review of International Studies* 46(3): 376–394.

Shouten, P. and Mayer M. 2017. Materiality. In: X. Guillaume and P. Bilgin eds. 2017. *Routledge Handbook of International Political Sociology*. London and New York: Routledge, pp. 309–318.

Walker, R. B. J. 1993. *Inside/Outside: International Relations as Political Theory*. Cambridge: Cambridge University Press.

Walker, R. B. J. 2010. *After the Globe, Before the World*. Abingdon: Routledge.

Waltz, K. N. 1979. *Theory of International Politics*. Reading, MA: Addison-Wesley Publishing.

Wight, C. 1999. They Shoot Dead Horses Don't They? Locating Agency in the Agent-Structure Problematique. *European Journal of International Relations*, 5(1), pp. 109–142.

CHAPTER 9

Feminism and the Discipline of International Relations

Zeynep Arıöz

1 Introduction

As a discipline, International Relations emerged after the First World War with the motivation to prevent the re-occurrence of the war and establish peace. In the beginning, the primary purpose of the discipline of International Relations was shaped around explaining why states fight and solving the problem of instability. Therefore, international relations studies have concentrated on explaining, understanding, and predicting the behaviour of states and their interactions. During the interwar period, studies focusing on collective security and international law became widespread in order to prevent future conflicts. In this process, the League of Nations was established, and Idealism had considerable support in the beginning. Realists criticized the group they called Idealist due to their optimistic appraisal of the possibility of cooperation in international politics. In this context, the First Great Debate of the discipline was experienced between Idealists and Realists. The Second World War provided a wide area of validity to Realism, which regards conflict and anarchy as permanent elements of inter-state relations, and Realism maintained its weight in the discipline throughout the Cold War. The Realist school of thought has described the international system, in which states are positioned as the main actors, as an area of the constant power struggle in which it is not possible to achieve permanent peace. According to this traditional understanding basically shared by neo-realists, states in the anarchic international system have to rely on their own power (self-help). Uncertainty and insecurity about the intentions and actions of other states prevent cooperation, and the system creates insecurity due to its structure.

This approach presented quite appropriate arguments for analysing the behaviour of states under nuclear threat throughout the Cold War. However, it did not seem possible to explain the new unipolar and cooperative structure of international politics from a traditional perspective after the Cold War. In addition to the integration movements like in Europe, fragmentations like in the case of Yugoslavia and the USSR have changed the agenda of international politics. During this period, low-intensity conflicts that emerged in states with ethnic and/or religious identity motivation, often considered weak or failed, including non-state actors, emerged as significant threats to the stability of the international system (Kaldor, 1999; Münkler, 2005). New transnational threats, ranging from cyber-attacks to international terrorism, infectious diseases, migration and human traffic, financial crises and environmental disasters, have paved the way for new perspectives as developments inexplicable with the basic arguments of traditional approaches. Globalization has accelerated this process even more by making traditional distinctions such as inside-outside, national-international, high politics-low politics meaningless.

Traditional approaches have been criticized for failing to provide a valid theoretical framework for evaluating new threats emerging in international relations after the end of Cold War. In particular, a wave of criticism has awakened in the discipline of International Relations against neo-realism, anarchy-system, and actor-state simplification. Therefore, space has been opened in the discipline for critical theories defending the inadequacy of theories that address the world we live in as a reality and explain it and focusing on what should be.

The discipline of International Relations has been theoretically dominated by realism, pluralism, and structuralism for a long time. Regardless of their differences, traditional approaches have defended the opportunity to explain the world impartially and assumed that International Relations are appropriate to be examined through scientific methods. Critical approaches have objected to this dominant positivist method in the discipline, which argues that it is possible to make a definite distinction between reality and values, subject and object, to address the world as a reality, and to explain it objectively.

These approaches, which are generally based on Robert Cox's (1981) distinction between problem-solving and critical theories, have caused the Third Great Debate of the discipline. The Third Great Debate,[1] to which many currents of thought and many different academic groups were parties, has taken place between positivist and post-positivist methods in general. In this debate, feminism has been positioned on the post-positivist front of the critical/problem-solving theory divide, on the critical side in general. Like critical theory, postmodernism, poststructuralism, and constructivism, which struggle against traditional International Relations, feminism has also objected to the

---

1   The Great Debate is also known as the inter-paradigm debate between liberalism, realism and marxism or realism, institutionalism and structuralism. The third debate is also considered important for historical trajectory of "neo-neo debate" which is taking place between neorealism and neoliberalism (Waever, 1996).

positivist methodology of traditional international relations. Although they have had different agendas, these approaches, which are generally positioned in the third debate, have investigated for whose benefit and for what purpose knowledge is built. Many feminists have shared this post-positivist ground when examining the relationship between power and knowledge (Tickner & Sjoberg, 2013b, pp. 206–207). Feminists have aimed to bring issues such as gender, women's rights, and masculine politics that have not been included in the discipline before to the agenda of international relations and to make women's experience visible in the history of international relations. Feminist scholars have taken their points of departure from the question, "Where are women in the agenda and theoretical framework of International Relations?" The other questions posed by feminists to re-evaluate the traditional understanding of International Relations are "'What work is gender doing?' and 'What about women?'" (Zalewski, 1995, p. 341).

2   The Historiography of the Feminist IR

In comparison with other fields of social sciences, feminism has been lately included in International Relations, which is regarded to be a new discipline itself. The entry of feminism into International Relations became possible in the critical atmosphere in which the traditional assumptions of the discipline that emerged after the Cold War were opened to discussion. Although the approach was accepted as a theory of the discipline only towards the end of the 1980s, the history of feminist movements in international relations fundamentally dates back to the First World War (WWI). However, Tickner and True (2018, p. 231), who have attributed ignoring/negligence on this issue to the discipline itself, have stated that "Feminism is not a recent development in international relations; rather, it is the field of international relations that has come late to feminism."

Similar to the fundamental motivation of the IR as a discipline, the effort to understand the causes of war and seek a lasting peace has found a response in women's movements. For example, the Hague Peace Conference was held in 1915 with the participation of more than 1000 women from many countries. By focusing on the causes of war and how it could be prevented, the conference conducted studies in this respect parallel to the agenda of the discipline's first period. At that conference in the middle of the First World War, feminists posed the same question as their contemporaries, "Where are the women?" (Jane et al., 2003, p. 68). At the conference, first, the International Committee of Women for Permanent Peace (ICWPP) and then the Women's International

League for Peace and Freedom (WILPF) were established. With WILPF, international cohesion has developed among women through conferences, congresses, and correspondence (Francesca, 1998).

Although international women's movements during the Cold War were limited to a certain extent in the context of the East-West ideological conflict, the *detente* period paved the way for the inclusion of alternative agendas in international politics. In the process that started with the Helsinki Final Act of 1975 and aimed to secure fundamental human rights, primarily for Western European states, the issue of women's rights/human rights started to be discussed worldwide. In the same year, the UN organized the World Conference on Women, which focused solely on the issue of women, and the "United Nations Decade for Women" was declared. Later, the "UN Development Fund for Women/UNIFEM- and United Nations International Research and Training Institute for the Advancement of Women/INSTRAW" were established under the umbrella of the UN. International platforms have provided the ground for feminists to question national-international and public-private distinctions and work on the codification of women's rights. The CEDAW/Convention on the Elimination of All Forms of Discrimination Against Women was adopted by the United Nations General Assembly in 1979. Women's movements started to show their influence in the international arena with the Nairobi Conference in 1985. The movement was brought further with the Beijing Conference, and the Beijing Declaration and the Platform for Action were unanimously accepted by 189 countries. The Declaration is still the key global policy paper on gender equality and women's empowerment (UNWOMEN, 2020). Thorburn (2000, pp. 2–4) suggests that the UN initiatives in question and the Women and Development (WID) approaches that investigate women's experience in development in the following process and that would later turn into Gender and Development (GAD), the changing agenda of international relations after the Cold War, the development of non-governmental international women's organizations are the main factors influencing the emergence of the feminist approach in International Relations.

Publications made since the 1980s are one of the important signs that feminism has started to take place in the discipline of International Relations. During this period, the "Feminist Theory and Gender Studies" section of the International Studies Association and the Gender and IR Working Group of the British International Studies Association have facilitated the institutional recognition of feminist scholars and their studies in IR (Zalewski, 2017). In 1988, in the UK, the Millennium – Journal of International Studies, focusing on the subject of 'Women and international relations' marked the beginning of feminist writing in International Relations as a discipline. In the said journal,

Tickner (1988, pp. 429–440) criticized Morgenthau's "political realism" for being based on male-dominated human nature and thus defining a partial international policy. In the same journal, Halliday (1988, pp. 419–428) questioned the silence of discipline of IR in the face of the gender agenda that was increasingly taking place in social sciences.

Many conferences and books in the late 1980s and early 1990s created a momentum for feminist International Relations studies. Two conferences organized under the name of "Women, the State and War: What Difference Does Gender Make?" at the USC/University of Southern California in 1989 and "Gender in International Relations" at Wellesley College in 1990 are important steps in the inclusion of the feminist approach in the field of IR (Tickner & Sjoberg, 2013a, p. 10). The conference was later turned into a book edited by Peterson, and the basic concepts of IR, such as state, sovereignty, security, and anarchy, were re-evaluated through the lens of gender. Peterson (1992a, p. 1) states that "these essays not only reveal how IR is gendered but also explore the implications of that gendering." The work of Enloe entitled *Bananas, Beaches and Bases*, which was published in 1989 and takes women's experience at the centre of international politics, is regarded as a historical step, a classic for feminist IR by many authors (Wibben, 2004; Steans, 2003). Peterson (1998, p. 581) described the book as "the first major intervention of feminist international relations." According to Zalewski (2017), "this work was not 'simply' about women;" it was about "how deeply the international political system was indebted to the work of women and the working of masculinity and femininity."

Enloe (2000a) interpreted many experiences of women who were made invisible in everyday local, especially defined areas, in which they were involved sometimes as nationalist wombs, diplomat wives, foreign currency source maids, tourism workers, and sometimes as prostitutes, as both political and international actions. Enloe (2000a, p. 7) transformed the way of thinking of international relations by directing the question, "where are the women?" adapted the motto of feminism "personal is political" to the discipline and brought women visibility in international relations with the claim "the personal is international" (p. 195).

An important feminist intervention in the discipline was directed by Tickner, and she gave her first studies on the lack of gender in the analysis and gender not being generally accepted as a parameter in IR. Tickner (1992, p. 1) directed the questions, "Why are there so few women in my discipline? If I teach the field as it is conventionally defined, why are there so few readings by women to assign to my students? Why is the subject matter of my discipline so distant from women's lived experiences?" and criticized the male-dominated character of the discipline. Likewise, Sylvester (1994) conducted research on the gender-exclusive framework of IR. Using a "lens" metaphor, Peterson and Runyan (1993) provided an alternative, gendered depiction of international politics. Aforementioned first studies created the feminist literature that re-evaluates international relations through gender analysis. In addition to international panels focusing on gender and feminist approaches in international relations, and courses in mainstream IR curricula, another sign that feminism has reached international politics is the increasing number of articles in international relations journals such as Foreign Affairs, International Organization, and SAIS Review. It is possible to say that feminist international relations are now accepted and approved by the academy as a sub-discipline of the field of International Relations, although it is considered that feminism has reached the field quite late compared to other disciplines (Thorburn, 2000, pp. 1–2).

3   Main Critiques of Feminist Approach Levied Against Conventional IR Theory

Feminist academicians first directed the question "Where are the women?" to the discipline of International Relations. However, they went beyond this and started to question how women are marginalized as economic, political, and social subjects in the agenda and theoretical framework of mainstream International Relations. Feminism has suggested re-evaluating the discipline of International Relations and world politics, primarily using the gender lenses. In this context, feminist intervention "is neither just about women, nor the addition of women to male-stream constructions; it is about transforming ways of being and knowing" (Peterson, 1992b, p. 205). Within this framework, feminist IR has addressed gendered and one-sidedness in the knowledge production process as the first task. By finding the basic concepts of the discipline such as state, security, and power as given, it has aimed to show that the inferences of the white man who claims to be rational are the basis in the knowledge of these concepts. Therefore, although there are differences in approach among feminist international relations scholars, most of them have positioned themselves in the post-positivist tradition (Tickner, 1997, p. 614).

Feminist IR started analysis with the criticism of the basic concepts and preconceptions of the International Relations discipline. This brought about the questioning of the basic assumptions of the Realist theory, which had dominated the discipline for a long time. Feminist criticism first showed the gendered nature of the basic concepts in Realist theory and suggested that realism constructs male-dominated roles as the foundation of political identity

(Steans, 1998, p. 39). In the traditional approach, the behaviour of states has been conceptualized largely based on ideas about 'human nature.' According to feminists, the rational person on which traditional approaches that have dominated International Relations for a long time are based is elite, white, and male. For example, human nature assumptions in the works of Morgenthau and Hobbes were actually based on male nature. In these works, which constitute the traditional story of international politics, it was accepted that the gender which runs the state and holds power is always male. This rhetoric associates danger with outside which was described with feminine expressions, and the discourse was based on gendered assumptions and dual distinctions from the very beginning (Tickner, 1999, pp. 44–47). Within this framework, another important classic of the field, the book of Waltz "Man, the State and War," is true to its name. Zalewski (2013, p. 98) asks a provocative question, "If a book titled Woman, State and War was written in the same year as Waltz's Man, State and War, what are its chances of claiming uncontested status half a century later in IR theory?"

Many feminists have aimed to show the need for gender analysis and reveal the place of women in international relations by indicating the absence of women and gender in International Relations with similar questions. Secondly, they have investigated how the discipline developed a masculine attitude, within the roots of International Relations, and the construction of knowledge (Stancich, 1998, p. 4). According to the feminist approach that aims to reveal the gendered dimensions of the discipline, the language used by traditional International Relations when defining the basic concepts is excluding women and their experiences. With its focus on real politics and high politics of war, the Western International Relations theorisation privileges issues consisting of men's experience. Characteristics such as power, endurance, autonomy, independence, and rationality have usually been associated with men and masculinity, and a correct international policy has been associated with these characteristics (Tickner, 1992, pp. 1–4). Feminists have explained this division with the concept of "gender," which they have defined as a socially and culturally constructed variable group, in which characteristics such as power, autonomy, rationality, and the public sphere are symbolically attributed to men and concepts such as weakness, dependence, sensuality, and the private sphere are attributed to women (Tickner, 1997, p. 614). Ultimately, human nature, through which the discipline focuses on high politics, the state, is based to explain international relations is masculine as a result of such a division. In this case, "high politics" areas such as diplomacy, war, state administration, international politics, and national security are regarded as men's domains. By attributing rationality, power, and autonomy to the state, traditional approaches have excluded or ignored women, who are defined with the opposite of these characteristics from international relations in many ways. In this context, feminists share common views at the point of seeing what is considered "mainstream" in International Relations as actually "malestream" (Youngs, 2004, p. 76).

According to the feminist approach, the discipline has been dominated by men for a long time, male scholars dominate it, and women's issues are excluded, and International Relations is patriarchal in terms of its history and practitioners as a type of relationship (Tickner & True, 2018). Many paradigms that have dominated the discipline for a long time, such as Realism, pluralism, and structuralism, have devoted themselves to seeing a certain part of the international picture ontologically and ideologically and consequently have been constrained theoretically and epistemologically (Zalewski & Enloe, 1995, p. 298). For example, traditional commentators, who have not taken the question, "Where are the women?" seriously in international relations, have not considered "the issues of femininity in the global banana trade, the tourism industry, or sweatshops" (Enloe, 2000a, p. xii). The traditional discipline of International Relations, which emphasizes war studies, has been reluctant to accept feminist intervention in particular. Thus, asking the question, "where are the women?" has become a method of dealing with International Relations in itself for feminists.

The main agenda of feminist IR is gender emancipation, which means liberating people from the pressure that prevents them from doing what they freely choose to do. While different feminisms have developed around this goal, they have common criticisms of traditional IR. Young states (2004, p. 76) that feminist analysis determines three fundamentals: The state and market are gendered in theory and practice with the masculine structure and assumptions. The conceptualization of economic and political units according to male-dominated terms ignores the contribution of women to economic and political life. The lack of attention to the gender category hides the social construction of male and female identity and roles. Based on this given area and focusing on the interaction and behaviour of states in the anarchic international environment, traditional International Relations is criticized for underestimating the picture. Enloe (2000a, p. 1) states "But if we employ only the conventional, ungendered compass to chart international politics, we are likely to end up mapping a landscape peopled only by men, mostly élite men. The real landscape of international politics is less exclusively male."

Feminists argue that Western political theory, embroidered with masculine elements from Ancient Greece to Machiavelli, dominates traditional IR focusing on understanding the behaviour of states in the international arena. Myths such as the public-private sphere distinction in the origin of Greek city-states, in which the city-state appears as a male political domain for a free, male citizen, give information about Western political theory (Pettman, 1996, p. 6). While the person in the public sphere is responsible, rational, and shares his police life, his integral citizenship, the person in the private sphere is not fully rational and shares a limited virtue. In this typology, women are completely included in the private, non-public sphere (Elshtain, 1974, pp. 456–457). This traditional understanding underlies the exclusion of women from the history of war and international relations. According to feminists, international relations ignore the entire humanity experience by putting men's experiences in a privileged position. The aim of feminists regarding International Relations is to show that the international system has a Western-centric and patriarchal structure and reveal that the discipline is a type of relationship in which marginal groups excluded from the history of the discipline are involved as well as states. Therefore, they struggle with this limited ontology by including the previously ignored experiences of particular groups such as ethnic groups, women, and children, in relation to understanding the functioning of the international system (Zalewski & Enloe, 1995, p. 295).

Another common criticism of feminist IR of traditional IR is regarding the epistemology of the discipline. Tickner (2001, p. 12) states that scientific theories claiming the impartiality of truths and universal objectivity hide a gendered epistemological tradition. The epistemology, determining what can we know and what is worth knowing, supervises our way of understanding international relations. Knowledge constructed according to dichotomies such as rational-emotional, objective-subjective, global-local, and public-private – the first is privileged and associated with masculinity, the second is associated with femininity – spontaneously reduces the value of certain types of knowledge (Tickner, 2001, p. 133). Poststructuralist feminism, in particular, focuses on and investigates the mentioned linguistic manifestations of gender and gender-based dichotomized linguistic constructions. Poststructuralists are interested in how dichotomized linguistic constructions serve to strengthen masculine dominance. Femininity and masculinity constructions legitimize the public-private distinction, and these constructions are confirmed and maintained through discourse and practices (Tickner & Sjoberg, 2013a, p. 6). Feminist IR shows that distinctions in International Relations, such as domestic-international, order-hierarchy, centre-periphery, national-international, are constructed with the same hierarchy logic.

Another fundamental criticism of feminist IR is related to the traditional security conceptualization. Security is mostly associated with power capacity in international relations. The concept of security is explained by dominance, control over physical resources and possibilities and the capacity to move these resources over others in accordance with their own will. This definition creates two sides, exercising power and submitting to power: A rational, active side that is inclined to violence due to its nature and a passive side. Based on this dichotomy, feminists have primarily questioned the premises of power and security dominated by a masculine language and certain actors. These characteristics, which are referred to as power, autonomy, competence, rationality, and realism in International Relations, are very effective in security studies. All these characteristics have been associated with masculinity (Tickner, 2004, p. 44). Within this framework, feminist IR has primarily aimed to make women visible in the field of security and to create a new security perception, including women's experience. According to feminists, it is clear that a male-dominated language prevails in studies on security in International Relations. Ollapally (2004, pp. 9–10) states that "thinking on international security has long been dominated by men in Western societies, who have tended to define the global system in Realist politico-military terms, tracing its roots to Thucydides." Traditional security positions the state as the primary actor as the provider and protector of security. It draws the distinction between national and foreign policy with sharp lines and puts national security in the top order. In their current form, Blanchard states (2003, p. 1289) that "national security discourses are typically part of the elite world of masculine high politics," because practices included in 'high' politics mostly exclude women's experiences of violence. The traditional understanding of security ignores women and positions them as objects or victims. This approach is dangerous because it strengthens the perception that women do not have control over their own lives and conceals the insecurities they experience (Riddel, 2004). Most feminists are reluctant to accept the essentialist and reductionist concept of peaceful women and aggressive men (Tickner, 1992, p. 52). If women are regarded as merely peacekeepers, this will maintain militarized masculinity and cause the exclusion of women from national security (Hooper, 2001, p. 84). Furthermore, associating women with peace will reproduce the existing distinction between the private and public sphere and limit women's experiences to the private sphere. Likewise, the preserved-protective distinction is denied by feminists. This distinction legitimizes violence while affirming men's power and dominance over women. It makes women a target. A preservation discourse creates an illusion in this sense (Sjoberg, 2006, p. 902). In this context, feminists claim that situations specific to women's experiences, such as being a refugee or a victim of rape, in international relations are not collateral damages but the result of certain strategies (Enloe, 2000b).

According to feminists, taking the state as the main point of departure for security is problematic since the state already represents certain gendered prejudices. In this context, security is always partial, according to feminists (Sylvester, 1994, p. 183). These gendered inequalities embedded in state practices are the most important threat to security, and military-oriented security policies damage women the most. Most feminists regard the military as a threat to the security of especially women and other vulnerable groups, rather than regarding the military capacity as a safeguard against external threats to the state (Stancich, 1998, p. 4; Tickner, 2001, p. 62). The traditional approach, which bases security on dichotomies such as inside-outside, protective-protected, peaceful-aggressive, and active-passive, cannot include insecurities at the micro-level in the analysis. For example, rape is often not considered in security studies as a side effect of war, not as a part of war culture. However, feminists claim that when considering the experiences of women, it is possible to see that rape is used as a deliberate means of war during the war and that rape has a long history in armed conflicts (Zalewski, 1995; Goldstein, 2001; Enloe, 2000a).

In this context, feminist criticism has focused on the taken-for-granted assumptions about epistemology and ontology of the discipline. Traditional approaches limiting international relations to inter-state relations have been criticized primarily for being Eurocentric. Tickner (1992, p. 5) states that the language used by traditional approaches to IR to develop an objective, rational, and universal theory based on ahistorical laws of human nature is based on a Western-centred historical worldview, by benefiting from the experiences of several elite men. The conceptualization of self-interested, rational and competitive "mankind" is the starting point of traditional approaches. In its current form, Peterson (1998, p. 581) defined International Relations as the study of interstate and seemingly anarchic relations dominated by Anglo and European-based male practitioners and conducted through masculine constructions such as the army and the state. Feminists have sought ways to combat the ontology of the mainstream by drawing attention to the limited ontology of international relations based on sovereign states supposed to operate in an anarchic sphere. They have opposed the traditional approach that regards the international system as a structure consisting of states, "No children are ever born, and nobody ever dies" (Tickner, 1999, p. 46). While the state has been the basic unit of the traditional International Relations, feminist IR has presented gender as the unit to be studied in international relations. In this context, feminist approaches in IR generally adopt three different ontologies: The first one is based on sex, the second one is based on gender, and the third one has started with an ontology based on both. Three separate epistemologies have accompanied this ontology, and as a result, different feminist approaches have emerged. These have generally taken place in feminist international relations as empiricist/rationalist, standpoint and postmodern (Hansen, 2010, p. 18).

3.1   *Empiricist/Rationalist Feminism*
Empiricist/rationalist feminism examines the gendered structure at the core of states and the interstate system. Within this framework, it takes the state as the central actor in empiricist/rationalist feminism, which defines International Relations as both an empirical field of application and a discipline. Empiricist/rationalist feminism regards women and men as biological empiricist categories. The research agenda has been formed on the possible effects of gender and state on each other. It basically focuses on the causes of war and foreign policy attitudes of states, and while doing this, it employs quantitative methods by adding gender to the analysis (Hansen, 2010, pp. 19–20). The approach has investigated the harmful and often destructive effects of patriarchal states and modern international relations on women's lives. Feminist experimenters have claimed that International Relations is dominated by gender blind and masculine values and paid attention to using scientific standards to investigate women's actions unacceptable in the field (Keohane, 1989, p. 248). Empiricist feminism has demonstrated through empirical research the false assumption that men's experiences can apply to both men and women in international politics and the denial or misrepresentation of women's presence in international politics (True, 2005, p. 216). Such studies have mostly shed light on the relationship between gender and development, globalization, and political economy (Newland, 1988; Waylen, 1997; Kardam, 1991).

3.2   *Standpoint Feminism*
Standpoint feminism argues that the conceptions of masculinity and feminity are socially constructed and these categories are constantly reproduced in social practices. Standpoint feminism originates from a post-Marxist tradition. It explicitly criticizes the state as a set of patriarchal practices. Its main criticism is towards the historical distinction between the public-private sphere on which the patriarchal state is based. This distinction causes women to be marginalized in political, economic, and cultural spheres (Hansen, 2010, pp. 21–23). Therefore, standpoint feminism claims that when we pay attention to the "subordinate" segment of society, we can have a more accurate understanding of how the world and its rules are functioning. The approach tries to improve our understanding of the existing practice of international relations by analysing the central concepts of International Relations influenced by the gendered constructions of international society. Standpoint feminism claims that

to develop a correct understanding of international relations, it is necessary to make the experiences of subordinate people – in this case, women in international relations – visible (Keohane, 1989, p. 245).

3.3   Postmodern Feminism

Like most contemporary feminist perspectives, postmodern feminism defines itself upon reaction to liberal feminism. Liberal feminists assume that the equality of men and women can be achieved through legal regulations. Liberals have attracted attention to the secondary position of women in global politics and focused on developing policies for the inclusion or representation of women in the policymaking process (Tickner & Sjoberg, 2013b, p. 208). According to Zalewski (1993, p. 116), liberal feminism in its current form is the most easily accepted version of feminism as the "add women and stir." However, postmodern feminism claims that the basis of discrimination against women is deeper than legal restrictions. These restrictions are in the economic, social, and cultural structure of society, and they do not end when legal restrictions are lifted. Reforms made to eliminate these restrictions will not go beyond superficial arrangements and will preserve the existing masculine structure (Tickner, 1992, pp. 14–15). They find the idea of providing equal opportunities to women in "a system created for men by men" with various arrangements/corrections inadequate and misleading. They recommend changing the basic norms for a fundamental change (Tickner & Sjoberg, 2013a, p. 6). Postmodern feminists also criticize liberal feminists for their aim to adapt women to a currently male-based system. Although most of the feminists welcome women-inclusive practices, the main problem here is the implicit acceptance of the traditional (expressed as 'malestream') agenda and is related to the acceptance of "plus, the acceptance of the standard of 'human', which is, by historical default, most often elite, white and male" (Zalewski, 2017). Postmodern feminism not only incorporates gender into international relations but suggests a rethinking of the basic assumptions and dichotomies on which the modern state is based. It draws attention to the importance of gender, femininity, and masculinity categories in the identity construction of the modern state (Walker, 1992). According to postmodern feminism, the public/private distinction causes the political marginalization of women. The similar categorical boundaries created for the nation state, which depends significantly on this distinction, continue to construct the discipline of International Relations as a masculine field. Therefore, "this perspective has refused to accept international/domestic and public/private boundaries to politics as relevant" (Hooper, 2001, pp. 219–220).

4   The Main Premises of the Feminist IR Approach

The main premises of feminist International Relations are based on the concept of gender. There are three basic approaches regarding gender and sex.
The first one is a constructivist approach that distinguishes between sex and
gender and recognizes that gender is constructed through social interaction
and changes according to context. Another one is the essentialist approach
that claims that gender behaviour originates directly from sex. Accordingly,
male and female behaviours arise from sex. Another basic approach is the discursive approach. According to it, gender is a product of discourses (Shepherd,
2010, p. 8).

Feminist IR has generally argued that there is a distinction between gender and sex. The vast majority of feminists who address gender as a socially
"constructed" element/variable act with a constructivist ontology (Locher &
Prügl, 2001). Hooper states (2001, p. 35) that "gender is neither a thing nor a
property of individual character. It is a property of collectivities, institutions,
and historical processes." According to Sylvester (1994, p. 4), "men and women
are socially constructed." Peterson indicates (1992b, p. 194) that "gender is not
"simply a trait of individuals but an institutionalized feature of social life."

As can be understood from the definitions mentioned above, the concept
of gender, in general, refers not to biological differences between men and
women but to culturally defined and shaped characteristics of masculinity
and femininity that may vary according to time and place. Feminism suggests
placing gender at the centre of this research while seeking ways to make wom-
en's experiences visible in international relations. According to the feminist
approach, gender, as the main unit of analysis, will reveal invisible experiences
in the discipline while re-analysing global politics, economy, and international
security. The feminist approach argues that many experiences that are ignored
and qualified as the private sphere to make a more accurate picture of international politics have international significance. The claim that private is polit-
ical/international makes visible many experiences that are confined to the
private sphere, ignored but essentially have an international equivalent. For
example, for the whole of the international system, the purchase and sale of
approximately three million women or young girls per year across borders and
the contribution of women working in the service sector outside of their countries to the country's economy make sense (Enloe, 2000a, p. xiii). In many jobs
that are devalued/feminized by gender hierarchies in the global economy, factories, export areas, and assembly lines, women constitute the majority of the
cheap labour force. To understand this situation, it is necessary to see the legit-
imizing internalizations created by gender. Here, "gendered division of labour"

serves to make women's work invisible and worthless. For example, women who set out to seek employment across state borders, who are mostly maids or babysitters, or who are waiting in their own countries for 'tourists' coming from outside are among the sources of its global flow. Organizations such as banks, business agencies, and airline companies also play a role in internationalizing these resources (Pettman, 2001, pp. 588–591). In international tourism, the undeniable place of prostitution in the global economy, which has become a commercial commodity, requires reopening of what is private and what is international to discussion (Steans, 1998, p. 137).

The claim that private is international also reveals the relationship between militarism, structural violence, and everyday life. The feminist approach, which tries to make this relationship visible, paves the way for re-evaluating the scope of threats to international security by removing many insecurities experienced by women during the periods of war and peace from being "private." In this context, feminism suggests a new security approach. Feminists claim that military states can pose a threat even to their own people and that people can be deprived of the most basic economic, social, and political rights and find the traditional understanding of security, which is defined on the basis of the army and military power capacities, incomplete. According to feminists, threats to security such as domestic violence, rape, poverty, and environmental degradation are just as dangerous as war (Tickner & Sjoberg, 2013b). Therefore, feminists associate achieving real security with moving away from a negative, state-centred and protection-oriented understanding of security. Within this framework, security is defined as being away from physical and structural violence. The feminist approach addresses security as a positive and emancipatory concept in the sense of the improvement of social and economic conditions. Thus, many 'private' issues representing the direct relationship between gender and security, such as camp pursuits, rape, refugees, migrant camps, and exile, which have not been considered before, are brought to the agenda of security studies. Feminists have often been positioned on the "widening" side in new security debates by adding these experiences that the traditional approach does not include in 'high' policies to the security agenda (Blanchard, 2003, p. 1292). Feminists have reconstructed security on women's experiences of violence by associating the gender lens with violence at national, international, and local levels (Hoogensen & Rottem, 2004). For example, women who have been raped and displaced during the war experience the same fear, maltreatment, and deprivation in refugee camps. This situation is a proof that violence spreads everywhere in the context of its relationship with gender and is not limited only to war. There is continuity between women's exposure to physical violence during and after the war and the hunger, poverty, health problems, and economic deprivation they experience during the 'peace' period (Cockburn, 2004).

Feminists suggest re-evaluating security by considering the nature of modern warfare. Especially the civilian-front distinction, which is the equivalent of militarism's idea of the private and public spheres in the war field, has become invalid in modern wars. During these wars, while violence is normalized as a permanent possibility, individuals lose control over their own lives, and violence occurs in many forms such as mass slaughter, rape, hunger, pillaging, enslavement, refugee camps, and exile (Münkler, 2005). The feminist approach takes many forms of violence out of the private sphere and suggests making them the subject of security. Feminists explain security by a decrease in all forms of structural violence (Tickner, 1997, p. 624). Feminists have conceptualized security as the elimination of all forms of violence with the emphasis on structural violence, emancipating individuals from social, physical, economic, and political constraints, maintaining their own control over their lives, and achieving positive peace that expresses development, not just the absence of armed conflicts.

5   The New Theoretical Openings and Research Directions

The feminist approach in International Relations has evaluated gender as a whole of certain expected behaviours and characteristics in comparison with sex. New ideas on the gender/sex distinction have been recently developed in feminist theory. Butler (2006, pp. xv, 191) argues that gender is performative. The performativity refers continuing construction of identity through "stylized repetition of acts" and "performativity is not a singular act, but a repetition and a ritual, which achieves its effects through its naturalization in the context of a body." Within this framework in which it is not possible to mention a single gender experience, it has been argued that gendered power relations exist in every period of social and political life since gender is lived and performed differently in different contexts (Tickner & Sjoberg, 2013a, p. 4). Especially poststructuralist feminists have focused on the performative and linguistic indicators of gender. Fausto (2005, p. 1495) has put forward her claim that gender and sex are not separate but co-constituted -an approach that is becoming increasingly accepted among feminists- and the claim that "our bodies physically imbibe culture."

According to feminists, gender not only expresses a difference but also reveals a hierarchical power relationship. The concept of hegemonic masculinity was proposed by Connel (1995, p.77), who claimed that this hierarchy also exists within the masculinities: "Hegemonic masculinity can be defined as the configuration of gender practice which embodies the currently accepted answer to the problem of the legitimacy of patriarchy, which guarantees (or is taken to guarantee) the dominant position of men and the subordination of women." The concept was developed to describe the ideal masculinity at the top of the power hierarchy (above both women and other men). Hegemonic masculinity characterizes the domination over both women and non-dominant types of masculinity. Maruska (2010, p. 248) brought a new interpretation to the concept of hegemonic masculinity and introduced the concept of hypermasculinity: "Hypermasculinity goes further than this (*hegemonic masculinity*) and refers to aggressive and bellicose behaviour." Maruska states (2010, p. 239) that hegemonic masculinity has started to become hypermasculine in international politics after 9/11: "in short, hypergendered behaviour is generally understood to be characterized by extreme behaviour within gender roles, brought about by a reaction to some internal or external threat." Enloe (2017, pp. 16–19) determined that the dominance of patriarchal values in international politics followed the examples of "masculinized authoritarian leadership" worldwide during this period. Enloe indicates that this shows the continuity of the patriarchal system: "It's Not All About Trump' it's about Patriarchy. It can be updated and modernized. It is stunningly adaptable."

The relationship between technology and gender roles has recently been the new area of interest of feminist approaches. The potential of cyberspace to change sex-gender stereotyping 'in-real-life' is discussed. The effects of virtual representations on gender perception are the subject of feminist research. Franklin indicates (2010, p. 340) that "not only sex-gender roles in everyday life but also political institutions, formal, informal, and 'virtual' economies, public and private spheres, and socio-cultural relations are increasingly configured by and through information and communication technologies." In this sense, virtually different genders are produced and performed in a wide range from computer game characters to virtual icons. Franklin (2010, p. 326) makes an addition to the famous slogan of Enloe in this context. "If the personal is not only political but also international then ... must also be virtual." Likewise, Rowle (2010) drew attention to the relationship of gender, which is shown through virtual representations, with popular culture and, ultimately, world politics. For example, she drew attention to how the Hollywood film industry maintains the US hegemony and the function of preserving masculine-military values through virtual representations. Cyberfeminism (Hawthorne & Klein, 1999), which evaluates the relationship between technology and gender from a radical perspective, creates new discussion areas in IR. Approaches that evaluate the results of internet technologies empowering women and their

transformative effects on social movements through gender present new theoretical expansions to international relations (Batmanghelichi & Mouri, 2017;
Stephan, 2013; Gajjala R, 1999).

Feminists have recently presented studies that reveal international relations as a feminist narrative instead of feminist criticism to create an international relations perspective on their behalf and on their own (Zalewski, 2013;
Wibben, 2011; Enloe, 2016). According to Zalewski (2010, p. 40), the question
of what the contribution of the feminist approach to international relations is
already misleading because "Feminism simply (if not uncontroversially) both
does and produces IR."

6   Conclusion

The discipline of International Relations has been resistant to gender studies from the very beginning. Prior to feminist intervention, IR as a discipline
has paid little attention to issues related to identity construction policies and
has been structured to exclude identity politics (Hooper, 2001, p. 89). However,
during the post-Cold War period, new agendas such as human rights, environment, migration, identity, culture, and gender have forced the scope of
the discipline to change. Feminists have also tried to expand this context by
asking the question, "Where are women in international relations?" Within
the framework of the third debate, feminists have criticized IR for being male-
dominated and gender-insensitive by claiming that the discipline is "highly
gendered rather than gender neutral" (Tickner, 1999, p. 45). According to the
feminist approach, the hierarchical dichotomies that dominate traditional
international relations, especially the distinction between the public and private spheres, rooted in Western political philosophy, have constructed the state
administration and international politics as male-dominated areas belonging
to males for a long time. Within this framework, the feminist intervention has
focused primarily on revealing the gendered prejudices embedded in the discipline of International Relations, making women's experience visible, and
forming a feminist theory of international relations. However, the incomplete
establishment of the feminist literature and basic distinctions within the
feminist approach prevent it from developing a common terminology. The
elusiveness of feminist epistemology causes the marginalization of feminist
approaches within the discipline. Feminist IR is criticized for remaining within
its own borders, not being able to develop a comprehensible language even on
gender issues, not being able to present concrete solutions, too much advocacy
of women, and focusing on women's experience (Stancich, 1998; Thorburn,

2000; Weber, 2005). However, the concept of gender has already proven itself as a unit of analysis that is considered nationally and internationally in the discipline of International Relations. Domestic violence, systematic rapes, violations of women's bodily integrity, violations of sexual and reproductive rights have started to be included as human rights in the UN resolutions and international conventions. The UN Security Council's decision numbered 1325 (UNSCR, 2000) and the International Criminal Court's evaluation of rape as a crime against humanity show that the gender dimension of the war is internationally acknowledged. Through feminist intervention, gender issues are freed from being marginal and are increasingly placed on the agenda of mainstream international relations.

References

Batmanghelichi, K. S. & Mouri, L., 2017. Cyberfeminism, Iranian Style: Online Feminism in Post-2009 Iran. *Feminist Media Histories,* 3(1), p. 50–80.

Blanchard, E. M., 2003. Gender, International Relations, and the Development of Feminist Security Theory. *Signs: Journal of Women in Culture and Society,* 28(4), pp. 1289–1312.

Butler, J., 2006. *Gender Trouble, Feminism and the Subversion of Identity.* London: Routledge.

Cockburn, C., 2004. The Continuum Of Violence: A Gender Perspective On War And Peace. In: W. Giles & J. Hyndman, ed. *Sites of Violence: Gender and Conflict Zones.* Berkeley: University of California Press, pp. 24–44.

Connell, R. W., 1995. *Masculinities.* Berkeley: CA: University of California Press.

Cox, R., 1981. Social Forces States and World Orders: Beyond International Relations Theory. *Millenium: Journal of International Relations,* 10(2), pp. 126–155.

Elshtain, J. B., 1974. Moral Woman and Immoral Man: A Consideration of Public Private Split and Its Political Ramification. *Politics&Society,* 4(4), pp. 453–473.

Enloe, C., 2000a. *Bananas, Beaches and Bases: Making Feminist Sense of International Politics.* London: University Of California Press.

Enloe, C., 2000b. *Maneuvers: The International Politics of Militarizing Women's Lives.* Berkeley: University of California Press.

Enloe, C., 2016. Flick of the Skirt: A Feminist Challenge to IR's Coherent Narrative. *International Political Sociology,* 10(4), p. 320–331.

Enloe, C., 2017. *The Big Push Exposing and Challenging the Persistence of Patriarchy.* Berkeley: University of California Press.

Fausto-Sterling, A., 2005. The Bare Bones of Sex: Part 1 – Sex and Gender. *Signs,* 30(2), pp. 1491–1527.

Francesca, M., 1998. Feminisms and Transnationalism. *Gender and History*, 10(3), pp. 569–580.

Franklin, M. I., 2010. Sex, Gender and Cyberspace. In: L. J. Shepherd, ed. *Gender Matters In Global Politics A feminist introduction to International Relations*. New York: Routledge, pp. 326–346.

Gajjala R, M. A., 1999. Cyberfeminism, technology, and international "development". *Gend Dev.*, 7(2), pp. 8–16.

Goldstein, S. J., 2001. *War and Gender: How Gender Shapes The War System and Vice Versa*. Cambridge: Cambridge University Press.

Halliday, F., 1988. Hidden From International Relations: Women and the International Arena. *Millennium: Journal of International Studies*, 17(3), p. 419–428.

Hansen, L., 2010. Ontologies, Epistemologies, Methodologies. In: L. J. Shepherd, ed. *Gender Matters in Global Politics a Feminist Introduction to International Relations*. New York: Routledge, pp. 17–27.

Hawthorne, S. & Klein, R., 1999. *CyberFeminism: Connectivity, Critique and Creativity*. Melbourne: Spinifex Press.

Hoogensen, G. & Rottem, S. V., 2004. Gender Identity and Subject of Security. *Security Dialogue*, 35(2), p. 155–171.

Hooper, C., 2001. *Manly States Masculinities*. New York: Columbia University Press.

Jane, A., Emily, G. B., Harriet, H. A. & Alice, H., 2003. *Women at The Hague: The International Congress of Women and Its Results*. Place of publication unknown: University of Illions Press.

Kaldor, M., 1999. *New and old Wars: Organized Violence in A Global Era*. Stanford: Stanford University Press.

Kardam, N., 1991. *Bringing Women in: Women's Issues in International Development Programs*. Place of publication unknown: Lynne Rienner Pub.

Keohane, R., 1989. International Relations Theory: Contributions of Feminist Standpoint. *Millennium*, 18(2), pp. 245–253.

Locher, B. & Prügl, E., 2001. Feminism and Constructivism: World Aparts or Sharing the Middle Ground?. *International Studies Quarterly*, 45(1), pp. 111–129.

Maruska, J. H., 2010. When are states hypermasculine?. In: L. Sjoberg, ed. *Gender and International Security*. London: Routledge, pp. 235–255.

Münkler, H., 2005. *The New Wars*. Cambridge: Polity Press.

Newland, K., 1988. From Transnational Relationships to International Relations: Women in Development and the International Decade for Women. *Millennium*, 17(3), pp. 507–516.

Ollapally, D. M., 2004. Rethinking Gender and International Security: Balancing Global and Regional Perspectives. *Indian Journal of Gender Studies*, 11(1), pp. 9–26.

Peterson, S. & Runyan, A. S., 1993. *Global Gender Issues*. Virginia:Westview Press.

Peterson, V. S., 1992a. *Gendered States: Feminist (re)visions of International Relations Theory.* Boulder& London: Lynne Rienner.

Peterson, V. S., 1992b. Transgressing Boundaries: Theories of Knowledge, Gender and International Relations. *Millennium,* 21(2), p. 183–206.

Peterson, V. S., 1998. Feminism and International Relations. *Gender and History,* 10(3), pp. 581–589.

Pettman, J. J., 1996. *Worlding Women a Feminist International Politics.* London: Routledge.

Pettman, J. J., 2001. Gender Issues. In: B. John & S. Steve, ed. *The Globalization of World Politics: an Introduction to International Relations.* New York: Oxford University Press, pp. 582–598.

Riddel, K., 2004. *Female Empowerment as a Means of Security.* Canberra, Oceanic Conference on International Studies Organising Committee.

Rowley, C., 2010. Popular Culture and the Politics of the Visual. In: L. J. Shepherd, ed. *Gender Matters In Global Politics: A Feminist Introduction to International Relation.* New York: Routledge, pp. 309–325.

Shepherd, L. J., 2010. Sex or Gender? Bodies in World Politics and Why Gender Matters. In: L. J. Shepherd, ed. *Gender Matters in Global Politics .* New York: Routledge, pp. 3–16.

Sjoberg, L., 2006. Gendered Realities of the Immunity Principle: Why Gender Analysis Needs Feminism. *International Studies Quarterly,* 50(4), pp. 889–910.

Stancich, L., 1998. Discovering Elephants and a Feminist Theory of International Relations. *Global Society,* 12(1), pp. 125–140.

Steans, J., 1998. *Gender and International Relations.* New Jersey: Rutgers University Press.

Steans, J., 2003. Engaging from the margins: feminist encounters with the mainstream of International Relations. *British Journal of Politics and International Relations,* 5(3), pp. 428–454.

Stephan, R., 2013. *Cyberfeminism and its Political Implications for Women in the Arab World.* [Online] Available at: https://www.e-ir.info/2013/08/28/cyberfeminism-and -its-political-implications-for-women-in-the-arab-world/ [Accessed 02 09 2020].

Sylvester, C., 1994. *Feminist Theory and International Relations in a Postmodern Era.* New York: Cambridge University Press.

Thorburn, D., 2000. Feminism Meets International Relations. *SAIS Review,* 20(2), pp. 1–10.

Tickner, J. A., 1992. *Gender in International Relations Feminist Perspectives on Achieving Global Security.* New York: Columbia University Press.

Tickner, J. A., 1988. Hans Morgenthau's Principles of Political Realism: A Feminist Reformulation. *Millennium – Journal of International Studies,* 17(3), pp. 429–440.

Tickner, J. A., 1997. You Just Don't Understand: Troubled Engagements between Feminists and IR Theorists. *International Studies Quarterly,* 41(4), pp. 611–632.

Tickner, J. A., 1999. Searching for the Princess? Feminist Perspectives in International Relations. *Harvard International Review*, Issue Fall, pp. 44–48.

Tickner, J. A., 2001. *Gendering World Politics Issues and Approaches in the Post-Cold War Era.* New York: Columbia University Press.

Tickner, J. A., 2004. Feminist Responses to International Security Studies. *Peace Review,* 16(1), pp. 43–48.

Tickner, J. A. & Sjoberg, L., 2013a. Introduction: International Relations through Feminist Lenses. In: J. A. Tickner & L. Sjoberg, ed. *Feminism and International Relations: Conversations about the Past, Present and Future.* London: Routledge, pp. 1–21.

Tickner, A. J. & Sjoberg, L., 2013b. Feminism. In: T. Dunne, M. Kurki & S. Smith, ed. *International Relations Theories.* New York: Oxford University Press, pp. 205–222.

Tickner, J. A. & True, J., 2018. A Century of International Relations Feminism: From World War I Women's Peace Pragmatism to the Women, Peace and Security Agenda. *International Studies Quarterly,* 62(2), p. 221–233.

True, J., 2005. Feminism. In: S. Burchill, et al. ed. *Theories of International Relations.* New York: Palgrave, pp. 213–234.

UNSCR, 2000. *Resolution 1325.* [Online] Available at: http://unscr.com/en/resolutions/doc/1325 [Accessed 06 09 2020].

UNWOMEN, 2020. *World Conferences on Women.* [Online] Available at: https://www.unwomen.org/en/how-we-work/intergovernmental-support/world-conferences-on-women [Accessed 06 09 2020].

Waever, O., 1996. The Rise and Fall of the Inter- Paradigm Debate. In: S. Smith, K. Booth & M. Zalewski, ed. *International Theory: Positivism and Beyond.* Cambridge: Cambridge University Press, pp. 149–185.

Walker, R., 1992. Gender and Critique in the Theory of International Relations. In: S. Peterson, ed. *Gendered States: Feminist (Re)Visions of International Relations Theory.* Boulder: Lynne Rienner, pp. 179–202.

Waylen, G., 1997. Analysing Women in the Politics of the Third World. *Review of Japanese Culture and Society,* Cilt 9, pp. 1–14.

Weber, C., 2005. *International Relations Theory: A Critical Introduction.* London: Roudledge.

Wibben, A. T., 2004. Feminist International Relations: Old Debate and New Directions. *The Brown Journal of World Affairs,* 10(2), pp. 97–114.

Wibben, A. T. R., 2011. *Feminist Security Studies A Narrative Approach.* New York: Routledge.

Youngs, G., 2004. Feminist International Relations: a contradiction in terms? Or: why women and gender are essential to understanding the world 'we' live in. *International Affairs,* 80(1), pp. 75–87.

Zalewski, M., 1993. Feminist Theory and International Relations. In: M. Bowker & R. Brown, ed. *From Cold War to collapse: theory and world politics in the 1980s.* Cambridge: Cambridge University Press, pp. 115–144.

Zalewski, M., 1995. Well What Is the Feminist Perspective on Bosnia. *International Affairs,* 71(2), pp. 339–356.

Zalewski, M., 2010. Feminist International Relations: Making Sense. ... In: L. J. Shepherd, ed. *Gender Matters In Global Politics A feminist introduction to International Relations.* New York: Routledge, pp. 28–43.

Zalewski, M., 2013. *Feminist International Relations 'Exquisite Corpse' (Interventions).* New York: Routledge.

Zalewski, M., 2017. Feminist Approaches To International Relations. In: P. R. H. G. Editorial, ed. *The Age of Perplexity: Rethinking the World we Knew.* Madrid: BBVA OpenMind.

Zalewski, M. & Enloe, C., 1995. Questions about Identity in International Relations. In: K. Booth & S. Smith, ed. *International Relations Theory Today.* Cambridge: Polity Press, pp. 279–305.

CHAPTER 10

Non-Western International Relations Theories

Pınar Akgül

1   Introduction

The common belief is that IR is a Western discipline (Acharya and Buzan, 2007). The problems addressed and their possible solutions are believed to be Western-oriented and so that academic production is primarily conducted by Western scholars and institutions. Deriving from the works of Western philosophers such as Hobbes and Kant, theories of realism and liberalism have become the conventional approaches of IR (Rumelili, 2014). This traditional view, however, has been questioned. According to revisionists, the story of Westphalia is a historical myth, creating a foundational basis in history for particular realist or traditional social theories (Jackson and Sørensen, 2013). Another significant criticism, which forms the foundation of this chapter, argues that Westphalia and related events built the hegemony of the West in the world politics. The traditional view glorifies Western values and generalises them as fundamental principles that every state must obey (Hobson, 2004). In other words, Western centrism establishes parochialism (Rumelili, 2014); it is unable to respond to the questions of the whole world, particularly the non-Western world.

Non-Western IR[1] theories has recently emerged to challenge this generalisation and parochialism. Why is a non-Western approach important? Acharya (2014) outlines three reasons. First, majority of the members of the international system are non-Western countries. Second, after the end of WWII, whether inter-state or intra-state, conflicts mostly have taken

---

1   The term non-Western IR is also controversial. Although there are different terms to define non-Western IR (Acharya, 2011, 2014), such as post-Western (Shani, 2008; Vasilaki, 2012) or Third World (Tickner, 2003a), this article prefers to use Non-Western as it is defined by Acharya (2011, p.621).

"I use the term 'non-Western' partly as a term of convenience, rather than to reflect any particular ideology. The term is also useful to interrogate the idea of 'Western', which has been so dominant, pervasive (and less questioned by critics of 'non-Western'), in the mainstream IRT, and as a point of reference to engage theorists, such as the founders of the English School, who used these concepts ('Western' or 'European') to lay out their own beliefs about the foundations and evolution of international relations."

place in non-Western areas. Finally, a large majority of these conflicts had their own origins. Thus, they should be examined through their own lenses, because at some point conventional IR theories (IRTs) are not capable of explaining them. The general tendency regarding non-Western areas is to neglect their circumstances and values as well as their history and political theory (Acharya and Buzan, 2019). On the contrary, it is expected that scholars will examine their issues via Western theories. The Teaching Research and International Politics Project (TRIP) survey presents the most comprehensive database of information on the discipline of IR, indicating teaching and research practices and views on foreign policy issues among IR scholars. In the 2014 TRIP survey, conducted with IR scholars from 32 countries (19 from Western and 13 from non-Western countries), 66.98% agreed or strongly agreed that IR is a Western/North American-dominated discipline (Wemheuer-Vogelaar et al., 2016). Western IR scholars are named as the most influential scholars in the field, while non-Western scholars are neglected. Furthermore, Western scholars are seen as theory producers while non-Western scholars are for theory testing (Tickner, 2013; Wemheuer-Vogelaar et al., 2016).

While Western-oriented theories are considered the only instruments providing a clear picture on world politics, non-Western scholars often argue that conventional IRTs are not able to respond to their problems. As Tickner (2003a) argues, every state has its own features, and thereof, making such generalisations questions the internationality of the discipline of IR. Tickner (2016) questions Western dominance on knowledge and suggests challenging it. One way of doing this would be to develop non-Western IRTs, which non-Western IR scholars have attempted to do, and to derive insights from local history, culture or dynamics. Non-Western IRTs are intertwined with the efforts to challenge Western centrism.

The aim of this chapter is to elaborate non-Western IR theories. It starts with the history of non-Western thinking in IR. It outlines why scholars believe there is a requirement for non-Western IR theories in the field. It continues with the critiques of conventional IRTs and how non-Western IR thinking diverges from them. The problems of Western-centred IR can be explained by three headings: ethnocentrism (i.e. North American-centrism and Eurocentrism), false universalism and agency denial (Acharya and Buzan, 2019). The third section addresses the main premises of non-Western IRTs, giving examples of global IR and theoretical initiatives from Chinese thought. Finally, new theoretical openings and research directions triggered by non-Western IR theories are briefly outlined.

2   The History of Non-Western IR Thinking

Non-Western IR thinking is a relatively new research area. Although the concept started to be discussed in the 1990s, it is only since the 2000s and in particular from 2007 that it has become a widely known concept. The efforts of
Amitav Acharya cannot be ignored in this regard. Acharya (2000) outlined the
problem of acknowledgment of the non-Western world in contemporary IR.
IR theories and concepts give insights into so-called world politics, including
all states but essentially ignoring and excluding the non-Western world. Thus,
over-generalisation and exclusion creates the problem of representation in IR.
Acharya addresses this problem using the term ethnocentrism, describing it as
"one of the most pernicious forms of exclusion in IR theory" (2000, p.18). This
concept is further elaborated in the second part.

In a special issue of *International Relations of the Asia-Pacific* in 2007,
Acharya and Barry Buzan helped non-Western IR to receive worldwide notice.
Inspired by Wight's (1966) article 'Why there is no international theory?',
they titled their article 'Why is there no non-Western international relations
theory?'. They emphasise the Western hegemonic power in IR, arguing that
this power ignores the realities and practices of the non-Western world and
weakens the discipline with over-generalisations. The authors claim that conventional IR thinking is very much focused on Western notions and utilises
Western concepts and history. This parochialism makes the discipline of IR not
international but Western. Acharya and Buzan (2007, p.288) state that:

> there is now a substantial body of theory about international relations
> (IRs), but that almost all of it is produced by and for the West, and rests
> on an assumption that Western history *is* world history. The puzzle for us
> is that the almost exclusively Western sources of international relations
> theory conspicuously fail to correspond to the now global distribution of
> its subjects.

The authors suggest that rather than making simplifications, generalising
Western notions and practices to include the non-Western world, is a complex
task. They attempt to broaden the discipline by including non-Western contributions, taking into account local history and culture, the ideas of national
leaders, distinctive local and regional interaction patterns, and the writings of
scholars working on different regions and global politics.

Acharya and Buzan also analyse the underdevelopment of IR outside of
the West and the dominance of the West in the field. The first reason for this
is that Western IRTs discovered the right path for understanding IR. Second,

they have acquired hegemonic status in the Gramscian sense, meaning they operate largely unconsciously regardless of their truth. Third, non-Western theories exist but are hidden. This is due to language and cultural barriers, or as they are accepted as the studies outside of the Western-defined realm. The fourth reason is that local conditions (historical, cultural, political, and institutional) prevent the production of IRT in non-Western areas. Finally, the West had a big head start, and the non-Western world is in the process of catching up (Acharya and Buzan, 2007, pp. 293–301).

Acharya and Buzan also stress the requirement of bringing area studies and IR together. In a 2010 book they evaluated the topic with other scholars studying non-Western IRTs. Chapters range across cases from China, India, Japan, Korea, South Asia, Indonesia, and the Islamic world, all based on non-Western concerns in IRTs and concepts, analysing current academic initiatives in detail. A decade later Acharya and Buzan (2017) revisited the issue and claimed that nothing had changed: IR was still dominated by the West.

Acharya was elected as the first non-Western President of the International Studies Association (ISA) in 2014. In his ISA Convention speech, he pointed out the deficiency of conventional IR thinking and suggested a global IR, aiming to combine East and West. Acharya claimed that the discipline of IR was not able to reflect the voices, experiences, knowledge claims and contributions of non-Western societies and states, and on the contrary had a tendency to marginalise them.

Acharya (2014) described the division between West and non-West, giving the example of *sahib* and *muhab* in Indian culture. During the colonial era, British universities in India had two different teaching forms. While Indian teachers (mostly Persians called Munshis) taught local language, history and culture and earned less, British scholars taught Western subjects and earned more. It was expected that Munshis would be informants, while British scholars were rule-makers, setting the agenda. Acharya argued that this division still exists in the discipline today, in institutions, in publishing outlets, in universities and among scholars. While Western scholars are *sahibs* setting the agenda, non-Western scholars are *munshis*, the informants. Acharya (2014) also remarks that there have been insufficient studies on colonisation and decolonisation, which in fact should be as salient as the world wars, the European international order, the American superpower or the Cold War. Giving the example of the Cold War, which has been accepted as a long peace, scholars ignored conflict and tension in the Third World, which in reality meant there was no peace in the world. The same is valid in IR thought; current studies focus on Thucydides, Machiavelli, Hobbes, Locke and Kant, not on Ashoka, Kautilya, Sun Tzu, Ibn Khaldun, Frantz Fanon or other non-Westerners.

Arlene Tickner has further indicated the ignorance of non-Western dimensions in the discipline. Taking into account so-called universal IRTs and concepts, Tickner indicates the failure of IR to see the Third World. The author (2003a) argues that in order to enhance knowledge of global politics and build an inclusive discipline, it is necessary to take into consideration what she calls the Third World's interpretation of that subject matter. In an edited collection, Tickner and Ole Wæver (2009) broadened the debate and focused on how the world is understood differently around the world. They emphasise that IR is not only for Western issues and so should not only be conducted by Western scholars (core), but should also cover non-Western issues and be conducted by non-Western scholars (periphery):

> Looking at IR in different settings, both as scholarship in its own right and within the framework of a critical understanding of the discipline as a whole, would deepen our comprehension of and receptivity to knowledge produced around the world. IR at the center would be better understood too, given that core-periphery relations are an integral part of the social structures that produce knowledge there. Therefore, studying academic practice in the less influential parts of the world does not just explain deviation from a proto-global, Western normality. It also provides key insights into how 'really existing IR' as canonised at the center (on behalf of an abstract, universal disciplinary ideal) is not produced by a global discipline that is only temporarily represented by a geographically defined forerunner, but is actually the local product of a particular geo-epistemological perspective.
>
> TICKNER and WÆVER, 2009, p.2

They are interested in social and intellectual structures, including both the political and social environment, and people, particularly scholars. The book explores the role of geographical and epistemological factors, focusing on Latin America, Africa, China, Japan, Korea, Taiwan, South Asia, Iran, Arab countries, Israel, Turkey, Russia, Central and Eastern Europe, Anglo-core, Western Europe, and the USA. The authors focus on the reasons for the lack of notice given to non-Western IR, claiming that language differences/barriers, financial funding problems and a lack of cooperation with non-Western scholars hamper dialogue between the two sides.

In his 2004 book John Hobson discusses the neglected influence of Eastern civilisation on the current understanding of the West. He argues that due to interaction with Eastern culture via trade or politics, the West built modern Western civilisation, using Eastern institutions, technologies and ideas.

Colonisation of Eastern land, labour and markets also contributed to the European identity. In other words, "the East enable[d] the rise of the West through two processes: diffusionism/assimilationism and appropriation-ism" (Hobson, 2004, p.2). Rather than the East being a marginal or a passive bystander, they are at the forefront of the story of progress in world history and their contribution should be admitted.

In a 2007 article, Hobson argued that Western thinking is racist and criti-cised the Eurocentrism in IR. All IRTs and concepts, according to Hobson, are problematic, since they are Eurocentric and fail to accurately comprehend the non-Western world. According to Hobson (2007) the West has constructed a self-image that separates itself from the East; the East is the other. The West in this sense defined itself as the ruler of world politics and torchbearer of global political and economic developments, while the Eastern other represented the regressive and antithetical. This is reflected in academia. Rather than challeng-ing this stance, Hobson argues, scholars invite it.

3   The Main Critiques of Conventional IR Theory

Robert Cox (1981, p.128), in an influential article, claimed that "theory is always *for* someone and *for* some purpose". In other words, theorisation is a politi-cal act and theories often serve to meet the expectations of people and their purposes. Theory relates to the theorist's position in time and place (Hobson, 2007). Thus, even though all conventional IRTs, in particular realism, liberal-ism and the English school, claim that they are universal, Acharya and Buzan (2007) argue that in reality they speak for the West and in the interest of main-taining its power, prosperity and influence. According to Acharya and Buzan, it is rational for China or Japan or any other non-Western state to form their own theories, since conventional IRTs do not comfortably fit with their practices.

Non-Western IR thinking, rather than criticising specific theories or con-cepts, targets all theories and concepts. The fundamental criticism behind their argument is that all theories and concepts are Western-/Eurocentric and so priorities, problems, solutions or premises are insufficient for meeting expectations, solving problems and understanding the situation in the non-Western world. IRTs are rooted in European history and Western traditions of social theory and practice (Acharya and Buzan, 2010).

Classical realism and neorealism are also frequently criticised. Since their focus is on state sovereignty, national interest and military power (Tickner, 2003a), these theories "project onto the rest of world history their basic Europe-derived story of international anarchy and balance of power as a permanent, universal structural condition" (Acharya and Buzan, 2010, p.7). Seeing non-great powers as irrelevant to study, realist theorists often neglect or reject non-Western areas; for example, Waltz (1979, cited in Tickner, 2003a, p.301) stated that "it would be [...] ridiculous to construct a theory of international politics based on Malaysia and Costa Rica".

Liberalism and neoliberalism had faced similar criticisms. They have clear roots in European political and economic theories. In particular, liberal principles of individualism and the market came out of Western practices but are presented as universal values (Acharya and Buzan, 2010). The English school is also criticised for being a Western theory. The concept of "international society" can be found in European history, having formed in Europe and expanded to take over the world (Acharya and Buzan, 2010). In other words, this is how Europe remade the world. In this regard, very little work has been done on the non-Western world.

Critical theory, in particular the ideas of Marx, is also criticised by non-Western thinking, according to which Marx's theory illustrates all the hallmarks of a Eurocentric worldview (Hobson, 2004). Marxism assumes that the West is unique and enjoyed a developmental history which is absent in the non-West/East, and so Marx claims that the East has no progressive history (Hobson, 2004). For instance, Marx defined China as a rotting semi-civilisation (1862, cited in Hobson, 2004, p.12). The same is true for India. Thus, Marxism is Western-oriented and cannot address non-Western issues.

Constructivism and postmodernism also have roots in Western philosophy of knowledge and social theory. Constructivism, in addressing issues of norms, ideas, cultures and identities, has contributed to the development of non-Western IR thinking. This is because it looks at local dimensions, paving the way for the emergence of non-Western areas as a subject of study. However, it remains largely a Western-centric enterprise (Acharya and Buzan, 2017), neglecting issues of race and pre-Westphalian civilisations in Asia, the Middle East or anywhere that might contribute new insights from the outside of the West (Acharya and Buzan, 2017; 2019).

Postcolonialism, compared with the above-stated theories, is significant in terms of illustrating the experiences and practices and noticing the voices of the non-Western world. It makes the non-West visible. Many non-Western postcolonial scholars direct criticisms at their Western counterparts. For instance, Gayatri Spivak and Edward Said criticised Foucault for neglecting the central role of imperialism in the making of Europe (Acharya and Buzan, 2010). However, postcolonialism has some deficiencies, including its authenticity. It is framed within cultural discourses originating from the West (Dirlik, 1994). Thus, it needs to solve this problem.

In terms of concepts in IR, war and conflict are the main study areas. In conventional IR, war and conflict are perceived as an inter-state character affair particularly in the Global South (Tickner, 2003a). This lack of understanding also occurs in relation to security. In particular, during the Cold War, it was argued that the concept of national security only refers to security problems coming from outside of the state, but this was problematic because it ignored internal rebellion or secessionist movements within countries, quite ordinary among African states (Barkawi and Laffey, 2006). For instance, Western scholars claim there is no reason to study African national security challenges because they are different from their notion of national security.

The state, particularly state weakness is another concept that is misunderstood. According to Western notions, state weakness relates to the question of legitimacy (Buzan, 1991), where states lack a national identity: socio-political cohesion is weak and there are security problems. Third World countries in particular are thus defined as weak, quasi, failed or incomplete states. However, it is often ignored that state weakness in the Third World is the historical result of the imperial past/colonisation, "which harnessed state-building processes to global capitalist dynamics in ways that hampered the consolidation of the state" (Tickner, 2003a, p.318). These imperialist and capitalist features also influence state sovereignty and autonomy. In conventional IR thinking, the Treaty of Westphalia is accepted as the milestone for the principles of sovereignty and autonomy, the exclusion of external threats, and respect for territories. However, Third World examples indicate that domestic developments also need to be considered (Tickner, 2003a). In short, taking the arguments above into account in terms of categorising these critiques, there are three significant deficiencies in contemporary IR according to non-Western IR thinking: Western-centrism, false universality and agency denial.

Western centrism is common in the current methodological and conceptual understanding, which results from focusing on Western interests and notions. Before clarifying it, however, it is necessary to understand ethnocentrism. Ethnocentrism has various definitions, derived from anthropology, sociology and politics. In terms of IR, according to Booth (1979, cited in Acharya, 2000, p.3) ethnocentrism is "as a term to describe feelings of group centrality and superiority ... a technical term to describe faulty methodology in social sciences [and] a synonym for being "culture-bound". Acharya (2000) claims that ethnocentrism creates ignorance and exclusion. In other words, IR prefers to ignore non-Western others, and examines issues from a single perspective; often non-Western experiences are viewed as 'inferior'.

Western centrism refers to both North American and European centrism. Regarding narrowing down the concept of Western-centrism, North

American-centrism within the discipline in particular is often criticised. Critics argue that current debates in the discipline take into account American foreign policy agenda premises and are shaped and conducted by American scholars. Hoffmann argued in 1977 that IR had become a science when the USA became a superpower in world politics (Hoffmann, 1977). In doing so, the USA also gained influence over academia and the power to shape the IR discipline. Intellectual dispositions, political circumstances and institutional opportunities are important factors in the development of IR as an American-centred field, which has a different methodological and conceptual framework, rejecting historical and philosophical approaches while prioritising scientific methods.

Some scholars opposed American-centrism in IR. Smith (2002) argued that since American-centred IRTs adopt scientific approaches, they were only able to see a small part of global politics – the US perspective – and avoided to see many inequalities. These epistemological approaches at the same time limit pluralism. Wæver (1998) looked at the issue from the qualitative side, examining four US and three European scientific journals published between 1970 and 1995, concluding that while 88% of the articles in the US journals were written by American scholars, this decreased to 40% in the European ones. In terms of meta-theoretical approaches, while the US journals were based on rationalist approaches, the European ones were based on reflexivity.

Even though Smith and Wæver's criticisms do not specifically target Western-centrism, but only American-centrism, American and European IR represent the same parochialism, and thus are gathered under the name of Western-centrism. Since the end of the 1990s criticism of American-centrism, influenced by the positivism and post-positivism debate, turned into criticism of Western-centrism. Critiques depend on two points: contributions of periphery scholars are not represented in conventional IRTs, and theories are inefficient in explaining developments in the non-Western areas (Rumelili, 2014).

Using the same method as Wæver, Aydınlı and Mathews (2000) examined seven US scientific journals from 1990 to 1997. They showed that when excluding the USA, Canada, Western Europe, Israel and Australia, non-Western articles composed only 3.28% of the total; with USA-settled foreign scholars this reached 10.47%. The authors indicate a core-periphery division in IRT, with the periphery less recognised than the core.

When examining the reasons why periphery scholars are not sufficiently represented in IR, the hierarchical division in between theory and case analysis is prominent (Aydınlı and Mathews, 2000). Thus, the current IR limits the publication from the peripheries. Periphery scholars in the Western universities are pushed to study their own country by their supervisors (Rumelili,

2014). Conditions in the periphery also push scholars away from conceptual studies.

False universality means that Western norms, values or practices are accepted as universal standards, while non-Western ones seen as particularisms, aberrations or inferiorities (Acharya and Buzan, 2019). Subjects and practices of contemporary IRTs are extensions of European diplomatic history and contemporary American foreign policy. Concepts like democracy, human rights, the contemporary state system and the regional/international order are defined by and derived from Westerners and expected to be adopted and followed by non-Westerners. If the latter reject them, it means they are undemocratic or do not respect human rights (Sen, 1998). In this sense, according to non-Western IR, Western states are able to hold their own values as universal.

Agency denial is related to false universality because it involves the West denying agency to the non-Western world. According to this notion, the non-West can only be an object, not a subject. This parochial approach ignores the achievements and contributions of the non-Western world. The "Non-West are seen as customers, rather than producers, passive recipients rather than active borrowers, of theoretical knowledge claims" (Acharya and Buzan, 2019, p.286). Acharya (2011) challenges this so-called universal view, stating that when defining agency in both material and ideational dimensions, non-Western societies also have agency. In general, the role of non-Western states in the international system has been conceptualised as one of rebellion and dissent, but when analysing the period of the Cold War, for example, non-Western states played a conformist and supportive role (Ayoob, 1998). They have contributed to the making of international rules and norms, by modifying and adapting European norms of sovereignty and combining them with pre-existing local beliefs and practices: this is called localisation. In other words, actors borrow or select norms from global applications – transnational norms – and modify or localise them in accordance with their concerns (Acharya, 2004).

4 The Main Premises of Non-Western IRTs

Conventional IRTs and concepts clearly do not meet the expectations of the non-Western world. In this sense, the non-West needs to develop its own theories in order to meet its purposes. Historically the non-Western world had different priorities than the West. For instance, while the West's key issues are war and peace, such as nuclear war, the Cold War, European integration or energy crises, the key issues in the non-West are anti-colonialism, anti-racism, development and regionalism (Acharya and Buzan, 2019). Thus, using Western lenses on non-Western areas is problematic.

According to non-Western studies, in order to emancipate IR, periphery scholars should form generalisable concepts and theories inspired by their historical and political developments, rather than utilising conventional IR concepts. Acharya and Buzan (2007) call this new conceptual approach *sub-systemic*, while Aydınlı and Mathews (2008) call it *homegrown*. Sub-systemic studies, according to Acharya and Buzan, develop Asian, African and Middle East IR theories as alternatives to Western approaches. They claim that "area studies should be a main location for subsystem theorising" (Acharya and Buzan, 2010, p.5). Such theory may not necessarily be theorised by non-Western scholars, but this materially indicates it as non-Western. Homegrown refers to a theory stemming from local experiences. It might utilise existing theories, but local experiences must be added to the analysis. Its difference from the theoretical application of existing theories is that it might "address an existing body of literature, but [often] finds a gap or inconsistency in that literature and then adds to that existing literature with concepts derived out of the local context and case" (Aydınlı and Mathews, 2008, p.702).

Finally, cultural and environmental conditions have paved the way for non-Western academic contributions. Every state asks different questions and presents alternative information. However, this presentation should not mean portraying the non-Western world as exotic, pure or idealised, which is a result of a Western-centred viewpoint (Rumelili, 2014).

It has become a necessity for the non-Western world to develop their own theories. The most important element that non-Western IRT brings to current IR study is locality. In other words, local culture, local history and local civilisation are the elements that scholars are required to take into account. This method considers the local dynamics of each state, which shape their political, economic or security aspects.

Apart from locality, global IR is another significant element offered by non-Western IR thinking. Accepting that Western IR was the first academic discipline attempting to understand and theorise the dynamics of world politics, and that the main ideas in IR were rooted in European history and the rise of West as a world power, since the world has become more global, IR should be global too. Rather than suggesting a new theory, global IR aims to transcend the divide between the West and 'the Rest'. In this regard, Global IR has six dimensions:

- It is founded upon a pluralistic universalism: not 'applying to all' but recognizing and respecting the diversity in us.

- It is grounded in *world* history, not just Greco-Roman, European, or US history.
- It subsumes, rather than supplants existing IR theories and methods.
- It integrates the study of regions, regionalisms, and Area studies.
- It eschews exceptionalism.
- It recognizes multiple forms of agency beyond material power, including resistance, normative action, and local constructions of global order.

  ACHARYA, 2014, pp. 649–52

Regarding the first dimension, IR needs a new understanding of universality. We have seen that universality refers in conventional IRTs to a specific area, the West, and corresponds closely to the Enlightenment universalism. Acharya (2014) defines Western universalism as monistic universalism. It brings arbitrary standard-setting, gatekeeping, and marginalising of alternative narratives, ideas and methodologies (Acharya, 2011). Pluralistic universalism is needed, comprehending IR as a large, overarching canopy with multiple foundations. In this regard, scholars use more and different approaches and so one can see many theories, cultures, civilisations and ideas. A pluralist view of theory has a harder, positivist, rationalist, materialist and quantitative understanding on the one side, and on the other it is reflective, social, constructivist and post-modern as well as normative theory (Acharya and Buzan, 2010).

Second, global IR should look at world history, not only Western history. World history means combining a holistic perspective with local histories (Acharya and Buzan, 2019). When world history is analysed, one needs to take into consideration of at least 5,000 years of development in all civilisations and societies, and to avoid modern definitions of concepts like human rights, sovereignty and power.

Third, some theories have made great efforts in understanding the non-West, while others have neglected it. Global IR suggests rethinking contemporary IRTs, taking into account non-Western knowledge, ideas and norms. Fourth, regional dimensions should not be seen as a challenge but an opportunity. Global IR suggests acknowledgment of regional diversities and agencies because regions are dynamic, purposeful and socially constructed spaces. Fifth, exceptionalism is a salient problem of contemporary IR thought. It suggests the superiority of one side over another, which therefore justifies the dominance of the powerful over the weak. Global IR suggests breaking these boundaries.

Sixth, contemporary IR needs to accept non-Western actors as agents that can be active and capable of make changes in world politics. Global IR suggests agency "goes beyond military power and wealth and avoids privileging trans-national norm entrepreneurship" (Acharya, 2014, p.651). In this sense, it should be material and ideational.

Later, Acharya and Buzan add a new dimension to Global IR, which is responding "to the increasing globalisation of the world not only in terms of the diffusion of wealth, power and cultural authority, but also in terms of rising interdependence and shared fates" (2019, p.300). It refers that globalisation helps IR with increasing the interconnection and interdependence.

Within these dimensions there are several elements that can contribute to challenging and improving IR, as stated in the global IR agenda. These elements are based around the need to:

- Discover new patterns, theories, and methods from world histories.
- Analyse changes in the distribution of power and ideas after 200 plus years of Western dominance.
- Explore regional worlds in their full diversity and interconnectedness.
- Engage with subjects and methods that require deep and substantive integration of disciplinary and area studies knowledge.
- Examine how ideas and norms circulate between global and local levels.
- Investigate the mutual learning among civilizations, of which there is more historical evidence than there is for the 'clash of civilizations'.

ACHARYA, 2014, pp. 652–56

Since the Westphalia mindset is still powerful in IR and forms the international system and order, there is a tendency to neglect non-Western systems and orders, such as the fourteenth century BC Amarna system in East Asia, or the Mandala system in South-east Asia (Acharya, 2014). These systems among others also need to be taken into account. Different regions present different concepts and practices of power, legitimacy and international orders, helping to rethink and elaborate contemporary definitions (Tickner, 2003a).

The international system has changed dramatically since the end of the Cold War. Today the world is much more complex than it is portrayed by the Western-centric understanding sees. The rising and great powers are more diverse and geographically dispersed, and are predominately non-Western. There are also significant regional powers, international institutions, non-state actors and multinational corporations. Acharya (2014, p.653) calls this new order as the multiplex world, "comprising *multiple* key actors/producers/directors (including shape-shifting villains like terrorist groups) whose relationships are defined by *complex* forms of interdependence." Thus, the revised model should take into account these new powers' distinct and diverse cultural and historical experiences in order to understand the current world order. Therefore, examinations only through European or Western history are not explanatory.

The concept of regionalism also needs revision. While classical regionalism sees European institutions or cooperation initiatives as the foundation of regionalism, with the new regionalism, which takes constructivist dimensions like community building into consideration, non-Western initiatives can also be realised. However, it also has some deficiencies regarding regional orders. Thus, rather than simply putting the concept of 'integration' into regionalism studies need to consider various forms of regional initiatives around the world. The same is true for area studies. Rather than dividing the field into two, i.e. 'disciplinary area studies', focusing mainly on IRTs, and 'transnational and comparative regional studies', focusing on issues affecting regions, scholars should admit this false division.

Finally, the understanding of civilisation needs to be revised. Rather than a narrow, a-historical, colonialist and strategic understanding, as in Samuel Huntington's 'clash of civilisations' and standard of civilisation, the concept should be considered in plural form, including the relations and interactions, with all its dimensions.

As stated above, since non-Western countries have their own priorities and concerns, conventional IRTs have deficiencies in fitting to these countries. For instance, as Acharya and Buzan (2010, p.3) state,

> Neither China nor Japan fit comfortably into realism or liberalism. China is trying to avoid being treated as a threat to the status quo as its power rises, and the moves to develop a Chinese school of IR are focused on this problem. Japan is seeking to avoid being a 'normal' great power and its status as a 'trading state' or 'civilian power' is a direct contradiction of realist expectations. ASEAN [Association of South-east Asian Nations] defies the realist, liberal and English School logic that order is provided by the local great powers. South Korea and India perhaps fit more closely with realist models, yet neither seems certain about what sort of place it wants for itself in international society.

Such countries have attempted to build their own theories. There are non-Western contributions to conventional IRTs, but they are often seen as soft or hidden theories (Acharya and Buzan, 2010). Acharya and Buzan (2019) and Eun (2019) argue that the decline of US power in world politics is reflected in the theoretical framework of IR, as non-Western theoretical developments have found an academic platform. Even though mainstream IRTs are still significant, non-Western approaches are now non-negligible. These new studies, contrary to mainstream theories, include a wider range of theoretical approaches. Non-Western IRT has "served a crucial purpose in generating debate [and drawn] a good deal of attention to the parochialism of IR" (Acharya and Buzan, 2019, p.297).

The tendency of non-Western theoretical initiatives is to point out non-Western cultures, histories and norms; various countries have formed their IR contexts in this way (Biltekin, 2014), such as Africa (Lavelle, 2005; Nkiwane, 2001), Japan (Inoguchi, 2010; Ong, 2004), India (Behera, 2010; Zaman, 2006), Latin America (Tickner, 2003b, 2008) and Russia (Sergonuinin, 2009; Tsygankov, 2008). Chinese efforts can be given as key examples of non-Western IRT. Having long intellectual traditions, culture and history, the Chinese role in IR is *sine qua non*. At the very beginning, however, as Qin (2010, pp. 36–41) argues, there were no Chinese IRTs due to "unconsciousness of "international-ness" in the traditional Chinese worldview; the dominance of the Western IR discourse in the Chinese academic community; and the absence of a consistent theoretical core in the Chinese IR research". During this period Wang (2009) states that Chinese scholars copied Western theories. With the rise of China in world politics (Wang, 2009), Chinese IR has gained great impetus. Qin (2007, p.313) states that "Chinese IR theory is likely and even inevitable to emerge along with the great economic and social transformation that China has been experiencing". Chinese scholars aim to change the Western conceptualisation of China as a threat and to present a vision of a harmonious world (Wang, 2009). Chinese theoretical initiatives are based on 'Chinese characteristics', referring to Confucianism, Tianxia (All-Under-Heaven) system, Marxism and the Chinese tributary system[2] (Qin, 2007, 2011; Wang, 2009; Wan, 2012). Qin Yaqing's relational theory (2016), Yan Xuetong's moral realism (2011) and super-ficial friendship (2010), and Zhao Tingyang's Tianxia theory (2009) are some important examples.

Relational theory argues that existing mainstream IRTs have problems in explaining how the world functions, because they prioritise individual actors' rationality over social processual relationality (Eun, 2020). Eun (2020) argues

---

2 Deriving its background from ancient Chinese history, the system refers to an "emperor-prince system with the emperor overriding the land while princes governing in their respec-tive fiefdoms within the land" (Qin, 2007, p.322). It is an unequal system but benign and its essence is "the radiation of the ego, China as the "I" at the center while other tributary states at the periphery paid tributes to the center" (Qin, 2007, p.323). This, however, prevented China from going beyond its borders.

that, as in Chinese culture, it needs to be the other way around. Qin (2016) states that relationality determines human actors' existence and meaning; actors can exist only as 'actors-in-relation'. Thus, one needs to study relations rather than actors. The relational theory of world politics emphasises the primacy of social context and action (Acharya, 2019). The theory uses *zhongyong* dialectics – inclusivity, complementarity, harmony – which is derived from *ying* and *yang* and the meta-relationship as epistemological foundations. The latter is the simplest method of representing relationships and the former helps understanding and interpreting meta-relationships (Qin, 2016).

Xuetong's moral realism takes into account Chinese traditional thought and history, asking why only some rising states can achieve their goals and why a hegemon cannot remain so forever (2011; Acharya, 2019). Moral realism addresses the 'kingly way' (Wang Dao), which "stresses the moral values of righteousness and benevolence over the legalistic Western values of equality and democracy" (Acharya, 2019, p.475). Morality is as important as power, capacity and interest in policy making (Xuetong, 2011). Xuetong (2010) also presents the concept of superficial friendship, giving the example of Chinese-USA relations since the Cold War. The nature of the relationship is determined "according to the consistence of two countries' knowledge of their interest relations and the reality" (2010, p.280). A superficial friendship means that the two countries imagine they have more mutually favourable than unfavourable interests, when the reality is the opposite (Xuetong, 2010, p.280). In other words, states pursue a policy of pretending to be friends. In this scenario, states delude themselves that they are friends and often cover up conflict, resuming a superficial friendship in the short term with new friendly rhetoric (Xuetong, 2010). This causes, however, instability in the relationship.

The philosophical world system concept of Tianxia, in the Chinese mind, does not refer to the natural world or a geographically defined area but combines nature, super-nature (god) and morality (Qin, 2007; 2010). Tingyang's Tianxia system aspires to "harmony" through a universal agreement in the "hearts" of all people" (2005, cited in Eun, 2020, p.3). Tingyang (2009) develops notions of world society, worldness and world order basing on Tianxia system. Thus rather than signifying a state, the world is more important, and so world-building is more important than nation-building (Tingyang, 2009). Tianxia focuses on the unity of the physical world (land), the psychological world (public opinion) and the political world (world institutions) (Wang, 2009, p.111). The state as seen in the Westphalian nation-state model is believed to be the cause of international conflict and state failures (Eun, 2020). While Western thinkers often ask, 'who are you', causing a division between 'us' and 'other', Chinese thinkers ask, 'who are we', seeing the whole world as one family (Wang, 2009).

Thus, Western thought is prone to fighting, while Chinese thought reveals that harmonious co-existence is possible (Tingyang, 2009).

5   New Theoretical Openings and Research Directions

There are criticisms to global IR and non-Western IRTs. Scholars have discussed the validity of existing IRTs in explaining contemporary developments in the non-Western world. Ikenberry and Mastanduno (2003) argue that especially since China has re-evaluated its foreign policy and integrated itself more into the Europe-derived international system, there is no necessity to divide the discipline into West and non-West, because contemporary theories explain non-Western developments very well. Mearsheimer (2016) asserts that since American dominance is 'benign', there is nothing wrong with its dominance in the discipline. However, non-Western IR challenges parochialism in current IR and is "interested in exploring IR's inadequacy for understanding key global problems of concern to the periphery and the ways in which the discipline has unfolded in distinct non-core settings" (Tickner, 2013, p.636). Non-Western IR studies aim to broaden the discipline, adding new insights, methods and dynamics. They also aim to reveal the Gramscian hegemony of Western thinking and mobilise alternative approaches, histories and philosophies (Buzan, 2016) – to make IR an international rather than a Western discipline.

The aim of IR theory is to ensure explanation of world events and thereof, it should be applicable worldwide. However, conventional IRTs lack universality. Non-Western IR brings the Rest in and makes their voices audible. Locality is a salient contribution of non-Western IR studies, opening new theoretical and research directions. Locality encourages exploration of "indigenous histories, classical philosophy and religious traditions, the ideas of national leaders, the writing of contemporary scholars, and foreign policy practices of modern states and norms and process dynamics of regional interactions" (Acharya and Buzan, 2017, p.356). Dependency theory is an example; it challenges classical understandings of development as an organising principle in international politics, asserting that "underdevelopment and poverty are the result of political, economic and cultural influences exerted on such countries from the outside" (Benabdallah et al., 2017, p.128). It reveals unfair and exploitative relationships between the Global North and the Global South. Moreover, ideas of human development and human security, which introduced by Mahbub ul-Haq of Pakistan and Amatya Sen of India (Acharya, 2014); Nehru and fellow Asian and African leaders' non-alignment movement, which ensured the neutrality of

Asian and African states in regard to the US and Soviet blocs during the Cold War (Acharya and Buzan, 2010).

Furthermore, African scholars redefine the concept of agency. African agency has multiple dimensions: "as a collective international actor; as a collection of states with (in the 'broadest of sweeps') a shared history; and as a discursive presence, used both Africans and outsiders, in international politics and policy" (Brown, 2012 cited in Acharya and Buzan, 2019, p.251). These dimensions reflect on regionalism such as in the formation of the African Union, security management, and Africa's relations with the outside world. Other examples of non-Western theoretical and conceptual initiatives are; using notions of Nishida, who systematises a Chinese dialecticism into an Eastern-inspired 'logic of emptiness' focusing on building an identity that emerge through a coexistence of opposites; Ong (2004) studies building a theory with 'Japanese characteristic'; Ibn Khaldoun in concept of 'assabbiyya' argues "the state emerged as an outcome not of anarchy but of human cooperation, based on reason, social solidarity with an emphasis on group consciousness and social cohesion" (Tadjbakhsh, 2010, p.190); and Kautilya, father of Indian *realpolitik*, in his book *Arthashastra* states notions on administration; law, order and justice; taxation, revenue and expenditure; foreign policy; defence and war (Zaman, 2006). In addition, his theory of Mandala (sphere or circle of influence, interest, and ambitions) assumes and is prepared for world of eternally warring states by stressing 'perpetual preparedness' or punishment and sanction (Behera, 2010). All above-stated new concepts and theories derive their conceptual background from local history, politics and culture.

Non-Western IR studies have also introduced new understanding of area studies and regionalism. Rather than the contemporary understanding of area studies, in which it is perceived as theory-testing, in non-Western thinking area studies are utilised for theory-building (Acharya, 2014). In terms of the role of non-Western thinking in regionalism, ASEAN is an example (Acharya, 2004). Although the Western understanding of regionalism has Eurocentric terms – the integration process of the EU is accepted as the great success of regional integration and often seen as a universal standard – ASEAN challenges with its localisation. Thus, new conceptualisation of regionalism, with the inclusion of the non-Western world, will mean more diversity, including issues such as migration, the environment or internal conflicts, rather than only the classical understanding, where such issues as trade liberalisation or conflict management are prominent (Acharya, 2014).

6   Conclusion

Raising questions about comprehensive understanding and frameworks reveals the necessity of revising the discipline of IR. Questions are often linked to the general truths and concerns that the discipline claims, and its universal solutions to problems. It is often claimed that IR cannot provide universality, that on the contrary it only explains or studies a small part of the world. It is largely defined by Western great powers, and by a view of history that is the extension of European/Western history. However, IR is expected to be a truly international discipline. These concerns, especially with the rise of non-Western countries in world politics, pave the way for an increase in non-Western voices in the discipline. Since the millennium, scholarship has articulated the need for a more inclusive IR, representing those voices from the non-Western world.

It is argued that the universal standards or explanations of IR are not universal but rather efforts preserving the hegemony of the West over the Rest. Conventional IRTs and concepts often reflect the interests and perspectives of the dominant West – Western-centrism – while marginalising the non-West. There is also a tendency to neglect the agency of the non-Western world, since it is seen as an object rather than subject.

Non-Western IR studies have attempted to find solutions to this parochialism, such as considering local dimensions in history, culture and civilisation. This has provided new research areas and allowed us to hear voices of the non-Western world. Another solution is global IR, an extension of non-Western IR. It is not a theory but a way of conceptualising and reshaping the discipline, which aims to displace Western-dominated knowledge. It encourages mainstream IRTs to admit ideas, experiences and insights from the non-Western world.

There have been great efforts by non-Western IRT initiatives to explain and to help the West to understand the non-Western world. Different countries have developed their own theoretical approaches, deriving from local dimensions. Theory is for some people and for a purpose, and in order to understand states' realities one needs to look from their perspective. Pluralism in IR helps to develop the discipline, as well as making it as 'international' as its name suggests. Non-Western IR studies have diversified the discipline, adding new insights and dynamics. They have also broadened research areas and methods through concentration on local dimensions, which help ensuring plurality and diminish parochialism.

While critiques of non-Western IRTs emphasise that plurality might derail the discipline's vantage point, or that Chinese efforts in this regard might build their own hegemonic logic of dominance over Asia and risk inviting 'nativism'

(Chen, 2011), these initiatives do encourage greater pluralism and have helped for global IR (Acharya, 2019). Conventional IRTs in Western thought are now more aware of non-Western theories and thought in world politics. The aim of both Western and non-Western IRTs should be to form a general theory and further efforts should be spent to interrogate the gap between them. The West/ non-West binary has to end, and the creation of new platforms should provide cross-cultural dialogue between both sides.

References

Acharya, A., 2000. Ethnocentrism and Emancipatory IR Theory. In: S. Arnold, and J.M. Bier, eds. (Dis)placing Security: Critical Re-evaluations of theBoundaries of Security Studies. Toronto: York University, Centre for International and Strategic Studies. pp. 1–18.

Acharya, A., 2004. How Ideas Spread: Whose Norms Matter? Norm Localisation and Institutional Change in Asian Regionalism. International Organisation, 58(2), pp. 239–275.

Acharya, A., 2011. Dialogue and Discovery in Search of International Relations Theories beyond the West. Millennium: Journal of International Studies, 39(3), pp. 619–637.

Acharya, A., 2014. Global International Relations (IR) and Regional Worlds: A New Agenda for International Studies. International Studies Quarterly,58(2014), pp. 647–659.

Acharya, A., 2019. From Heaven to Earth: "Cultural Idealism" and "Moral Realism" as Chinese Contributions to Global International Relations. Chinese Journal of International Politics, 2019, pp. 467–494.

Acharya, A., Buzan, B., 2007. Why is there no non-Western international relations theory? An Introduction. International Relation of the Asia-Pacific, 7(2007), pp. 287–312.

Acharya, A. and Buzan, B. eds., 2010. Non-Western International Relations Theory: Perspectives on and Beyond Asia. Oxon:Routledge.

Acharya, A., Buzan, B., 2017. Why is there no non-Western international relations theory? Ten years on. International Relation of the Asia-Pacific, 17(2017), pp. 341–370.

Acharya, A. and Buzan, B. 2019. The Making of Global International Relations: Origins and Evolution of IR at its Centenary. Cambridge: Cambridge University Press.

Aydınlı, E., Mathews, J., 2000. Are the Core and Periphery Irreconcilable? The Curious World of Publishing in Contemporary International Relations. International Studies Perspective, 1(2000), pp. 289–303.

Aydınlı, E., Mathews, J., 2008. Periphery theorizing for a truly internationalised discipline: spinning IR theory out of Anatolia. Review of International Studies, 34(2008), pp. 693–712.

Ayoob, M. 1998. Subaltern Realism: International Relations Theory Meets the Third World. In: S.G. Neuman, ed. 1998. *International Relations Theory and the Third World*. New York: St. Martin's Press. pp. 31–54.

Barkawi, T., Laffey, M., 2006. The Postcolonial Moment in Security Studies. *Review of International Studies*, 32(2), pp. 329–352.

Benebdallah, L., Adetula, V., and Murillo-Zamora, C. 2017. Global South Perspective. In: S. McGlinchey, R. Walters, and C. Scheinpflug, eds. 2017. *International Relations Theory*. Bristol:E-International Relations Publishing. pp. 125–130. Available at https://www.e-ir.info/publication/international-relations-theory/ [Accessed 30 August 2020].

Behera, N. C., 2010. Re-imagining IR in India. In A. Acharya and B. Buzan, eds.2010. *Non-Western International Relations Theory: Perspectives on and Beyond Asia*. Oxon: Routledge, pp. 92–116.

Biltekin, G. 2014. Özgün teori inşası ve batı-dışı uluslararası ilişkiler teorileri. In: R. Gözen, ed. 2014. *Uluslararası İlişkiler Teorileri*. İstanbul: İletişim Yayınları. pp. 517–565.

Buzan, B. 1991. *People, States and Fear: An Agenda for International Security Studies in the Post-Cold War*. Boulder, CO: Lynne Rienner Publishers.

Buzan. B., 2016. Could IR be different?*International Studies Review*,0(2016), pp. 155–157.

Booth, K. 1979. *Strategy and Ethnocentrism*. London: Croom Helm.

Chen, C. C., 2011. The absence of non-western IR theory in Asia reconsidered. *International Relations of the Asia- Pacific*, 11(2011), pp. 1–23.

Cox, R. W., 1981. Social forces, states and world orders: beyond international relations theory. *Millennium: Journal of International Studies*, 10(2), pp. 126–155.

Dirlik, A., 1994. The Postcolonial Aura: Third World Criticism in the Age of Global Capitalism. *Critical Inquiry*, 20(2), pp. 328–356.

Eun, Y., 2019. Opening up the debate over 'non-western' international relations. *Politics*, 39(1), pp. 4–17.

Eun, Y., 2020. Non-Western International Relations Theorisation: Reflexive Stocktaking. *E-International Relations*. 12.04.2020. Available at https://www.e-ir.info/2020/04/12/non-western-international-relations-theorisation-reflexive-stocktaking/ [Accessed 06.05.2020].

Hobson,J. M., 2004. *The Eastern Origins of Western Civilisation*. Cambridge: Cambridge University Press.

Hobson, J. M., 2007. Is critical theory always for the white West and for Western imperialism? Beyond Westphilian towards a post-racist critical IR. *Review of International Studies,* 33(2007), pp. 91–116.

Hoffmann, S., 1977. An American Social Science: International Relations. *Daedelus,* 106(3), pp. 41–60.

Ikenberry, G. J., MastandunoM. 2003. Conclusion: Images of Order in the Asia-Pacific and the Role of the United States. In: G.J. Ikenberry, and M. Mastanduno, eds. 2003.

International Relations Theory and the Asia-Pacific. New York: Columbia University Press. pp. 421–439.

Inoguchi, T., 2010. Why are there no non-Western theories of international relations?: The case study of Japan. In A. Acharya and B. Buzan, eds. 2010. *Non-Western International Relations Theory: Perspectives on and Beyond Asia.* Oxon: Routledge, pp. 51–68.

Jackson, R., Sørensen, G. 2013. *Introduction to International Relations: Theories and Approaches.* 5th ed.Oxford: Oxford University Press.

Lavelle,K. C., 2005. Moving in from the periphery: Africa and the study of international political economy. *Review of International Political Economy,* 2(2), pp. 364–379.

Mearsheimer, J., (2016). Benign Hegemony. *International Studies Review,* 0(2016), pp. 147–149.

Nkiwane, T. C., 2001. Africa and international relations: regional lessons for a global discourse. *International Political Science Review,* 22(3), pp. 279–290.

Ong, G. G., 2004. Building an IR theory with 'Japanese characteristic': Nishida Kitaro and Emptiness. *Millennium: Journal of International Studies,* 33(1), pp. 35–58.

Qin, Y., 2007. Why there is no Chinese international relations theory?. *International relations of the Asia-Pacific,* 7(3), pp. 313–340.

Qin, Y. 2010. Why there is no Chinese international relations theory?. In: A. Acharya, and B. Buzan, eds. 2010. *Non-Western International Relations Theory: Perspectives on and Beyond Asia.* Oxon: Routledge. pp. 26–50.

Qin, Y., 2011. Development of international relations theory in China: Progress through debates. *International relations of the Asia-Pacific,* 11(2), pp. 231–257.

Qin, Y., 2016. A Relational Theory of World Politics. *International Studies Review,*18(2016), pp. 33–47.

Rumelili, B., 2014. Batı Merkezcilik ve Postkolonyalizm. In: E. Balta, ed. 2014.*Küresel Siyasete Giriş: Kavramlar, Teoriler ve Süreçler,* İstanbul: İletişim. pp. 203–220. Available at https://avys.omu.edu.tr/storage/app/public/gurhan.unal/131581/ Bat%C4%B1%20Merkezcilik%20ve%20Postkolonyalizm%20Bahar%20Rumelili .pdf [Accessed 23.04.2020].

Sen, A., 1998. Universal Truths: Human Rights and the Westernizing Illusion. *Harvard International Review,* 20(3), pp. 40–43.

Sergouinin, A., 2009. Russia: IR at crossroads. In: A.B. Tickner and O. Wæver, eds. 2009. *International Relations Scholarship around the World.* New York: Routledge. pp. 223–241.

Shani, G., 2008. Toward a Post-Western IR. The Umma, Khalsa Panth, and Critical International Relations Theory. *International Studies Review,*10(4), pp. 722–734.

Smith, S., 2002. The United States and the Discipline of International Relations: Hegemonic Country, Hegemonic Discipline. *International Studies Review,* 4(2), pp. 67–85.

Tadjbakhsh, S., 2010. International Relations theory and the Islamic worldview. In A. Acharya and B. Buzan, eds. 2010. *Non-Western International Relations Theory: Perspectives on and Beyond Asia.* Oxon: Routledge, pp. 174–196.

Tickner,A. B., 2003a. Seeing IR Differently: Notes from the Third World. *Millennium: Journal of International Studies,* 32(2), pp. 295–324.

Tickner,A. B., 2003b. Hearing Latin American voices in IR. *International Studies Perspectives,* 4(4), pp. 325–350.

Tickner, A. B., 2008, Latin American IR and the primacy of lo práctico. *International Studies Review,* 10(4), pp. 735–748.

TicknerA. B., 2013. Core, periphery and (neo)imperialist International Relations. *European Journal of International Relations,* 19(3), pp. 627–646.

Tickner, A.B. and Wæver, O. eds.2009. *International Relations Scholarship around the World.* New York: Routledge.

Tickner, A. J., 2016. Knowledge is Power: Challenging IR's Eurocentric Narrative. *International Studies Review,* 18(2016), pp. 157–159.

Tingyang, Z., 2009. A political world philosophy in terms of all-under-heaven (tianxia). *Diogenes,* 56(1). pp. 5–18.

Tsagankov, A. P., 2008. Self and other in international relations theory: learning from Russian civilisational debates. *International Studies Review,* 10(4), pp. 762–775.

Vasilaki, R., 2012. Provincialising IR? Deadlocks and Prospects in Post-Western IR Theory. *Millennium – Journal of International Studies,* 41, pp. 3–22.

Waltz, K.N. 1979. *Theory of International Politics.* New York: McGraw-Hill.

Wan, M., 2012. Introduction: Chinese traditions in international relations. *Journal of Chinese Political Science,* 17(2), pp. 105–109.

Wang, Y. 2009. China: between copying and constructing. In: A.B. Tickner, and O. Wæver, eds. 2009. *International Relations Scholarship around the World.* New York: Routledge. pp. 103–119.

Wemheuer-Vogelaar W., Bell, N. J., Morales, M. N., and Tierney, M. J., 2016. The IR of the Beholder: Examining Global IRUsing the 2014 TRIP Survey. *International Studies Review,* 0(2016), pp. 1–17.

Wæver, O. 1998. The Sociology of a Not So International Discipline: American and European Developments in International Relations. *International Organization,* 52(4), pp. 687–727.

Xuetong, Y., 2010. The Instability of China-US Relations. *The Chinese Journal of International Politics,* 3(2010), pp. 263–292.

Xuetong, Y. 2011. *Ancient Chinese Thought, Modern Chinese Power.* Princeton: Princeton University Press.

Zaman, R. U. 2006. Kautilya: The Indian Strategic Thinker and Indian Strategic Culture. *Comparative Strategy,* 25(3), pp. 231–247.

CHAPTER 11

Green Theory in IR

A Theory for a Green World

Altuğ Günar

1   Introduction

The rise of environmental concerns on a global scale in the 1960s has increased the importance of Green Theory in International Relations. Escalating global environmental crises have encouraged and prompted states to take various precautions at the international level. However, the beginning of addressing environmental issues in a disciplinary way is based on the analogy of "the tragedy of the commons" as suggested by Garrett Hardin. According to Hardin, the commons face a major daily threat due to misuse. In parallel with Hardin's contribution, a series of conferences held by the United Nations in 1972 increased environmental awareness in global politics.

While these actions, which may be regarded as the first wave of the development of Green Theory, mainly focused on basic concepts such as the role of the state and market mechanisms, more global and universal trends emerged during the second wave. However, the theory has developed in the third wave of the process and focused on a fundamental question that approached traditional theories critically. In parallel with this development process, following the activities of "The Club of Rome" and the publication of the report "Limits to Growth" (Meadows, Meadows, Rangers and Behren, 1972) in the 1970s, the foundation of the magazine "The Ecologist" was regarded as a milestone in terms of Green Theory. After 1980s and 1990s, the full development of this theory has been realized with the works of leading figures such as John S. Dryzek, Robyn Eckersley, Val Plumwood and Andrew Dobson.

The Green Theory established its theoretical framework on three claims. The most notable one is to accept ecocentrism which puts environment at the center, unlike other IR theories that adopt a human-centered worldview. At this point, the theory, which differs from the mainstream IR theories, provides quite a radical perspective. Another claim of the Green Theory is the hypothesis that growth is limited. In this context, the theory states that it is impossible to maintain development or growth at the expense of depletion of resources. Finally, according to Green Theory, a decentralized approach needs to be adopted, given that it is easier to make a change within hierarchical organizations. As central organizations give authority to more local organizations, it will become easier for democratic organizations to be accountable, and it will be much easier to prevent environmental crises.

Mainstream theories of International Relations have ignored serious environmental issues. These theories gave priority to high policy areas, particularly security, peace and independence; however, the recognition of the ecological approach to the environmental issues on a global scale caused a critical reconsideration of mainstream theories. In this context, by raising a radical question about whether the theoretical green state is the right actor in the prevention of environmental crises, it provokes a discussion about the roles of states as the main actors of international relations. Besides, in discussing whether the state is the right actor for a green revolution, the Green Theory is opposed to the concept of "sustainability" and states that the concept is suggested as an approach for controlling outcomes of industrialization. Therefore, the theory stands against modernity and highlights direct democracy through strengthening local organizations rather than central ones. The Green Theory continues to develop International Relations as a scientific field. Nevertheless, it still has not been regarded as a theory of the field. Although it is obvious that Green Theory has made significant progress in its journey over the last twenty years, it is claimed that it has come to a dead end. The weakest points of the theory are that some fundamental concepts in the field of global regulations are still controversial and it does not develop a concrete approach to the role of the state.

The main aim of this study is to discuss the basic tenants of the Green Theory of International Relations. In this regard, the first part analyzes the historical development and the pioneer sources of the theory, and the second part strives to determine the position of the theory among International Relations theories by approaching Green Theory as a critical perspective of International Relations. The final section aims to provide a holistic evaluation of the Green Theory by stating its fundamental principles and research directions.

2   Historical Background: Development of Green Theory

It is claimed that Green Theory dates back to Ancient Greece in terms of its historicization. Indeed, there is a claim that the Greek Philosopher Xenophon proposed the principles of the "Gaia Hypothesis",[1] which covers significant

---

1 Gaia Hypothesis is the principle that implied the world should be best understood as a complex system and living including a self-regulating mechanism. The term was first put

components of the theory 2000 years before the green policy was scientifically suggested (Richardson, 2005, p.3).

With the political and intellectual developments in the 17th century, (*Newton's laws of physics and the nation-state*) which put forward the concept of modernity, ecology continued to play a role in social theory. The development of capitalism followed the developments that focus on two main concepts, science and politics. As a result, organic bonds between societies were replaced by individuals who pursue their self-interests and are fighting for their lives in a world where competition is constantly increasing. Understanding of specified developments led to the emergence of pragmatic theories in the 18th and early 19th century, and the reorganization of the world where humans live was accepted as its natural consequence. However, contemporary growth and power theories and approaches to sustainable development, backed by technological and scientific developments, were used to access goods with high added value and wider markets. As a result of this situation, the violation of human rights increased dramatically following ecological crises. The role of the state became quite limited within this process and could not go beyond bringing the outcomes under control, and supervisory power/authority remained weak against ecological destruction (Lafferiere and Stoett, 1999, p.3–4).

E. F. Schumacher, a prominent figure of Green Theory, indicated uncontrolled industrialization as the main problem (2011, p.67–69). He drew our attention to six main and "anti-nature" factors that create natural destruction. He asserted that in the 19th century, "evolution", "competition", "natural selection", "the survival of the fittest", "the concept of mass production based on a Marxist interpretation of history", "Descartes' and Newton's philosophy of science related to relativity and scientific thinking and putting forward the idea of empirical information" produce anti-nature actions (Democratic Socialist Party, 1999, p.98). The development of an ecological approach in the 18th and 19th centuries is also associated with the romanticization of postmodern culture. Non-materialistic ideas arising in the context of criticizing enlightenment ideas were able to be defined through romanticization. Thus, the ecological approach emerged as a modernization response to the material changes in societies. The emergence of modern environmentalism developed after American romantic philosophers evaluated the value of nature with a non-pragmatic approach in the 19th century and led to a radical nature movement in the late 19th and early 20th centuries. Based on the notion of "the great

---

by James Lovelock. For Lovelock, the existence of the planetary system depends on whether humankind and other living organisms destroy the planet. For more information: (Heywood, 2014, p.79).

chain of being"[2] which is opposite to rationalism, all organisms in nature are connected to an ecological spirit in a semi-religious manner. Thus, American romantics gave all living creatures a divine role in nature and led to the emergence of different movements in the USA. The best known of these trends are the Sierra Club and the Audubon Society (Newel, 2019, p.23–24).

Despite of these pre-mature developments, the real story of Green Theory has began in the 1960s with public sensitivity based on the destruction of the environment all around the world. The public became aware of the destruction of the environment with the "tragedy of the commons", an analogy/idea/concept put forward by the USA ecologist Garrett Hardin about the overuse of resources of a farm (Dyer, 2017, p.84). According to the analogy, due to farmers' overuse of the resources in a limited area for grazing their animals, the available resources will be consumed in the end, and no one will be able to graze their animals using available resources due to overconsumption. Also, with the rise in the number of animals, the resources will be exhausted. In such a situation, shepherds will focus on gaining profit and will start calculating the benefits and losses of adding more animals to their herd. Two situations arise as a result of the calculation made by the shepherd. In the first case, the shepherd's income will increase by adding more animals. In the second case, there will be a high consumption of resources, which will cause excessive consumption of resources and the shepherd will logically decide to add a new animal to the herd so that the number of animals will increase steadily. This is the logical conclusion that all shepherds will draw, not one single shepherd. In this way, the tragedy of the commons will arise and result in the destruction of natural resources by shepherds who put the interest of the freedom of the commons in a world of limited resources (Hardin, 1968, p.1244).

Another study that has importance for Green Theory and raises great awareness in the international arena is *Silent Spring*, written by Rachel Carson in 1965. After the publication of *Silent Spring*, the industrial agriculture and chemical industries seriously opposed the ideas in the book and claimed that it included wrong propositions and statements in many aspects. However, Carlson's work led to the emergence of a major environmental movement, firstly among ecologists, and brought many communities interested in the protection of the environment together. Thus, the work made a great contribution to the rise of the green movement on a global scale and had a worldwide impact (Stoll, 2020). Carlson's work mentioned the dangers of pesticide

---

2   This is the expression that describes the hierarchical creation of live. It can be explained as
    a "The great chain of being" or "ladder of life" which are commonly used for describing the
    existence step by step. For more information see. (Barlow, 1997, p.44).

use in the USA and caused the pesticide policy in the USA to be changed and then later regulated. Following these developments, Carlson's work was instrumental in the foundation of the Environmental Protection Agency in the USA (Beyond Cruie, n.d).

The studies triggering the development of Green Theory increased at a remarkable rate in the 1970s. The increasing environmental destruction, reaching a level that can no longer be ignored, has resulted in a rise in green awareness globally. In particular, the report "Limits to Growth", commissioned by the Club of Rome in 1972, the British "Blueprint for Survival" (The Ecologist, 1972) and "Small is Beautiful", (Schumacher, 2011; 1973) written by Schumacher, are regarded as the leading works of Green Theory. The works produced by Schumacher made him the global green movement pioneer. Schumacher adopted a vision for improving the quality of life (Spretnak and Capra, 1985, p.163).

After *The Ecologist* magazine's issue "A Blueprint for Survival" was published in 1972, missing parts of the theoretical framework and model of Green Theory has begun to be completed. Following the publication of this issue, it was expressed that there was a need for the world to undergo a serious green revision and environmental reform process. The magazine clearly showed the terrible environmental issues that the world was facing and had a huge impact around the world before the Stockholm Conference held in 1972. Addressing the problems that the world was facing explicitly revealed the necessity of taking radical precautions concerning the environment (Hubbard, 2012). During this period, coupled with the publication of *The Ecologist* and the report "The Limits of Growth", a very comprehensive intellectual atmosphere known as the "Great Doomsday Debate" emerged in terms of Green Theory (Richardson, 2005, p.4). These developments led to the rise of green parties all over Europe, prompted many theorists to consider a new model of society for the future, and led the theory to philosophically build on the basis of "self-sufficiency", "appropriate technology", "decentralization" and "balanced population" policies.

Another milestone for Green Theory is the "Gaia" hypothesis formulated by James Lovelock. According to this hypothesis, the world is made up of two different types of organisms. The first type of organism make up the geochemistry of the planet and regulate the geochemistry structures of the planet humans live in. The world itself comprises the second type. As a matter of fact, the world has a structure that can organize itself and adapt itself to various situations. With the Gaia hypothesis, a huge leap was made in natural sciences and the world is considered as a totality of global systems (Litfin, 2005, p.508–509).

Green Theory arrived on the agenda of International Relations with the steps taken by the United Nations (UN)[3] in 1972 when the UN held the "United Nations Conference on the Human Environment." As Earth Day was celebrated for the first time in 1970, nation-states have started to pay attention to environmental issues and measures began to be implemented at the national level. The conference held by the UN had crucial importance since it led nation states to address the causes and effects of environmental damage on a global scale, and it had a major role in the emergence of environmental awareness in the UN. The UN Environment Program focused on the main issues indicated in the "Stockholm Declaration" after 1972 (Birnkman, Garren and Liu, 2013, p.9). The biggest environmental benefit was the foundation of the UN Environment Program in 1972, which drew attention to the relationship between economic development and environment and, notably, to the issues of climate change, environmental governance, efficient use of resources and energy sources (Garen and Brinkmann, 2018, p.7).

Due to the issues addressed by the mainstream theories of International Relations, environmental issues or issues related to the environment have never been included in "high politics". While the main starting point of mainstream theories was the relationship or conflict between states, especially the matter of security, other issues were ignored. This situation has changed in the 1970s and afterwards; a group of academicians have raised their concerns on the depletion of the ozone layer and, in particular, climate change in the international area, and it was the first time that the biodiversity of the world, humanity's natural habitat, was recognized as being under threat. The green awakening in International Relations revealed the "blindness" of mainstream theories to environmental issues and provided a basis for the development of other theories. "Gender blindness" in International Relations theories proposed by feminism came into existence and developed as a result of a critical approach to the current theories. The Green Theory, on the other hand, enriched its critical approach over time and broadened its scope by making use of neo-Marxism. The Green Theory of International Relations

---

3 Environmental activities carried out by the UN are chronologically as follows: 1972 UN Conference on the Human Environment, 1983 World Commission on Environment and Development, 1992 UN Conference on Development and Environment, 1994 Barbados Activity Program, 1997 UN General Assembly Special Session, 1999 Barbados Activity Program +5, 2002 World Summit on Sustainable Development, 2012 UN Conference on Sustainable Development. For more information visit: https://sustainabledevelopment.un.org/content/documents/4607Background%20paper%20on%20review%20of%20national%20SD%20assessments.pdf.

also reinterpreted the fundamental principles discussed by the mainstream theories. It reconsidered the notions such as "security" and redefined the fundamental concepts of "sustainable development", environmental justice and "ecological security", through objecting to the main assumptions of the mainstream scholarship (Eckersley, 2007, p.248).

In the 1980s, the dramatic increase in concerns about the environment and the biological structure of the world not only affected natural sciences but also revealed themselves as an outcome of the re-assessment of the theories within social sciences. In this context, by entering into a new questioning process in International Relations, the first wave of Green Theory has started. In this process, while the meaning of "green" was directly associated with environmental problems, the theory started to take place among International Relations theories in the 1990s. The great transformation that the world underwent in the relevant period resulted in a critical consideration of transatlantic capitalism and the Soviet-style system by Green Theory. Green Theory thinkers opposed the ideas of modernization and progress in the first wave and focused on the ecological effects of these concepts (Ercandırlı, 2014, p. 496).

After the 1980s and 1990s, the Green Theory developed in the context of the works of Dryzek, Eckersley, Plumwood and Dobson and formed its theoretical basics. Participatory democracy appeared as a central factor within the Green Theory, and decentralization strived to get the opportunity to develop stronger democratic trends, such as paying attention to citizen participation or grassroots participation in politics. Participatory democracy created a favorable environment for the best expression of the values and concerns represented by Green Theory. Concepts such as direct citizen participation, social justice concerns and ecological awareness have recently strengthened the theory's tendency to deliberative democracy (Peters, 2019, p.133).

Along with the rise of parties that brought to the fore environmental concerns in global politics, new social movements made contact with peace and feminism approaches and caused concerns about the quality of life to be placed at the center of human life. The new understanding of politics that started to emerge in this way and found a place in the ecological approach has begun to manifest itself in all social areas associated with direct democracy, such as concerns for developing countries and disarmament. The parties that brought to the fore green concerns started to rise in the states with left-leaning and corporatist tradition, especially in advanced welfare states. In this period, the increase of environmental issues globally resulted in the rise of green policy and its politicization. Concerns about the state of the ozone layer, climate change and many natural crises such as increased acid rain were regarded as proof of a great global natural destruction in the 1980s. Chernobyl and similiar nuclear disasters were enough to raise global awareness of environmental decline and crises. Especially at the conference held in Toronto in 1988, the environmental crises that the world was facing were compared to a nuclear weapon (Newell, 2019, p.21–22).

In this context, the first wave of the Green Theory has focused on the difference of ecology and political theory. Outstanding studies; Jonathan Porritt's (1984) "Seeing Green: The Politics of Ecology Explained", David Pepper's (1984) "The Roots of Modern Environmentalism", Spretnak and Capra's (1985) "Green Politics: The Global Promise", John S. Dryzek's (1987) "Rational Ecology: Environment and Political Economy", Andrew Dobson's (1990) "Green Political Thought", Robyn Eckersley's (1992) "Environmentalism and Political Theory: Towards an Ecocentric Approach", Robert Paehlke's (1989) "Environmentalism and the Future of Progressive Politics" and finally Tim Hayvard's "Ecological Thought: An Introduction" were among the works that marked the first wave of Green Theory (Barry, 2014, p.4).

The second wave of Green Theory included more cosmopolitan and transnational trends compared to its first wave and drew attention to ecological disproportions related to the fundamental concepts, such as theories of the state and market (Eckersley, 2013, p.271). The Green Theory focused on establishing relationships with other theories in the second wave and expanding its theoretical scope. In this context, it is seen that the Green Theory is included in the debates between liberalism, feminism, critical theory and other IR theories. Prominent studies of Green Theory in the second wave are: John Barry's (1999) "Rethinking Green Politics: Nature Virtue and Progress", Mary Mellor's (1992) "Breaking The Boundaries: Towards a Feminist Green Socialism", Ariel Salleh's (1997) "Ecofeminism as Politics Nature Marx and the Postmodern", Marcel Wissenburg's (1998) "Green Liberalism: The Free and the Green Society", Anver De-Shalit's "Why Posterity Matters: Environmental Policies and Future Generations", Biran Doherty and Marius de Geus's (1996) "Democracy and Green Political Thought: Sustainability, Rights and Citizenship", Saral Sarkar's (1999) "Eco-Socialism or Eco-Capitalism?: A Critical Analysis of Humanity's Fundamental Choices", and finally William M. Lafferty and James Meadowcroft's (1996) "Democracy and the Environment: Problems and Prospects" (Barry, 2014, p.4).

As with other new theories in International Relations, the Green Theory has also come into existence in the "third wave" of the process. Therefore, in parallel with other theories, Green Theory tended to adopt a critical approach to the issues drawing on many disciplines. The Green Theory of International Relations is supported by intergovernmental and non-governmental organizations, scientists, and academicians for the protection of the environment at the international level. This situation has led to the foundation of political parties called "green" in the political systems of nation-states. It can be seen that Green Theory significantly influences International Relations and scientific institutions and international policy making as it aims to make inequity between the North and the South more sustainable through international trade, debt and aid (Eckersley, 2013, p.274). In the third wave, the Green Theory has turned to case studies which was multi-disciplinary and therefore is opened to other disciplines. As a matter of fact, it is difficult to situate the issues included in the Green Theory on a single intellectual level. For this reason, The Green Theory should be included and combined with the ideological structures outside of political theory. Otherwise, it is quite difficult for the Green Theory to reach a theoretical depth. Therefore, it has adopted an interdisciplinary perspective in the third wave process. In this respect, during the third wave John Barry's "The Politics of Actually Existing Unsustainability" (2012), Molly Scott Cato's (2012) "Green Economics: An Introduction to Theory Policy and Practice", Andy Dobson's (2003) "Citizenship and the Environment", Mathew Humprey's (2008) "Ecological Politics and Democratic Theory: The Challenge to the Deliberative Ideal (Extremism and Democracy)", Graham Smith's (2003) "Deliberative Democracy and the Environment", Simon A. Hailwood's (2004) "How to be Green Liberal: Nature Value and Liberal Philosophy", Tim Hayward's (2005) "Constitutional Environmental Rights" and Tim Jackson's "Prosperity without Growth: Economics for a Finite Planet" appeared to be out. As can be seen from the studies, Green Theory has tried to explain the green thoughts that were put forward by acting in a wide range of disciplines during the third wave process, and specifically focused on the criticism of economic growth. These trends created more agenda during the global economic crisis in 2008 and discussions on green development gained momentum. The report, published in 2008 by the "Green New Deal Group" in particular, served as a theory machine by introducing new visions and perspectives to the Green Theory (Barry, 2014, p.4).

Subdivisions within the Green Theory may be helpful to better understand the environmental issues. In this context, to ensure a better comprehension of the current issues of Green Theory, "regime theories" may be useful to understand global ecological issues with the concept of international political economy. Moreover, "green cosmopolitanism" may make new trends such as environmental justice and "green democracy" more understandable. It is crucial to state that these subdivisions are based on the neo-Gramscian critical theory of International Relations and Habermas' cosmopolitan discourse ethics (Eckersley, 2013, p.274).

It is important to draw attention also to the distinctions between the concepts of the Green Theory and environmentalism in terms of understanding the Green International Relations theory. This difference is crucially important especially for understanding the main premises of the Green Theory. Since environmentalists accept social, economic and normative structures of current global political structures as they are, they struggle with existing environmental issues within the system. On the other hand, the Green Theory as opposed to the main structures accepted by environmentalists, claims that the current global political structure is the main cause of environmental crises. The Green Theory discusses the need to go beyond these structures. It is a remarkable point that the approach adopted by environmentalists is quite compatible with the theoretical framework created by neo-liberal institutionalism (Paterson, 2005, p.236).

The distinction between environmentalism and ecology has become clear with the development of Green Theory. Recent works about the theory have made significant contributions to this issue. This broad theoretical framework within Green Theory has resulted in some divisions in the Theory. In this context, the theory can take various forms such as eco-feminism, deep ecology, eco-socialism, eco-anarchism and bio-regionalism (Newell, 2019, p.28–31). There are different approaches in the philosophical and epistemological origins of the Green Theory. It can be seen that the elements of universalism are found in deep ecology, those of spiritualism in the green radicalism/anarchism approach, those of structuralism in ecological socialism and deterministic elements in ecologic feminism (Newell, 2019, p.27).

3 The Main Critiques Levied against Conventional IR Theory

Criticisms of Green Theory to mainstream International Relations may be divided into six areas including state authority, conflict and violence, institution and world order, peace and security, inequality and justice, identity and community.

The first critique on state authority addresses whether state authority loses power due to environmental crises and whether responses to natural crises need global measures. It is extremely difficult to resolve global environmental crises within the context of the nation-state; large-scale global problems like climate change, global warming, etc. bring states together, and cooperation gains a capacity to develop a new understanding of sovereignty (Steans, Pettiford, Diez and El-Anis, 2013, p.218). Discussions about the loss of state sovereignty started to come to the forefront in the 1970s. The relations of multinational companies with the state, which were gaining power at that time, were the basis of these discussions. Later, a balance was tried to be struck between the state and transnational relations. At this point, it is necessary to distinguish between economic interdependence and ecological interdependence. Ecological interdependence does not cause serious problems for state authority such as economic interdependence (Litfin, 1997, p.170). For French, environmental problems threaten all nations and therefore necessitate a global governance system to deal with global environmental problems by making international agreements between states (French, 1992, p.6).

By challenging the traditional understanding of the state in International Relations, Green Theory takes on more radical forms. At some point, the Green Theory opposes the state for anarchic reasons. The understanding of the state adopted by Weber is regarded as a problematic structure by the Green Theory. The state is a hierarchical structure within itself, as well as a structure that gathers all other hierarchical institutions within itself. Although the state is a dynamic of modern society, it provides the dynamic power that ensures the continuation of modern society causing environmental crises (Paterson, 2000, p.62).

This criticism of Green Theory toward state authority is not accepted by Realists. According to Realists, the state holds the power of sanction to prevent environmental crises and even stands out as the sole actor that has the power in this matter. As the state is the dominant actor in the formulation and implementation of foreign policy, its sovereignty is protected by the rules of international law, when it becomes a party to the international treaty. For this reason, international environmental treaties reinforce the authority of the state and even strengthen the state authority. While some green theorists disagree with such thoughts of Realists, some have justified and supported the idea of state negotiations. However, this support is given to a state that could ensure the redistribution of resources existing in the world. Some Green Theory thinkers have argued that by promoting the existence of stronger state authority at the international level, the state will play an active role in the redistribution of resources globally with the negotiating authority. With this role of the state, the idea of allocating resources from the rich to the poor regions is expressed. Even if there is not a certain contradiction, Green Theory considers the state as "fatality" and opposes the authority's point of view. Hence, the Green Theory argues that a source of authority should be created at the regional and global levels; therefore, state structures remain either enormous/bulky or fractional (Steans, Pettiford, Diez and El-Anis, 2010, p.219).

In International Relations, reasons for environmental crises are dependent on climate change, and it is concerned that environmental degradation will have various consequences socially. Hence, there is a concern about how mainstream International Relations theories will explain this situation when worse environmental crises are faced. Environmental issues will be ordinarily overlooked within a theoretical framework based on power, and interests for power politics will be the main causes of environmental crises. Today, strength or other variations of power are still calculated with the gross domestic product, which is an economic measuring index. Within this context, the "ecological footprint" is associated with GDP; therefore, the dependence of a nation-state on power is at the same time the main catalyst of environmental crises (Mathai, 2013). Even though Green Theory critically attacks the hierarchies in state structures, the most of the Green theorists consider the state structure an authority to make more environmental arrangements as the sole solution. Hence, it is stated that various structures can be established to cope with global environmental problems, such as "democratic citizenship" (Pennington, 2008, p.431).

The Second critique of the Green Theory addresses the nature of the conflict and violence. The Green Theory states that peace cannot be established on a military basis. Even if military peace is established, it will feed on an ecological crisis, and state leaders cannot act logically for a long time. Thus, the approach of Realism towards the nature of the conflict cannot be accepted (Laferriere and Stoett, 1999, p.100). According to the Green Theory the problems experienced in supplying resources such as water that directly constitute the basic need of human beings can cause conflicts and tensions between states. Diseases caused by the decrease in water resources, overfishing and excessive consumption of seafood seriously damage the global ecological structure and result in economic difficulties for countries. As a matter of fact, it is stated that such damage to the ecological structure can cause changes in social structures, as social movements gain radical forms and may reveal new social classes, as well as increase social conflicts and divisions. In this context, ethnic conflicts may confront states in the context of social divisions. At the same time, situations such as protecting regionally owned resources have the potential to cause conflicts that may bring states against each other. In a country suffering from famine, people will start to migrate for better living conditions and will decide to migrate to the countries and regions where resources are more abundant. When all these situations are accompanied by factors such as the fragility of democratic structures and the lack of strength of civil society, the legitimacy of the political structures of the states may weaken with the worsening environmental conditions. Since this situation renders democratic mechanisms dysfunctional, change may lead to violent incidents, unlike the political way (Steans, Pettiford, Diez and El-Anis, 2010, p.219–220).

The third critique of the Green Theory on conventional IR Theory is on the understanding of the institution and world order. In this respect, the concept that needs to be addressed is the concept of "sustainability". The idea of managing the development, industrialization and economic growth of countries has been criticized by radical sections of the Green Theory. According to the Green Theory, most of the conferences and the systems or institutions established by the UN are only based on a fiction that the society will progress. A structure has been established based on the idea of preserving the existing order. As a matter of fact, this accepted "managerial" understanding is the product of a vision that envisages changing the development in the context of the strategies adopted from time to time rather than being a problem. This situation brings up two important concepts. The first one is "shallow environmentalism" which implies that environmental problems can be overcome by realizing reforms within existing structures. The second concept, "deep environmentalism", states that the source of ecological degradation is the existing systems accepted as consumption and production models. Deep environmentalism claims that environmental crises cannot be prevented unless there is a radical change. After the Rio Summit, the concept of "sustainable development" was not reconsidered, but it was emphasized that the management style should be changed. However, at the World Environment and Development Commission meeting held in 1987, the concept was left ambiguously and not defined. The Green Theory believes that responding the environmental crisis in the current situation regarding global order and institutions is only possible with radical changes. As a matter of fact, according to the Greens, today's world order is based on a consumption culture and industrialization based on the strengthening of capitalism. Since this structure is oppressive, it also becomes oppressive in social relationships (Steans, Pettiford, Diez and El-Anis, 2010, p.220–223).

The fourth critique of the Green Theory to traditional International Relations Theory is related with understanding of peace and security in conventional IR Theories. The Green theory claims that peace can not be achieved unless oppressive practices are abolished. Based on the view that all organisms should live in harmony, which is one of the main premises of the theory, perpetual peace indicates that all organisms in the universe live in harmony. Therefore, according to the Green Theory, it is a must to change the visions of understanding the world in order to achieve international peace. In terms of security, the Green Theory states that most of the resources go to armament due to the importance given to military resources. It also examines the issue from a broad perspective that addresses the impact of current conflicts on the environment. States' dedication to military spending may cause impoverishment.

As a matter of fact, the use or testing of chemical and biological weapons seriously affects the ecological system in the world (Steans, Pettiford, Diez and El-Anis, 2010, p.223–224).

The fifth critique of the Green Theory to mainstream IR is on inequality and justice. The Green Theory claims that systems built on inequality cause environmental problems. For this reason, it is stated that relations structured in an oppressive and unjust way should be terminated. In this regard, it was concretely associated with the Environment and Development Conference held by the UN in 1992, which presents that there is a connection between poverty and environmental degradation. The quality of life of people who are poor or who live in disadvantaged regions of the world decreases in direct proportion to environmental degradation. The division of agricultural lands while they are being used in the production process can cause an unequal sharing, resulting in the accumulation of more resources in the hands of a lesser segment of the society. In this context, the Green Theory focuses on how resources should be distributed over the concept of social justice. However, according to the Green Theory, the concepts of justice and "sustainable development" cannot be considered complementary. For this reason, while states design an ecologically sustainable society, they also cause a situation where there are inequalities in which some people have much more resources. The fairness of a society does not mean that environmental collapse will not occur. The main problem arises in relation to the overconsumption paradigm. The justice issue cannot be explicitly addressed in the international arena. Although the idea that international justice can be achieved with a certain authority is accepted as an easy problem at first, the international justice problem has a much more complex structure. Considering global warming, even if it is thought that the most developed countries of the world are effective on global warming, will it be possible to compensate for the damages that have occurred before? Or is global warming really recognized as a problem internationally? Most attempts to ensure justice in global environmental problems have pursued the fair, acting on statistical values such as emissions. Although the Green Theory attaches importance to the issue of justice, they foresee that unless there is justice, inequality will increase and its success will decrease (Steans, Pettiford, Diez and El-Anis, 2010, p.225–226).

The sixth critique of the Green Theory is on identity and community. Green Theory's view on community is quite different than the mainstream IR Theories' perception. Indeed, the Green Theory suggests that the concept of community should be considered at a local and, global level. In this context, the concept that is accepted as "community" according to the Green Theory actually includes all the people of the world and non-human living species.

The Green Theory supports diversity by criticizing industrialized society and development and stating that differences must be preserved. Mary Midgley's work "Animal and Why they Matter" is of great importance in terms of expanding the concept of community. As a matter of fact, it was stated by Midgley that the concept of community can be expanded by accepting them as sensitive beings in their animals. From the point of view that Green Theory deals with the concept of community, they argue that it will not be enough to just expand it, and their understanding of identity should be reconsidered. In this regard, eco-feminist ideas came to the fore and drew attention to self and identity problems. They developed an alternative perspective based on the concept of "ecological self" introduced by Freta Matthews. In this context, self and identity construction are interrelated, and this duality has inherently been problematic (Steans, Pettiford, Diez and El-Anis, 2010, p.226–227).

4   Main Principles of the Green Theory

The development of the International Relations literature on the basic acknowledgements and assumptions of Green Theory took place in the 1990s. Green political theory and global ecology also contributed to the constitution of the main principles of Green Theory on global policy. While green political theory provides the theory with a canonical structure to explain the Green Theory in International Relations, global ecology provides a descriptive base for Green Theory to explain situations. Within this scope, it is accepted that the theory focuses on two main approaches. Green Theory literature in International Relations established its main principles with the contributions of Wolfgang Sachs, Pratap Chatterjee, Matthias Finder, Vandana Shiva, etc. and focused on the emergence of environmental crises and protection of the environment. In this sense, the World Summit of the United Nations Conference on Environment and Development (UNCED) held in 1992 is considered as a milestone. This summit was very important in terms of ensuring that environmental problems are taken seriously by the part of public opinion and political decision-makers. It is also accepted as a major fiasco since it was the last collaboration established by elites for the environment (Paterson, 2005, p.238).

The main assumptions of Green Theory can be divided into three themes: 1- Ecocentrism, 2-Limits to Growth, and 3-Decentralization of Power. Ecocentrism (an approach putting nature at the center of the universe), which is commonly associated with environmentalist tendencies, resulted from criticisms of anthropocentrism (an approach putting humans at the center of the universe) and is used for all non-anthropocentric theories/systems (Leib, 2001, p.28). Ecocentrism is one of the most important central assumptions of the Green Theory. In the concrete sense of the word, Green Theory approaches existing structures by putting a worldview that prioritizes nature at the center of the theory instead of a worldview that prioritizes human. With the simplest meaning, ecocentrism does not just include the near environment of microorganisms but all environmental relations. Within this context, the world does not just consist of substances, and it is more logical to recognize or approach it as a "phenomenon or body of phenomena". From this point of view, Green Theory opposes the anthropocentric approach that is at the center of mainstream theories. According to Green Theory, an anthropocentric approach ignores the fact that creatures in the world, including living and non-living creatures, humans and nonhuman creatures, are in relation to each other. There is no discrimination among all creatures existing in the world, and there is a sequence of dynamic relations. Scientific revolutions also explicitly oppose anthropocentric claims and cause important effects on ecocentric approaches. Hence, the ecocentric approach has a more coherent relationship with modern sciences. Rather than being anti-science, ecocentric philosophers apply modern science while opposing the anthropocentric approach. In this sense, philosophers that adopt the ecocentric approach are not anti-science but oppose scientism (Eckersley, 1992, p.49–51).

Ecocentrism is also accepted as emancipation writ large. Within this context, it is not accepted that only humans have an effect on nature and the world. All creatures in the world are also accepted as securing justice between humans and other species (Benton, 2007, p.88). Therefore, humankind is not accepted as the sole commander of nature. All creatures are given autonomy within the network of ecological relations. Therefore, ecocentrism has four main ethical features. By having features like protection of resources, human prosperity ecology, preservationism and emancipation of animals, ecocentrism distinguishes itself from other moral approaches. Protection of resources means recognition of all human interests in an unhumanitarian world. Human prosperity ecology, on the other hand, means protection of interests of unhumanitarian communities. Preservationism signifies the protection of interests of humans and nonhuman creatures. Lastly, emancipation of animals refers to all organisms and ecosystems in the atmosphere being recognized with a holistic approach (Paterson, 2005, p.239).

The second main assumption of the Green Theory is that growth has limits (*limits to growth*). More clearly, the Green Theory claims that there are limits to the growth of human communities. The concept was brought forward first in the book *Limits to Growth* written in 1972. Scientists from ten different countries came together in Rome in 1968 and established the Club of

Rome. They wanted to draw the attention of policymakers to understand all economic, political, natural and social phenomena in the global system and encourage new fields of policy. In line with this purpose, they focused on a goal, "estimating the situation of human beings" and tried to get to the bottom of the complex problems that humankind faced at the time. They launched a project bringing various problems forward, such as "poverty in the midst of abundance", "losing faith in institutions", "ecocide", "uncontrolled urban development", "unemployment", etc.

The concept of "limits to growth" also means that resources existing in the world limit growth. In other words, growth is not eternal on a planet with limited resources. The report drafted as part of the project conducted by the Club of Rome in 1972 included an estimation within a model it adopted considering the situation in that period (Newell, 2019, p.79). According to the existing situation in 1972, the report suggested that current growth would end within 100 years if the world population, industrialization, pollution and food production continued rising. It also stated that population and industrial capacity would face a serious decline (Meadows, Meadows, Rangers and Behren, 1972, p.23). Concerning the report, it was specified that various raw materials existing in the world would run out rapidly and pollution would exceed the environment's absorption capacity, causing a large downfall at the beginning of the 2100s (Paterson, 2005, p.239).

The ideas of Green Theory about limits to growth are addressed in three dimensions. Technology constitutes the first of these dimensions; however, according to Green Theory, technology will not ensure sustainability on limits to economic, political or social growth. In other words, it will not be possible to create a sustainable society. The second dimension is that societies which are being industrialized rapidly face serious devastation due to ignoring threats for a long time. The third and last dimension is that problems arising from growth are connected; thus, it becomes complicated to solve the problems. The solution to a problem will not ensure that other problems associated with this problem are solved (Dobson, 2007, p.53–54). At this point, the term "sustainability" is important in terms of Green Theory. However, Green Theory contests the ordinary meaning of the term sustainability. Sustainability refers to methods that use resources logically or rationally to prevent them from being damaged (Merriam-webster, 2020). It suggests that the existing meaning of the term sustainability refers to a reduction of energy, economic production and resources in industrialized countries (Paterson, 2005, p.240).

The term sustainability drew attention in the 1980s, and the term "sustainable development" stood out. Within this context, ecologists created various models and tried to explain how the ecological environment had transformed in response to shocks and crises and assessed them using these models. In this sense, methods for using natural resources rationally and increasing efficiency were used in a wide variety of areas of the ecosystem, such as sustainable areas and resource management. The term sustainability was defined as the ability of a system to return after relevant processes. Hence, a serious question has arisen over this concept, which can be accepted as the status quo, about the systems that are not complex and non-status quo. The term was criticized by both the social sciences and ecological sciences. With the rise of ideas about the term sustainable development, a uniform concept addressing political goals from the economy to the environment arose (Scoones, 2016, p.319). The term sustainability was defined in the document "World Conservation Strategy" in various forms. In this document, a scope was created for the term development, and it was defined as the mobilization of world facilities for human goals. "Protection" was defined as the protection of resources to realize human needs. While natural resources may disappear due to their nature, they are also "renewable". Therefore, protection arises as a natural necessity. The strategy document addresses protection and sustainable development on the basis of such resources and emphasizes that protection and sustainable development are inseparable and vital for humans living in rural areas (World Conservation Strategy, 1980, p.18). However, Green Theory transparently disputes this term in this point and notes that it is necessary to handle natural systems aggregately so that the ecological system of the world can be sustainable. It stresses that goals set to meet human needs must be handled in any dimensions that include production and are designed by considering ecological systems. To explain this more concretely, Green Theory opposes opinions put forward within the context of the sustainability of economic efficiency to protect ecological integrity. In this sense, it objects to orthodox opinions that anticipate the sake of societies and points out the importance of respecting the integrity of the biosphere. It suggests that consumption tendencies will undergo a change and specifies that "passivity in consumption" will change into "creativity" in terms of work and leisure times, which are humans' sources of satisfaction (Lee, 1995, p.116).

The third assumption of the Green Theory is the belief in decentralized structure of authority. Decentralized systems, namely the assignment of central decision-making structures to local authorities usually have advantages; it is also important in terms of "autonomy" and democratic accountability. It is also seen that the decentralized approach has advantages in terms of envrioment. Hence, the abovementioned advantage is important to small communities that are dependent on local sources and facilities. In this way, they will protect the environment more, consider the environment as their home and care for it by conceptualizing it less. Therefore, it is thought that disregarding local communities, which are deemed as one of the reasons for natural crises in the environment, can be overcome. In this sense, the term "bioregionalism" stands out (Dyer, 2018, p.3).

Before discussing bioregionalism, it is necessary to understand the term "bioregion." "Bioregion" is derived from the Greek and Latin languages. The word is a combination of the terms "bios", which means *life* in Greek and "regire", which means *managing* in Latin. In this sense, bioregions refer to areas in the world that are biologically important and home to various animal species and life forms. Bioregionalism was derived from bioregions, is defined as "governments of the world"; it is a concept that aims to protect the whole ecological system with a decentralized structure and aims to help people in this structure. The term bioregionalism arose in the 1970s as a socio-political concept. The term bioregion was originally defined by Van Newkirk (1975, p.108) as a "... biologically significant areas of the Earth's surface which can be mapped and discussed as distinct existing patterns of plant, animal, and habitat ..." Later, Berg and Dasmann (Berg and Dasmann, 1977, p.399) underlined the cultural dimension of the bioregion and indicated that it "refers both to geographical terrain and a terrain of consciousness- that a place and the ideas that have developed about how to live in that place." Following that the term detailed widely by Dasmann (1984) in his remarkable work titled "Environmental Conservation." The term bioregionalism is based on an environment-oriented point of view and focuses on the considerable transformation of human behaviors within the scope of ecological balance (Francese, 2016, p.21–22). The roots of the term defined as bioregionalism today dates back to the first indigenous people. Hence, indigenous people applied most methods before the term was defined and experienced many factors related to the term bioregionalism. However, with population growth and the rise of technological possibilities, economic and social models adopted by human communities caused damage to the lifestyles of indigenous people and started to prevent such methods (McGinnes, 1999, p.2–3). From this point of view, the Green Theory also puts forward the mainframe for worldview. According to Green Theory, the nation-state is incapable of managing new developments arising regionally and globally, especially sustainability since it is too big or too small (Paterson, 2005, p.242).

5   Research Directions for Green Politics

To build a green-friendly world is the one of the goals of the Green Theory. However, the Green Theory must cooperate with the structures that it has challenged in the past. To achieve this goal, a wide range of support is needed beyond environmentalism. It has to form a coalition strategically, including trade unions and private sector representatives that the theory has opposed in the past (Newel, 2019, p.220). While the green literature approached post-structuralism in the context of modern society criticism, the theory was fed by critical theory in the context of criticism to capitalism. There are also social constructivists among Green Theory thinkers. The theory has also been seriously interested in feminism. This trait of the Green Theory has caused it to become a post-positivist theory. As a matter of fact, at the center of the Green Theory is the reconstruction of the relationship between man and nature. As a matter of fact, in this context, the concept of "ecological self" put forward by Freta (1991) tries to connect with nature (Steans, Pettiford, Diez and El-Anis, 2010, p.243).

Eco-radicals are in favor of radical changes on how to establish green state, which is the main problem of the Green Theory. As a matter of fact, eco-radicals believe that the state has failed to resolve environmental crises which are the root cause. In other words, the state, as a part of modern society, is the cause of the environmental crisis. There is no consensus among the eco-radicals regarding how to replace the state structure. Current discussions include the nature and scope of the measures and reforms to be taken against environmental crises. In this context, it is stated that eco-radicals have gone too far in their thinking. It is claimed by eco-radicals that ideas based on reform are very optimistic by modernists. Between these two extreme poles, there is a debate about what the concept of a green state (Eckersley, 2004) should encompass and what would be considered more sustainable (Jackson, Sorensen, 2013, p. 293).

It is thought that future studies of the Green Theory will be realized towards the visible effects of the world we live in. Its emergence in empirical studies on theory in the 3rd wave process confirms this situation. The environmental concerns of the period also shape the zeitgeist, and today humanity faces a future climate change and where available resources, especially, have come to an end. Although this is the result of the accepted carbon-based capitalist consumption and production system, it also clearly shows that the system has come to an end. In terms of the Green Theory, it is stated that the subject of the studies in the next stage may be the tendencies towards the transition to the post-carbon society with low carbon tendency. The establishment of a post-carbon society economically and socially is accepted as a necessity by the Green Theory. In this context, ecological-realists draw attention in recent studies. Ecological realists firmly state that such a lifestyle is not sustainable (Barry, 2014, p.12).

The harsh expression of the failure of politicians and the most powerful countries in the face of the disasters the world faces, as Cormac McCarthy has set it up in his work "The Road",[4] stands out in the green literature. In particular, terms such as "climate chaos", "carbon-constrained world", "food and climate insecurity" were used quite frequently in this period. Again, during this period, announcements such as "100 Months to Save the World" tried to express the emergency of the world in the face of environmental disasters. In this context, it can be argued that the Green Theory has recently focused on green realism analyzes. At the same time, the whole world, especially multinational companies, remains silent in the face of the unsustainable deterioration of the planet where humanity lives. Although the whole world is a single voice in conferences and all other actions on global warming, and support becomes shallow when it comes to changing people's lifestyle. Another stop of this green realism idea that emerged in green thought has been in the UK and Ireland. "Dark Mountain"[5] project is an ecological reality project that tries to show that humanity lives in uncertainty and chaos. On the same plane, James Lovelock (2009) stands out with his striking thoughts in the context of ecological reality in his work "The Vanishing Face of Gaia: A Final Warning". According to Lovelock, emission values are calculated based on statistical values by turning them into a commodity today.

6   Conclusion

The story of Green Theory taking its place in International Relations has started in the 1960s. However, its history dates back to ancient Greece. The term "tragedy of the commons" put forward by Garret constitutes an important starting point for the theory. Even if a series of global environmental conferences held by the UN in the 1970s contributed to the development of the theory, they were far from effective. However, the theory had an opportunity to develop with the publication of "The Limits of Growth" report and the foundation of

---

4   The work depicts a post-apocalyptic situation. The characters in the novel have no names. The story is a passing dystopia in a ruined America. For more information: Aylin Alkaç, "Ethics of Being in Cormac McCarthy's The Road The Ethics of Being in Cormac McCarthy's Road Novel", Gaziantep University Journal of Social Sciences, 2019, pp. 71–80.

5   The main purpose of the project is to investigate the origins of the complexity of the world by moving away from the culture faced by humanity and the factors that prevent ecological and social disintegration. According to the Dark Mountain project, humanity is in a period of great uncertainty and chaos.

The Ecologist magazine during this period. In this sense, the contributions of Dryzrk, Eckersley, Plumwood and Dobson in the 1980s and 1990s, when the theory developed, basically caused a kind of germination period and the theory entered into a process of building itself on very powerful democratic terms, such as advanced democracy, participative democracy, etc.

The ecocentric point of view adopted by Green Theory radically separates it from mainstream theories of International Relations since it suggests a basis for limits to development and prioritizes decentralized structures. With such basic principles, Green Theory critiques the centralized position of the state, which is perceived as the main actor of International Relations and addresses the functions of the state to prevent environmental crises by starting from the question of whether the state is a beneficial actor or not. Also, by opposing the term sustainability, the theory denies the elimination of the environment for the sake of development and claims that terms like sustainability just focus on results and are related to controlling current results. Also, by objecting to hierarchical structures, the theory claims that it is necessary to prioritize decentralized structures and change authority from centralized to localized, as more manageable and democratic systems can be built in this way.

The Green Theory offers a different world reading with an ecocentric point of view located at the center of the theory, unlike the other theories of International Relations. Today, an increase in the number of environmental disasters provides a significant opportunity for the development of Green Theory. However, its weaknesses and uncertain position on basic concepts cause it to remain weak against mainstream theories of International Relations.

The natural and environmental crises that humankind faces today show how important environmental issues are in areas of high policy, such as peace, conflict, etc., and especially security in terms of International Relations. Hence, while the emergence of concepts like green security, the regulation of state development plans using green perspectives and the race to build a nature-friendly, greener world continues without slowing down, the perspective suggested by Green Theory is still ignored.

To summarize, the Green Theory was on the rise in International Relations in the 1960s and preferred to develop its aspect of study by re-addressing concepts and issues at the center of International Relations theory from its perspective. The Green Theory put the ecocentric point of view at the center of the process of explaining international relations, world politics and interstate relations. It is based on the idea that development must have been limited by suggesting that development cannot be sustained or realized in a controlled manner despite environmental disasters. Lastly, Green Theory stresses that environmental disasters cannot be controlled through hierarchical structures, prioritizes decentralized structure and directs its field of studies to new horizons for combining a new democratic form with a green state understanding by orienting to advanced understandings of democracy.

References

Barry, J. 1999. Rethinking Green Politics: Nature, Birtue, Progress. London: Sage.

Barry, J. 2014. Green Political Theory In: Geoghean, V. and Vilford, R. (eds). *Political Ideologies: An Introduction.* London: Routledge.

Berg, P. Dasmann, R. 1977. Reinhabiting California. *The Ecologist,* 7(10), pp. 399–401.

Barlow, C. 1997. *Green Space, Green Time: The Way of Science.* Berlin: Springer-Verlag.

Benton, T. 2007. Deep Ecology. In: Pretty, J. Ball, A. S. Benton, T. Guivant, J. Lee, D. R. Orr, D. Pfeffer M. J. and Ward, H. ed. 2007. *The Sage Handbook of Environment and Society.* Sage Publications.

Beyond Curie, n.d. [online] Available at: https://www.beyondcurie.com/rachel-carson/, [Accessed 17 September 2020].

Brinkmann, R., Garren, S., Liu, W. 2013. *Global Sustainable Development Report 2013: A Review of National Sustainable Development Assessments,* [online] Available at: https://sustainabledevelopment.un.org/content/documents/4607Background%20paper%20on%20review%20of%20national%20SD%20assessments.pdf.

Browning, E. V. n.d. Xenophon (430–354 B.C.E). Internet Encyclopedia of Philosophy. [online] Available at: https://iep.utm.edu/xenophon/ [Accessed 25 October 2020].

Democratic Socialist Party. 1999. *Environment Capitalism & Socialism.* Sydney: Resistance Books.

Denis, M. J. 2019. Green IR Theory and Domestic Wars: Revisiting Environmental Conflicts in Africa. *International Journal of Research and Innovation in Social Sciences,* 3(9), pp. 166–171.

Dobson, A. 2007. Green Political Thought. London: Routledge.

Dobson, A., MacGregor, S., Torgerson, D. 2009. Trajectories of Green Political Theory. *Contemporart Political Theory,* 8(3) 2009, pp. 317–350.

Dyer, H. C. 2017. Green Theory. In ed. McGlinchey, S., Walters, R., Scheinplug, C., *International Relations Theory.* E-International Relations Publishing, [online] Available at: https://www.e-ir.info/publication/international-relations-theory/ [Accessed 10 September 2020] pp. 84–90.

Eckersley, R. 2004. *The Green State Rethinking Democracy and Sovereignty.* The MIT Press.

Eckersley, R. 2007. Green Theory. In: Dunne, T., Kurki, M., Smith, S. ed. 2007. International Relations Theories, United Kingdom: Oxford University Press.

Eckersley, R. 2013. Green Theory. In: Dunne, T., Kurki, M., Smith, S. ed. 2013. *International Relations Theories Discipline and Diversity*, United Kingdom: Oxford University Press.

Francese, D. 2016. *Technologies for Sustainable Urban Design and Bioregionalist Regeneration*. Routledge.

Ercandırlı, Y. 2014. Yesil Teori. In: Gözen, R. 2014. Uluslararası İlişkiler Teorileri. İletişim Yayınları. pp. 413–516.

French, H. F. 1992. *After the Earth Summit: The Future of Environmental Governance*. Worldwatch Institute. 1992.

Garen, S. J., Brinkmann, R. 2018. Sustainability Definitions, Historical Context and Frameworks. In: Brinkmann, R. and Garren, S.J. ed. 2018. *The Palgrave Handbook of Sustainability Case Studies and Practical Solutions*. Palgrave Macmillan. pp. 1–18.

Hardin, G. 1968. The Tragedy of the Commons. *Science, 162(3859)*, pp. 1243–1248.

Heywood, A. 2014. *Global Politics*. New York, NY: Palgrave Macmillan.

Homer-Dixon, T. F. 1991. Threshold: Environmental Changes as Causes of Acute Conflict. *International Security*, 6(2), pp. 76–116.

Hubbard, B. 2012. The Ecologist January 1972: A Blueprint for Survival. [online] Available at: https://theecologist.org/2012/jan/27/ecologist-january-1972-blueprint-survival, [Accessed 19 September 2020].

Laferriere, E. and Stoett, P. J. 1999. *International Relations Theory and Ecological Thought Towards a Synthesis*. London: Routledge.

Lafferiere, E. and Stoett, P. J. 1999. *International Relations Theory and Ecological Thought Towards A Synthesis*. London: Routledge.

Lee, K. 1995. To De-Industrialize-Is It So Irrational?. In: ed. Dobson, A. and Lucardie, P. ed. 1995. *The Politics of Nature Explorations in Green Political Theory*, London: Routledge.

Leib, L. H. 2011. *Human Rights and the Environment: Philosophical Theoretical and Legal Perspectives*, Netherlands: Martinus Nijhoff Publishers.

Litfin, K. T. 1997. Sovereignty in World Ecopolitics. *Mershon International Studies Review*, 41(2), pp. 167–204.

Litfin, K. T. 2005. Gaia Theory: Intimations for Global Environment Politics. In: Dauvergbe, P. 2005. ed. *Handbook of Global Environemntal Politics*, Cheltenham: Edward Elgar.

Matthews, F. 1991. *The Ecological Self*. London: Routledge.

Midgley, M 1998. *Animals and Why They Matter*. Athens, GA: University of Georgia Press.

Maslow, S. and Nakamura, A. 2008. Constructivism and Ecological Thought: A Critical Discussion on the Prospects for a Greening of IR Theory. *Interdisciplinary Information Sciences*, 14(2), pp. 133–144.

Mathai, M. V. 2013. Will the Environment Survive International Relations? [online] Available at: https://ourworld.unu.edu/en/will-the-environment-survive-intern ational-relations, [Accessed 21 September 2020].

McGinnis, M. V. 1999. A Rehersal to Bioregionalism. In: McGinnis, M.V. *Bioregionalism,* London: Routledge.

Meadows, D. H., Meadows, D. L., Rangers, J., Behren, W. W. 1972. *The Limits to Growth A Report for the Club of Rome's Projects on the Predicament of Mankind.* New York: Universe Books.

Merriam-Webster. 2020. [online] Available at: https://www.merriam-webster.com/dic tionary/sustainability, [Accessed 21 September 2020].

Newel, P. 2019. *Global Green Politics.* Cambridge: Cambridge University Press.

Newell, P. 2019. What is Green Politics? In Global Green Politics, Cambridge: Cambridge University Press.

Newkirk, A. V. 1975. Bioregions: Towards Bioregional Strategy for Human Cultures. *Enviromental Conservation,* 2(2), pp. 108.

Paterson, M. 2000. *Understanding Global Environmental Politics Domination Accumulation Resistance.* Great Britain: Palgrave Macmillian.

Paterson, M. 2005. Green Politics. In: *Theories of International Relations.* Palgrave-Macmillan.

Pennington, M. 2008. Classical Liberalism and Ecological Rationality: The Case for Polycentric Environmental Law. *Environmental Politics,* 17(3), pp. 431–448.

Peters, M. 2019. Can Democracy Solve the Sustainability Crisis? Green Politics, Grassroots Participation and the Failue of the Sustainability Paradigm. *Educational Philosophy and Theory,* 51(2), pp. 133–141.

Porritt, J. 1984. Seeing Green: The Politics of Ecology Explained. Oxford: Basil Blackwell.

Richardson, D. 2005. Philosophical Programmatic and Electoral considerations. In: D. Richardson, Chris Rootes ed. 2005. *The Green Challenge The development of Green Parties in Europe,* Routledge, pp. 3–16.

Roby Eckersley, R. 1992. *Enviromentalism and Political Theory Toward an Ecocentric Approach.* London: UCL Press.

Steans, J., Pettiford, L., Diez, T. and El-Anis, I. 2010. *An Introduction to International Relations Theory: Perspectives and Themes.* Harlow: Pearson Longman.

Schumacher, E. F. (1973). Small is beautiful: Economics as if people mattered. *London: Blond & Briggs.*

Schumacher, E. F. (2011). *Small is beautiful: A study of economics as if people mattered.* Random House.

Scoones, I. 2016. The Politics of Sustainability and Development. *The Annual Review of Environment and Resources,* 41, pp. 293–319.

Spretnak, C. and Capra, F. 1985. *Green Politics: The Global Promise.* London: Paladin, Grafton Books.

Steans, J. Pettiford, L. Diez, T. El-Anis, I. 2013. *An Introduction to International Relations Theory: Perspectives and Themes.* USA: Routledge.

Stoll, M. 2020. Rachel Carson's Silent Spring a Book That Changed the World. [online] Available at: http://www.environmentandsociety.org/exhibitions/rachel-carsons-silent-spring/introduction, [Accessed 15 September 2020].

The Ecologist. 1972 A Blueprint for Survival. 2 (1) [online] Available at: https://www .resurgence.org/magazine/ecologist/issues1970-1979.html, [Accessed 20 September 2020].

United Nation. 1993. Report of the United Nations Conference on Environment and Development. New York: United Nations Publications.

World Conservation Strategy Living Resource Conservation for Sustainable Development. 1980. [online] Available at: https://portals.iucn.org/library/efiles/documents/wcs-004.pdf, [Accessed 25 September 2020].

Jackson, R. Sorensen, G. 2013. *Introduction to International Relations Theories and Approaches.* Oxford: Oxford University Press.

CHAPTER 12

Epilogue

Engin Sune and M. Kürşad Özekin

Emerged as a separate theoretical discipline at the beginning of the 20th century, International Relations has tended to be a western-centric, men-dominated, state-bound and power-obsessed realm of inquiry that seeks to provide universally valid explanations of inter-state relations and political behavior on a global level. To a large extent, the main driver for the inception of IR as a rigorous academic discipline was credited the unprecedented scale of conflict and human loss in the World War I. Indeed, the extreme devastation and catastrophe of the war brought into our vocabulary the term "total war" which signifies the willingness of contenders to make sacrifice in any and all civilian-associated infrastructure and resources to obtain a complete victory. The great catastrophe of total war in turn is claimed to led many to search for a new international order on liberal values that would make security and lasting peace possible. Braced up by US President Woodrow Wilson's Fourteen Points, liberal international theorists in the U.S. and British universities shared the general conviction that a more peaceful and just world order could be constructed by democratizing inter-state relations, transferring the liberal principles of rule of law and mutual respect to the realm of international politics and constructing international institutions designed to overcome the malign effects of anarchical nature of international politics.

A major theme uniting liberal international theorists was optimism and positive view on the human nature that people can learn from their mistakes for a better state of mutual existence. Drawing on a pre-existing body of European philosophy, particularly on liberal ideas of John Locke, Hugo Grotius, Samuel von Pufendorf and Immanuel Kant, liberal IR theory committed to a shared belief that rationally chosen, self-regarding action of mankind could achieve political progress to develop good will, common interest, and universal values in preventing international conflicts and making the world a more peaceful place for future generations. This "idealist" or "progressivist" thinking indeed constituted a crucial underpinning for the peace-making efforts during the interwar period and led to the creation of League of Nations, representing a case of how theory and practice are interwoven. Reaching a high point in the interwar years, the liberal IR theorists have generally been credited as the founders of IR as an academic discipline.

Nevertheless, although a brief period of relative peace prevailed throughout the 1920s, and even Germany and Japan had been members of the League of Nations, neither of this could prevent the decline of the post-1918 settlement. With the breakdown of the League of Nations and the aggressive revisionism of Germany, Italy and Japan, the ascendency of political idealism and liberal internationalism witnessed a devastating setback. The real-life crises of the post-1918 international order led up to another catastrophe in human history with the outbreak of the Second World War during which over 50 million people were killed- more than five times the number killed in the previous world war. Indeed, the Second World War not only dramatically changed the agenda of world politics, but also marked an important milestone in IR scholarship. The visionary world view of moral idealism and liberal internationalism, that ruled over the discipline's early years, received a fierce attack by political realist, leading to what would later come to recognize as the first 'discipline-defining debate' in International Relations' history. Although, there is no single theory that goes under the name of realism, virtually all classical realists share the presupposition that power politics prevails the game in inter-state relations and that the matter of morality is irrelevant in the sphere of international politics.

Mostly dwelling on the longstanding tradition of Western political philosophers such as Thucydides, Niccolò Machiavelli and Thomas Hobbes, classical realists believe that innate selfishness of humankind, its inability to trust others and its insatiable appetite for power leads to repetitive outcomes and predictable patterns of behavior that are constant for all times and all places. As humans are organized in the states-system, their basic characteristics in turn impinge on state behavior. In that respect, under the condition of self-help system in which no supreme authority is capable of arbitrating inter-state disputes and enforcing international order, mistrust, fear and insecurity drive states to act selfishly, and strive for survival, power and domination to detriment of others. Emerged as a conservative response to liberal international thought, the core premises of Realism found greater respect within academic and policy circles. In the decade or so after the World War Two, the realist explanation of IR has become the most dominant theoretical perspective in the discipline, offering easily adoptable insights particularly for the world of policymaking and statecraft until today.

Nevertheless, during the late 1950s and 1960s, IR scholarship acquired a distinctively empiricist tone with rise of behavioralism, leading to the second major disciplinary debate between traditionalists or normative analysts and behavioralists or positivists. Coming late to IR, at least compared to other fields of political science, behavioralism rejects interpretive, historical and moral analyses in favor of measurable, testifiable and scientific method to generate supposedly neutral or "objective" knowledge of international politics. Mostly rooted in positivist hypothetical-deductive methodology, behavioralists have searched for a more precise and "scientifically rigorous" approach to theorize international affairs by emulating as much as possible the methodologies of natural sciences. The quest for precision and universally valid theory of International Relations has led many turn their attention from historical analyses and human nature to models, analogies, metaphors and system analysis to explain regularities and patterns of state behavior similar to laws observed in natural sciences. Thus, behavioralism has gradually established a strong presence in the field of International Relations, forcing the traditional approaches to take a more "scientific" direction in the late 1970s by seeking for precision and rigor in their analyses.

Having a long-term impact on the study of international relations, behavioralist turn in IR did not only contribute to theoretical advancement of the discipline, but also deeply affected the mainstream IR that traditional approaches of realism and liberalism were compelled to relaunch more 'scientific' versions by adopting more precise and formula-like assertions which could be easily reduced to simple analytical and testifiable explanations. Along with the behavioralist turn, the basic tenets and assumptions of classical approaches such as Realism and Liberalism were reformulated relying on models and concepts barrowed from economics, rational choice theory and expected utility of firm and markets theories. As a result, throughout the 1970s, the field of International Relations was increasingly marked by a renewed debate, mainly called 'the inter-paradigm debate' or 'the third debate'.

As mainstream theories, both realism and liberalism have indeed continued to hold the sway over the domain of IR scholarship. However, by the late 1970s, each has given rise to a "neo" form that utilizes more scientifically robust methods to understand the world politics. Adopting a more "scientific" form of inquiry, neorealists have sought for a falsifiable, parsimonious theory of IR that is amenable to generate testable hypotheses. While retaining recognizable realist assumptions such as centrality of power politics, the lack of a rulemaking and rule-enforcing authority and skepticism about the relevance of morality to international politics, neorealists discount human nature as a meaningful variable for the sake of theoretical parsimony. Capitalizing on analogies from microeconomics and oligopoly theory, they rather propose that the structure of the inter-state system as a whole is the primary determinant of international political outcomes. In doing so, neorealists have moved the intention away from expounding idiosyncratic motivations of government and instead examined the structural imperatives of international system to which all states are subjected as rational units whose functions are more or less similar. Likewise, neoliberals have also sought to present a more parsimonious and stripped-down reformulation of liberal conception of international relations. While neoliberals share the neorealist position that the international system is essentially anarchic, they come to different conclusions. They claim that anarchy does not necessarily lead to competition and conflict as neorealists keen to argue. Relying on models borrowed from rational choice approaches and game theory, they rather explain behavior and policy choices of states both in conflict and co-operative situations, arguing that international regimes and institutions have a critical role in mitigating the adverse consequences of power politics and anarchy.

Although realist and liberal IR theories and their neo forms scrutinize each other's proposals for flaws and limitations, they all see the world in the similar way: a universally valid-international order of sovereign states interacting under ostensibly anarchic conditions. Indeed, despite the alleged intellectual discord, these two competing but fairly similar bodies of theory came to form a disciplinary framework for the mainstream IR scholarship. Throughout the 1980s, both underwent a self-limiting reconstruction towards an anti-metaphysical, theoretical position by which they increasingly became compatible with each other. Both see the international as always 'of' something out there, which exists independently of its apprehension and take the existing world order and its prevailing social and power relations for granted as the given framework for action. As IR orthodoxy, neither of these approaches has challenged the existing social structures and dominant classes and their implications for international politics, nor do they address class, gender and racial inequalities that prevail in the international arena. Thus, in the mainstream IR theorizing, the prevailing political interests of the time, as defined by the ruling classes, acquire disciplinary dominance and hegemony at the expense of dissent voices and interests of subaltern groups.

However, from the early 1980s onwards, a diverse set of schools of thought in IR have progressively challenged the mainstream theorizing of international relations and offered alternative forms of analysis that have developed under the banner of critical IR approaches. Constituting a very broad and heterogeneous group of theories, critical IR approaches share an overall commitment to challenging the immutability of the current world order as well as the acceptability of its dominant power relations and practices. In stark contrast to the established theories of mainstream IR scholarship, critical approaches place themselves above the prevailing power relations and dominant social order and questions how that order came into existence. Being self-consciously normative and reflective, the critical approaches do not take the prevailing international order as an unchangeable natural fact but seek to problematize existing power relations and dominant social structures asking whether and how they might be transcended. In this sense, they have not only served a critical function in questioning the very foundations of world politics and its unequal power relations but also pursued a normative and emancipatory interest in identifying the prospects for new forms of social and political order hopping that humanity could be free from marginalization, vulnerability, exploitation and any other kinds of social domination.

No doubt, the expansion of critical IR scholarship has overall widened the disciplinary boundaries of the field in epistemological and ontological terms and allowed a greater space for the dissent voices of marginalized and oppressed to be heard. Thanks to the wider intellectual plurality which has prospered by the rise of the critical IR scholarship, International Relations theory today looks very different than what it was twenty or thirty years ago. However, despite the mantra that IR celebrates theoretical diversity, critical IR approaches still take a back seat in the terrain of intellectual currents and policy circles. Thus, bringing the self-reflective and emancipatory power of critical IR scholarship into the front, this book has sought to reveal the achievements of a wide variety of critical approaches in International Relations theory, discuss the barrage of criticism and theoretical openings they levied against the IR orthodoxy and suggest future potential of critical IR scholarship to improve not only our explanatory possibilities, but also our ethical and practical horizons.

In this sense, as indicated in the introductory chapter, four main concerns have been occupied our research agenda for launching this book. The first was to examine the current state of International Relations theory in relation to a wide range of critical approaches and to assess the extent to which the critical approaches, in all its various guises, have transcended and moved away from the intellectual dominance of the mainstream IR scholarship.

Regarding this objective, chapters on various strands of critical scholarship have put forth that conventional IR theories are under an intellectual attack from different ontological and epistemological stands generated in distinct fields of social sciences. Apart from their critiques on the foundational themes in IR literature, Marxism and imperialism theory posed a challenge to mainstream IR scholarship within the field of International Political Economy. Additionally, chapters on dependency school and uneven and combined development (UCD) demonstrated the various critiques generated in the field of development studies against current state of IR theory. Similarly, while feminism attacked to the mainstream IR with the intellectual heritage emerged out of corpus of gender studies, green theory revealed the position of environmental studies vis a vis traditional IR literature. In fact, these critiques are not only limited to different fields of social sciences but also alternative voices from different geographies have been rising against conventional IR scholarship by challenging Western centrism of the field, as it revealed by the chapters on Postcolonialism and non-Western IR.

This intellectual attack from various fields of social sciences sheds light on two broad facts on social sciences and social reality in general. First of all, disciplinary boundaries in social sciences are so artificial that capturing the essence of a social reality by concentrating merely on the international sphere ends up on a wild goose chase regarding the complex interactions among different social layers. As chapter 8 on International Political Sociology revealed, the boundaries between IR and other disciplines such as sociology, political science, and criminology limit our understandings of power, authority, and sovereignty. Thereof, the critical approaches to international relations also acknowledged limits and boundaries themselves as a unit of analysis. Secondly, the increasing interest on the field of International Relations in various fields of social sciences proves that contextualizing the international sphere is central in understanding any aspect of current social condition. Regarding the developments that took place since 1970s, the process of globalization dialectically integrated different segments of societies, which turned the field of IR into one of most sophisticated fields of social sciences, especially with the contributions of theories that aim to frame their own counter-narratives.

In this context, regarding the first concern of the book, each separate chapter exposed the current state of IR theory that is constantly being challenged by the critical approaches. Despite their late arrival to the field, which was triggered by the dominance of ahistorical conceptualizations of the "international", critical approaches gave a new impulse to International Relations. They created new centers of gravity that investigate the issues that have been neglected by the conventional accounts. With their focus on the relations of dominance and subordination in the world, critical approaches revealed the material and ideational hierarchies embedded in global social structures. While overwhelming concentration of the conventional approaches on state as the main actor of world politics leaves no space for an alternative ontological understanding of IR, it limits the whole field into discussions on politics among great powers. Various critical approaches within the scope of this book, on the other hand, discussed how naturalizing such power relations covers hierarchical, racist and colonial character of international relations by excluding the experiences of the "other" states, people, groups or planet in general. Furthermore, while mainstream IR theories are primarily occupied with policy areas such as security, peace or sovereignty and naturalize their perspective with the claim of being scientific through their positivist methodology, critical approaches to IR paved the way for new units of analysis in IR such as class, gender, race and environment, by challenging the concepts that are taken for granted.

The second main concern of the book was to provide a series of further reflections on dissent voices of marginalized in the contemporary theory of the international, assuming an emancipatory moral purpose for the betterment of human affairs based on more just and equal terms. Regarding this, the book has sought to uncover how power relations exclude certain points of view based on their race, class, gender, sexuality and or geographical location. By drawing the boundaries of the field of IR and fixing upon the basic concepts of the discipline such as state, security or power, the mainstream approaches legitimized and naturalized their own narratives. Therefore, each separate chapter of the book revealed the possible alternative narratives of IR by raising the voice of those excluded and silenced.

The exclusion of certain points of view from the circles of IR was exposed by the second chapter on Marxism which stressed that these non-material inequalities in terms of representation, ideas and culture are interconnected with material inequalities imposed by the capitalist world system. On the other hand, in the third chapter imperialism theory, as a sub-school of Marxism, proclaimed total exclusion of studies on imperialism since the field of IR has been disproportionally dominated by the problem-solving theories. While the mainstream narratives on IR crystalize the origins of the field with the first great debate between Idealists and Realists, the third chapter on imperialism revealed that the first generation of imperialism studies have been conducted before the so-called debate. Moreover, those studies on imperialism have also concentrated on traditional issues that the first debate was concerned with and strived to explain the underlying causes of the First World War with their emphasis on inter imperial rivalries. Despite of this, imperialism theory has not been widely acknowledged as a theory of IR due to its critical stand that challenged the existing world order and power relations. Similarly, another sub-school of Marxism, the Dependency School, has exposed how these power relations exclude the non-core actors as the agencies of the global structure and transform mainstream IR literature as a Western-centric initiative that merely concentrates on the relations among core nations. In this sense, the fourth chapter uncovered the voices of excluded geographies as it revealed the negligence of the periphery and the impact of global structures on those peripheral social formations within conventional IR accounts. In a similar vein, in the fifth chapter another sub-study within Marxist tradition, the theory of Uneven and Combined Development, criticized narratives on

European exceptionalism within mainstream IR. While the chapter presented the impact of interaction between uneven societies on the cumulative history of humanity, it put forth a non-Eurocentric account on the genesis of capitalism and global system.

Developing an understanding of the "international" by augmenting the dissent voices of those marginalized in contemporary IR theory is not only limited to the Marxist variants of critical theories. In chapter six, by exploring the subjectivity of the representations of most conventional actors and issues of IR, poststructuralism revealed how particular cultures of violence as well as their state-centric and masculine nature are reproduced. In this regard, in order to discuss the possibility of alternative representations, the theory strived to display what is kept out of sight by the mainstream narratives of IR. In a similar line, Postcolonial theory in chapter seven, discussed the exclusion of the agency of Global South from the conventional IR theories, which undermine the role of "the others" located in the Third World. Therefore, postcolonial IR scholars shed light on the ideas, perspectives, experiences and practices of those non-core actors who have been neglected by the conventional accounts of the discipline since their analysis is largely rooted in the experiences of the West countries and the Global North. Correspondingly, International Political Sociology in chapter eight, pointed out another form of exclusion that is based on artificial lines drawn by the mainstream IR narratives in between different disciplines and segments of social life. With its emphasis on the transitivity of the lines between different categories, levels of analysis and disciplines, international political sociology has opened IR field to the possible contributions from other fields of social sciences that has been silenced by mainstream narratives, which reduced the science of international relations to the analysis of interactions among atomistic states.

Without any doubt, exclusion of certain points of view based on their geographical location, race, class or gender is one of the central themes of the feminist scholarship. In this regard, chapter nine on feminism discussed the exclusion of gender out of analysis by the conventional theories of IR which marginalize women as economic, political, and social subjects. Thereof, feminism strived to reveal the place of women in international relations by indicating the absence of women and gender in theory and policymaking in the field of International Relations. Accordingly, feminist scholarship asserted that the rational person, which is associated with the rational state by the mainstream understandings, is elite, white and male that excludes other agencies. In fact, exclusion of other agencies and perspectives, especially non-Western ones, was also the main starting point for Non-Western IR theories, as it is presented in chapter ten. The theory exposed the exclusion of non-Western countries, which compose the majority of the members of the international system, and the negligence of circumstances and values of the "others" in conventional IR theories. Additionally, non-Western IR theory pointed to the exclusion of non-Western scholars from the field since the mainstream IR theories extensively deal with Western-oriented problems and solutions. Therefore, non-Western IR theories challenged the fake universality of the field by raising the dissent voices of the non-Western world. It is not only certain geographies but also environment and environmental concerns are also totally excluded from the field of IR as argued by the Green Theory in chapter eleven. The theory criticized human-centered perspectives dominant in mainstream IR theories and suggested an ecocentric world view that locates environment at the center of analysis. Through establishing a relationship between environmental problems and overall global inequalities, Green theory revealed how local communities disproportionally influenced from the global power relations. Thus, the theory aimed to bring the environmental problems triggered by national and international social structures into the agenda of International Relations through divulging how individual and social life are directly shaped by the ecological balance.

Following these reflections on dissent voices of marginalized in the contemporary theory of the international, the third main concern of the book was to discuss the major theoretical openings and achievements of various critical approaches and to assess their respective strengths and weaknesses vis a vis the parochial theories of the International Relations scholarship. Regarding this, each chapter presented a very detailed account on how distinct strands of critical scholarship developed a different understanding of the "international" through their relentless critique to mainstream IR theories.

In this sense, Marxism in the second chapter challenged the distinction between national boundaries and international sphere; the tendencies of excessive specialization and disciplinary exclusion between the fields of economics, sociology, political science, philosophy and International Relations; and the fundamental notions of IR such as nation, state, sovereignty, power, war, peace and international law that are taken for granted by the conventional IR theories. The Marxist theory, on the other hand, reformulated these concepts by concentrating on their relation with the social and historical relations of production, underlying class relations and the structure of global economy. Furthermore, against the fallacy methodological individualism dominant in traditional IR theories, Marxism aimed to capture the essence of the complex relationship between economic, political and ideological structures within the totality of global capitalist system.

Similarly, another offspring of the Marxist tradition, Imperialism theory, in the third chapter criticized conventional approaches' depiction of IR as a world structure organized according to the principle of formal sovereign equality between nation states. The theory, on the other hand, uncovered the embedded inequalities and hierarchies hidden behind the principle of formal sovereign equality of states. In accordance with the Marxist critique, imperialism theory inclined to avoid atomistic accounts of the international by perceiving the social and material world as a single system organized by the capitalist social relations and under the dominance of Western capitalist states. In this regard, the theory also refuted the concept of anarchy developed by the mainstream IR narratives and underlined the hierarchies embedded into the whole international system, where unequal relations among the geographies are prevalent.

Dependency theory, as another strand of Marxist critical scholarship, also criticized the mainstream IR theories since they are explaining the international politics as it is. In chapter four the dependency theory, on the other hand, problematized the very foundations of asymmetries and hierarchical power relations in existing international order both in economic and political terms. In this regard, rather than taking nation-state or the international system as a level of analysis as the mainstream approaches, the dependency theory critically examined the interplay between nation-states, social classes and world capitalist system. As a product of the postcolonial move and the nativist reaction to the perceived immutability of existing structures in the social world, the dependency theory revealed how this perception serves to sustain inequalities of power and wealth between and within nations. As a Marxian-inspired critical theory, dependency approach also placed itself above the prevailing power relations and dominant social order to offer an emancipatory alternative to the existing international structures.

In line with other strands of Marxist inspired theories, in chapter five theory of Uneven and Combined Development commenced its critique with the analytical separation between domestic and international spheres in conventional IR approaches. In this regard, UCD concentrated critically on the reified understanding of the international in mainstream narratives and strived to develop a sociological definition of the international with the concept of "inter-societal relations". The chapter on UCD outplayed the neo-realist understanding of anarchy by reconceptualizing it as an emergent phenomenon of social development, under which multiple societies with different levels of development are interacting. In this sense, the theory transcended conventional approaches of IR as it developed a historical and sociological understanding of the international where multiple societies coexist and interact unevenly.

Poststructuralism as another strand of critical scholarship developed a critical stand not only against foundational theoretical approaches, but against any approach with a universal truth claim in International Relations. As discussed in chapter six, poststructuralism attempted to display how configurations on symbols and representations produce and reproduce power relations in IR. Thereof, the theory focused on the mainstream representations of the concepts such as war, peace or state competition in order to reveal that these concepts are discursive artefacts rather than timeless and objective facts. With its emphasis on the subjectivity of representations, poststructuralist turn disclosed the power-knowledge relationship in order to challenge the objectivity of science allegations by the positivistic epistemological stands in mainstream IR.

Another influential approach that challenged the foundations of conventional IR scholarship is the Postcolonial IR theory as presented in chapter seven. The theory criticized conventional theories of international relations for their relative neglect of questions concerning inequality and justice and asserted that these theories pay no attention to the role of history, ideology, culture in shaping state power and practices in international relations. Thereof, postcolonial approaches strive to surmount the mainstream approaches by questioning the inequalities, hierarchies and oppressions triggered by material and ideational legacies of colonialism. Similar to other critical approaches, as discussed above, postcolonial accounts of IR do not acknowledge that the world system is organized anarchically and underline how rooted hierarchies are shaped by (and shape) different power relations stemming from race, class, and gender.

International political sociology, likewise, brought new theoretical outsets and achievements into the field of IR by questioning the presupposed formal sovereign equality between the states and opening the sovereignty problematique to the theoretical debate, in chapter eight. In doing that the theory put forth how binaries between inside/outside, as alleged by the mainstream narratives, constitute our views on possibilities and limits of political life. The theory discredited these binaries or dichotomies as it presupposes that power operates in multiple contexts within the state boundaries and international sphere. Furthermore, with its analysis on power and authority, the theory investigated the politics of exception and security practices by opening new ontological discussions among IR theorists and critical security scholars.

The encounter between mainstream IR theories and feminist theory, on the other hand, commences with latter's accusation of the former for being a "malestream" perspective. Feminist theory, in chapter nine, criticized conventional IR theories for producing gendered and one-sided knowledge regarding the study of IR. Thereof, feminist theory through taking gender as a unit of analysis, firstly suggested a re-evaluation of the discipline of International Relations and world politics, which is dominated by mainstream theories that construct male-dominated roles to the political identity. Furthermore, similar to the other strands of critical scholarship discussed above, feminist theory also challenged the positivistic epistemological stands in IR since it believes that the claims on the impartiality of truths and universal objectivity hide gendered nature of knowledge production. Within this framework, Feminist IR strived to make women visible in the international relations and generate a new theoretical approach in IR that takes into account the experiences and perspectives of women.

Non-Western IR theories similarly aimed to make another excluded actor, the non-Western world, visible in the field of International Relations by questioning the internationality of the whole IR discipline in chapter ten. Regarding this, non-Western IR perspectives castigated not only mainstream IR theories but also Marxist theories for their illustration of all the hallmarks of a Eurocentric worldview. Reflecting upon how IR theories are rooted in European history and Western traditions of social theory and practice, non-Western IR theories revealed that priorities, problems, solutions or premises of mainstream narratives are insufficient to meet expectations, problems or perspectives of the non-Western world. In this sense, non-Western theories aimed to emancipate IR from the Western dominance and go beyond conventional approaches by forming generalizable concepts and theories inspired by historical and political experiences of non-core geographies.

An akin refusal of mainstream IR narratives for their exclusion of actors and themes apart from state and security is evident in Green Theory as discussed in the last chapter. By questioning the role and authority of states in environmental crises and natural disasters, the theory aimed to open new horizons in IR theories especially in terms of challenging power, interest or military security as the central issues concerning state relations. Similar to the feminist theory which elaborated the notion of gender in IR, Green theory strived to include environment and ecology into the agenda of theoretical discussion in the field. Based on this objective, with the notion of ecocentrism that locates environment at the center of the universe, the Green theory transcended mainstream IR scholarship by challenging not only the state-centric conceptualizations but also the human-centric worldview.

Last but not least, the fourth concern of the book was to display the future research directions within critical IR scholarship and to discuss prospective contributions that various critical approaches offer to move beyond the current confines of IR theory. Regarding this grand objective, each separate chapter introduced and explored the new research directions and current studies that make use of theoretical findings and conceptual framework of the approach that is under inquiry.

The second chapter on Marxism, for instance, presented how Marxist theoretical discussions in IR have paved the way for new studies concentrating on the relationship between capitalism and geopolitics. The chapter also set forth new studies developing Marxist concepts of imperialism, hegemony and transnationalization. The third chapter on imperialism likewise revealed the studies on new imperialism which especially focus on the relationship between neoliberalism and imperialism. In this regard, theory of imperialism has generated new concepts and studies on sub-imperialisms, cultural imperialism, humanitarian imperialism and peace building. Furthermore, the chapter discussed how the theory of imperialism inspired a group of study centered around the discussions on globalization. Another theoretical school that triggered new studies on globalization is the dependency school as discussed in chapter four. The dependency perspective has offered an integrated and comprehensive social science framework that combines analysis of economic structures and imperatives of world economy with a focus on class configurations, state-society relations and modes of national integration into world economy. In accordance with this, the theory inspired new studies discussing divergences in development in the contemporary era of globalization, which reflects how asymmetrical power relations in the contemporary global capitalist system generate forms of 'new' or 'neo' dependency. Similar to the other Marxist traditions, Uneven and Combined Development triggered new studies especially on geopolitics that scrutinize the relationship between capitalism and the state system. These new studies not only questioned the nature plurality of states under capitalist system but also challenged Eurocentrism in IR as it was visible in their alternative reading on the so-called 'Rise of the West'.

Akin to the Marxist variants of critical theories, Post-positivistic theories also generated a new corpus of current theoretical studies in IR. As discussed in chapter six, poststructuralist studies led to new discussions and interpretations on security, war and militarization; political economy and development; postcolonial and environmental politics; UN, humanitarian intervention and international law; and lastly foreign policy, national identity and citizenship. In a similar vein, postcolonial narratives generated new studies on globalization, foreign policy, war, security, weapons of mass destruction, international law, international political economy, race, humanitarian intervention and subjecthood, which concentrate on how colonialism and imperialism have continued to shape these issues. International political sociology, on the other hand, led to new theoretical openings in IR, which mostly sprouted up the discussions on "post-truth" regimes of knowledge and their implication. In addition to these new research directions, feminist discussions on gender stimulated further studies in IR, such as the investigations on the concept of hegemonic masculinity or those questioning the relationship between technology and gender roles. Equivalently, the concept of locality, which is a salient contribution of non-Western IR studies, encouraged new explorations of indigenous histories, classical philosophy and religious traditions, the ideas of national leaders, the writing of contemporary scholars, and foreign policy practices of modern states. Lastly, Green Theory, opened up new and current theoretical horizons in critical IR scholarship which reconstruct the relationship between man and nature by discussing the scope of measures and reforms to be taken against environmental crises.

Overall, with these four broad objectives our book diverged from the existing studies in the field of critical IR scholarship with its content, the organization of chapters and its contribution to the literature with its meticulous focus on the current theoretical openings and research directions in each school of thought. Even though there are significant studies within the critical IR scholarship that scrutinize theorists, concepts and configurations in critical IR thinking and that concentrate on the concepts of emancipation, power and other excluded subject matters (see Roach 2020, 2008; Linklater 1989; Edkins 2009, 2019; Rengger and Thirkell-White 2007; Jones 2001), this whole book provides a very detailed account that extends our knowledge on different strands of critical IR scholarship. Regarding this, the content of the book is incommensurable with the existing works as they are seldomly organized in a way to depict different schools of thought in critical IR thinking. It is generally very uncommon to encounter with chapters on dependency school, uneven and combined development or international political sociology as distinct schools in books on critical IR theories. Moreover, compared to the existing literature, our book treated imperialism as a critical theory of IR and analyzed Marxism and its sub-theories such as dependency, imperialism and UCD separately. Furthermore, with the detailed historiographical examinations and literature reviews of each different theoretical school in separate chapters, we are convinced that this book provides main philosophical foundations and premises of different stands in critical IR scholarship. Based on this framework, we believe the whole book provides a valuable resource to be familiarized with further studies in the critical IR scholarship as each chapter presented the most current studies developing the theoretical school analyzed and we hope that this study itself will also encourage new critical studies within the field of IR.

References

Edkins, Jenny 2009 *Critical Theorists and International Relations,* London: Routledge.

Edkins, Jenny 2019 *Routledge Handbook of Critical International Relations*, London: Routledge.

Jones, Richard Wyn 2001 *Critical Theory and World Politics*, Boulder, CO: Lynne Rienner Publishers.

Linklater, Andrew 1989 *Beyond Realism and Marxism,* London: Palgrave.

Rengger, Nicholas John and Tristram Benedict Thirkell-White, 2007 *Critical International Relations Theory after 25 Years*, Cambridge: Cambridge University Press.

Roach, Steven C. (ed.) 2020, *Handbook of Critical International Relations*, Cheltenham Edward Elgar Publishing.

Roach, Steven C. 2008 *Critical Theory and International Relations: A Reader*, London: Routledge.

Index

CPSIA information can be obtained
at www.ICGtesting.com
Printed in the USA
JSHW051548221022
31896JS00004B/4

9 781642 598049